THE CHICAGO OF EUROPE

MARK TWAIN

The Chicago of Europe

And Other Tales of Foreign Travel

EDITED AND INTRODUCED BY

PETER KAMINSKY,

EXECUTIVE PRODUCER, THE MARK TWAIN PRIZE
FOR AMERICAN HUMOR

UNION SQUARE PRESS
An imprint of Sterling Publishing Co., Inc.

New York / London
www.sterlingpublishing.com

STERLING and the distinctive Sterling logo are registered trademarks of Sterling Publishing Co., Inc.

LIBRARY OF CONGRESS CATALOGING-IN-PUBLICATION DATA

Twain, Mark, 1835-1910.
  The Chicago of Europe, and other tales of foreign travel / Mark Twain ; edited and introduced by Peter Kaminsky.
    p. cm.
  Includes bibliographical references and index.
  ISBN 978-1-4027-5869-0 (hc-trade cloth : alk. paper) 1. Twain, Mark, 1835-1910--Travel. I. Kaminsky, Peter. II. Title.
  PS1302.K28 2009
  818'.409--dc22

                                                                    2009006805

10   9   8   7   6   5   4   3   2   1

Published by Sterling Publishing Co., Inc.
387 Park Avenue South, New York, NY 10016
© 2009 by Peter Kaminsky
Distributed in Canada by Sterling Publishing
c/o Canadian Manda Group, 165 Dufferin Street
Toronto, Ontario, Canada M6K 3H6
Distributed in the United Kingdom by GMC Distribution Services
Castle Place, 166 High Street, Lewes, East Sussex, England BN7 1XU
Distributed in Australia by Capricorn Link (Australia) Pty. Ltd.
P.O. Box 704, Windsor, NSW 2756, Australia

Book Design by BTDNYC

Manufactured in the United States of America
All rights reserved

Sterling ISBN 978-1-4027-5869-0

For information about custom editions, special sales, premium and corporate purchases, please contact Sterling Special Sales Department at 800-805-5489 or specialsales@sterlingpublishing.com.

For JFK

from the town of Narev

in present-day Poland

In the midst of his transports came an officer into the room, followed by the abbe, and a file of musketeers. "There," said he, "are the two suspected foreigners." At the same time he ordered them to be seized and carried to prison. "Travelers are not treated in this manner in the country of El Dorado," said Candide.

—from *Candide*, by Voltaire

CONTENTS

Contents

Contents

PART VI: AFRICA, INDIA, AND
THE HOLY LAND

Contents

PART VII: FANTASIES

PART VIII: A FINAL NOTE

INTRODUCTION:
MARK TWAIN'S
OWN LETTERS FROM
THE EARTH

In the fall of 1995, I went to the White House with three close friends to pitch an idea to the Clinton administration's White House social secretary, Ann Stock. We came to propose a new award recognizing the role of humor in our nation's life. The glut of national awards for novelists, biographers, great moviemakers, architects, economists, relief pitchers, and defensive linemen could leave one with the impression that nearly everyone in public life spends their evenings in tuxedos and designer dresses handing out or tearfully accepting statuettes. But where was the national recognition for those who helped to lighten our spirits in times of scandal, fear, and a tanking stock market? Where was our Pulitzer Prize for comedy?

There was none, which was why we went to the White House to propose such an award: an all-star tribute to George Burns, who was about to celebrate his hundredth birthday.

"What will you call it?" Ann asked.

It was a no-brainer really. How could you not call it the Mark Twain Prize? Everyone likes Twain. At the height of the Cold War, even the Russians and the Red Chinese liked Twain. Just say the words "Mark Twain Prize" out loud—it sounds like an award that has been around forever.

"Sold!" Ann said. But neither she nor we had counted on Grand Inquisitor Ken Starr and his obsessive (and ultimately fruitless) pursuit of alleged Whitewater misdoings. The Clinton White House did not think that involving itself in the world of comedy and unpredictably opinionated comedians made for good politics in the upcoming election year.

Introduction

We feared that our surefire idea was dying on the vine. But then Ann left the scandal-beset West Wing and took a job at the Kennedy Center. She had not forgotten our idea and arranged a meeting for us with the center's senior staff.

Our pitch took about a minute: Humor is popular. You need more humor in Washington. Pretty much everyone in America likes our great comics. So let's have an award, invite a lot of funny people, and call it the Kennedy Center Mark Twain Prize for American Humor.

"Sold!" they said.

By that point, George Burns had departed the scene (he died in March 1996), but the Mark Twain Prize lived on, going that first year to the brilliant—and gravely ill—Richard Pryor. It was a ribald and rousing evening of comedy; "the funniest night ever in Washington, D.C.," many said, perhaps as much a recognition of the low bar for humor in our nation's capital as it was a tribute to our show.

Nonetheless, the idea stuck. The Mark Twain Prize is now in its twelfth year and has been presented to Pryor, Carl Reiner, Jonathan Winters, Bob Newhart, Whoopi Goldberg, Lily Tomlin, Lorne Michaels, Neil Simon, Steve Martin, Billy Crystal, posthumously to George Carlin in 2008, and to Bill Cosby in 2009.

Not only is Twain's legacy the inspiration for the award, but it has been part of the ceremony every year. Alluding to Richard Pryor's near-fatal free-basing accident in year one, presenter Robin Williams recalled it was Twain who said, "The source of humor itself is not joy but sorrow." In explaining why a gloves-off antiwar sketch had been cut from a Lily Tomlin network special in the 1970s, playwright Eve Ensler observed that Twain also received a thumbs-down from "the suits" at his publishers when he submitted his scathing antijingoist poem "War Prayer." Just six weeks after 9/11, Whoopi Goldberg travelled to a still-numb Washington to accept the Twain Prize and recalled that it was Twain who first remarked, "Against the assault of laughter, nothing can stand."

So that's how the Twain Prize was born, which explains how I, as one of its creators, have come to be asked to survey and select from Mark Twain's writings on travel. Apart from being exceptionally good at travel writing, Twain was also among the first modern travel writers. Before him, there really was no such creature as the casual American traveler or anything we would recognize as modern travel writing in the American vein. This is not to say that Twain single-handedly and consciously created a new form of literature. It is much closer to the truth to say that he was a peerless observer of his fellow humans and that he happened to come of age just at the time that the steamboat and railroad made it relatively easy for someone struck with a will-o'-the-wisp to light out for a pleasure trip to a distant place.

In earlier times, those who wrote of their travels were more likely to be cast from the Marco Polo mold of intrepid adventurers whose memoirs were a mixture of fact interlaced with fable whenever things got boring. It made for a good read, and if you were stuck for a colorful idea, you could pretty much say what you wanted because who was going to fact-check you anyway? Alexander the Great's horse was actually a unicorn? There was a warrior king in the Ethiopian outback, still very much alive, who had once dined with St. John the Evangelist? Apparently, all it took for such "facts" to enter the historical record was that some sunstruck monk had sworn them to be true.

There were so few sources to verify or disprove the wildest reports and the tallest tales that merely having traveled qualified *anyone* to write *anything* without fear of contradiction. In those olden times, travel to foreign lands required a major commitment. Itineraries of a few months, such as the ones Twain undertook when he set out for Hawaii in 1866 or his grand tour of Europe and the Holy Land in 1867, would have taken years to complete. Where the medieval pilgrim or the Renaissance merchant might have encountered kidnappers, slavers, cannibals, and cutthroats along the way, Twain's traveling contemporaries often risked nothing worse than indigestion or an ill-informed tour guide.

By Twain's time, travel and travel writing had passed from the province of adventurers and explorers and had acquired the character of amusing and interesting everyday letters to one's friends and family. As Twain observed in *A Tramp Abroad*:

> Seventy or eighty years ago Napoleon was the only man in Europe who could really be called a traveler; he was the only man who had devoted his attention to it and taken a powerful interest in it; he was the only man who had traveled extensively; but now everybody goes everywhere; and Switzerland, and many other regions which were unvisited and unknown remotenesses a hundred years ago, are in our days a buzzing hive of restless strangers every summer.

Technological advances that made travel less rigorous and more affordable—the steamboat, its ocean-going brother the steamship, and the railroad—all occurred around the time of Twain's birth in 1835. In the next thirty years, tracks were laid across the continents, ocean travel became an affair of weeks rather than months and years, and communications, following the invention of the telegraph, became nearly instantaneous. In such a world, shrunk more in those few decades than in the previous ten thousand years, facts were checkable, tall tales were easily cut down to size, and a traveler could pretty much get from anywhere to anywhere else.

Before Twain the man, gave us his travel writing, Clemens the boy looked on in wonderment as the watery highway of the Mississippi flowed past his ramshackle boyhood hometown, Hannibal, Missouri. To us, Hannibal has come to signify small-town America in the years when our national character—full of hope, not entirely trusting of outsiders, and eager for new experiences—was being born. To Twain, though, it was a small, circumscribed place, somewhere to leave just as soon as he could. The river called to him, stirred his soul, and eventually became the highway that transformed the spirit of young hayseed Sam Clemens into the clear, penetrating, guileless voice of Mark Twain.

The picture that Twain paints of that little town and his youthful spirit in *Life on the Mississippi* is so vital and full of excitement that the reader can believe for just a moment that he or she, too, is a young boy stuck in

Introduction

Nowheresville, when, with the booming blast of a ship's claxon, a steamboat arrives, serving up a glimpse of all the romance, riches, and adventures the wider world has to offer. Little Hannibal and its young inhabitants are awakened from their provincial slumber, if only for a few minutes. The feeling of wonder Twain conveys reminds me of nothing so much as Richard Dreyfuss's character when he sees the aliens walk down the gangplank from their spacecraft in *Close Encounters of the Third Kind*. "Take me with you!" his eyes seem to beg. If you want to understand what Mark Twain felt, consider his words as he relives those moments when the steamboat came to town:

> After all these years, I can picture that old time to myself now, just as it was then: the white town drowsing in the sunshine of a summer's morning; the streets empty, or pretty nearly so; one or two clerks sitting in front of the Water Street stores, with their splint-bottomed chairs tilted back against the wall, chins on breasts, hats slouched over their faces, asleep—with shingle-shavings enough around to show what broke them down; a sow and a litter of pigs loafing along the sidewalk, doing a good business in watermelon rinds and seeds; two or three lonely little freight piles scattered about the "levee," a pile of "skids'" on the slope of the stone-paved wharf, and the fragrant town drunkard asleep in the shadow of them; two or three wood flats at the head of the wharf, but nobody to listen to the peaceful lapping of the wavelets against them; the great Mississippi, the majestic, the magnificent Mississippi, rolling its mile-wide tide along, shining in the sun; the dense forest away on the other side; the "point" above the town, and the "point" below, bounding the river-glimpse and turning it into a sort of sea, and withal a very still and brilliant and lonely one. Presently a film of dark smoke appears above one of those remote "points," instantly a negro drayman, famous for his quick eye and prodigious voice, lifts up the cry, "S-t-e-a-m-boat a-comin'!" and the scene changes! The town drunkard stirs, the clerks wake up, a furious clatter of drays follows, every house and store pours out a human contribution,

and all in a twinkling the dead town is alive and moving. Drays, carts, men, boys, all go hurrying from many quarters to a common center, the wharf. Assembled there, the people fasten their eyes upon the coming boat as upon a wonder they are seeing for the first time. And the boat is rather a handsome sight, too. She is long and sharp and trim and pretty; she has two tall, fancy-topped chimneys, with a gilded device of some kind swung between them; a fanciful pilot-house, a glass and "gingerbread," perched on top of the "texas" deck behind them; the paddle-boxes are gorgeous with a picture or with gilded rays above the boat's name; the boiler deck, the hurricane deck, and the texas deck are fenced and ornamented with clean white railings; there is a flag gallantly flying from the jack-staff; the furnace doors are open and the fires glaring bravely; the upper decks are black with passengers; the captain stands by the big bell, calm, imposing, the envy of all; great volumes of the blackest smoke are rolling and tumbling out of the chimneys—a husbanded grandeur created with a bit of pitch pine just before arriving at a town; the crew are grouped on the forecastle; the broad stage is run far out over the port bow, and an envied deck-hand stands picturesquely on the end of it with a coil of rope in his hand; the pent steam is screaming through the gauge-cocks, the captain lifts his hand, a bell rings, the wheels stop; then they turn back, churning the water to foam, and the steamer is at rest. Then such a scramble as there is to get aboard, and to get ashore, and to take in freight and to discharge freight, all at one and the same time; and such a yelling and cursing as the mates facilitate it all with! Ten minutes later the steamer is under way again, with no flag on the jack-staff and no black smoke issuing from the chimneys. After ten more minutes the town is dead again, and the town drunkard asleep by the skids once more.

When Twain was seventeen years old, he left Hannibal, but to the extent that each of us is inescapably a product of a time and a place, Hannibal never left him. As shrewd as Huck, as friendly as Tom, Twain sized up new places and new experiences as carefully and as skeptically as the pennywise dry-goods merchant in Hannibal might have done as he felt the heft of a bolt of bombazine on offer from a fast-talking riverboat peddler.

Twain drifted into writing, as many do, because, to quote Clark Gable's character in *The Misfits* when asked why he put up with the punishing profession of capturing wild horses, "It beats wages." His early pieces are interesting, if only because they offer a glimmer of the writer he was to become. Had his output stopped after a few years of these occasional reports on his travels for small-town papers, it's likely no one would have long remembered Mark Twain. In fact, he wasn't even called Mark Twain at that time. His early writings either appeared under his own name, Samuel Clemens, or bore such fanciful bylines as Adrastus W. Epaminondas Perkins and Thomas Jefferson Snodgrass. It was under this last *nom de plume* that he published his first travel piece in the Keokuk Iowa *Daily Post* in 1856 ("Goin' to the Theater in the Big City"). Adopting the voice of the rube, which he would later perfect and add depth to with Huck Finn, he described a visit to the theater in St. Louis in a pitch-perfect example of a deadpan bumpkin humbling the sophisticates.

Though Twain wouldn't adopt his pen name until 1864, the transformation of Sam Clemens into Mark Twain began in the four years he spent as a river pilot on the Mississippi, from 1857 to 1861. This was his university among the travelers and traders, the carousers and hard-bitten crewmen, the colorful men and women of the river towns. Getting out on the river, literally into the flow of a larger world, was nothing short of transformational for the small-town boy; he wrote this:

> I became a new being, and the subject of my own admiration. I was a traveler! A word never had tasted so good in my mouth before. I had an exultant sense of being bound for mysterious lands and distant climes which I never have felt in so uplifting a degree since. I was in such a glorified condition that all ignoble feelings departed out of me, and I was able to look down and pity the untraveled with a compassion that had hardly a trace of contempt in it.

Introduction

You see this same sense of enthusiasm in the letters that he sent back to his family during his riverboat days. They also reveal an increasingly confident writer and perspicacious observer of places and people. For example, there is an 1859 letter that he sent to his sister from New Orleans (see page 14). Even at this early date, it shows all the depth of observation and curiosity that would come to characterize Twain's travel writing for the rest of his life. It's not the breezy insouciance of *Innocents Abroad* quite yet, but it is very good. Think "I Want to Hold Your Hand" with the promise but not yet the polish of *Sgt. Pepper's.*

The Civil War destroyed commerce on the Mississippi and abruptly ended Sam Clemens's riverboat career. It was a small setback for river boating and a huge boon for American literature that Clemens headed west, following his brother Orion, who took up a federal post in Nevada. The milieu of instant-millionaire miners (and equally instantly destitute ones), dance-hall girls, gun-toting desperadoes, and blowhard politicos made for a colorful cast of characters in the stories Clemens began to file for the *Virginia City Territorial Enterprise.* Though these pieces were conceived as newspaper stories and not pure travel writing, Clemens had begun his career of reporting on new places, new people, and new experiences. Read today, these dispatches today, they are as much a window into far-off places as are his writings from Florence and Jerusalem.

Much of this material, along with his subsequent work for the *Sacramento Union,* would appear later in *Roughing It,* which, although it covers his early experiences in the West, was first published in 1872. Twain had originally organized the material as a lecture. So, rather than heavily excerpting that book, as most collections of his work do, I thought readers would like to see one of the two existing transcriptions of the actual lecture. After flipping a coin, I settled on the one that appeared in the *(Lansing Michigan) State Republican* in 1871 (see page 31).

Another piece that drew on his experience in the West is the flat-out comedic "The Killing of Julius Caesar Localized" (see page 48). It presents Caesar's assassination as it might have appeared had Twain reported on it for the Virginia City paper. Apart from the fun of it, I think it sheds a light on one of Twain's gifts as a travel reporter: Wherever he went, he could relate events to the everyday experiences of his American readers, always driving home the more general theme that there are scalawags, charlatans, and miscreants everywhere.

By 1866, West Coast newspaper editors knew they could rely on Twain for a steady output of entertaining writing. The *Sacramento Union* agreed to foot the bill for a trip to Hawaii; in return, they received twenty-six columns. More important for our story, he used his columns as a basis for his first public lecture. At that event, in San Francisco on October 2, Twain expected at best a half-filled auditorium, mostly the result of papering the seats with friends and friends of friends. Instead, it was a sell-out crowd.

Flush with success, he added sixteen dates to his lecture tour, and it was at this time that the familiar Mark Twain persona took form— perspicacious, outrageous, flamboyant. In an era when there was no TV and no radio (no recorded anything), public lecturing was big-time showbiz. Twain, an authentic, unbamboozled, funny American truthteller was a bracing and entertaining tonic for a nation seeking to move past the legacy of death and destruction wrought by the Civil War.

From this point on, Twain realized that anytime he needed some extra cash, he could write about and talk about travel. The high-paying banquet circuit was hungry for good speakers, and Twain was the best. His observations on New York, Boston, Philadelphia, and other American locales (often delivered as after-dinner speeches) are as full of fun and brio as anything that appeared in his more famous travel books. Though he was writing about New York for the *California Alta* in 1867 (see page 78), his shrewd observations on city life could have been penned yesterday:

> The old, genuine, traveled, cultivated, pedigreed aristocracy of New York, stand stunned and helpless under the new order of things. They find themselves supplanted by upstart princes of Shoddy, vulgar and with unknown grandfathers. The incomes, which were something for the common herd to gape at and gossip about once, are mere livelihoods now—would not pay Shoddy's house-rent. They move into

remote new streets up town, and talk feelingly of the crash which is to come when the props are knocked from under this flimsy edifice of prosperity.

On the heels of his triumph as a lecturer, Twain, bankrolled by the *California Alta,* signed on as correspondent with a group traveling to Europe and the Holy Land on an oceangoing paddle wheeler, *The Quaker City.* If it seems odd that a tour of the Holy Land was tacked on to the end of a fun European jaunt, I suspect the reason is that Americans back then still saw themselves as a puritanical people, distrustful of pleasure for pleasure's sake. The idea of traveling simply for enjoyment was morally ambiguous. The high-minded bona fides for this trip were secured when it was announced that abolitionist Henry Ward Beecher was to be among the party. Although he eventually bailed out, visiting the actual places where the famous scenes of the Bible transpired was thought to be ennobling enough to ensure that the trip would be justified as a sort of religious pilgrimage.

In his accounts of this visit to the Old World, Twain is simultaneously awestruck, like the young boy in Hannibal entranced by the approach of a smoke-puffing paddle wheeler, and eager to cut through the fawning reverence of pomp and majesty with which his compatriots deferred to Europe. He cleverly damns with excessive praise, using descriptions as gushing as the most effusive travel agency brochure, whether depicting the wonders of Versailles in *The Innocents Abroad* (see page 295) or portraying St. Paul's Cathedral in a fictionalized guidebook that appears in his unpublished *English Journals* (see page 180). Likewise, no one but Twain could have taken the tragedy of Heloise and Abelard and reduced it to a sitcom domestic mishap, as he did in *The Innocents Abroad* (see page 298), which was his first best seller and the product of his Quaker City trip.

Though *The Innocents Abroad* was the first work exploring Twain's concurrently rapt and sardonic view of Europe, its mores, and its languages, it wasn't his last. As a writer—that is, someone who made his living through the use of language—he was both fascinated and confounded by the infernal goulash of European languages, and he took every opportunity to let his readers know it both in this book and through the rest of his work: See *Italian without a Master* (page 308) and *The Awful German Language* (page 203), where he wrote, "My philological studies have satisfied me that a gifted person ought to learn English (barring spelling and pronouncing) in thirty hours, French in thirty days, and German in thirty years. It seems manifest, then, that the latter tongue ought to be trimmed down and repaired. If it is to remain as it is, it ought to be gently and reverently set aside among the dead languages, for only the dead have time to learn it."

While Twain loved the art, the history, and the culture of Europe, he was loath to risk being confused with his Euro-worshipping countrymen, who were, as he was, among the first generation of middle-class tourists. Nowhere did he demonstrate this contrast more fully than in "The American Vandal Abroad" (see page 173), a speech retrieved by one of his biographers, Albert Bigelow Paine.

On the one hand, Twain presents, and eviscerates, the kind of boob who pinballs from monument to monument and from Titian to Tintoretto, as if he were checking off bird sightings on a nature walk, rarely stopping to experience what it is he is seeing:

> The Vandal goes to see the ancient and most celebrated painting in the world, *The Last Supper.* We all know it in engravings: the disciples all sitting on one side of a long, plain table and Christ with bowed head in the center—all the last suppers in the world are copied from this painting. It is so damaged now, by the wear and tear of three hundred years, that the figures can hardly be distinguished. The Vandal goes to see this picture—which all the world praises—looks at it with a critical eye, and says it's a perfect old nightmare of a picture and he wouldn't give forty dollars for a million like it (and I indorse his opinion), and then he is done with Milan.

On the other hand, just a few pages later, Twain gives us an appreciation of the beauty of Venice that is as wondrous and lyrical as anything written by John Ruskin:

Introduction

[U]nder the mellow moonlight the Venice of poetry and romance stood revealed. Right from the water's edge rose palaces of marble; gondolas were gliding swiftly hither and thither and disappearing suddenly through unsuspected gates and alleys; ponderous stone bridges threw their shadows athwart the glittering waves. There were life and motion everywhere, and yet everywhere there was a hush, a stealthy sort of stillness, that was suggestive of secret enterprises of bravos and of lovers; and clad half in moonbeams and half in mysterious shadows, the grim old mansions of the republic seemed to have an expression about them of having an eye out for just such enterprises as these. At that same moment music came stealing over the waters—Venice was complete.

Contrast this with his descriptions of the Holy Land. In reading his reports, one feels that Twain regarded that part of his trip the way a twelve-year-old boy might receive the news that, instead of playing baseball on a hot summer day, he would have to put on an itchy suit to attend a Sunday school lecture on the evils of tobacco and alcohol. A perfect example is Twain's reporting on a visit to the Sea of Galilee (see page 351):

If these unpeopled deserts, these rusty mounds of barrenness, that never, never, never do shake the glare from their harsh outlines, and fade and faint into vague perspective; that melancholy ruin of Capernaum; this stupid village of Tiberias, slumbering under its six funereal plumes of palms; yonder desolate declivity where the swine of the miracle ran down into the sea, and doubtless thought it was better to swallow a devil or two and get drowned into the bargain than have to live longer in such a place; this cloudless, blistering sky; this solemn, sailless, tintless lake, reposing within its rim of yellow hills and low, steep banks, and looking just as expressionless and unpoetical (when we leave its sublime history out of the question) as any metropolitan reservoir in Christendom—if these things are not food for rock me to sleep, mother, none exist, I think.

Introduction

With the publication of *Innocents Abroad* in 1869, followed by that of its prequel, *Roughing It,* in 1872, Twain's repertoire of travel writing reached its pinnacle. He was, by turns, the mistrustful Yank, the lyrical vagabond, the lover of art, the hater of art lovers, the humanist, the misanthrope. He would produce two more pure travel books—*A Tramp Abroad* (1880) and *Following the Equator* (1897)—which have Twain the traveler at his best but also, for long stretches, Twain the writer at his less than greatest. Lengthy passages in both books are quoted directly from tour books and local legends, and while they up the page count, they add little to the books.

A Tramp Abroad, some observers have suggested, was occasioned by Twain's desire to get out of America for a while after what he felt was the most disastrous public appearance of his life, a speech on the occasion of John Greenleaf Whittier's seventieth birthday. William Dean Howells was there, as were Ralph Waldo Emerson and, of course, Whittier. Twain had no idea that it was such a serious event and essentially winged it, mocking the Eastern literary establishment. It was, by all accounts, a total bomb and a great embarrassment. In its aftermath, Twain decided to take the family to Europe, financing the trip with another book. Although he was clearly out of sorts, and even downright grumpy, the real and brilliant Twain could not help but shine through as well. His nonascent of the Matterhorn (see page 246) reads like a Europeanized version of his trip to Lake Tahoe in *Roughing It*: lyrical, personal, big in scope, yet full of carefully chosen detail. Likewise, the journey described in "Rafting Down the Neckar," in *A Tramp Abroad* (see page 255), in its bold outlines, could have been written by any number of people, but not with the same feel for the rhythms of a riverscape and the variety of people and places that the author of *Huckleberry Finn* and *Life on the Mississippi* brought to such a journey.

Following the Equator, like the companion lecture tour that financed his around-the-world travels to Australia, India, and Africa, was written to help him climb out of the mountain of debt into which he had fallen as a result of his ruinous investment in a supposedly revolutionary printing technology. Added to that was the devastating loss of his daughter Susie in 1896 as he was about to start writing the book. Doing the only thing that he knew how to do to preserve his sanity, he soldiered through a manuscript that he described as having been written "in hell" but which he hoped came off as an "excursion through heaven." It is neither, but, even in this desperately written volume, the curious world traveler comes through. The tragic yet comic story of Australia's aborigines, "The Weet-Weet" (see page 163), is the work of a man familiar with racial injustice but at the same time not blind to the foibles of all races.

This collection concludes with a section of whimsical pieces. "Captain Stormfield's Visit to Heaven" is as fanciful as the travels of Swift's *Gulliver* (with a bit of Baron Munchausen thrown in). "Letters from the Earth," the putative reports on humanity sent back from heavenly messenger Lucifer (before he was excused from archangeldom), reminds me in its fierce deadpan of Voltaire's *The Huron,* where a Native American "savage" writes about his encounter with "civilized" Europe. And speaking of savages, you will never find more droll barbarism than "Cannibalism in the Cars," where, day after day, a railway car full of congressmen debate which of their number would make the more appropriate meal for the rest of the snow-bound group.

When my grandpa Jan, who was a printer and poet by trade, died, my brother Don placed a copy of *Letters from the Earth* in his grave. We are not a religious family, and in our home, the collected works of Mark Twain—a faux calfskin set popular in workingmen's libraries of the 1930s—occupied the place on our bookshelves that is reserved for Scripture in others. Grandpa loved Twain for his humanism and for his blasphemous irreverence. We wouldn't have had the one without the other. I trust, and hope, you will find both between the covers of this book.

— **Peter Kaminsky**
Brooklyn
January 2009

PART I

The Mississippi

The Lure of the River

FROM *Life on the Mississippi,* CHAPTER XXX

One cannot see too many summer sunrises on the Mississippi. They are enchanting. First, there is the eloquence of silence; for a deep hush broods everywhere. Next, there is the haunting sense of loneliness, isolation, remoteness from the worry and bustle of the world. The dawn creeps in stealthily; the solid walls of black forest soften to gray, and vast stretches of the river open up and reveal themselves; the water is glass-smooth, gives off spectral little wreaths of white mist, there is not the faintest breath of wind, nor stir of leaf; the tranquility is profound and infinitely satisfying. Then a bird pipes up, another follows, and soon the pipings develop into a jubilant riot of music. You see none of the birds; you simply move through an atmosphere of song which seems to sing itself. When the light has become a little stronger, you have one of the fairest and softest pictures imaginable. You have the intense green of the massed and crowded foliage near by; you see it paling shade by shade in front of you; upon the next projecting cape, a mile off or more, the tint has lightened to the tender young green of spring; the cape beyond that one has almost lost color, and the furthest one, miles away under the horizon, sleeps upon the water a mere dim vapor, and hardly separable from the sky above it and about it. And all this stretch of river is a mirror, and you have the shadowy reflections of the leafage and the curving shores and the receding capes pictured in it. Well, that is all beautiful; soft and rich and beautiful; and when the sun gets well up, and distributes a pink flush here and a powder of gold yonder and a purple haze where it will yield the best effect, you grant that you have seen something that is worth remembering.

More River Thoughts

From *Adventures of Huckleberry Finn,* CHAPTER XIX

The first thing to see, looking away over the water, was a kind of dull line—that was the woods on t'other side; you couldn't make nothing else out; then a pale place in the sky; then more paleness spreading around; then the river softened up away off, and warn't black any more, but gray; you could see little dark spots drifting along ever so far away—trading scows, and such things; and long black streaks—rafts; sometimes you could hear a sweep screaking; or jumbled up voices, it was so still, and sounds come so far; and by and by you could see a streak on the water which you know by the look of the streak that there's a snag there in a swift current which breaks on it and makes that streak look that way; and you see the mist curl up off of the water, and the east reddens up, and the river, and you make out a log-cabin in the edge of the woods, away on the bank on t'other side of the river, being a woodyard, likely, and piled by them cheats so you can throw a dog through it anywheres; then the nice breeze springs up, and comes fanning you from over there, so cool and fresh and sweet to smell on account of the woods and the flowers; but sometimes not that way, because they've left dead fish laying around, gars and such, and they do get pretty rank; and next you've got the full day, and everything smiling in the sun, and the song-birds just going it!

Steam Boat Magic and a Small Town Boy

From *Life on the Mississippi,* CHAPTER IV

When I was a boy, there was but one permanent ambition among my comrades in our village on the west bank of the

Mississippi River. That was, to be a steamboatman. We had transient ambitions of other sorts, but they were only transient. When a circus came and went, it left us all burning to become clowns; the first negro minstrel show that came to our section left us all suffering to try that kind of life; now and then we had a hope that if we lived and were good, God would permit us to be pirates. These ambitions faded out, each in its turn; but the ambition to be a steamboatman always remained.

. . . After all these years I can picture that old time to myself now, just as it was then: the white town drowsing in the sunshine of a summer's morning; the streets empty, or pretty nearly so; one or two clerks sitting in front of the Water Street stores, with their splint-bottomed chairs tilted back against the wall, chins on breasts, hats slouched over their faces, asleep—with shingle-shavings enough around to show what broke them down; a sow and a litter of pigs loafing along the sidewalk, doing a good business in watermelon rinds and seeds; two or three lonely little freight piles scattered about the "levee"; a pile of "skids" on the slope of the stone-paved wharf, and the fragrant town drunkard asleep in the shadow of them; two or three wood flats at the head of the wharf, but nobody to listen to the peaceful lapping of the wavelets against them; the great Mississippi, the majestic, the magnificent Mississippi, rolling its mile-wide tide along, shining in the sun; the dense forest away on the other side; the "point" above the town, and the "point" below, bounding the river-glimpse and turning it into a sort of sea, and withal a very still and brilliant and lonely one. Presently a film of dark smoke appears above one of those remote "points"; instantly a negro drayman, famous for his quick eye and prodigious voice, lifts up the cry, "S-t-e-a-m-boat a-comin'!" and the scene changes! The town drunkard stirs, the clerks wake up, a furious clatter of drays follows, every house and store pours out a human contribution, and all in a twinkling the dead town is alive and moving. Drays, carts, men, boys, all go hurrying from many quarters to a common center, the wharf. Assembled there, the people fasten their eyes upon the coming boat as upon a wonder they are seeing for the first time. And the boat IS rather a handsome sight, too. She is long and sharp and trim and pretty; she has two tall, fancy-topped chimneys, with a gilded device of some kind swung between them; a fanciful pilot-house, a glass and "gingerbread," perched on top of the "texas" deck behind them; the paddle-boxes are gorgeous with a picture or with gilded rays above the boat's name; the boiler deck, the hurricane deck, and the texas deck are fenced and ornamented with clean white railings; there is a flag gallantly flying from the jack-staff; the furnace doors are open and the fires glaring bravely; the upper decks are black with passengers; the captain stands by the big bell, calm, imposing, the envy of all; great volumes of the blackest smoke are rolling and tumbling out of the chimneys—a husbanded grandeur created with a bit of pitch pine just before arriving at a town; the crew are grouped on the forecastle; the broad stage is run far out over the port bow, and an envied deckhand stands picturesquely on the end of it with a coil of rope in his hand; the pent steam is screaming through the gauge-cocks, the captain lifts his hand, a bell rings, the wheels stop; then they turn back, churning the water to foam, and the steamer is at rest. Then such a scramble as there is to get aboard, and to get ashore, and to take in freight and to discharge freight, all at one and the same time; and such a yelling and cursing as the mates facilitate it all with! Ten minutes later the steamer is under way again, with no flag on the jack-staff and no black smoke issuing from the chimneys. After ten more minutes the town is dead again, and the town drunkard asleep by the skids once more.

The Face of the Water

From *Life on the Mississippi,* CHAPTER IX

The face of the water, in time, became a wonderful book—a book that was a dead language to the uneducated passenger, but which told its mind to me without reserve, delivering its most cherished secrets as clearly as if it uttered them with a voice. And it was not a book to be read once and thrown aside, for it had a new story to tell every day. Throughout the long twelve hundred miles there was never a page that was void of interest, never one that you could leave unread without loss, never one that you would want to skip, thinking you could find higher enjoyment in some other thing. There never was so wonderful a book written by man; never one whose interest was so absorbing, so unflagging, so sparkingly renewed with every reperusal. The passenger who could not read it was charmed with a peculiar sort of faint dimple on its surface (on the rare occasions when he did not overlook it altogether); but to the pilot that was an *italicized* passage; indeed, it was more than that, it was a legend of the largest capitals, with a string of shouting exclamation points at the end of it; for it meant that a wreck or a rock was buried there that could tear the life out of the strongest vessel that ever floated. It is the faintest and simplest expression the water ever makes, and the most hideous to a pilot's eye. In truth, the passenger who could not read this book saw nothing but all manner of pretty pictures in it painted by the sun and shaded by the clouds, whereas to the trained eye these were not pictures at all, but the grimmest and most dead-earnest of reading-matter.

Now when I had mastered the language of this water and had come to know every trifling feature that bordered the great river as familiarly as I knew the letters of the alphabet, I had made a valuable acquisition. But I had lost something, too. I had lost something which could never be restored to me while I lived. All the grace, the beauty, the poetry had gone out of the majestic river! I still keep in mind a certain wonderful sunset which I witnessed when steamboating was new to me. A broad expanse of the river was turned to blood; in the middle distance the red hue brightened into gold, through which a solitary log came floating, black and conspicuous; in one place a long, slanting mark lay sparkling upon the water; in another the surface was broken by boiling, tumbling rings, that were as many-tinted as an opal; where the ruddy flush was faintest, was a smooth spot that was covered with graceful circles and radiating lines, ever so delicately traced; the shore on our left was densely wooded, and the somber shadow that fell from this forest was broken in one place by a long, ruffled trail that shone like silver; and high above the forest wall a clean-stemmed dead tree waved a single leafy bough that glowed like a flame in the unobstructed splendor that was flowing from the sun. There were graceful curves, reflected images, woody heights, soft distances; and over the whole scene, far and near, the dissolving lights drifted steadily, enriching it, every passing moment, with new marvels of coloring.

I stood like one bewitched. I drank it in, in a speechless rapture. The world was new to me, and I had never seen anything like this at home. But as I have said, a day came when I began to cease from noting the glories and the charms which the moon and the sun and the twilight wrought upon the river's face; another day came when I ceased altogether to note them. Then, if that sunset scene had been repeated, I should have looked upon it without rapture, and should have commented upon it, inwardly, after this fashion: This sun means that we are going to have wind to-morrow; that floating log means that the river is rising, small thanks to it; that slanting mark on the water refers to a bluff reef which is going to kill somebody's steamboat one of these nights, if it keeps on stretching out like that; those tumbling "boils" show a dissolving bar and a changing channel there; the lines and circles in the slick water over yonder are a warning that that troublesome place is shoaling up dangerously; that silver streak in the shadow of the forest is the "break" from a new snag, and he has located himself in the very best place he could have found to fish for steamboats; that tall dead tree, with a single living branch, is not going to last long, and then how is a body ever going to get through this blind place at night without the friendly old landmark.

No, the romance and the beauty were all gone from the river. All the value any feature of it had for me now was the amount of usefulness it could furnish toward compassing the safe piloting of a steamboat. Since those days, I have pitied doctors from my heart. What does the lovely flush in a beauty's cheek mean to a doctor but a "break" that ripples above some deadly disease. Are not all her visible charms sown thick with what are to him the signs and symbols of hidden decay? Does he ever see her beauty at all, or doesn't he simply view her professionally, and comment upon her unwholesome condition all to himself? And doesn't he sometimes wonder whether he has gained most or lost most by learning his trade?

Goin' to the Theater in the Big City (A Letter from "Thomas Jefferson Snodgrass," 1856)

FROM *Keokuk Saturday Post,* NOVEMBER 1, 1856

CORRESPONDENCE

Saint Louis, Oct. 18, 1856

MISTER EDITORS—

I want to enlighten you a leetle. I've been to the Theater—and I jest want to tell you how they do things down here to Saint Louis—the Mound City, as they call it, owin to its proximity to the Iron mountain and Pilot Knob.

Last night as I was a settin in the parlor of my Dutch boardin house in Fourth street (I board among the crouters so as to observe human natur in a forren aspeck) one of my hairy friends proposed that we mought as well go down and see Mr. Nealy play Julius Cesar. Now I had see Mr. Belding's Atheneum in Keokuk, and allers had a hankerin to get inside of it—so I told the Dutchman (who is for all the world like other humans, eats like 'em, looks something like 'em, and drinks a good deal more like 'em) that I was anxious to patronize the Drammer.

We hadn't gone more'n about six squares till we come to a tremenjous dirt-colored house, with carriages, and omnibuses, and niggers, and penut boys tearin around in front of it, indiscriminate like, and Dutch (I couldn't put in his name without using up too many of your type) said that was the place. We bought some green tickets and follered some fellers up nigh unto four hundred flights of stairs, and finally got into the concern, which was built into three or four round stories, with men and fiddlers in the first, along with a right smart chance of ragged boys, eatin penuts and cussin like militia majors. The second story had men and gals in it, and above there was nothing but masculine genders. We very naturally went into the second story, and got round where the side of the house (least ways I thought it was part of the house) was painted to represent Alexandria, or Venice, or some other small village settin in the water.

Gee Whillikens! Mister Editors, if you could a been there jest then, you'd a thought that either old Gabriel had blowed his horn, or else there was houses to rent in that locality. I reckon there was nigh onto forty thousand people setting in that theatre—and sich an other fannin, and blowin, and scrapon, and gigglin, I hain't seen since I arrived in the United States. Gals! Bless your soul, there was gals there of every age and sex, from three months up to a hundred years, and every cherubim of 'em had a fan and an opery glass and a-tongue—probably two or three of the latter weepon, from the racket they made. No use to try to estimate the oceans of men and mustaches—the place looked like a shoe brush shop.

Presently, about a thousand fellers commenced hammerin on the benches and hollerin "Music," and then the fiddlers laid themselves out, and went at it like forty millions of wood sawyers at two dollars and a half a cord. When they got through the people hollered and stamped and whistled like they do at a demercratic meeting, when the speaker says something they don't understand. Well, thinks I, now I've got an old coarse comb in my pocket, and I wonder if it wouldn't take them one-hoss fiddlers down a peg and bring down the house, too, if I'd jest give 'em a tech of "Auld Lang Syne" on it. No sooner said than done, and out come the old comb and a piece of paper to put on it. I "hem'd and haw'd" to attract attention, like, and commenced Doo-doo—do-doo—do-doo. "He, he, he," snickered the gals. "Ha, ha, ha," roared the mustaches. "Put him out." "Let him alone." "Go it, old Country." "Say, when did you get down?" and the devil himself couldn't a hearn that comb. I tell you now, I was riled. I throwed the comb at a little man that wasn't sayin nothin and ris right up. "Gentlemen and Ladies," says I, "I want to explain. I'm a peacable stranger from Keokuk, and my name is Thomas Jefferson Snodgrass—" "Go it, Snodgrass." "Oh, what a name." "Say, old Country, whar'd you get that hat?" Darn my skin if I wasn't mad. I jerked off my coat and jumped at the little man and, says I, "You nasty, sneakin degenerate great grandson of a ring tailed monkey, I kin jest lam—" "Hold on there, my friend, jest pick up your coat and follow me," says a military lookin gentleman with a club in his hand, tappin me on the shoulder. He was a police. He took me out and after I explained to him how St. Louis would fizzle out if Keokuk got offended at her, he let me go back, makin me promise not to make any more music durin the evening. So I let 'em holler their darndest when I took my seat, but never let on like I heard 'em.

Pretty soon a little bell rung, and they rolled up the side of the house with Alexandria on it, showin a mighty fine city, with houses, and streets, and sich, but nary a fire plug—all as natural as life. This was Rome. Then a lot of onery lookin fellers come a tearin down one of the streets, hurrayin and swingin their clubs, and said they were going to see Julius Cesar come into town. After this they shoved Rome out of the way, and showed the inside of a splendid palace, they call it, and then some soldiers with bob-tailed tin coats on (high water coats we used to call 'em in Keokuk) come in, then some gals (with high water dresses on), and then some more soldiers, and so on, gals and soldiers and soldiers and gals, till it looked like all the Free Masons and Daughters of Temperance in the world had turned out. Finally Mr. Cesar hisself come in with a crown on, folks called it, but it looked to my unsofisticated vision like a hat without any crown about it. He had a little talk with Antony, durin which he was uncommon severe on a Mr. Cashus (who was a standin within three feet of him, but the derned fool didn't hear a word of it) reflectin on his personal appearance—saying he had a "lean and hungry look," which was mighty mean in him to say, though he was in fact, for the feller couldn't a looked more like a shadder if he'd a boarded all his life at a Keokuk hotel. It's no use expatiating on every thing they done, so I'll jest mention a few of the things which I happened to see when the gal that sot in front of me took her turkey's tail head dress out of the way a minute to say somethin to the owner of an invisable mustash that had got wilted by coming out into the night air.

Arter a spell, a lot of fellers come out, along with Mr. Cashus, and they all laid their heads together like as many lawyers when they are gettin ready to prove that a man's heirs ain't got any right to his property. Presently Mr. Brutus come a marchin in as grand as a elephant in a menagerie of monkeys, and then the people stamped like Jehu. I kinda liked his looks. He 'peared like a man and a gentleman. The gal with the turkey's tail clapped her spy-glass to her eye, and says, "Ther's Brutus—oh, what a mien he has." I didn't like that, so leanin forward, says I, "Madam, beggin your pardon, them other fellers is a consarned sight meaner'n him. There's that Cashus—" "Hold your tongue, sir," yelled the wilted mustasch—and in half a second there was enough double-barrelled opery glasses leveled at me to a blowed me into chunks no bigger'n a mustard seed if they'd only been loaded. Rememberin the music scrape, I dried up and kept quiet, letten the fellers in the lower story holler at me as much as they wanted. Dr. H. had been settin purty close to me, and I thought I'd get him to explain this time, but I found he'd gone out between the acts to see a intimate friend, and hadn't got back yet. Cashus and the other fellers was for killin Cesar and makin sausage meat of him cause they couldn't be kings and emperors while he was alive, but Brutus didn't like that way of doin the thing—he jist wanted to kill him like a christian, jist for the good of Rome. Then the people stomped again. It 'peared to me kind of curus that they should kick up sich a noise every time any body raved around and ripped out somethin hifalutin, but went half asleep when anybody was tellin about poor Cesar's virtues.

Arter that, Misses Brutus come out when the other fellars was gone, and like Mr. Clennam at the Circumlocution Office, she "wanted to know." But it warn't no use—Brutus warn't going to publish jest then, and it 'pears that wimmin was the only newspapers they had in those days. You see all them fellers was conspirators, got together to conspirit a little again Cesar, and Brutus didn't consider it healthy to tell the secret to everybody. (Mr.

Editors, as I'm acquainted with a right smart chance of gals in Keokuk, why, if it's jest as convenient, I'd ruther you wouldn't send your paper only to the men, this week.) At last it come time to remove Mr. Cesar from office, like they say the Buchaneers are going to do the Fremonsters extinguish him entirely—so all the conspirators got around the throne, and directly Cesar come steppin in, putting on as many airs as if he was mayor of Alexandria. Arter he had sot on the throne awhile they all jumped on him at once like a batch of Irish on a sick nigger. He fell on the floor with a percussion that would a made him feel like he'd been ridin bare back on a Keokuk livery stable horse for a month, if he'd lived. When he drapped, the turkey tailed gal flinched, and grunted a sympathetic "ugh," and everybody in the neighborhood laughed at her. But it wasn't the gal's fault—she had for once got wrapped up in the play, and I spose that was the only part she entirely comprehended, cause I seen her slip down in the street the other day.

Finally, the play was done, and I reached over to the wilted mustache, and says I: "Squire, can you tell me what Mr. Cesar's agoin to play next?" He wheeled hisself around sudden, and says he: "Don Cesar—he be damn'd, sir." "Oh, gracious sakes, don't swear so hard," says I, horrerfied. "I ain't swearin," says he, and he pinted out the play on the bill of fare—"I said Don Cesar de Bazan, sir." I seen through it, then, in a minnit, so I told him it was sufficient—no apologies wasn't necessary.

I changed my seat now, and took a pew in front, so I could see plumb back into the kitchen of the concern, if they should take away the cities and woods and things. Proppin my feet up on the railin, I thought I'd take it comfortable like. Jest then, them fellers in the pit, as they call it (and I guess, Mr. Editors, some of 'em'll get into a dern sight deeper pit than that, afore you git to heaven) went to hollerin "Boots. Boots. Boots," like all natur. Thinks I, that's fun, and I went to hollerin too, though I didn't know what it meant. When I got at it they all pitched in louder'n ever, and that gal like to a shook all her tail feathers out a laughin. Dutch says to me, "Take your feet down, you dern ledderhet, it's you vot makes all dish fuss." Dang my buttons if I wasn't a rarin and chargin when I found they was makin fun of me, and I ris right up, puttin my hat on the extreme side of my head, and stickin my thums in the armholes of my vest, and commenced a little oration, so—"Gentlemen and Ladies—I'm a peacable stranger from Keokuk, and my name is Thomas Jefferson—" "Put him out." "Hurrah for old Keokuk." "Go it, Snodgrass," yelled the purgatory fellers, and in a twin-klin a couple of police had sot me down in the street, advisin me to go to the devil and not come back there any more. Now, Mister Editors, Saint Louis may fizzle out and be derned.

Yours, with lacerated feelins,
—Thomas Jefferson Snodgrass

Mardi-Gras in New Orleans (A Letter to Pamela A. Moffett, 1859)

March 11, 1859, New Orleans, LA

It has been said that a Scotchman has not seen the world until he has seen Edinburgh; and I think that I may say that an American has not seen the United States until he has seen Mardi-Gras in New Orleans.

I posted off up town yesterday morning as soon as the boat landed, in blissful ignorance of the great day. At the corner of Good-Children and Tchoupitoulas streets, I beheld an apparition!—and my first impulse was to dodge behind a lamp-post. It was a woman—a hay-stack of curtain calico, ten feet high—sweeping majestically down the middle of the street (for what pavement in the world could accommodate hoops of such vast pro-portions?). Next I saw a girl of eighteen, mounted on a fine horse, and dressed as a Spanish Cavalier, with long rapier, flowing curls, blue satin doublet and half-breeches, trimmed with broad white lace—(the balance of her dainty legs cased in flesh-colored silk stockings)—white kid gloves— and a nodding crimson feather in the coquettishest little cap in the world.

She removed said cap and bowed low to me, and nothing loath, I bowed in return—but I couldn't help murmuring, "By the beard of the Prophet, Miss, but you've mistaken your man this time—for I never saw your silk mask before—nor the balance of your costume, either, for that matter." And then I saw a hundred men, women and children in fine, fancy, splendid, ugly, coarse, ridiculous, grotesque, laughable costumes, and the truth flashed upon me—"This is Mardi-Gras!" It was Mardi-gras—and that young lady had a perfect right to bow to, shake hands with, or speak to, me, or any body else she pleased. The streets were soon full of "Mardi-gras," representing giants, Indians, nigger minstrels, monks, priests, clowns—birds, beasts—everything, in fact, that one could imagine. The "free-and-easy" women turned out en masse—and their costumes and actions were very trying to modest eyes. The finest sight I saw during the day was a band of twenty stalwart men, splendidly arrayed as Comanche Indians, flying and yelling down the street on horses as finely decorated as themselves. It was worth going a long distance to see the performances of the day—but bless me! how insignificant they seemed in comparison with those of the night, when the grand torchlight procession of the "Mystic Krewe of Comus" was added. At half past seven in the evening I went up to St. Charles street, and found both its pavements, for many squares, packed and jammed with thousands of men and women, waiting to see the Mystic Krewe. I managed to get an eligible place near the middle of the street opposite the St. Charles Hotel, where I waited—yes, I waited—standing on both feet as long as I could—then on one—then on t'other—and was just preparing to stand on my head awhile, when a shout of "Here they come!" kept me still in the proper position of a box of glassware. But it was a false alarm—and after a while we had another false alarm—and then another—each repetition stirring up the impatience and anxiety of the crowd and setting it to heaving and surging at a fearful rate. At last the distant tinkling of lively music was heard—and then the tag-end of a great huzza that had battered nearly all the life out of itself by butting against many squares of hard brick houses before it reached us—and again the tinkling music, and again the faint huzza—and five thousand people near me were tip-toeing and bobbing and peeping down the long street, and wondering why the devil it didn't come along faster—if it ever expected to get in sight. Impatience was growing, now—for ever so far away down the street we could see a flare of light spreading away from a line of dancing colored spots. They approached faster, then, and pretty soon, we took up the fainting huzza, and breathed new life into it. And here was the procession at last. The torches were of all colors, but their shapes represented the spots on a pack of cards—an endless line of hearts, and clubs, &c. The procession was led by a mounted Knight Crusader in blazing gilt armor from head to foot, and I think one might never tire of looking at the splendid picture. Then followed tall, grotesque maskers representing some ancient game—then an odd figure covered with checks, with a huge chess board and chessmen for a hat—then another quaint fellow gleaming in backgammon stripes, with two great dice for a hat—then the kings of each suit of cards dressed in royal regalia of ermine, satin and gold—then queer figures representing various other games—then the Queen of the Fairies, with an winged troop of beauties, in airy costumes at her heels—then the King and Queen of the Genii, I suppose (eight or ten feet high) with vast rolls of flaxen curls, bowing majestically to the crowd—followed by a couple of infinitesimal dwarfs—and again by other genii, in costumes grotesque, hideous and beautiful in turn—then figures whose bodies were vast drums, trumpets, clarinets, fiddles, &c.,—followed by others whose bodies were pitchers, punch-bowls, goblets, &c., terminated by two tremendous and very unsteady black wine bottles—then gigantic chickens, turkeys, bears, and other beasts and birds—then a big Christmas tree, followed by Santa Claus, with fur cap, short pipe, &c., and surrounded by a great basket filled with toys—and then—well, I don't remember half. There were transparencies, marking the divisions, with a band of music to each. Under "May-day" was a beautifully decorated May-tree and a May-pole—after "Twelfth-Night" followed a troupe of the most outrageously hideous figures, half-beast, -half-human, that one could imagine—Santa Claus and his crew followed "Christmas"—the games, &c., followed "Comus at his old English tricks, and again," and if there were any other transparencies, I have forgotten them. The long procession blazed with bran-new silk and satin, and the whole thing seemed to have been gotten up without any regard to cost.

Certainly New Orleans seldom does things by halves....

My love to all,
Your brother
Sam

A Tour of New Orleans

FROM *Life on the Mississippi*, CHAPTER XLIV

The old French part of New Orleans—anciently the Spanish part— bears no resemblance to the American end of the city: the American end which lies beyond the intervening brick business-center. The houses are massed in blocks; are austerely plain and dignified; uniform of pattern, with here and there a departure from it with pleasant effect; all are plastered on the outside, and nearly all have long, iron-railed verandas running along the several stories. Their chief beauty is the deep, warm, varicolored stain with which time and the weather have enriched the plaster. It harmonizes with all the surroundings, and has as natural a look of belonging there as has the flush upon sunset clouds. This charming decoration cannot be successfully imitated; neither is it to be found elsewhere in America.

The iron railings are a specialty, also. The pattern is often exceedingly light and dainty, and airy and graceful—with a large cipher or monogram in the center, a delicate cobweb of baffling, intricate forms, wrought in steel. The ancient railings are hand-made, and are now comparatively rare and proportionately valuable. They are become BRIC-A-BRAC.

The party had the privilege of idling through this ancient quarter of New Orleans with the South's finest literary genius, the author of *The*

Grandissimes. In him the South has found a masterly delineator of its interior life and its history. In truth, I find by experience, that the untrained eye and vacant mind can inspect it, and learn of it, and judge of it, more clearly and profitably in his books than by personal contact with it.

With Mr. Cable along to see for you, and describe and explain and illuminate, a jog through that old quarter is a vivid pleasure. And you have a vivid sense as of unseen or dimly seen things—vivid, and yet fitful and darkling; you glimpse salient features, but lose the fine shades or catch them imperfectly through the vision of the imagination: a case, as it were, of an ignorant near-sighted stranger traversing the rim of wide vague horizons of Alps with an inspired and enlightened long-sighted native.

We visited the old St. Louis Hotel, now occupied by municipal offices. There is nothing strikingly remarkable about it; but one can say of it as of the Academy of Music in New York, that if a broom or a shovel has ever been used in it there is no circumstantial evidence to back up the fact. It is curious that cabbages and hay and things do not grow in the Academy of Music; but no doubt it is on account of the interruption of the light by the benches, and the impossibility of hoeing the crop except in the aisles. The fact that the ushers grow their buttonhole-bouquets on the premises shows what might be done if they had the right kind of an agricultural head to the establishment.

We visited also the venerable Cathedral, and the pretty square in front of it; the one dim with religious light, the other brilliant with the worldly sort, and lovely with orange-trees and blossomy shrubs; then we drove in the hot sun through the wilderness of houses and out on to the wide dead level beyond, where the villas are, and the water wheels to drain the town, and the commons populous with cows and children; passing by an old cemetery where we were told lie the ashes of an early pirate; but we took him on trust, and did not visit him. He was a pirate with a tremendous and sanguinary history; and as long as he preserved unspotted, in retirement, the dignity of his name and the grandeur of his ancient calling, homage and reverence were his from high and low; but when at last he descended into politics and became a paltry alderman, the public "shook" him, and turned aside and wept. When he died, they set up a monument over him; and little by little he has come into respect again; but it is respect for the pirate, not the alderman. To-day the loyal and generous remember only what he was, and charitably forget what he became.

Thence, we drove a few miles across a swamp, along a raised shell road, with a canal on one hand and a dense wood on the other; and here and there, in the distance, a ragged and angular-limbed and moss-bearded cypress, top standing out, clear cut against the sky, and as quaint of form as the apple-trees in Japanese pictures—such was our course and the surroundings of it. There was an occasional alligator swimming comfortably along in the canal, and an occasional picturesque colored person on the bank, flinging his statue-rigid reflection upon the still water and watching for a bite.

And by-and-bye we reached the West End, a collection of hotels of the usual light summer-resort pattern, with broad verandas all around, and the waves of the wide and blue Lake Pontchartrain lapping the thresholds. We had dinner on a ground-veranda over the water—the chief dish the renowned fish called the pompano, delicious as the less criminal forms of sin.

Thousands of people come by rail and carriage to West End and to Spanish Fort every evening, and dine, listen to the bands, take strolls in the open air under the electric lights, go sailing on the lake, and entertain themselves in various and sundry other ways.

We had opportunities on other days and in other places to test the pompano. Notably, at an editorial dinner at one of the clubs in the city. He was in his last possible perfection there, and justified his fame. In his suite was a tall pyramid of scarlet cray-fish—large ones; as large as one's thumb—delicate, palatable, appetizing. Also deviled whitebait; also shrimps of choice quality; and a platter of small soft-shell crabs of a most superior breed. The other dishes were what one might get at Delmonico's, or Buckingham Palace; those I have spoken of can be had in similar perfection in New Orleans only, I suppose.

In the West and South they have a new institution—the Broom Brigade. It is composed of young ladies who dress in a uniform costume, and go through the infantry drill, with broom in place of musket. It is a very pretty sight, on private view. When they perform on the stage of a theater, in the blaze of colored fires, it must be a fine and fascinating spectacle. I saw them go through their complex manual with grace, spirit, and admirable precision. I saw them do everything which a human being can possibly do with a broom, except sweep. I did not see them sweep. But I know they could learn. What they have already learned proves that. And if they ever should learn, and should go on the war-path down Tchoupitoulas or some of those other streets around there, those thoroughfares would bear a greatly improved aspect in a very few minutes. But the girls themselves wouldn't; so nothing would be really gained, after all.

The drill was in the Washington Artillery building. In this building we saw many interesting relics of the war. Also a fine oil-painting representing Stonewall Jackson's last interview with General Lee. Both men are on horseback. Jackson has just ridden up, and is accosting Lee. The picture is very valuable, on account of the portraits, which are authentic. But, like many another historical picture, it means nothing without its label. And one label will fit it as well as another—

First Interview between Lee and Jackson.

Last Interview between Lee and Jackson.

Jackson Introducing Himself to Lee.

Jackson Accepting Lee's Invitation to Dinner.

Jackson Declining Lee's Invitation to Dinner—with Thanks.

Jackson Apologizing for a Heavy Defeat.

Jackson Reporting a Great Victory.

Jackson Asking Lee for a Match.

It tells *one* story, and a sufficient one; for it says quite plainly and satisfactorily, "Here are Lee and Jackson together." The artist would have made it tell that this is Lee and Jackson's last interview if he could have done it. But he couldn't, for there wasn't any way to do it. A good legible label is usually worth, for information, a ton of significant attitude and expression in a historical picture. In Rome, people with fine sympathetic natures stand up and weep in front of the celebrated *Beatrice Cenci the*

Day before her Execution. It shows what a label can do. If they did not know the picture, they would inspect it unmoved, and say, "Young girl with hay fever; young girl with her head in a bag."

I found the half-forgotten Southern intonations and elisions as pleasing to my ear as they had formerly been. A Southerner talks music. At least it is music to me, but then I was born in the South. The educated Southerner has no use for an r, except at the beginning of a word. He says "honah," and "dinnah," and "Gove'nuh," and "befo' the waw," and so on. The words may lack charm to the eye, in print, but they have it to the ear. When did the r disappear from Southern speech, and how did it come to disappear? The custom of dropping it was not borrowed from the North, nor inherited from England. Many Southerners—most Southerners—put a y into occasional words that begin with the k sound. For instance, they say Mr. K'yahtah (Carter) and speak of playing k'yahds or of riding in the k'yahs. And they have the pleasant custom—long ago fallen into decay in the North—of frequently employing the respectful "Sir." Instead of the curt Yes, and the abrupt No, they say "Yes, Suh," "No, Suh."

But there are some infelicities. Such as "like" for "as," and the addition of an "at" where it isn't needed. I heard an educated gentleman say, "Like the flag-officer did." His cook or his butler would have said, "Like the flag-officer done." You hear gentlemen say, "Where have you been at?" And here is the aggravated form—heard a ragged street Arab say it to a comrade: "I was a-ask'n' Tom whah you was a-sett'n' at." The very elect carelessly say "will" when they mean "shall"; and many of them say, "I didn't go to do it," meaning "I didn't mean to do it." The Northern word "guess"—imported from England, where it used to be common, and now regarded by satirical Englishmen as a Yankee original—is but little used among Southerners. They say "reckon." They haven't any "doesn't" in their language; they say "don't" instead. The unpolished often use "went" for "gone." It is nearly as bad as the Northern "hadn't ought." This reminds me that a remark of a very peculiar nature was made here in my neighborhood (in the North) a few days ago: "He hadn't ought to have went." How is that? Isn't that a good deal of a triumph? One knows the orders combined in this half-breed's architecture without inquiring: one parent Northern, the other Southern. To-day I heard a schoolmistress ask, "Where is John gone?" This form is so common—so nearly universal, in fact—that if she had used "whither" instead of "where," I think it would have sounded like an affectation.

We picked up one excellent word—a word worth traveling to New Orleans to get; a nice, limber, expressive, handy word—*lagniappe*. They pronounce it "lanny-yap." It is Spanish—so they said. We discovered it at the head of a column of odds and ends in the Picayune, the first day; heard twenty people use it the second; inquired what it meant the third; adopted it and got facility in swinging it the fourth. It has a restricted meaning, but I think the people spread it out a little when they choose. It is the equivalent of the thirteenth roll in a "baker's dozen." It is something thrown in, gratis, for good measure. The custom originated in the Spanish quarter of the city. When a child or a servant buys something in a shop—or even the mayor or the governor, for aught I know—he finishes the operation by saying—

"Give me something for lagniappe."

The shopman always responds; gives the child a bit of licorice-root, gives the servant a cheap cigar or a spool of thread, gives the governor—I don't know what he gives the governor; support, likely.

When you are invited to drink, and this does occur now and then in New Orleans—and you say, "What, again?—no, I've had enough"; the other party says, "But just this one time more—this is for lagniappe." When the beau perceives that he is stacking his compliments a trifle too high, and sees by the young lady's countenance that the edifice would have been better with the top compliment left off, he puts his "I beg pardon—no harm intended," into the briefer form of "Oh, that's for lagniappe." If the waiter in the restaurant stumbles and spills a gill of coffee down the back of your neck, he says, "For lagniappe, sah," and gets you another cup without extra charge.

The Scene of the Battle: Vicksburg

From *Life on the Mississippi,* CHAPTER XXXIV

We used to plow past the lofty hill-city, Vicksburg, down-stream; but we cannot do that now. A cut-off has made a country town of it, like Osceola, St. Genevieve, and several others. There is currentless water—also a big island—in front of Vicksburg now. You come down the river the other side of the island, then turn and come up to the town; that is, in high water: in low water you can't come up, but must land some distance below it.

Signs and scars still remain, as reminders of Vicksburg's tremendous war experiences; earthworks, trees crippled by the cannon balls, cave-refuges in the clay precipices, etc. The caves did good service during the six weeks' bombardment of the city—May 8 to July 4, 1863. They were used by the non-combatants—mainly by the women and children; not to live in constantly, but to fly to for safety on occasion. They were mere holes, tunnels, driven into the perpendicular clay bank, then branched Y shape, within the hill. Life in Vicksburg, during the six weeks was perhaps—but wait—here are some materials out of which to reproduce it:

Population, twenty-seven thousand soldiers and three thousand non-combatants; the city utterly cut off from the world—walled solidly in, the frontage by gunboats, the rear by soldiers and batteries; hence, no buying and selling with the outside; no passing to and fro; no God-speeding a parting guest, no welcoming a coming one; no printed acres of world-wide news to be read at breakfast, mornings—a tedious dull absence of such matter, instead; hence, also, no running to see steamboats smoking into view in the distance up or down, and plowing toward the town—for none came, the river lay vacant and undisturbed; no rush and turmoil around the railway station, no struggling over bewildered swarms of passengers by noisy mobs of hackmen—all quiet there; flour two hundred dollars a barrel, sugar thirty, corn ten dollars a bushel, bacon five dollars a pound, rum a hundred dollars a gallon; other things in proportion: consequently, no roar and racket of drays and carriages tearing along the streets; nothing for them to do, among that handful of non-combatants of exhausted means; at three o'clock in the morning, silence; silence so dead that the measured tramp of a sentinel can be heard a seemingly impossible distance; out of hearing of this lonely sound, perhaps the stillness is absolute: all in a moment come ground-shaking thunder-crashes of artillery, the sky is cobwebbed with the crisscrossing red lines streaming from soaring bomb-shells, and a rain of iron fragments descends upon the city; descends upon the empty streets: streets which are not empty a moment later, but mottled with dim figures of frantic women and children scurrying from home and bed toward the cave dungeons—encouraged by the humorous grim soldiery, who shout "Rats, to your holes!" and laugh.

The cannon-thunder rages, shells scream and crash overhead, the iron rain pours down, one hour, two hours, three, possibly six, then stops; silence follows, but the streets are still empty; the silence continues; by-and-bye a head projects from a cave here and there and yonder, and reconnoitres, cautiously; the silence still continuing, bodies follow heads, and jaded, half smothered creatures group themselves about, stretch their cramped limbs, draw in deep draughts of the grateful fresh air, gossip with the neighbors from the next cave; maybe straggle off home presently, or take a lounge through the town, if the stillness continues; and will scurry to the holes again, by-and-bye, when the war-tempest breaks forth once more.

There being but three thousand of these cave-dwellers—merely the population of a village—would they not come to know each other, after a week or two, and familiarly; insomuch that the fortunate or unfortunate experiences of one would be of interest to all?

Those are the materials furnished by history. From them might not almost anybody reproduce for himself the life of that time in Vicksburg? Could you, who did not experience it, come nearer to reproducing it to the imagination of another non-participant than could a Vicksburger who did experience it? It seems impossible; and yet there are reasons why it might not really be. When one makes his first voyage in a ship, it is an experience which multitudinously bristles with striking novelties; novelties which are in such sharp contrast with all this person's former experiences that they take a seemingly deathless grip upon his imagination and memory. By tongue or pen he can make a landsman live that strange and stirring voyage over with him; make him see it all and feel it all. But if he wait? If he make ten voyages in succession—what then? Why, the thing has lost color, snap, surprise; and has become commonplace. The man would have nothing to tell that would quicken a landsman's pulse.

Years ago, I talked with a couple of the Vicksburg non-combatants—a man and his wife. Left to tell their story in their own way, those people told it without fire, almost without interest.

A week of their wonderful life there would have made their tongues eloquent for ever perhaps; but they had six weeks of it, and that wore the novelty all out; they got used to being bomb-shelled out of home and into the ground; the matter became commonplace. After that, the possibility of their ever being startlingly interesting in their talks about it was gone. What the man said was to this effect:

> It got to be Sunday all the time. Seven Sundays in the week—to us, anyway. We hadn't anything to do, and time hung heavy. Seven Sundays, and all of them broken up at one time or another, in the day or in the night, by a few hours of the awful storm of fire and thunder and iron. At first we used to shin for the holes a good deal faster than we did afterwards. The first time, I forgot the children, and Maria fetched them both along. When she was all safe in the cave she fainted. Two or three weeks afterwards, when she was running for the holes, one morning, through a shell-shower, a big shell burst near her, and covered her all over with dirt, and a piece of the iron carried away her game-bag of false hair from the back of her head. Well, she stopped to get that game-bag before she shoved along again! Was getting used to things already, you see. We all got so that we could tell a good deal about shells; and after that we didn't always go under shelter if it was a light shower. Us men would loaf around and talk; and a man would say, "There she goes!" and name the kind of shell it was from the

THE CHICAGO OF EUROPE

sound of it, and go on talking—if there wasn't any danger from it. If a shell was bursting close over us, we stopped talking and stood still— uncomfortable, yes, but it wasn't safe to move. When it let go, we went on talking again, if nobody hurt—maybe saying, "That was a ripper!" or some such commonplace comment before we resumed; or, maybe, we would see a shell poising itself away high in the air over-head. In that case, every fellow just whipped out a sudden, "See you again, gents!" and shoved. Often and often I saw gangs of ladies prom-enading the streets, looking as cheerful as you please, and keeping an eye canted up watching the shells; and I've seen them stop still when they were uncertain about what a shell was going to do, and wait and make certain; and after that they sa'ntered along again, or lit out for shelter, according to the verdict. Streets in some towns have a litter of pieces of paper, and odds and ends of one sort or another lying around. Ours hadn't; they had *iron* litter. Sometimes a man would gather up all the iron fragments and unbursted shells in his neighborhood, and pile them into a kind of monument in his front yard—a ton of it, some-times. No glass left; glass couldn't stand such a bombardment; it was all shivered out. Windows of the houses vacant—looked like eye-holes in a skull. *Whole* panes were as scarce as news.

We had church Sundays. Not many there, along at first; but by-and-bye pretty good turnouts. I've seen service stop a minute, and every-body sit quiet—no voice heard, pretty funeral-like then—and all the more so on account of the awful boom and crash going on outside and overhead; and pretty soon, when a body could be heard, service would go on again. Organs and church-music mixed up with a bombardment is a powerful queer combination—along at first. Coming out of church, one morning, we had an accident—the only one that happened around me on a Sunday. I was just having a hearty handshake with a friend I hadn't seen for a while, and saying, "Drop into our cave to-night, after bombardment; we've got hold of a pint of prime wh—." Whiskey, I was going to say, you know, but a shell interrupted. A chunk of it cut the man's arm off, and left it dangling in my hand. And do you know the thing that is going to stick the longest in my memory, and outlast everything else, little and big, I reckon, is the mean thought I had then? It was "the whiskey *is saved*." And yet, don't you know, it was kind of excusable; because it was as scarce as diamonds, and we had only just that little; never had another taste during the siege.

Sometimes the caves were desperately crowded, and always hot and close. Sometimes a cave had twenty or twenty-five people packed into it; no turning-room for anybody; air so foul, sometimes, you couldn't have made a candle burn in it. A child was born in one of those caves one night. Think of that; why, it was like having it born in a trunk.

Twice we had sixteen people in our cave; and a number of times we had a dozen. Pretty suffocating in there. We always had eight; eight belonged there. Hunger and misery and sickness and fright and sorrow, and I don't know what all, got so loaded into them that none of them were ever rightly their old selves after the siege. They all died but three of us within a couple of years. One night a shell burst in front of the hole and caved it in and stopped it up. It was lively times, for a while, digging out. Some of us came near smothering. After that, we made two openings—ought to have thought of it at first.

Mule meat. No, we only got down to that the last day or two. Of course it was good; anything is good when you are starving.

This man had kept a diary during—six weeks? No, only the first six days. The first day, eight close pages; the second, five; the third, one—loosely written; the fourth, three or four lines; a line or two the fifth and sixth days; seventh day, diary abandoned; life in terrific Vicksburg having now become commonplace and matter of course.

The war history of Vicksburg has more about it to interest the general reader than that of any other of the river-towns. It is full of variety, full of incident, full of the picturesque. Vicksburg held out longer than any other important river-town, and saw warfare in all its phases, both land and water—the siege, the mine, the assault, the repulse, the bombardment, sickness, captivity, famine.

The most beautiful of all the national cemeteries is here. Over the great gateway is this inscription:

HERE REST IN PEACE 16,600 WHO DIED FOR THEIR
COUNTRY IN THE YEARS 1861 TO 1865.

The grounds are nobly situated; being very high and commanding a wide prospect of land and river. They are tastefully laid out in broad terraces, with winding roads and paths; and there is profuse adornment in the way of semi-tropical shrubs and flowers, and in one part is a piece of native wild-wood, left just as it grew, and, therefore, perfect in its charm. Everything about this cemetery suggests the hand of the national Government. The Government's work is always conspicuous for excellence, solidity, thoroughness, neatness. The Government does its work well in the first place, and then takes care of it.

By winding-roads—which were often cut to so great a depth between perpendicular walls that they were mere roofless tunnels—we drove out a mile or two and visited the monument which stands upon the scene of the surrender of Vicksburg to General Grant by General Pemberton. Its metal will preserve it from the hackings and chippings which so defaced its predecessor, which was of marble; but the brick foundations are crumbling, and it will tumble down by-and-bye. It overlooks a picturesque region of wooded hills and ravines; and is not unpicturesque itself, being well smothered in flowering weeds. The battered remnant of the marble monument has been removed to the National Cemetery.

PART II

The West

"Roughing It" Lecture

From *The (Lansing Michigan) State Republican,* December 21, 1871. [Transcribed text of Mark Twain's lecture, given December 14, 1871.]

Ladies and Gentlemen: By request, I will ask leave to introduce the lecturer of the evening, Mr. Clemens, otherwise Mark Twain—a gentleman whose great learning, whose historical accuracy, whose devotion to science, and whose veneration for the truth, are only equaled by his high moral character and his majestic presence. I refer in these vague and general terms to myself. I am a little opposed to the custom of ceremoniously introducing a lecturer to an audience, partly because it seems to me that it is not entirely necessary, I would much rather make it myself. Then I can get in all the facts.

But it is not really the introduction that I care for—I don't care about that—that don't discommode me—but it's the compliments that sometimes go with it. That's what hurts. It would hurt anybody. The idea of a young lady being introduced into society as the sweetest singer or the finest conversationalist! You might as well knock her in the head at once. I never had but one public introduction that seemed to me just exactly the thing—an introduction brimful of grace. Why, it was a sort of inspiration. And yet the man who made it wasn't acquainted with me; but he was sensible to the backbone, and he said to me: "Now you don't want any compliments?" Of course I did not want any compliments at all. He said: "Ladies and gentlemen—I shan't fool away any unnecessary time in this introduction. I don't know anything about this man; at least I only know two things: One is, that he has never been in the penitentiary; and the other is, I don't know why." Such an introduction as that puts a man at his ease right off.

I must not forget to make the announcement of the next lecture, the second of course, to be delivered by President Angell of the State University on Tuesday evening, the 26th of December. I don't know what his subject is going to be, but it will be good and well handled no doubt. In fact I forgot to ask what the subject is going to be.

Now when I first started out on this missionary expedition, I had a lecture which I liked very well, but by-and-by I got tired of telling that same old stuff over and over again, and then I got up another lecture, and after that another one, and I am tired of that: so I just thought tonight I would try something fresh, if you are willing. I don't suppose you care what a lecturer talks about if he only tells the truth—at intervals. Now I have got a book in press (it will be out pretty soon), over 600 octavo pages, and illustrated after the fashion of the *Innocents Abroad*. Terms—however I am not around canvassing for the work. I should like to talk a little of that book to you tonight. It is very fresh in my mind, as it is not more than three months since I wrote it. Say 30 or 40 pages—or if you prefer it the whole 600.

Ten or twelve years ago, I crossed the continent from Missouri to California, in the old overland stagecoach, a good while before the Pacific Railway was built. Over 1,900 miles. It was a long ride, day and night, through sagebrush, over sand and alkali plains, wolves and Indians, starvation and smallpox—everything to make the journey interesting. Had a splendid time, a most enjoyable pleasure trip, in that old stagecoach. We were bound for Nevada, which was then a bran' new Territory nearly or about as large as the state of Ohio. It was a desolate, barren, sterile, mountainous, unpeopled country, sagebrush and deserts of alkali. You could scarcely cast your eye in any direction but your gaze would be met by one significant object, and that was the projecting horns of a dried, shrunken carcass of an ox, preaching eloquent sermons of the hardships suffered by those emigrants, where a soil refused to clothe its nakedness, except now and then a little rill (or, as you might call it, a river) goes winding through the plain. Such is the Carson River, which clothes the valley with refreshing and fragrant hayfields. However, hay is a scant crop, and with all the importations from California the price of that article has never come under $300 per ton. In the winter the price reaches $800, and once went up to $1,200 per ton, and then the cattle were turned out to die, and it is hardly putting the figure too strong to say that the valleys were paved with the remains of these cattle.

It is a land where the winters are long and rigorous, where the summers are hot and scorching, and where not a single drop of rain ever falls during eleven tedious months; where it never thunders, and never lightens; where no river finds its way to the sea or empties its waters into the great lakes that have no perceptible outlet, and whose surplus waters are spirited away through mysterious channels down into the ground. A territory broad and ample, but which has not yet had a population numbering 30,000, yet a country that produced $20,000,000 of silver bullion in the year 1863, and produces $12,000,000 to $16,000,000 every year, yet the population has fallen away until now it does not number more than 15,000 or 18,000. Yet that little handful of people vote just as strongly as they do anywhere, are just as well represented in the Senate of the United States as Michigan, or the great state of New York with her 3,000,000 or 4,000,000 of people. That is equality in representation.

. . . In our journey we kept climbing and climbing for I don't know how many days and nights. At last we reached the highest eminence—the extreme summit of the great range of the Rocky Mountains, and entered the celebrated South Pass. Now the South Pass is more suggestive of a straight road than a suspension bridge hung in the clouds though in one place it suggests the latter. One could look below him on the diminishing crags and canyons lying down, down, down, away to the vague plain below, with a crooked thread in it which was the road, and tufts of feathers in it which were trees—the whole country spread out like a picture, sleeping in the sunlight, and darkness stealing over it, blotting out feature after feature under the frown of a gathering storm—not a film or shadow to mar the spectator's gaze. I could watch that storm break forth down there; could see the lightnings flash, the sheeted rain drifting along the canyon's side, and hear the thunder crash upon crash reverberating among a thousand rocky cliffs. This is a familiar experience to traveling people. It was a miracle of sublimity to a boy like me, who could hardly say that he had ever been away from home a single day in his life before.

We visited Salt Lake City in our journey. Carson City, the capital of Nevada, had a wild harem-scarem population of editors, thieves, lawyers, in fact all kinds of blacklegs. Its desperadoes, gamblers, and silver miners went armed to the teeth, every one of them dressed in the roughest kind of costumes, which looked strange and romantic to me and I was fascinated.

Now, instead of making a tedious description, I will say that they had a curious and peculiar breed of horses out there. I will give you the main points in regard to a little personal adventure which I had with one of these horses, leaving your imaginations to do the rest. Everybody rode horseback there. They were most magnificent riders. I thought so at least. I soon learned to tell a horse from a cow, and I was just burning with impatience to learn more. I was determined to have a horse to ride, and just as the thought was rankling in my mind an auctioneer came along on a beast crying him for sale, going at 22, 22, horse, saddle, and bridle. I could hardly resist. There was a man standing there. I was not acquainted with him (he turned out to be the auctioneer's brother). He observed to me, "That is a remarkable horse to be going at that price." I said I had half a notion to buy it. He said: "I know that horse—know him perfectly well. You are a stranger, and you may think that he is an American horse. He's nothing of the kind; he's a genuine Mexican plug; that's what he is." Well, I didn't know what a "genuine Mexican plug" was, but there was something about that man's way of saying it that I made up my mind to have that horse if it took every cent I had, and I said: "Has he any other advantages?" Well, he just hooked his forefinger into the breast pocket of my army shirt, led me off one side, and said in a low tone that no one else could hear, said: "He can outbuck any horse in this part of the country. Yes," he repeated, "he can outbuck any horse in America." The auctioneer was crying him at 24, 24, going at 24. I said, 27—"and sold." I took the "genuine Mexican plug," paid for him, put him in the livery stable, had him fed, then I let him rest until after dinner, when I brought him out into the plaza, where some of the citizens held him by the head while others held him down by the tail, and I got on him. As soon as they had let go, he put all his feet together in a bunch. He let his back sag down and then he arched it suddenly and shot me 180 yards into the air. I wasn't used to such things, and I came down and lit in the saddle, then he sent me up again and this time I came down astride his neck, but I managed to slide backward until I got into the saddle again. He then raised himself almost straight up on his hind legs and walked around awhile, like a member of Congress, then he came down and went up the other way, and just walked about on his hands as a schoolboy would, and all the time kept kicking at the sky. While he was in this position I heard a man say to another, "But don't he buck!" So that was "bucking." I was very glad to know it. Not that I was particularly enjoying it, but I was somewhat interested in it and naturally wanted to know what the name of it was. While this performance was going on, a sympathizing crowd had gathered around, and one of them remarked to me: "Stranger, you have been taken in. That's a genuine Mexican plug," and another one says: "Think of it! You might have bought an American horse, used to all kinds of work, for a very little more money." Well I didn't want to talk. I didn't have anything to say. I sat down. I was so jolted up, so internally, externally, and eternally mixed up, gone all to pieces. I put one hand on my forehead, the other on my stomach; and if I had been the owner of 16 hands I could have found a place for every one of them. If there is a Californian in this audience he knows what a Mexican plug is, and he knows that I have hardly exaggerated that exasperating creature.

Now if you would see the noblest, loveliest inland lake in the world, you should go to Lake Tahoe. It is just on the boundary line between California and Nevada. I have seen some of the world's celebrated lakes and they bear no comparison with Tahoe. There it is, a sheet of perfectly pure, limpid water, lifted up 6,300 feet above the sea—a vast oval mirror framed in a wall of snowclad mountain peaks above the common world. Solitude is king, and in that realm calm silence is brooding always. It is the home of rest and tranquility and gives emancipation and relief from the griefs and plodding cares of life. Could you but see the morning breaking there, gilding those snowy summits and then creeping gradually along the slopes until it sets, the lake and woodlands, free from mist, all agleam, you would see old Nature, the master artist, painting these dissolving views on the still water and finally grouping all these features into a complete picture. Every little dell, the mountains with their dome-turned pinnacles, the cataracts and drifting clouds, are all exquisitely photographed on the burnished surface of the lake, suffused with the softest and richest color. This lake is ten miles from Carson City, and in company with a friend we used to foot it out there, taking along provisions and blankets—camp out on the lake shore two or three weeks at a time; not another human being within miles of us. We used to loaf about in the boat, smoke and read, sometimes play seven-up to strengthen the mind. It's a sinful game, but it's mighty nice. We'd just let the boat drift and drift wherever it wanted to. I can stand a deal of such hardship and suffering when I'm healthy. And the water was so wonderfully clear. Where it was 80 feet deep the pebbles on the bottom were just as distinct as if you held them in your hand; and in that clear white atmosphere it seemed as if the boat was drifting through the air. Out in the middle it was a deep dark indigo blue, and the official measurement made by the State Geologist of California shows it to be 1,525 feet deep in the center. You can imagine that it would take a great many churches and steeples piled one upon another before they would be perceptible above its surface. You might use up a great deal of ecclesiastical architecture in that way. Now, notwithstanding that lake is lifted so high up among the clouds, surrounded by the everlasting snowcapped mountain-peaks, with its surface higher than Mt. Washington in the East, and notwithstanding the water is pretty shallow around the edges, yet the coldest winter day in the recollection of humanity was never known to form ice upon its surface. It has no feeders but the little mountain rills, yet it never rises nor falls. Donar Lake, close by, freezes hard every winter. Why Lake Tahoe does not is a question which no scientist has ever been able to explain.

If there are any consumptives here I urge them to go out there, renew their age, make their bodies hale and hearty, in the pure, magnificent air of Lake Tahoe. If it don't cure you I'll bury you at my own expense. It will cure you. I met a man there—he had been a man once, but now he was only a shadow, and a very poor sort of shadow at that. That man took the thing very deliberately. He had fixed up things comfortable while he did stay, but he was in dead earnest. Thought he was going to die sure, but he made a sickly failure of it. He had brought along a plan of his private graveyard, some drawings of different kinds of coffins, and he never did anything but sit around all day and cipher over these plans, to get things to suit him, and try to find out which coffin would be the most becoming. Well, I met that man three months afterward. He was chasing mountain sheep over mountains seven miles high with a Sharp's rifle. He didn't get them, but he was chasing them just the same. He had used up his graveyard plans for wadding and had sent home for some more. Such a cure as that was! Why, when I first saw that man his clothes fitted him about as a circus tent fits the tentpole; now they were snug to him; they stuck to him like postage stamps, and he weighed a ton. Yes, he weighed more than a ton, but I will throw in the odd ounces, I'm not particular about that, eleven I think it was. I know what I am talking about, for I took him to the hay scales and weighed him myself. A lot of us stood on there with him. But I hope you won't mind my nonsense about it. It was really a wonderful cure, and if I can persuade any consumptive to go out there I shall feel at any rate that I have done one thing worth having lived to accomplish. And if there is a consumptive in this house I want to say to him: Shoulder your gun, go out there and hunt. It's the noblest hunting ground on earth. You can hunt there a year and never find anything—except mountain sheep; but you can't get near enough to them to shoot one. You can see plenty of them with a spyglass. Of course you can't shoot mountain sheep with a spyglass. It is our American Shamwah (I believe that is the way that word is pronounced—I don't know), with enormous horns, inhabiting the roughest mountain fastnesses, so exceedingly wild that it is impossible to get within rifleshot of it. There was no other game in that country when I was there—except seven-up; though one can see a California quail now and then—a proud, stately, beautiful bird, with a curved and graceful plume on top of its head. But you can't shoot one. You might as well try to kill a cast-iron dog. They don't mind a mortal wound any more than a man would mind a scratch.

I had supposed in my innocence that silver mining was nice, easy business, and that of course all you had to do was to pick it up, and that you could tell it from any other substance on account of its brightness and its white metallic look. Then came my disenchantment; for I found that silver was merely scattered through quartz rock. Gold is found in cement veins, in quartz veins, loosely mingled with the earth, in the sand in beds of rivers, but I never heard of any other house or home for silver to live in than quartz rock. This rock is of a dull whitish color faintly marbled with blue veins. A fine powder of silver ore makes these blue veins and this yields $30 in bullion. A little dab of silver that I could crowd in my mouth came out of this 2,000 pounds of solid rock. I found afterward that $30 rock was mighty profitable. Then they showed me some more rock which was a little more clouded, that was worth $50 a ton. The bluer and darker the rock the richer it was. Sometimes you could find it worth $400, $500, and $600 a ton. At rare intervals rock can be found that is worth $1,500 and $2,000 per ton, and at rarer intervals you would see a piece of quartz that had a mass of pure silver in its grip, large as a child's head—more than pure, because it always had a good deal of gold mixed up in its composition. The wire silver is Nature's aristocratic jewelry. The quartz crystallizes and becomes perfectly clear, just as clear and faultless as the diamond, and almost as radiant in beauty. Nature, down there in the depths of the earth, takes one of these quartz rocks, shapes a cavity, and right in its heart imprisons a delicate little coil of serpentine, pure white, aristocratic silver.

It was uphill work, this silver mining. There were plenty of mines but it required a fortune to work one; for tons of worthless rock must be ground to powder to get at the silver. I was the owner of a hundred silver mines, yet I realized that I was the poorest man on earth. Couldn't sell to anybody; couldn't pay my board; so I had to go to work in a quartz mill at ten dollars per week. I was glad to get that berth, but I couldn't keep it. I don't know why; I was the most careful workman they ever had. They said so. I took more pains with my work than anybody else. I was shoveling sand-tailings as they call it. It is silver bearing rock that has been ground up and worked over once. It is then saved and worked over again. I was so particular about it that I have sat still for one hour and a half and studied about the best way to shovel that sand; and if I couldn't cipher it out in my mind I wouldn't go shoveling around recklessly—I would leave it alone until the next day. Many a time when I have been carrying sand from one pile to another 30 or 40 feet apart I would get started with a pailful when a splendid idea would strike me and I would carry that sand right back and sit down and think about it. Like as not I would get so absorbed in it as to go to sleep. I most always go to sleep when I am excited.

I knew there was a tiptop splendid way to move that sand from one pile to another and I told the boss so. "Well," he replied, "I am all-fired glad to hear it," and you never saw a man so kind of uplifted as he was. He seemed as if a load had been lifted from his breast—a load of sand.

I said to him: "What you want now is to get a cast-iron pipe about 14 feet in diameter—boiler iron will do—and about 42 feet long. Have one end raised up 35 or 40 feet, and then you want to have a revolving belt. Work it with the waste steam from the engine. Have a chair fastened to that belt and let me sit in that chair. Have a Chinaman to load up that big box, pass it to me as I come around, and I will up it into that pipe." You never saw a man so overcome with admiration. He discharged me on the spot. He said I had too much talent to be fooling away my time in a quartz mill.

If you will permit me, I would like to illustrate the ups and downs of fortune in the mining country with just a little personal experience of my own. I had a cabinmate by the name of Higby—a splendid good fellow. One morning the camp was thrown into a fearful state of excitement, for the "Wide West" had struck a lead black with native silver and yellow with gold. The butcher had been dunning us a week or two. Higby went up and brought a handful away and he sat studying and examining it, now and then soliloquizing in this manner: "That stuff never came out of the Wide West in the world." I told him it did, because I saw them hoist it out of the shaft. Higby went away by himself, and came back in a couple of hours perfectly overcome with excitement. He came in, closed the door, went and looked out of the window to make sure there was nobody in the neighborhood, and said to me, "We are worth a million of dollars. The Wide West be hanged— that's a blind lead." Said I: "Higby, are you really in earnest? Say it again: say it strong, Higby." He replied: "Just as sure as I am standing here, it's a blind lead. We're rich." Poverty had vanished and we could buy that town and pay for it, and six more just like it. A blind lead is one that doesn't crop out above the ground like an ordinary quartz lead. The Wide West had simply tapped it in their shaft and we had discovered it. It belonged to us. It was our property and there wouldn't anybody in the camp dispute that fact. We took into partnership the foreman of the Wide West, and the Wide West had to stop digging. We were the lions of Esmeralda. People wanted to lend us money; other people wanted to sell us village lots on time; and the butcher brought us meat enough for a barbecue and went away without his pay.

Now there is a rule that a certain amount of work must be done on a new claim within the first ten days, or the claim is forfeited to any one who may first take it up. Now I was called away to nurse an old friend who was dangerously ill up at the Nine Mile Ranch, and I just wrote a note and threw it into the window telling Higby where I was gone. The fellow I went to nurse was an irascible sort of fellow, and while carrying him from the vapor bath because I let my end of him fall we had a quarrel and I started for home. When I reached there, I saw a vast concourse of people over at the claim and the thought struck me that we were richer than ever, probably worth two million certain. Presently I met Higby looking like a ghost, and says I: "What on earth is the matter." "Well," he says, "you didn't do the work on the mine. I depended on you. The foreman's mother dying in California, he didn't do the work, our claim is forfeited and we are ruined. We haven't a cent." We went home to the cabin. I looked down at the floor. There was my note, and beside it was a note from Higby, telling me that he was going away to look for another mine which wouldn't have amounted to anything even if he had found it, in comparison with our claim.

It don't seem possible that there could be three as big fools in one small town, but we were there, and I was one of them. For once in my life I was absolutely a millionaire for just ten days by the watch. I was just ready to go into all kinds of dissipation and I am really thankful that this was a chapter in the history of my life, although at the time of course I did a great deal of weeping and gnashing my teeth. When I lost that million my heart was broken and I wanted to pine away and die, but I couldn't borrow money enough to live on while I did so, and I had to give that up. Everything appeared to go against me. Of course, I might have suicided, but that was kind of disagreeable.

I had written a few letters for the press, and just in the nick of time I received a letter from the *Virginia City Daily Enterprise* offering me $25 a week to go and be a reporter on that paper. I could hardly believe it, but this was no time for foolishness and I was in for anything. I never had edited anything, but if I had been offered the job of translating Josephus—from the original Hebrew—I should have taken it. If I had translated Josephus I would have thrown in as many jokes as I could for the money and made him readable. I would have had a variety, if I had to write him all up new.

Well, I walked that 130 miles in pretty quick time and took the berth. Have you ever considered what straits reporters are sometimes pushed to in furnishing the public with news? Why, the first day items were so scarce, I couldn't find an item anywhere and just as I was on the verge of despair, as luck would have it, there came in a lot of emigrants with their wagon trains. They had been fighting with the Indians and got the worst of it. I got the names of their killed and wounded, and then by-and-by there was another train came in. They hadn't had any trouble and of course I was disappointed, but I did the best I could under the circumstances. I cross-questioned that boss emigrant and found that they were going right on through and wouldn't come back to make trouble, so I got his list of names and added to my killed and wounded, and I got ahead of all the other papers. I put that wagon train through the bloodiest Indian fight ever seen on the plains. They came out of the conflict covered with glory. The chief editor said he didn't want any better reporter than I was. I said: "You just bring on your Indians and fetch out your emigrants, leave me alone, and I will make the fur fly. I will hang a scalp on every sagebush between here and the Missouri border." That was all first rate, but by-and-by items got low again and I was downhearted. I was miserable, because I couldn't strike an item. At last fortune favored me again. A couple of dear delightful desperadoes got into a row right before me and one of them shot the other. I stepped right up there and got the victim to give me his last words exclusively for the *Enterprise,* and I added some more to them so as to be sure and get ahead of the other papers, and then I turned to the desperado. Said I, "You are a stranger to me, sir, but you have done me a favor which I can never sufficiently thank you for. I shall ever regard you as a benefactor." And I asked him if he could lend me half a dollar. We always borrowed a piece whenever we could—it was a public custom. The thought then struck me that I could raise a mob and hang the other desperado, but the officers got ahead of me and took him into custody. They were down on us and would always do any little mean thing like that, to spite us. And so I was fairly launched in literature, in the business of doing good. I love to do good. It is our duty. I think when a man does good all the time his conscience is so clear. I like to do right and be good, though there is a deal more fun in the other thing.

Now you see by my sort of experience a man may go to bed at night not worth a cent and wake up in the morning to find himself immensely wealthy, and very often he is a man who has a vast cargo of ignorance. To illustrate my point I will give you a story about a couple of these fresh nabobs whose names were colonels Jim and Jack. Colonel Jim had seen considerable of the world, but Colonel Jack was raised down in the backwoods of Arkansas. These gentlemen after their good luck suddenly determined on a pleasure trip to New York; so they went to San Francisco, took a steamer, and in due time arrived in the great metropolis. While passing along the street, Colonel Jack's attention was attracted by the hacks and splendid equipages he saw, and he says: "Well I've heard about these carriages all my life and I mean to have a ride in one. I don't care what it costs." So Colonel Jim stepped to the edge of the sidewalk and ordered a handsome carriage. Colonel Jack says: "No, you don't. None of your cheap turnouts for me. I'm here to have a good time, and money's no object. I'm going to have the best rig this country affords. You stop that yellow one there with the pictures on it." So they got into the empty omnibus and sat down. Colonel Jack says: "Well! Ain't it gay? Ain't it nice? Windows and pictures and cushions, till you can't rest. What would the boys think of this if they could see us cut such a swell in New York? I wish they could see us. What is the name of this?" Colonel Jim told him it was a barouche. After a while he poked his head out in front and said to the driver, "I say, Johnny, this suits me. We want this shebang all day. Let the horses go." The driver loosened the strap and passed his hand in for the fare. Colonel Jack, thinking that he wanted to shake hands, shook him heartily and said: "You understand me. You take care of me and I'll take care of you." He put a $20 gold piece into the driver's hand. The driver says: "I can't change that." Colonel Jack replied: "Put it into your pocket, I don't want any change. We're going to ride it out." In a few minutes the bus stopped and a young lady got in. Colonel Jack stared at her. Pretty soon she got out her money to pay the driver. Colonel Jack says: "Put up your money, Miss; you are perfectly welcome to ride here just as long as you want to, but this barouche is chartered and we can't let you pay." Soon an old lady got in. Colonel Jack told her to "sit down. Don't be at all uneasy, everything is paid for and as free as if you were in your own turnout, but you can't pay a cent." Pretty soon two or three gentlemen got in, and ladies with children.

Colonel Jack says, "Come right along. Don't mind us. Free blowout." By and by the crowd filled all the seats and were standing up, while others climbed up on top. He nudged Colonel Jim and says: "Colonel, what kind of cattle do they have here? If this don't bang anything I ever saw. Ain't they friendly, and so awful cool about it, but they ain't sociable." But I have related enough of that circumstance to illustrate the enormous simplicity of these unfledged biddies of fortune.

When I told the chairman of the society this evening that I wanted to change my subject he said it was a little risky; he didn't know about it, but I pleaded so hard and said the only reason was I didn't want to talk that Artemus Ward lecture because it had been printed in the papers. I told him that I would put in a little scrap from that Artemus Ward lecture, just enough to cover the advertisement, and then I wouldn't be telling any lies. Besides this anecdote had a moral to it. Well, the moral got him.

As nearly as I can cipher it out, the newspaper reporter has got us lecturers at a disadvantage. He can either make a synopsis or do most anything he wants to. He ought to be generous, and praise us or abuse us, but not print our speeches. Artemus Ward was bothered by a shorthand reporter and he begged him not to do him the injustice to garble his speech. He says, "You can't take it all down as I utter it." The reporter said, "If you utter anything I can't take down I will agree not to print the speech." Along in the lecture he tipped the reporter the wink and then he told the following anecdote:

(Whistle wherever the stars occur. If you can't, get somebody that can.)

He said that several gentlemen were conversing in a hotel parlor and one man sat there who didn't have anything to say. By and by, the gentlemen all went out except one of the number and the silent man. Presently the silent man reached out and touched the gentleman and says: "** I think, Sir, I have seen you somewhere before. I am not ** sure where it was or ** when it was ** but I know I have seen you." The gentleman says: "Very likely: but what do you whistle for?" **" I'll tell you all about it. ** I used to stammer ** fearfully and I courted a ** girl ** and she wouldn't ** have me because I was afflicted with such an ** infirmity. I went to a doctor and ** he ** told me that every time I went to stammer ** that I must whistle, which I did, and it completely cured me. But don't you know that ** girl ** wouldn't have me at last, for she ** said that **she wouldn't talk to a man that whistled as I did. ** She'd as soon hold a conversation with a wheelbarrow that wanted ** greasing."

Ladies and gentlemen, For three or four days I have had it in my mind to throw away that other lecture, but I never had the pluck to do it until tonight. The audience seemed to look friendly, and as I had been here before I felt a little acquainted. I thought I would make the venture. I sincerely thank you for the help you have given me, and I bid you goodnight.

Among the Miners

From *Roughing It,* CHAPTER LVII

It was in this Sacramento Valley that a deal of the most lucrative of the early gold mining was done, and you may still see, in places, its grassy slopes and levels torn and guttered and disfigured by the avaricious spoilers of fifteen and twenty years ago. You may see such disfigurements far and wide over California—and in some such places, where only meadows and forests are visible—not a living creature, not a house, no stick or stone or remnant of a ruin, and not a sound, not even a whisper to disturb the Sabbath stillness—you will find it hard to believe that there stood at one time a fiercely-flourishing little city, of two thousand or three thousand souls, with its newspaper, fire company, brass band, volunteer militia, bank, hotels, noisy Fourth of July processions and speeches, gambling hells crammed with tobacco smoke, profanity, and rough-bearded men of all nations and colors, with tables heaped with gold dust sufficient for the revenues of a German principality—streets crowded and rife with business—town lots worth four hundred dollars a front foot—labor, laughter, music, dancing, swearing, fighting, shooting, stabbing—a bloody inquest and a man for breakfast every morning—everything that delights and adorns existence—all the appointments and appurtenances of a thriving and prosperous and promising young city—and now nothing is left of it all but a lifeless, homeless solitude. The men are gone, the houses have vanished, even the name of the place is forgotten. In no other land, in modern times, have towns so absolutely died and disappeared, as in the old mining regions of California.

It was a driving, vigorous, restless population in those days. It was a curious population. It was the only population of the kind that the world has ever seen gathered together, and it is not likely that the world will ever see its like again. For observe, it was an assemblage of two hundred thousand young men—not simpering, dainty, kid-gloved weaklings, but stalwart, muscular, dauntless young braves, brimful of push and energy, and royally endowed with every attribute that goes to make up a peerless and magnificent manhood—the very pick and choice of the world's glorious ones. No women, no children, no gray and stooping veterans—none but erect, bright-eyed, quick-moving, strong-handed young giants—the strangest population, the finest population, the most gallant host that ever trooped down the startled solitudes of an unpeopled land. And where are they now? Scattered to the ends of the earth—or prematurely aged and decrepit—or shot or stabbed in street affrays—or dead of disappointed hopes and broken hearts—all gone, or nearly all—victims devoted upon the altar of the golden calf—the noblest holocaust that ever wafted its sacrificial incense heavenward. It is pitiful to think upon.

It was a splendid population—for all the slow, sleepy, sluggish-brained sloths staid at home—you never find that sort of people among pioneers—you cannot build pioneers out of that sort of material. It was that population that gave to California a name for getting up astounding enterprises and rushing them through with a magnificent dash and daring and a reck- . lessness of cost or consequences, which she bears unto this day—and when she projects a new surprise, the grave world smiles as usual, and says, "Well, that is California all over."

But they were rough in those times! They fairly reveled in gold, whisky, fights, and fandangoes, and were unspeakably happy. The honest miner raked from a hundred to a thousand dollars out of his claim a day, and what with the gambling dens and the other entertainments, he hadn't a cent the next morning, if he had any sort of luck. They cooked their own bacon and beans, sewed on their own buttons, washed their own shirts—blue woollen ones; and if a man wanted a fight on his hands without any annoying delay, all he had to do was to appear in public in a white shirt or a stove-pipe hat, and he would be accommodated. For those people hated aristocrats. They had a particular and malignant animosity toward what they called a *biled shirt*.

It was a wild, free, disorderly, grotesque society! Men—only swarming hosts of stalwart men—nothing juvenile, nothing feminine, visible anywhere!

In those days miners would flock in crowds to catch a glimpse of that rare and blessed spectacle, a woman! Old inhabitants tell how, in a certain camp, the news went abroad early in the morning that a woman was come! They had seen a calico dress hanging out of a wagon down at the camping-ground—sign of emigrants from over the great plains. Everybody went down there, and a shout went up when an actual, bona fide dress was discovered fluttering in the wind! The male emigrant was visible. The miners said:

"Fetch her out!"

He said: "It is my wife, gentlemen—she is sick—we have been robbed of money, provisions, everything, by the Indians—we want to rest."

"Fetch her out! We've got to see her!"

"But, gentlemen, the poor thing, she—"

"FETCH HER OUT!"

He "fetched her out," and they swung their hats and sent up three rousing cheers and a tiger; and they crowded around and gazed at her, and touched her dress, and listened to her voice with the look of men who listened to a memory rather than a present reality—and then they collected twenty-five hundred dollars in gold and gave it to the man, and swung their hats again and gave three more cheers, and went home satisfied.

Once I dined in San Francisco with the family of a pioneer, and talked with his daughter, a young lady whose first experience in San Francisco was an adventure, though she herself did not remember it, as she was only two or three years old at the time. Her father said that, after landing from the ship, they were walking up the street, a servant leading the party with the little girl in her arms. And presently a huge miner, bearded, belted, spurred, and bristling with deadly weapons—just down from a long campaign in the mountains, evidently-barred the way, stopped the servant, and stood gazing, with a face all alive with gratification and astonishment. Then he said, reverently:

"Well, if it ain't a child!" And then he snatched a little leather sack out of his pocket and said to the servant:

"There's a hundred and fifty dollars in dust, there, and I'll give it to you to let me kiss the child!"

That anecdote is true.

But see how things change. Sitting at that dinner-table, listening to that anecdote, if I had offered double the money for the privilege of kissing the same child, I would have been refused. Seventeen added years have far more than doubled the price.

And while upon this subject I will remark that once in Star City, in the Humboldt Mountains, I took my place in a sort of long, post-office single file of miners, to patiently await my chance to peep through a crack in the cabin and get a sight of the splendid new sensation—a genuine, live Woman! And at the end of half of an hour my turn came, and I put my eye to the crack, and there she was, with one arm akimbo, and tossing flap-jacks in a frying-pan with the other.

And she was one hundred and sixty-five years old, and hadn't a tooth in her head.

The Killing of Julius Caesar "Localized"

FROM *The Celebrated Jumping Frog of Calaveras County, and Other Sketches*

Being the only true and reliable account ever published; taken from the Roman *Daily Evening Fasces,* of the date of that tremendous occurrence.

Nothing in the world affords a newspaper reporter so much satisfaction as gathering up the details of a bloody and mysterious murder and writing them up with aggravating circumstantiality. He takes a living delight in this labor of love—for such it is to him, especially if he knows that all the other papers have gone to press, and his will be the only one that will contain the dreadful intelligence. A feeling of regret has often come over me that I was not reporting in Rome when Caesar was killed—reporting on an evening paper, and the only one in the city, and getting at least twelve hours ahead of the morning-paper boys with this most magnificent "item" that ever fell to the lot of the craft. Other events have happened as startling as this, but none that possessed so peculiarly all the characteristics of the favorite "item" of the present day, magnified into grandeur and sublimity by the high rank, fame, and social and political standing of the actors in it.

However, as I was not permitted to report Caesar's assassination in the regular way, it has at least afforded me rare satisfaction to translate the following able account of it from the original Latin of the Roman *Daily Evening Fasces* of that date—second edition:

Our usually quiet city of Rome was thrown into a state of wild excitement yesterday by the occurrence of one of those bloody affrays which sicken the heart and fill the soul with fear, while they inspire all thinking men with forebodings for the future of a city where human life is held so cheaply and the gravest laws are so openly set at defiance. As the result of that affray, it is our painful duty, as public journalists, to record the death of one of our most esteemed citizens—a man whose name is known wherever this paper circulates, and where fame it has been our pleasure and our privilege to extend, and also to protect from the tongue of slander and falsehood, to the best of our poor ability. We refer to Mr. J. Caesar, the Emperor-elect.

The facts of the case, as nearly as our reporter could determine them from the conflicting statements of eye-witnesses, were about as follows: The affair was an election row, of course. Nine-tenths of the ghastly butcheries that disgrace the city nowadays grow out of the bickerings and jealousies and animosities engendered by these accursed elections. Rome would be the gainer by it if her very constables were elected to serve a century; for in our experience we have never even been able to choose a dog-pelter without celebrating the event with a dozen knockdowns and a general cramming of the station-house with drunken vagabonds overnight. It is said that when the immense majority for Caesar at the polls in the market was declared the other day, and the crown was offered to that gentleman, even his amazing unselfishness in refusing it three times was not sufficient to save him from the whispered insults of such men as Casca, of the Tenth Ward, and other hirelings of the disappointed candidate, hailing mostly from the Eleventh and Thirteenth and other outside districts, who were overheard speaking ironically and contemptuously of Mr. Caesar's conduct upon that occasion.

We are further informed that there are many among us who think they are justified in believing that the assassination of Julius Caesar was a put-up thing—a cut-and-dried arrangement, hatched by Marcus Brutus and a lot of his hired roughs, and carried out only too faithfully according to the program. Whether there be good grounds for this suspicion or not, we leave to the people to judge for themselves, only asking that they will read the following account of the sad occurrence carefully and dispassionately before they render that judgment.

The Senate was already in session, and Caesar was coming down the street toward the capitol, conversing with some personal friends, and followed, as usual, by a large number of citizens. Just as he was passing in front of Demosthenes and Thucydides' drug store, he was observing casually to a gentleman, who, our informant thinks, is a fortune-teller, that the Ides of March were come. The reply was, "Yes, they are come, but not gone yet." At this moment Artemidorus stepped up and passed the time of day, and asked Caesar to read a schedule or a tract or something of the kind, which he had brought for his perusal. Mr. Decius Brutus also said something about an "humble suit" which he wanted read. Artemidorus begged that attention might be paid to his first, because it was of personal consequence to Caesar. The latter replied that what concerned himself should be read last, or words to that effect. Artemidorus begged and beseeched him to read the paper instantly!—(Mark that: It is hinted by William Shakespeare, who saw the beginning and the end of the unfortunate affray, that this "schedule" was simply a note discovering to Caesar that a plot was brewing to take his life.)—However, Caesar shook him off, and refused to read any petition in the street. He then entered the capitol, and the crowd followed him.

About this time the following conversation was overheard, and we consider that, taken in connection with the events which succeeded it, it bears an appalling significance: Mr. Papilius Lena remarked to George W. Cassias (commonly known as the "Nobby Boy of the Third Ward"), a bruiser in the pay of the Opposition, that he hoped his enterprise to-day might thrive; and when Cassias asked, "What enterprise?" he only closed his left eye temporarily and said with simulated indifference, "Fare you well," and sauntered toward Caesar. Marcus Brutus, who is suspected of being the ringleader of the band that killed Caesar, asked what it was that Lena had said. Cassias told him, and added in a low tone, "I fear our purpose is discovered."

Brutus told his wretched accomplice to keep an eye on Lena, and a moment after Cassias urged that lean and hungry vagrant, Casca, whose reputation here is none of the best, to be sudden, for he feared prevention. He then turned to Brutus, apparently much excited, and asked what should be done, and swore that either he or Caesar would never turn back—he would kill himself first. At this time Caesar was talking to some of the back-country members about the approaching fall elections, and paying little attention to what was going on around him. Billy Trebonius got into conversation with the people's friend and Caesar's—Mark Antony—and under some pretense or other got him away, and Brutus, Decius, Casca, Cinna, Metellus Cimber, and others of the gang of infamous desperadoes that infest Rome at present, closed around the doomed Caesar. Then Metellus Cimber knelt down and begged that his brother might be recalled from banishment, but Caesar rebuked him for his fawning conduct, and refused to grant his petition. Immediately, at Cimber's request, first Brutus and then Cassias begged for the return of the banished Publius; but Caesar still refused. He said he could not be moved; that he was as fixed as the North Star, and proceeded to speak in the most complimentary terms of the firmness of that star and its steady character. Then he said he was like it, and he believed he was the only man in the country that was; therefore, since he was "constant" that Cimber should be banished, he was also "constant" that he should stay banished, and he'd be hanged if he didn't keep him so!

Instantly seizing upon this shallow pretext for a fight, Casca sprang at Caesar and struck him with a dirk, Caesar grabbing him by the arm with his right hand, and launching a blow straight from the shoulder with his left, that sent the reptile bleeding to the earth. He then backed up against Pompey's statue, and squared himself to receive his assailants. Cassias and Cimber and Cinna rushed, upon him with their daggers drawn, and the former succeeded in inflicting a wound upon his body; but before he could strike again, and before either of the others could strike at all, Caesar stretched the three miscreants at his feet with as many blows of his powerful fist. By this time the Senate was in an indescribable uproar; the throng of citizens in the lobbies had blockaded the doors in their frantic efforts to escape from the building, the sergeant-at-arms and his assistants were struggling with the assassins, venerable senators had cast aside their encumbering robes, and were leaping over benches and flying down the aisles in wild confusion toward the shelter of the committee-rooms, and a thousand voices were shouting "Po-lice! Po-lice!" in discordant tones that rose above the frightful din like shrieking winds above the roaring of a tempest. And amid it all great Caesar stood with his back against the statue, like a lion at bay, and fought his assailants weaponless and hand to hand, with the defiant bearing and the unwavering courage which he had shown before on many a bloody field. Billy Trebonius and Caius Legarius struck him with their daggers and fell, as their brother-conspirators before them had fallen. But at last, when Caesar saw his old friend Brutus step forward armed with a murderous knife, it is said he seemed utterly overpowered with grief and amazement, and, dropping his invincible left arm by his side, he hid his face in the folds of his mantle and received the treacherous blow without an effort to stay the hand that gave it. He only said, "Et tu, Brute?" and fell lifeless on the marble pavement.

We learn that the coat the deceased had on when he was killed was the same one he wore in his tent on the afternoon of the day he overcame the Nervii, and that when it was removed from the corpse it was found to be cut and gashed in no less than seven different places. There was nothing in the pockets. It will be exhibited at the coroner's inquest, and will be damning proof of the fact of the killing. These latter facts may be relied on, as we get them from Mark Antony, whose position enables him to learn every item of news connected with the one subject of absorbing interest of to-day.

LATER: While the coroner was summoning a jury, Mark Antony and other friends of the late Caesar got hold of the body, and lugged it off to the Forum, and at last accounts Antony and Brutus were making speeches over it and raising such a row among the people that, as we go to press, the chief of police is satisfied there is going to be a riot, and is taking measures accordingly.

A Trip to Tahoe

FROM *Roughing It,* CHAPTERS XXII–III

I t was the end of August, and the skies were cloudless and the weather superb. In two or three weeks I had grown wonderfully fascinated with the curious new country and concluded to put off my return to "the States" awhile. I had grown well accustomed to wearing a damaged slouch hat, blue woolen shirt, and pants crammed into boot-tops, and gloried in the absence of coat, vest and braces. I felt rowdyish and "bully" (as the historian Josephus phrases it, in his fine chapter upon the destruction of the Temple). It seemed to me that nothing could be so fine and so romantic. I had become an officer of the government, but that was for mere sublimity. The office was an unique sinecure. I had nothing to do and no salary. I was private Secretary to his majesty the Secretary and there was not yet writing enough for two of us. So Johnny K—— and I devoted our time to amusement. He was the young son of an Ohio nabob and was out there for recreation. He got it. We had heard a world of talk about the marvellous beauty of Lake Tahoe, and finally curiosity drove us thither to see it. Three or four members of the Brigade had been there and located some timber lands on its shores and stored up a quantity of provisions in their camp. We strapped a couple of blankets on our shoulders and took an axe apiece and started— for we intended to take up a wood ranch or so ourselves and become wealthy. We were on foot. The reader will find it advantageous to go horse-back. We were told that the distance was eleven miles. We tramped a long time on level ground, and then toiled laboriously up a mountain about a thousand miles high and looked over. No lake there. We descended on the other side, crossed the valley and toiled up another mountain three or four thousand miles high, apparently, and looked over again. No lake yet. We sat down tired and perspiring, and hired a couple of Chinamen to curse those people who had beguiled us. Thus refreshed, we presently resumed the march with renewed vigor and determination. We plodded on, two or three hours longer, and at last the Lake burst upon us—a noble sheet of blue water lifted six thousand three hundred feet above the level of the sea, and walled in by a rim of snow-clad mountain peaks that towered aloft full three thousand feet higher still! It was a vast oval, and one would have to use up eighty or a hundred good miles in traveling around it. As it lay there with the shadows of the mountains brilliantly photographed upon its still surface I thought it must surely be the fairest picture the whole earth affords.

We found the small skiff belonging to the Brigade boys, and without loss of time set out across a deep bend of the lake toward the landmarks that signified the locality of the camp. I got Johnny to row—not because I mind exertion myself, but because it makes me sick to ride backwards when I am at work. But I steered. A three-mile pull brought us to the camp just as the night fell, and we stepped ashore very tired and wolfishly hungry. In a "cache" among the rocks we found the provisions and the cooking utensils, and then, all fatigued as I was, I sat down on a boulder and super-intended while Johnny gathered wood and cooked supper. Many a man who had gone through what I had, would have wanted to rest.

It was a delicious supper—hot bread, fried bacon, and black coffee. It was a delicious solitude we were in, too. Three miles away was a saw-mill and some workmen, but there were not fifteen other human beings throughout the wide circumference of the lake. As the darkness closed down and the stars came out and spangled the great mirror with jewels, we smoked meditatively in the solemn hush and forgot our troubles and our pains. In due time we spread our blankets in the warm sand between two large boulders and soon fell asleep, careless of the procession of ants that passed in through rents in our clothing and explored our persons. Nothing could disturb the sleep that fettered us, for it had been fairly earned, and if our consciences had any sins on them they had to adjourn court for that night, any way. The wind rose just as we were losing consciousness, and we were lulled to sleep by the beating of the surf upon the shore.

It is always very cold on that lake shore in the night, but we had plenty of blankets and were warm enough. We never moved a muscle all night, but waked at early dawn in the original positions, and got up at once, thoroughly refreshed, free from soreness, and brim full of friskiness. There is no end of wholesome medicine in such an experience. That morning we could have whipped ten such people as we were the day before—sick ones at any rate. But the world is slow, and people will go to "water cures" and "movement cures" and to foreign lands for health. Three months of camp life on Lake Tahoe would restore an Egyptian mummy to his pristine vigor, and give him an appetite like an alligator. I do not mean the oldest and driest mummies, of course, but the fresher ones. The air up there in the clouds is very pure and fine, bracing and delicious. And why shouldn't it be?—it is the same the angels breathe. I think that hardly any amount of fatigue can be gathered together that a man cannot sleep off in one night on the sand by its side. Not under a roof, but under the sky; it seldom or never rains there in the summer time. I know a man who went there to die. But he made a failure of it. He was a skeleton when he came, and could barely stand. He had no appetite, and did nothing but read tracts and reflect on the future. Three months later he was sleeping out of doors regularly, eating all he could hold, three times a day, and chasing game over mountains three thousand feet high for recreation. And he was a skeleton no longer, but weighed part of a ton. This is no fancy sketch, but the truth. His disease was consumption. I confidently commend his experience to other skeletons.

I superintended again, and as soon as we had eaten breakfast we got in the boat and skirted along the lake shore about three miles and disembarked. We liked the appearance of the place, and so we claimed some three hundred acres of it and stuck our "notices" on a tree. It was yellow pine timber land—a dense forest of trees a hundred feet high and from one to five feet through at the butt. It was necessary to fence our property or we could not hold it. That is to say, it was necessary to cut down trees here and there and make them fall in such a way as to form a sort of enclosure (with pretty wide gaps in it). We cut down three trees apiece, and found it such heart-breaking work that we decided to "rest our case" on those; if they held the property, well and good; if they didn't, let the property spill out through the gaps and go; it was no use to work ourselves to death merely to save a few acres of land. Next day we came back to build a house—for a house was also necessary, in order to hold the property. We decided to build a substantial log-house and excite the envy of the Brigade boys; but by the time we had cut and trimmed the first log it seemed unnecessary to be so elaborate, and so we concluded to build it of saplings. However, two saplings, duly cut and trimmed, compelled recognition of the fact that a still modester architecture would satisfy the law, and so we concluded to build a "brush" house. We devoted the next day to this work, but we did so much "sitting around" and discussing, that by the middle of the afternoon we had achieved only a half-way sort of affair which one of us had to watch while the other cut brush, lest if both turned our backs we might not be able to find it again, it had such a strong family resemblance to the surrounding vegetation. But we were satisfied with it.

We were land owners now, duly seized and possessed, and within the protection of the law. Therefore we decided to take up our residence on our own domain and enjoy that large sense of independence which only such an experience can bring. Late the next afternoon, after a good long rest, we sailed away from the Brigade camp with all the provisions and cooking utensils we could carry off—borrow is the more accurate word—and just as the night was falling we beached the boat at our own landing.

If there is any life that is happier than the life we led on our timber ranch for the next two or three weeks, it must be a sort of life which I have not read of in books or experienced in person. We did not see a human being but ourselves during the time, or hear any sounds but those that were made by the wind and the waves, the sighing of the pines, and now and then the far-off thunder of an avalanche. The forest about us was dense and cool, the sky above us was cloudless and brilliant with sunshine, the broad lake before us was glassy and clear, or rippled and breezy, or black and storm-tossed, according to Nature's mood; and its circling border of mountain domes, clothed with forests, scarred with land-slides, cloven by canons and valleys, and helmeted with glittering snow, fitly framed and finished the noble picture. The view was always fascinating, bewitching, entrancing. The eye was never tired of gazing, night or day, in calm or storm; it suffered but one grief, and that was that it could not look always, but must close sometimes in sleep.

We slept in the sand close to the water's edge, between two protecting boulders, which took care of the stormy night-winds for us. We never took any paregoric to make us sleep. At the first break of dawn we were always up and running foot-races to tone down excess of physical vigor and exuberance of spirits. That is, Johnny was—but I held his hat. While smoking the pipe of peace after breakfast we watched the sentinel peaks put on the glory of the sun, and followed the conquering light as it swept down among the shadows, and set the captive crags and forests free. We watched the tinted pictures grow and brighten upon the water till every little detail of forest, precipice and pinnacle was wrought in and finished, and the miracle of the enchanter complete. Then to "business."

That is, drifting around in the boat. We were on the north shore. There, the rocks on the bottom are sometimes gray, sometimes white. This gives the marvelous transparency of the water a fuller advantage than it has elsewhere on the lake. We usually pushed out a hundred yards or so from shore, and then lay down on the thwarts, in the sun, and let the boat drift by the hour whither it would. We seldom talked. It interrupted the Sabbath stillness, and marred the dreams the luxurious rest and indolence brought. The shore all along was indented with deep, curved bays and coves, bordered by narrow sand-beaches; and where the sand ended, the steep mountain-sides rose right up aloft into space—rose up like a vast wall a little out of the perpendicular, and thickly wooded with tall pines.

So singularly clear was the water, that where it was only twenty or thirty feet deep the bottom was so perfectly distinct that the boat seemed floating in the air! Yes, where it was even eighty feet deep. Every little pebble was distinct, every speckled trout, every hand's-breadth of sand. Often, as we lay on our faces, a granite boulder, as large as a village church, would start out of the bottom apparently, and seem climbing up rapidly to the surface, till presently it threatened to touch our faces, and we could not resist the impulse to seize an oar and avert the danger. But the boat would float on, and the boulder descend again, and then we could see that when we had been exactly above it, it must still have been twenty or thirty feet below the surface. Down through the transparency of these great depths, the water was not merely transparent, but dazzlingly, brilliantly so. All objects seen through it had a bright, strong vividness, not only of outline, but of every minute detail, which they would not have had when seen simply through the same depth of atmosphere. So empty and airy did all spaces seem below us, and so strong was the sense of floating high aloft in mid-nothingness, that we called these boat-excursions *balloon voyages*.

We fished a good deal, but we did not average one fish a week. We could see trout by the thousand winging about in the emptiness under us, or sleeping in shoals on the bottom, but they would not bite—they could see the line too plainly, perhaps. We frequently selected the trout we wanted, and rested the bait patiently and persistently on the end of his nose at a depth of eighty feet, but he would only shake it off with an annoyed manner, and shift his position.

We bathed occasionally, but the water was rather chilly, for all it looked so sunny. Sometimes we rowed out to the "blue water," a mile or two from shore. It was as dead blue as indigo there, because of the immense depth. By official measurement the lake in its centre is one thousand five hundred and twenty-five feet deep!

Sometimes, on lazy afternoons, we lolled on the sand in camp, and smoked pipes and read some old well-worn novels. At night, by the camp-fire, we played euchre and seven-up to strengthen the mind—and played them with cards so greasy and defaced that only a whole summer's acquaintance with them could enable the student to tell the ace of clubs from the jack of diamonds.

We never slept in our "house." It never recurred to us, for one thing; and besides, it was built to hold the ground, and that was enough. We did not wish to strain it.

By and by our provisions began to run short, and we went back to the old camp and laid in a new supply. We were gone all day, and reached home again about night-fall, pretty tired and hungry. While Johnny was carrying the main bulk of the provisions up to our "house" for future use, I took the loaf of bread, some slices of bacon, and the coffee-pot, ashore, set them down by a tree, lit a fire, and went back to the boat to get the frying-pan. While I was at this, I heard a shout from Johnny, and looking up I saw that my fire was galloping all over the premises! Johnny was on the other side of it. He had to run through the flames to get to the lake shore, and then we stood helpless and watched the devastation.

The ground was deeply carpeted with dry pine-needles, and the fire touched them off as if they were gunpowder. It was wonderful to see with what fierce speed the tall sheet of flame traveled! My coffee-pot was gone, and everything with it. In a minute and a half the fire seized upon a dense growth of dry manzanita chapparal six or eight feet high, and then the roaring and popping and crackling was something terrific. We were driven to the boat by the intense heat, and there we remained, spell-bound.

Within half an hour all before us was a tossing, blinding tempest of flame! It went surging up adjacent ridges—surmounted them and disappeared in the canons beyond—burst into view upon higher and farther ridges, presently—shed a grander illumination abroad, and dove again—

flamed out again, directly, higher and still higher up the mountain-side—threw out skirmishing parties of fire here and there, and sent them trailing their crimson spirals away among remote ramparts and ribs and gorges, till as far as the eye could reach the lofty mountain-fronts were webbed as it were with a tangled network of red lava streams. Away across the water the crags and domes were lit with a ruddy glare, and the firmament above was a reflected hell!

Every feature of the spectacle was repeated in the glowing mirror of the lake! Both pictures were sublime, both were beautiful; but that in the lake had a bewildering richness about it that enchanted the eye and held it with the stronger fascination.

We sat absorbed and motionless through four long hours. We never thought of supper, and never felt fatigue. But at eleven o'clock the confla-gration had traveled beyond our range of vision, and then darkness stole down upon the landscape again.

Hunger asserted itself now, but there was nothing to eat. The provi-sions were all cooked, no doubt, but we did not go to see. We were home-less wanderers again, without any property. Our fence was gone, our house burned down; no insurance. Our pine forest was well scorched, the dead trees all burned up, and our broad acres of manzanita swept away. Our blankets were on our usual sand-bed, however, and so we lay down and went to sleep. The next morning we started back to the old camp, but while out a long way from shore, so great a storm came up that we dared not try to land. So I baled out the seas we shipped, and Johnny pulled heavily through the billows till we had reached a point three or four miles beyond the camp. The storm was increasing, and it became evident that it was better to take the hazard of beaching the boat than go down in a hundred fathoms of water; so we ran in, with tall white-caps following, and I sat down in the stern-sheets and pointed her head-on to the shore. The instant the bow struck, a wave came over the stern that washed crew and cargo ashore, and saved a deal of trouble. We shivered in the lee of a boulder all the rest of the day, and froze all the night through. In the morning the tempest had gone down, and we paddled down to the camp without any unnecessary delay. We were so starved that we ate up the rest of the Brigade's provisions, and then set out to Carson to tell them about it and ask their forgiveness. It was accorded, upon payment of damages.

We made many trips to the lake after that, and had many a hair-breadth escape and blood-curdling adventure which will never be recorded in any history.

Off for San Francisco

FROM *Roughing It,* CHAPTER LVI

I will remark here, in passing, that all scenery in California requires distance to give it its highest charm. The mountains are imposing in their sublimity and their majesty of form and altitude, from any point of view—but one must have distance to soften their ruggedness and enrich their tintings; a Californian forest is best at a little distance, for there is a sad poverty of variety in species, the trees being chiefly of one monotonous family—redwood, pine, spruce, fir—and so, at a near view there is a wearisome sameness of attitude in their rigid arms, stretched down ward and outward in one continued and reiterated appeal to all men to "Sh!—don't say a word!—you might disturb somebody!" Close at hand, too, there is a reliefless and relentless smell of pitch and turpentine; there is a ceaseless melancholy in their sighing and complaining foliage; one walks over a soundless carpet of beaten yellow bark and dead spines of the foliage till he feels like a wandering spirit bereft of a footfall; he tires of the endless tufts of needles and yearns for substantial, shapely leaves; he looks for moss and grass to loll upon, and finds none, for where there is no bark there is naked clay and dirt, enemies to pensive musing and clean apparel. Often a grassy plain in California, is what it should be, but often, too, it is best contemplated at a distance, because although its grass blades are tall, they stand up vindictively straight and self-sufficient, and are unsociably wide apart, with uncomely spots of barren sand between.

One of the queerest things I know of, is to hear tourists from "the States" go into ecstasies over the loveliness of "ever-blooming California." And they always do go into that sort of ecstasies. But perhaps they would modify them if they knew how old Californians, with the memory full upon them of the dust-covered and questionable summer greens of Californian "verdure," stand astonished, and filled with worshipping admiration, in the presence of the lavish richness, the brilliant green, the infinite freshness, the spend-thrift variety of form and species and foliage that make an Eastern landscape a vision of Paradise itself. The idea of a man falling into raptures over grave and sombre California, when that man has seen New England's meadow-expanses and her maples, oaks and cathedral-windowed elms decked in summer attire, or the opaline splendors of autumn descending upon her forests, comes very near being funny—would be, in fact, but that it is so pathetic. No land with an unvarying climate can be very beautiful. The tropics are not, for all the sentiment that is wasted on them. They seem beautiful at first, but sameness impairs the charm by and by. Change is the handmaiden Nature requires to do her miracles with. The land that has four well-defined seasons, cannot lack beauty, or pall with monotony. Each season brings a world of enjoyment and interest in the watching of its unfolding, its gradual, harmonious development, its culminating graces—and just as one begins to tire of it, it passes away and a radical change comes, with new witcheries and new glories in its train. And I think that to one in sympathy with nature, each season, in its turn, seems the loveliest.

San Francisco, a truly fascinating city to live in, is stately and handsome at a fair distance, but close at hand one notes that the architecture is mostly old-fashioned, many streets are made up of decaying, smoke-grimed, wooden houses, and the barren sand-hills toward the outskirts obtrude themselves too prominently. Even the kindly climate is sometimes pleasanter when read about than personally experienced, for a lovely, cloudless sky wears out its welcome by and by, and then when the longed for rain does come it stays. Even the playful earthquake is better contemplated at a distance.

However there are varying opinions about that.

The climate of San Francisco is mild and singularly equable. The thermometer stands at about seventy degrees the year round. It hardly changes at all. You sleep under one or two light blankets Summer and Winter, and never use a mosquito bar. Nobody ever wears Summer clothing. You wear black broadcloth—if you have it—in August and January, just the same. It is no colder, and no warmer, in the one month than the other. You do not use overcoats and you do not use fans. It is as pleasant a climate as could well be contrived, take it all around, and is doubtless the most unvarying in the whole world. The wind blows there a good deal in the summer months, but then you can go over to Oakland, if you choose—three or four miles away—it does not blow there. It has only snowed twice in San Francisco in nineteen years, and then it only remained on the ground long enough to astonish the children, and set them to wondering what the feathery stuff was.

During eight months of the year, straight along, the skies are bright and cloudless, and never a drop of rain falls. But when the other four months come along, you will need to go and steal an umbrella. Because you will require it. Not just one day, but one hundred and twenty days in hardly varying succession. When you want to go visiting, or attend church, or the theatre, you never look up at the clouds to see whether it is likely to rain or not—you look at the almanac. If it is Winter, it will rain—and if it is Summer, it won't rain, and you cannot help it. You never need a lightning-rod, because it never thunders and it never lightens. And after you have listened for six or eight weeks, every night, to the dismal monotony of those quiet rains, you will wish in your heart the thunder would leap and crash and roar along those drowsy skies once, and make everything alive—you will wish the prisoned lightnings would cleave the dull firmament asunder and light it with a blinding glare for one little instant. You would give anything to hear the old familiar thunder again and see the lightning strike somebody. And along in the Summer, when you have suffered about four months of lustrous, pitiless sunshine, you are ready to go down on your knees and plead for rain—hail—snow—thunder and lightning—anything to break the monotony—you will take an earthquake, if you cannot do any better. And the chances are that you'll get it, too.

San Francisco is built on sand hills, but they are prolific sand hills. They yield a generous vegetation. All the rare flowers which people in "the States" rear with such patient care in parlor flower-pots and green-houses, flourish luxuriantly in the open air there all the year round. Calla lilies, all sorts of geraniums, passion flowers, moss roses—I do not know the names of a tenth part of them. I only know that while New Yorkers are burdened with banks and drifts of snow, Californians are burdened with banks and drifts of flowers, if they only keep their hands off and let them grow. And I have heard that they have also that rarest and most curious of all the flowers, the beautiful Espiritu Santo, as the Spaniards call it—or flower of the Holy Spirit—though I thought it grew only in Central America—down on the Isthmus. In its cup is the daintiest little facsimile of a dove, as pure as snow. The Spaniards have a superstitious reverence for it. The blossom has been conveyed to the States, submerged in ether; and the bulb has been taken thither also, but every attempt to make it bloom after it arrived, has failed.

I have elsewhere spoken of the endless Winter of Mono, California, and but this moment of the eternal Spring of San Francisco. Now if we travel a hundred miles in a straight line, we come to the eternal Summer of Sacramento. One never sees Summer-clothing or mosquitoes in San Francisco—but they can be found in Sacramento. Not always and unvaryingly, but about one hundred and forty-three months out of twelve years, perhaps. Flowers bloom there, always, the reader can easily believe—people suffer and sweat, and swear, morning, noon and night, and wear out their stanchest energies fanning themselves. It gets hot there, but if you go down to Fort Yuma you will find it hotter. Fort Yuma is probably the hottest place on earth. The thermometer stays at one hundred and twenty in the shade there all the time—except when it varies and goes higher. It is a U.S. military post, and its occupants get so used to the terrific heat that they suffer without it. There is a tradition (attributed to John Phenix) that a very, very wicked soldier died there, once, and of course, went straight to the hottest corner of perdition—and the next day he telegraphed back for his blankets. There is no doubt about the truth of this statement—there can be no doubt about it. I have seen the place where that soldier used to board. In Sacramento it is fiery Summer always, and you can gather roses, and eat strawberries and ice-cream, and wear white linen clothes, and pant and perspire, at eight or nine o'clock in the morning, and then take the cars, and at noon put on your furs and your skates, and go skimming over frozen Donner Lake, seven thousand feet above the valley, among snow banks fifteen feet deep, and in the shadow of grand mountain peaks that lift their frosty crags ten thousand feet above the level of the sea.

There is a transition for you! Where will you find another like it in the Western hemisphere? And some of us have swept around snow-walled curves of the Pacific Railroad in that vicinity, six thousand feet above the sea, and looked down as the birds do, upon the deathless Summer of the Sacramento Valley, with its fruitful fields, its feathery foliage, its silver streams, all slumbering in the mellow haze of its enchanted atmosphere, and all infinitely softened and spiritualized by distance—a dreamy, exquisite glimpse of fairyland, made all the more charming and striking that it was caught through a forbidden gateway of ice and snow, and savage crags and precipices.

A San Francisco Day Trip

From *The Golden Era* [SAN FRANCISCO], JULY 3, 1864

> *Early to bed, and early to rise,*
> *Makes a man healthy, wealthy and wise.*
>
> —BENJAMIN FRANKLIN

> *I don't see it.*
>
> —GEORGE WASHINGTON

Now both of these are high authorities—very high and respectable authorities—but I am with General Washington first, last, and all the time on this proposition.

Because I don't see it, either.

I have tried getting up early, and I have tried getting up late—and the latter agrees with me best. As for a man's growing any wiser, or any richer, or any healthier, by getting up early, I know it is not so; because I have got up early in the station-house many and many a time, and got poorer and poorer for the next half a day, in consequence, instead of richer and richer. And sometimes, on the same terms, I have seen the sun rise four times a week up there at Virginia, and so far from my growing healthier on account of it, I got to looking blue, and pulpy, and swelled, like a drowned man, and my relations grew alarmed and thought they were going to lose me. They entirely despaired of my recovery, at one time, and began to grieve for me as one whose days were numbered—whose fate was sealed—who was soon to pass away from them forever, and from the glad sunshine, and the birds, and the odorous flowers, and murmuring brooks, and whispering winds, and all the cheerful scenes of life, and go down into the dark and silent tomb—and they went forth sorrowing, and jumped a lot in the graveyard, and made up their minds to grin and bear it with that fortitude which is the true Christian's brightest ornament.

You observe that I have put a stronger test on the matter than even Benjamin Franklin contemplated, and yet it would not work. Therefore, how is a man to grow healthier, and wealthier, and wiser by going to bed early and getting up early, when he fails to accomplish these things even when he does not go to bed at all? And as far as becoming wiser is concerned, you might put all the wisdom I acquired in these experiments in your eye, without obstructing your vision any to speak of.

As I said before, my voice is with George Washington's on this question.

Another philosopher encourages the world to get up at sunrise because "it is the early bird that catches the worm."

It is a seductive proposition, and well calculated to trap the unsuspecting. But its attractions are all wasted on me, because I have no use for the worm. If I had, I would adopt the Unreliable's plan. He was much interested in this quaint proverb, and directed the powers of his great mind to its consideration for three or four consecutive hours. He was supposing a case. He was supposing, for instance, that he really wanted the worm—that the possession of the worm was actually necessary to his happiness—that he yearned for it and hankered after it, therefore, as much as a man could yearn for and hanker after a worm under such circumstances—and he was supposing, further, that he was opposed to getting up early in order to catch it (which was much the more plausible of the two suppositions). Well, at the end of three or four hours' profound meditation upon the subject, the Unreliable rose up and said: "If he were so anxious about the worm, and he couldn't get along without him, and he didn't want to get up early in the morning to catch him—why then, by George, he would just lay for him the night before!" I never would have thought of that. I looked at the youth, and said to myself, he is malicious, and dishonest, and unhandsome, and does not smell good—yet how quickly do these trivial demerits disappear in the shadow when the glare from his great intellect shines out above them!

I have always heard that the only time in the day that a trip to the Cliff House could be thoroughly enjoyed, was early in the morning; (and I suppose it might be as well to withhold an adverse impression while the flow-tide of public opinion continues to set in that direction.)

I tried it the other morning with Harry, the stock-broker, rising at 4 A.M. to delight in the following described things, to wit:

A road unencumbered by carriages, and free from wind and dust; a bracing atmosphere; the gorgeous spectacle of the sun in the dawn of his glory; the fresh perfume of flowers still damp with dew; a solitary drive on the beach while its smoothness was yet unmarred by wheel or hoof, and a vision of white sails glinting in the morning light far out at sea.

These were the considerations, and they seemed worthy a sacrifice of seven or eight hours' sleep.

We sat in the stable, and yawned, and gaped, and stretched, until the horse was hitched up, and then drove out into the bracing atmosphere. (When another early voyage is proposed to me, I want it understood that there is to be no bracing atmosphere in the programme. I can worry along without it.) In half an hour we were so thoroughly braced up with it that it was just a scratch that we were not frozen to death. Then the harness came unshipped, or got broken, or something, and I waxed colder and drowsier while Harry fixed it. I am not fastidious about clothes, but I am not used to wearing fragrant, sweaty horse-blankets, and not partial to them, either; I am not proud, though, when I am freezing, and I added the horse-blanket to my overcoats, and tried to wake up and feel warm and cheerful. It was useless, however—all my senses slumbered, and continued to slumber, save the sense of smell.

When my friend drove past suburban gardens and said the flowers never exhaled so sweet an odor before, in his experience, I dreamily but honestly endeavored to think so too, but in my secret soul I was conscious that they only smelled like horse-blankets. (When another early voyage is proposed to me, I want it understood that there is to be no "fresh perfume of flowers" in the programme, either. I do not enjoy it. My senses are not attuned to the flavor—there is too much horse about it and not enough eau de cologne.)

The wind was cold and benumbing, and blew with such force that we could hardly make headway against it. It came straight from the ocean, and I think there are ice-bergs out there somewhere. True, there was not much dust, because the gale blew it all to Oregon in two minutes; and by good fortune, it blew no gravel-stones, to speak of—only one, of any consequence, I believe—a three-cornered one—it struck me in the eye. I have it there yet. However, it does not matter—for the future I suppose I can manage to see tolerably well out of the other. (Still, when another early voyage is proposed to me, I want it understood that the dust is to be put in, and the gravel left out of the programme. I might want my other eye if I continue to hang on until my time comes; and besides, I shall not mind the dust much hereafter, because I have only got to shut one eye, now, when it is around.)

No, the road was not encumbered by carriages—we had it all to ourselves. I suppose the reason was, that most people do not like to enjoy themselves too much, and therefore they do not go out to the Cliff House in the cold and the fog, and the dread silence and solitude of four o'clock in the morning. They are right. The impressive solemnity of such a pleasure trip is only equalled by an excursion to Lone Mountain in a hearse. Whatever of advantage there may be in having that Cliff House road all to yourself, we had—but to my mind a greater advantage would lie in dividing it up in small sections among the entire community; because, in consequence of the repairs in progress on it just now, it is as rough as a corduroy bridge— (in a good many places), and consequently the less you have of it, the happier you are likely to be, and the less shaken up and disarranged on the inside. (Wherefore, when another early voyage is proposed to me, I want it understood that the road is not to be unencumbered with carriages, but just the reverse—so that the balance of the people shall be made to stand their share of the jolting and the desperate lonesomeness of the thing.)

From the moment we left the stable, almost, the fog was so thick that we could scarcely see fifty yards behind or before, or overhead; and for a while, as we approached the Cliff House, we could not see the horse at all, and were obliged to steer by his ears, which stood up dimly out of the dense white mist that enveloped him. But for those friendly beacons, we must have been cast away and lost.

I have no opinion of a six-mile ride in the clouds; but if I ever have to take another, I want to leave the horse in the stable and go in a balloon. I shall prefer to go in the afternoon, also, when it is warm, so that I may gape, and yawn, and stretch, if I am drowsy, without disarranging my horse-blanket and letting in a blast of cold wind.

We could scarcely see the sportive seals out on the rocks, writhing and squirming like exaggerated maggots, and there was nothing soothing in their discordant barking, to a spirit so depressed as mine was.

Harry took a cocktail at the Cliff House, but I scorned such ineffectual stimulus; I yearned for fire, and there was none there; they were about to make one, but the bar-keeper looked altogether too cheerful for me—I could not bear his unnatural happiness in the midst of such a ghastly picture of fog, and damp, and frosty surf, and dreary solitude. I could not bear the sacrilegious presence of a pleasant face at such a time; it was too much like sprightliness at a funeral, and we fled from it down the smooth and vacant beach.

We had that all to ourselves, too, like the road—and I want it divided up, also, hereafter. We could not drive in the roaring surf and seem to float abroad on the foamy sea, as one is wont to do in the sunny afternoon, because the very thought of any of that icy-looking water splashing on you was enough to congeal your blood, almost. We saw no white-winged ships sailing away on the billowy ocean, with the pearly light of morning descending upon them like a benediction—"because the fog had the bulge on the pearly light," as the Unreliable observed when I mentioned it to him afterwards; and we saw not the sun in the dawn of his glory, for the same reason. Hill and beach, and sea and sun were all wrapped in a ghostly mantle of mist, and hidden from our mortal vision. (When another early voyage is proposed to me, I want it understood that the sun in his glory, and the morning light, and the ships at sea, and all that sort of thing are to be left out of the programme, so that when we fail to see them, we shall not be so infernally disappointed.)

We were human icicles when we got to the Ocean House, and there was no fire there, either. I banished all hope, then, and succumbed to despair; I went back on my religion, and sought surcease of sorrow in soothing blasphemy. I am sorry I did it, now, but it was a great comfort to me, then. We could have had breakfast at the Ocean House, but we did not want it; can statues of ice feel hunger? But we adjourned to a private room and ordered red-hot coffee, and it was a sort of balm to my troubled mind to observe that the man who brought it was as cold, and as silent, and as solemn as the grave itself. His gravity was so impressive, and so appropriate and becoming to the melancholy surroundings, that it won upon me and thawed out some of the better instincts of my nature, and I told him he might ask a blessing if he thought it would lighten him up any—because he looked as if he wanted to, very bad—but he only shook his head resignedly and sighed.

That coffee did the business for us. It was made by a master-artist, and it had not a fault; and the cream that came with it was so rich and thick that you could hardly have strained it through a wire fence. As the generous beverage flowed down our frigid throats, our blood grew warm again, our muscles relaxed, our torpid bodies awoke to life and feeling, anger and uncharitableness departed from us and we were cheerful once more. We got good cigars, also, at the Ocean House, and drove into town over a smooth road lighted by the sun and unclouded by fog.

Near the Jewish cemeteries we turned a corner too suddenly, and got upset, but sustained no damage, although the horse did what he honestly could to kick the buggy out of the State while we were grovelling in the sand. We went on down to the steamer, and while we were on board, the buggy was upset again by some outlaw, and an axle broken.

However, these little accidents, and all the deviltry and misfortune that preceded them, were only just and natural consequences of the absurd experiment of getting up at an hour in the morning when all God-fearing Christians ought to be in bed. I consider that the man who leaves his pillow, deliberately, at sunrise, is taking his life in his own hands, and he ought to feel proud if he don't have to put it down again at the coroner's office before dark.

Now, for that early trip, I am not any healthier or any wealthier than I was before, and only wiser in that I know a good deal better than to go and do it again. And as for all those notable advantages, such as the sun in the dawn of his glory, and the ships, and the perfume of the flowers, etc., etc., etc., I don't see them, any more than myself and Washington see the soundness of Benjamin Franklin's attractive little poem.

If you go to the Cliff House at any time after seven in the morning, you cannot fail to enjoy it—but never start out there before daylight, under the impression that you are going to have a pleasant time and come back insufferably healthier and wealthier and wiser than your betters on account of it. Because if you do you will miss your calculation, and it will keep you swearing about it right straight along for a week to get even again.

Put no trust in the benefits to accrue from early rising, as set forth by the infatuated Franklin—but stake the last cent of your substance on the judgment of old George Washington, the Father of his Country, who said, "He couldn't see it."

And you hear me endorsing that sentiment.

San Francisco Weather and Other Natural Events

FROM *The Celebrated Jumping Frog of Calaveras County, and Other Sketches*

At the instance of several friends who feel a boding anxiety to know beforehand what sort of phenomena we may expect the elements to exhibit during the next month or two, and who have lost all confidence in the various patent medicine almanacs, because of the unaccountable reticence of those works concerning the extraordinary event of the 8th inst., I have compiled the following almanac expressly for the latitude of San Francisco:

Oct. 17.—Weather hazy; atmosphere murky and dense. An expression of profound melancholy will be observable upon most countenances.

Oct. 18.—Slight earthquake. Countenances grow more melancholy.

Oct. 19.—Look out for rain. It would be absurd to look in for it. The general depression of spirits increased.

Oct. 20.—More weather.

Oct. 21.—Same.

Oct. 22.—Light winds, perhaps. If they blow, it will be from the "east'ard, or the nor'ard, or the west'ard, or the suth'ard," or from some general direction approximating more or less to these points of the compass or otherwise. Winds are uncertain—more especially when they blow from whence they cometh and whither they listeth. N.B.—Such is the nature of winds.

Oct. 23.—Mild, balmy earthquakes.

Oct. 24.—Shaky.

Oct. 25.—Occasional shakes, followed by light showers of bricks and plastering. N.B.—Stand from under!

Oct. 26.—Considerable phenomenal atmospheric foolishness. About this time expect more earthquakes; but do not look for them, on account of the bricks.

Oct. 27.—Universal despondency, indicative of approaching disaster. Abstain from smiling, or indulgence in humorous conversation, or exasperating jokes.

Oct. 28.—Misery, dismal forebodings, and despair. Beware of all light discourse—a joke uttered at this time would produce a popular outbreak.

Oct. 29.—Beware!

Oct. 30.—Keep dark!

Oct. 31.—Go slow!

Nov. 1.—Terrific earthquake. This is the great earthquake month. More stars fall and more worlds are slathered around carelessly and destroyed in November than in any other month of the twelve.

Nov. 2.—Spasmodic but exhilarating earthquakes, accompanied by occasional showers of rain and churches and things.

Nov. 3.—Make your will.

Nov. 4.—Sell out.

Nov. 5.—Select your "last words." Those of John Quincy Adams will do, with the addition of a syllable, thus: "This is the last of earthquakes."

Nov. 6.—Prepare to shed this mortal coil.

Nov. 7.—Shed!

Nov. 8.—The sun will rise as usual, perhaps; but if he does, he will doubtless be staggered some to find nothing but a large round hole eight thousand miles in diameter in the place where he saw this world serenely spinning the day before.

PART III

Back East

Philadelphia: The First Visit

FROM *Muscatine Journal*, FRIDAY, DECEMBER 16, 1853

Philadelphia, Dec. 4th, 1853

There is very little news of consequence stirring just now. The steamer, due several days ago, has not yet arrived, and fears are entertained that something has befallen her. Mitchell, the Irish patriot, is the lion in New York at present. I suppose he will be here soon.

Philadelphia is one of the healthiest places in the Union. The air is pure and fresh—almost like the country. The deaths for the week are 147.

It was about 1682 that this city was laid out. The first settlers came over the year previously, in the *Sarah and John*, Capt. Smith. The city now extends from Southwark to Richmond—about five miles—and from the Delaware to the Schuylkill—something over two miles. The streets are wide and straight, and cross each other at right angles, running north and south and east and west. Penn's original design was to leave Front street free, and allow no buildings to be erected upon it. This would have afforded a beautiful promenade, as well as a fine view of the Delaware. But this plan was not carried out. What is now the crooked Dock street was once a beautiful brook, running through the heart of the city. In old times vessels came up this creek as high as Third street.

The old State House in Chesnut street, is an object of great interest to the stranger; and though it has often been repaired, the old model and appearance are still preserved. It is a substantial brick edifice, and its original cost was £5,600 ($28,000). In the east room of the first story the mighty Declaration of Independence was passed by Congress, July 4th, 1776.

When a stranger enters this room for the first time, an unaccountable feeling of awe and reverence comes over him, and every memento of the past his eye rests upon whispers that he is treading upon sacred ground. Yes, everything in that old hall reminds him that he stands where mighty men have stood; he gazes around him, almost expecting to see a Franklin or an Adams rise before him. In this room is to be seen the old "Independence Bell," which called the people together to hear the Declaration read, and also a rude bench, on which Washington, Franklin, and Bishop White once sat.

It is hard to get tired of Philadelphia, for amusements are not scarce. We have what is called a *free-and-easy*, at the saloons on Saturday nights. At a free-and-easy, a chairman is appointed who calls on any of the assembled company for a song or a recitation, and as there are plenty of singers and spouters, one may laugh himself to fits at a very small expense. Ole Bull, Jullien, and Sontag have flourished and gone, and left the two fat women, one weighing 764, and the other 769 pounds, to "astonish the natives." I stepped in to see one of these the other evening, and was disappointed. She is a pretty extensive piece of meat, but not much to brag about; however, I suppose she would bring a fair price in the Cannibal Islands. She is a married woman! If I were her husband, I think I could yield with becoming fortitude to the dispensations of Providence, if He, in his infinite goodness, should see fit to take her away! With this human being of the elephant species, there is also a "Swiss Warbler"—bah! I earnestly hope he may live to see his native land for the first time.

New York: The Overgrown Metropolis

From *San Francisco Alta California*, March 28, 1867

New York, Feb. 2nd, 1867

The only trouble about this town is, that it is too large. You cannot accomplish anything in the way of business, you cannot even pay a friendly call, without devoting a whole day to it—that is, what people call a whole day who do not get up early. Many business men only give audience from eleven to one; therefore, if you miss those hours your affair must go over till next day. Now if you make the time at one place, even though you stay only ten or fifteen minutes, you can hardly get to your next point, because so many things and people will attract your attention and your conversation and curiosity, that the other three quarters of that hour will be frittered away. You have but one hour left, and my experience is that a man cannot go anywhere in New York in an hour. The distances are too great— you must have another day to it. If you have got six things to do, you have got to take six days to do them in.

If you live below Twenty-fifth street, you are "down town;" and if you live anywhere between that and Seven Hundred and Seventy-fifth street (I don't know how far they run—have quit trying to find out), you will never get down town with out walking the legs off yourself. You cannot ride. I mean you cannot ride unless you are willing to go in a packed omnibus that labors, and plunges, and struggles along at the rate of three miles in four hours and a half, always getting left behind by fast walkers, and always apparently hopelessly tangled up with vehicles that are trying to get to some place or other and can't. Or, if you can stomach it, you can ride in a horse-car and stand up for three-quarters of an hour, in the midst of a file of men that extends from front to rear (seats all crammed, of course,)—or you can take one of the platforms, if you please, but they are so crowded you will have to hang on by your eye-lashes and your toe-nails.

I room in East Sixteenth street, and I walk. It is a mighty honest walk from there to anywhere else, and very destructive to legs, but then the omnibuses are too slow during this mixed rainy, snowy, slushy and hard-frozen weather, and the cars too full—there is never room for another person by the time they get this far down town. The cars do not run in Broadway, any how, and I do not like to wander out of that street. I always get lost when I do. The town is all changed since I was here, thirteen years ago, when I was a pure and sinless sprout. The streets wind in and out, and this way and that way, in the most bewildering fashion, and two of them will suddenly come together and clamp the last house between them so close, and whittle the end of it down so sharp, that it looms up like the bow of a steam ship, and you have to shut one eye to see it. The streets are so crooked in the lower end of town that if you take one and follow it faithfully you will eventually fetch up right where you started from.

New York: The Dreadful Russian Bath

FROM *San Francisco Alta California*, APRIL 5, 1867

New York, Feb. 23rd, 1867

I only got over a calamitous cold in the head yesterday, and to-day I felt like the breaking up of a hard winter. I had the blues; and a ceaseless drumming and ringing in the ears; and a deadening oppression of the brain, and a horrible sense of suffocation. The weather was cold, and the gases from the villainous coal fire were stifling. Beside all these little inconveniences, my thoughts persistently ran on funerals and suicide. I was in a fit frame of mind for any desperate enterprise, and with a reckless-ness that even stirred a sort of dull admiration within me, I resolved to go and take a bath.

In five minutes I was breasting the frosty wind and ploughing through the soft new snow, and in fifteen I stumbled upon the place where they keep the monster they call the Russian Bath. This was rather more than I bargained for, but I hesitated only a moment, and went in. I went up stairs, in the stylish building, and along a carpeted hall, and entered a large and sumptuously furnished and decorated drawing-room, with pictures hung round the walls, and a general air of comfort and luxury visible all about the place that could not be otherwise than exasperating to a man in my frame of mind. A very polite man entered my name in a book, taxed me a dollar and a quarter, took charge of my watch and portmonnaie, gave me a ticket and turned me over to an attendant, who conducted me into another part of the house and gave me a neat stateroom wherein to undress. When I came out of there, a fine healthy young descendant of Adam (I think he was a descendant of Adam because he hadn't anything on but a fig-leaf made of a rag), took me into a large apartment that was as hot as sin, and gave me a basin of cold water to wash my face in, and a cup of ice water to drink, and then left me. The place had a latticed floor, and a great plunge bath in the middle of it, and two long rows of high, broad marble benches running down the sides—a sort of stairways that reached half way up to the ceiling. The room began to fill with steam, and I began to sweat. I oozed drops of water from every pore as large as marbles—marbles of the small kind. I climbed up on one bench, and then on the next, and finally to the third— and the higher I went the hotter it got. The fog grew thicker and thicker, till the gas lights were only faint blurs in the mist. I could not breathe through my nose any more, because the steam was so thick; I had to inhale it through my mouth—and if I hadn't had a mouth like a ship's hatchway, I must have suffocated anyhow. I was a little scared, thinking about steam-boat explosions and such things, because I knew I was carrying about a hundred and sixty pounds of steam to the square inch, and if I ever shut down my throttle-valve for a single moment I was bound to collapse a flue. But it was a comfort to me to know that I had got such a head on by this time that if I did let go I would be likely to blow the most of that bath-house over into Jersey somewhere.

At this critical period Adam appeared, and I was uncommon glad to see him, notwithstanding he loomed so vaguely through the shrouding mist that I could not swear I saw him at all. He put me under a cold shower-bath and turned a deluge loose on me. But it felt good. Next he laid me on a marble bench, and soaped and scrubbed me all over with an implement that was rough for a brush but soft for a curry-comb. I got another shower-bath after this, and then the outcast stood me up and shot me in the back with a spray of hot water that made me face around—well, quick, as you might say—and instantly shot me with a spray of ice water—and when I whirled again I caught a blast of hot air above, a spray of hot water below, and a jet of ice water like a thousand needles in the middle. This operation makes a man get around as spry as anything I know of. But it is exquisite torture. Then this inhuman Russian posted me in a corner and discharged a volley of boiling hot and ice-cold streams of water against every part of my body. To say that this makes a man frisky, is to use language of unspeakable tameness. Then I was told to jump into the plunge bath. I said with some irony, that if I was to go into a furnace next, and afterwards into an ice-chest and then suffer an earthquake and be struck by lightning, I would prefer to tackle those outrages first and get them off my mind, if it would be all the same to the Russian Bath Company. But the foreigner said no, and looked perplexed—delicate sarcasm always perplexes a foreigner—and I plunged in. After this, I had to climb up on the marble benches and sweat and steam and cook again for fifteen minutes, and then Adam came back and put me through the same old complicated system of tortures again, winding up with a Niagara of a shower-bath that must have washed all my sins away—unless they had got caked on me—because I felt like a regenerated man a moment afterward. Adam took me into a room of gentler temperature next, and rubbed me down with coarse towels; laid me on a couch and rubbed me with his hands and kneaded me all over with his knuckles as if I were dough; and sprung all my joints and tried to pull my limbs out by the roots. Then he brushed me gently all over with a soft brush, and finally sat me up and scratched and scratched and scratched my head for ten minutes, with his finger nails; but I had him there—he never caught anything.

I dressed and went into the drawing room and got my valuables, and as the polite Superintendent insisted and insisted and insisted on my taking a drink with him—he asked me once, anyway—I did take just a small taste to make him happy, and went my way. I appreciated that young man, because politeness to a stranger is rare in New York.

The sharp wintry wind never felt so bracing or smelled so delicious as it did when I went striding up the street, and if there was anything dismal or cheerless about this old world, it was not present to any of my senses then. The Russian bath will do.

New York: Changes in the City

From *San Francisco Alta California,* April 5, 1867

New York, Feb. 23rd, 1867

They have increased the population of New York and its suburbs a quarter of a million souls. They have built up her waste places with acres upon acres of costly buildings. They have made five thousand men wealthy, and for a good round million of her citizens they have made it a matter of the closest kind of scratching to get along in the several spheres of life to which they belong. The brown-stone fronter and the rag-picker of the Five Points have about an even thing of it; the times are as hard for one as for the other; both struggle desperately to hold their places, and both grumble and grieve to much the same tune. What advantage there is, though, is all in favor of the rag-picker—he can only starve or freeze, but the other can lose caste, which is worse.

The old, genuine, travelled, cultivated, pedigreed aristocracy of New York, stand stunned and helpless under the new order of things. They find themselves supplanted by upstart princes of Shoddy, vulgar and with unknown grandfathers. The incomes, which were something for the common herd to gape at and gossip about once, are mere livelihoods now—would not pay Shoddy's house-rent. They move into remote new streets up town, and talk feelingly of the crash which is to come when the props are knocked from under this flimsy edifice of prosperity. And, to tell the truth, a part of the crash is already here; and the sooner it comes in its might and restores the old, sure, plodding prosperity, the better. Heavy failures are frequent, but people seem to dislike to talk about them—dread the subject, maybe. If everybody goes to Paris in the summer, that movement will not assist any in keeping up the present ruinous prices of living. Government is helping to bring the crash, too. She is drawing all idle capital away from public improvements and other great new enterprises. Her bonds pay better and surer interest than railroad investments, mortgages, etc., and the money is not taxed. People grumble bitterly that they cannot borrow money against such formidable competition as the U.S. Government. Everything is high. That was well enough in war time, when a million men in full employment under Government pay made help scarce and money plenty as dust. But now, with that million discharged, of course help is plenty and money scarce. Yet all hands conspire to keep up prices. No man can afford to be the first to make a move toward lowering the figures.

You pay twelve hundred dollars rental, now, for the dwelling you used to get for five or six hundred. For a store you pay—well, you pay all you can make, and then turn your stock of goods over to your landlord at the end of the year. One firm here had occupied the same premises many years— a firm of sixty years standing. They used to pay $3,000; during the war the figure went up to $6,000; was raised afterwards to $12,000; this year they were told they must pay $18,000 or move. They moved.

You pay $20 to $25 and $30 a week for the same sort of private board and lodging you got for $8 and $10 when I was here thirteen years ago. You can board and lodge at the best hotels in the city for the same money— $4.50 a day. Still, both the hotels and the boarding houses are all full.

Butter is worth sixty cents a pound, eggs sixty cents a dozen, and other things about the same. What they call good cigars are three or four for a dollar. A dozen raw oysters are worth from forty to eighty cents, according to where you buy them. An oyster stew is worth from twenty to forty cents. You pay twenty cents to get shaved; six cents to ride in the horse-cars and ten in the omnibuses. Beggars charge two cents now. Crossing-sweeps demand toll going and coming, both. An old woman had a peanut shelf in a contracted corner—rent, $25 a month; they raised her to $50; she stood the raise and continued business; then they raised her to $75, and this time they raised her out.

Simple, "straight" whiskey, gin, and such things, are fifteen cents; brandy and mixed beverages, twenty-five (and they don't know how to mix them—besides their whiskey is bound to make a temperance man of a toper in a year or kill him). If you order a glass of champagne, you must pay for the whole bottle. Peanuts, hickory nuts and roast chestnuts are twenty cents a pint—say $25 a bushel—used to be worth two or three dollars. A choice seat in the theatre costs $1.50, and I suppose they would tax you to let you blow your nose anywhere within the city limits. Hackmen charge you $2.50 to take you around the block, or $10 to $12 a day. Late at night they charge you what they please. Pew rent is just about as high as house rent. Therefore, few men can afford to indulge in matrimony and religion both. In a word, I find that with due moderation, a single man can get along after a fashion for forty to fifty dollars a week. God help the married ones! Independent! You never saw such an independent set in your life as landlords, barbers, bar-keepers and tradesmen are. They don't care a cent whether you go, stay, buy or let it alone. I think they have sent agents far and near and drummed up all the worthless barbers in the world and set them up in New York. I believe they sharpen their razors on the curbstone. They snatch all the beard out of your face in about two minutes, swab your jaws a little with a damp rag, put a microscopic drop of oil on your hair, give it one rub forward, another backward, and a third sideways, stack it up in a ragged pile on top of your head like a Street Commissioner's monument, and let you go. And you go, hoping your beard will never grow again.

But the popular bar-keeper is the serenest villain of the lot. You have seen a vile, infernal waiter stand staring at vacancy with his complacent, exasperating smirk, pretending he didn't know you had been trying to attract his attention for ten minutes—well, the popular bar-keeper mimics that to a charm. He even improves on it. When a party of gentlemen finally get him to notice them after much rattling of glasses, he don't bow and smile and say "What will you have, gentlemen?" But he turns languidly upon them with an expression of countenance obtrusively intended to inform them that he knew they were calling all the time, and then stares impertinently at them without a word. That means, "Well, if you are going to name your drinks, you had better do it, that's all!" It has a most excellent tendency—it soon stops people from drinking.

If a man asks the popular cigar-vendor "Which are the best?" he intimates that he isn't paid to choose cigars for people, or relieves his mind of some similar incivility. Prosperity is the surest breeder of insolence I know of.

New Yorkers are singular people, somehow or other. Here, in their own home, they have the name among strangers of being excessively unsociable; but take them in any part of the world, outside their State limits, and they are the most liberal, pleasant and companionable people you can find. However, if I take my personal experience instead of the evidence of others, I must confess that I cannot find any fault with them here in their home, any more than I could abroad.

New York: Street People

FROM *San Francisco Alta California*, AUGUST 4, 1867

New York, June 2nd, 1867

A few months ago "puzzles" were all the rage with the street peddlers. A man could not walk three blocks without having some new invention of a ten-cent puzzle offered him to tangle his brain with. There were puzzles consisting of iron rings with handles to them, and iron rings strung on a stick, and iron rings linked together, and forty other puzzle nuisances. People bought these things—thousands and hundreds of thousands of them—and figured at them till they got them apart, and then figured at them till they got them together again; and then they saw the vanity of such things and did no more invest in them. And so the puzzle mania died.

Then there was an irruption of blind people from somewhere. Blind people led by a friend; blind people led by dogs; blind people who felt their way with a stick; blind people who sat on doorsteps with horrid poetry labelled on their hats, and a tin cup alongside, with a penny nest-egg in it; blind men who tortured charity from foot passengers by grinding dismal music out of a thing like a mud turtle. The blind business was immensely popular—for three days. Everybody who had a blind friend borrowed him and trotted him out. It was a short-lived excitement, but it was fine while it lasted.

Next came a villain who shrieked and whistled like a mocking bird, and who almost split people's ears when he happened upon them unawares. He carried a basket full of vile inventions, which were able to make other people as capable of dispensing his kind of misery as himself. I have lost sight of him, latterly. He is dead, maybe. I hope so.

The popular rage now runs to little painted horses, clowns, chickens, etc., suspended from India-rubber strings. On every corner is a vagrant peddling these wonderfully trifling toys. No invention, since the game of croquet, has reached such miraculous triviality. And, by-the-way, this toy-on-a-string business had its origin in a thing invented by a Brooklyn man about two years ago, and which consisted of nothing more extraordinary than a ball attached to an elastic cord. Its sole virtue was that when expelled from one's hand, it returned again, provided the end of the string was firmly held. This gave great satisfaction to the performer. Everybody bought this toy and played with it—men, women and children—everybody neglected graver pursuits, and revelled in the fierce intoxication of this amusement. The happiness it occasioned was universal. The inventor found himself suddenly famous and as suddenly wealthy. But mark you the moral. The fates favored him only to deceive. They promised him a long life blessed with the comfort and the serenity that go with a competence honestly earned. But behold, an ex-policeman waylaid the favorite of fortune in the streets of Brooklyn at dead of night a week ago, and shot him to death with an air-gun. Riches will still take wings and fly away, and so also will life—and nothing can assist them in their flight better than an ex-policeman.

New York: Personal Ads

FROM *San Francisco Alta California,* JUNE 30, 1867

New York, May 19th, 1867

You may sit in a New York restaurant in the morning for a few hours, and you will observe that the very first thing each man does, before ordering his breakfast, is to call for the *Herald*—and the next thing he does is to look at the top of the first column and read the "Personals." Such is the fascination mystery has for the human race! Your man has not the least idea in the world that there is ever going to be a Personal in the paper that will be of private individual interest to himself, and he knows very well that he cannot make head or tail of those he finds there, and that as a vehicle for fun they do not amount to much—yet, as I have said, he is bound to read those "Personals" the very first thing. There is such a toothsome flavor of mystery about them! It is the whole secret. The advertising public appreciate the value of a word under that "Personal" head, and many are the dodges they invent to get an airing for their wares there. But it don't succeed. The ingeniously-worded squibs are ruthlessly set aside and buried in the midst of solid cases of advertisements in the desert wastes of the paper, where a man might hunt them with a blood-hound and not find them. True, I have seen three of these dodges win, lately, but they never hinted at a single attraction in the matters they were meant to advertise—mentioned places of business—that was all—nothing but the barest mention. For instance:

"Caroline—Be in the same place, at Worrell Sisters' performance, to-night. White rose, left temple. Do not fail, dearest.

Robert."

And again:

"If the gentlemanly manager of the New York theatre, who was smiled upon by a lady in the dress circle last night, and who was generously befriended by him in Philadelphia two years ago, will approach the footlights again to-night, he will recognize her by the lily in the parting of her hair."

And get smiled on again, likely, poor devil. Here is the third:

"The lady who left a pair of gloves at Mrs. Mills' Mammarial Balm and Bust Elevator establishment, Washington place, can have them returned by calling or sending address."

I will bet a million dollars, seller ten, no deposit, that that advertisement read "Celebrated Mammarial," etc., etc., etc., originally, and the *Herald* people scratched it out. That worried Mrs. Mills, no doubt. It must have made the old bust elevator feel a little humiliated. (Which reminds me that I have not been through the mammarial bust establishments yet. I must make a note of that. I might as well go there and get busted as any where else.)

The "sick" kind of personals are very frequent. For instance, this:

"Black Eyes—Oh, dear, how anxious I am to hear from you !
        —W. De Angelo."

And this:

"Henry—Don't kill me. Remember, Fourth Avenue car runs all night.
        —Sweet Kate."

That is suggestive, to say the least. She don't want to be killed, but if he is determined to do it, why, he knows where she puts up, and the Fourth avenue car offers every facility for murder.

And how is this?

"H.—Have recovered from accident. Will see you at the old place in Thirteenth street, between Sixth and Seventh avenues, on Friday, at half-past four, rain or shine.

—EMMA FRANCIS W."

She calls it an accident. Well, accidents will happen, even in the best regulated families.

But this is the usual style, and altogether the most nauseating:

"Six P.M., Bleecker Street car, up from Fulton Ferry. Will the lady who was embarrassed in making change and was kindly assisted by a gentleman, whom she smiled upon and who smiled upon her and bowed when she got out, please address Harold, Herald office, stating where an interview may be had?"

There seems to be a pack of wooden-headed louts about this town, who fall in love with every old strumpet who smiles a flabby smile at them in a street car, and forthwith they pop a personal into the *Herald,* beseeching an "interview"—a favor they could have had with infinitely less circumlocution if they were half as full of gab as they are of self-complacency. And behold, if a respectable woman dares to look at one of these by accident, or to see if he has got hind legs and a brass collar on, up comes the inevitable personal, with a lot of stuff in it about "the lady who kindly took notice of a gentleman," and so forth and so on, and the equally inevitable supplication for an "interview." Perdition catch these whelps! But how is this one?

"Mr. WM. F. Lawler, Late Landsman, U.S. Navy, will call at 271 Broadway, to receive some money.

—CHIPMAN, HOSMER & CO."

That has got a very comfortable ring about it, after all that gruel and nonsense. Only a landsman in the Navy, yet they call him "Mr." Lawler? That appears to me to suggest that Lawler is to receive something more than a month's back wages. These Broadway firms do not call a plebeian Mr. without due and sufficient cause.

And here is a sad one; it tells its own story:

"Mary—Come back home, and all will be forgiven. My old heart is breaking.

—YOUR MOTHER."

Many a New Yorker is proof against the seductions of the Cable's despatches, but none of them can resist the *Herald's* "Personals."

Plymouth Rock and the Pilgrims

FROM *Mark Twain's Speeches*

I rise to protest. I have kept still for years, but really I think there is no sufficient justification for this sort of thing. What do you want to celebrate those people for?—those ancestors of yours of 1620—the Mayflower tribe, I mean. What do you want to celebrate them for? Your pardon: the gentleman at my left assures me that you are not celebrating the Pilgrims themselves, but the landing of the Pilgrims at Plymouth Rock on the 22d of December. So you are celebrating their landing. Why, the other pretext was thin enough, but this is thinner than ever; the other was tissue, tinfoil, fish-bladder, but this is gold-leaf. Celebrating their landing! What was there remarkable about it, I would like to know? What can you be thinking of? Why, those Pilgrims had been at sea three or four months. It was the very middle of winter: it was as cold as death off Cape Cod there. Why shouldn't they come ashore? If they hadn't landed there would be some reason for celebrating the fact. It would have been a case of monumental leather-headedness which the world would not willingly let die. If it had been you, gentlemen, you probably wouldn't have landed, but you have no shadow of right to be celebrating, in your ancestors, gifts which they did not exercise, but only transmitted. Why, to be celebrating the mere landing of the

Pilgrims—to be trying to make out that this most natural and simple and customary procedure was an extraordinary circumstance—a circumstance to be amazed at, and admired, aggrandized and glorified, at orgies like this for two hundred and sixty years—hang it, a horse would have known enough to land; a horse—Pardon again; the gentleman on my right assures me that it was not merely the landing of the Pilgrims that we are celebrating, but the Pilgrims themselves. So we have struck an inconsistency here: one says it was the landing, the other says it was the Pilgrims. It is an inconsistency characteristic of your intractable and disputatious tribe, for you never agree about anything but Boston. Well, then, what do you want to celebrate those Pilgrims for? They were a mighty hard lot—you know it. I grant you, without the slightest unwillingness, that they were a deal more gentle and merciful and just than were the people of Europe of that day; I grant you that they are better than their predecessors. But what of that?—that is nothing. People always progress. You are better than your fathers and grandfathers were (this is the first time I have ever aimed a measureless slander at the departed, for I consider such things improper). Yes, those among you who have not been in the penitentiary, if such there be, are better than your fathers and grandfathers were; but is that any sufficient reason for getting up annual dinners and celebrating you? No, by no means—by no means. Well, I repeat, those Pilgrims were a hard lot. They took good care of themselves, but they abolished everybody else's ancestors. I am a border-ruffian from the State of Missouri. I am a Connecticut Yankee by adoption. In me, you have Missouri morals, Connecticut culture; this, gentlemen, is the combination which makes the perfect man. But where are my ancestors? Whom shall I celebrate? Where shall I find the raw material?

My first American ancestor, gentlemen, was an Indian—an early Indian. Your ancestors skinned him alive, and I am an orphan. Not one drop of my blood flows in that Indian's veins today. I stand here, lone and forlorn, without an ancestor. They skinned him! I do not object to that, if they needed his fur; but alive, gentlemen—alive! They skinned him alive—and before company! That is what rankles. Think how he must have felt; for he was a sensitive person and easily embarrassed. If he had been a bird, it would have been all right, and no violence done to his feelings, because he would have been considered "dressed." But he was not a bird, gentlemen, he was a man, and probably one of the most undressed men that ever was. I ask you to put yourselves in his place. I ask it as a favor; I ask it as a tardy act of justice; I ask it in the interest of fidelity to the traditions of your ancestors; I ask it that the world may contemplate, with vision unobstructed by disguising swallow-tails and white cravats, the spectacle which the true New England Society ought to present. Cease to come to these annual orgies in this hollow modern mockery—the surplusage of raiment. Come in character; come in the summer grace, come in the unadorned simplicity, come in the free and joyous costume which your sainted ancestors provided for mine.

Later ancestors of mine were the Quakers William Robinson, Marmaduke Stevenson, et al. Your tribe chased them out of the country for their religion's sake; promised them death if they came back; for your ancestors had forsaken the homes they loved, and braved the perils of the sea, the implacable climate, and the savage wilderness, to acquire that highest and most precious of boons, freedom for every man on this broad continent to worship according to the dictates of his own conscience—and they were not going to allow a lot of pestiferous Quakers to interfere with it. Your ancestors broke forever the chains of political slavery, and gave the vote to every man in this wide land, excluding none!—none except those who did not belong to the orthodox church. Your ancestors—yes, they were a hard lot; but, nevertheless, they gave us religious liberty to worship as they required us to worship, and political liberty to vote as the church required; and so I the bereft one, I the forlorn one, am here to do my best to help you celebrate them right.

The Quaker woman Elizabeth Hooton was an ancestress of mine. Your people were pretty severe with her—you will confess that. But, poor thing! I believe they changed her opinions before she died, and took her into their fold; and so we have every reason to presume that when she died she went to the same place which your ancestors went to. It is a great pity, for she was a good woman. Roger Williams was an ancestor of mine. I don't really remember what your people did with him. But they banished him to Rhode Island, anyway. And then, I believe, recognizing that this was really carrying harshness to an unjustifiable extreme, they took pity on him and burned him. They were a hard lot! All those Salem witches were ancestors of mine! Your people made it tropical for them. Yes they did; by pressure and the gallows they made such a clean deal with them that there hasn't been a witch and hardly a halter in our family from that day to this, and that is one hundred and eighty-nine years. The first slave brought into New England out of Africa by your progenitors was an ancestor of mine—for I am of a mixed breed, an infinitely shaded and exquisite Mongrel. I'm not one of your sham meerschaums that you can color in a week. No, my complexion is the patient art of eight generations. Well, in my own time, I had acquired a lot of my kin—by purchase, and swapping around, and one way and another—and was getting along very well. Then, with the inborn perversity of your lineage, you got up a war, and took them all away from me. And so, again am I bereft, again am I forlorn; no drop of my blood flows in the veins of any living being who is marketable.

O my friends, hear me and reform! I seek your good, not mine. You have heard the speeches. Disband these New England societies—nurseries of a system of steadily augmenting laudation and hosannaing, which, if persisted in uncurbed, may some day in the remote future beguile you into prevaricating and bragging. Oh, stop, stop, while you are still temperate in your appreciation of your ancestors! Hear me, I beseech you; get up an auction and sell Plymouth Rock! The Pilgrims were a simple and ignorant race. They never had seen any good rocks before, or at least any that were not watched, and so they were excusable for hopping ashore in frantic delight and clapping an iron fence around this one. But you, gentlemen, are educated; you are enlightened; you know that in the rich land of your nativity, opulent New England, overflowing with rocks, this one isn't worth, at the outside, more than thirty-five cents. Therefore, sell it, before it is injured by exposure, or at least throw it open to the patent-medicine advertisements, and let it earn its taxes.

Yes, hear your true friend—your only true friend—list to his voice. Disband these societies, hotbeds of vice, of moral decay—perpetuators of ancestral superstition. Here on this board I see water, I see milk, I see the wild and deadly lemonade. These are but steps upon the downward path. Next we shall see tea, then chocolate, then coffee—hotel coffee. A few more years—all too few, I fear—mark my words, we shall have cider! Gentlemen, pause ere it be too late. You are on the broad road which leads to dissipation, physical ruin, moral decay, gory crime and the gallows! I beseech you, I implore you, in the name of your anxious friends, in the name of your suffering families, in the name of your impending widows and orphans, stop ere it be too late. Disband these New England societies, renounce these soul-blistering saturnalia, cease from varnishing the rusty reputations of your long-vanished ancestors—the super-high-moral old iron-clads of Cape Cod, the pious buccaneers of Plymouth Rock—go home, and try to learn to behave! However, chaff and nonsense aside, I think I honor and appreciate your Pilgrim stock as much as you do your-selves, perhaps; and I endorse and adopt a sentiment uttered by a grandfa-ther of mine once—a man of sturdy opinions, of sincere make of mind, and not given to flattery. He said: "People may talk as they like about that Pilgrim stock, but, after all's said and done, it would be pretty hard to improve on those people; and, as for me, I don't mind coming out flatfooted and saying there ain't any way to improve on them—except having them born in Missouri!"

First Visit to Boston

FROM *San Francisco Alta California*, JULY 25, 1869

New York, July, 1869

I reached Boston about seven in the morning on a certain Sunday. There was no need of an almanac whereby to discover that Sunday was the day. No—there was Sunday in the still air; there was Sunday in the absence of hurrying feet and anxious faces; there was Sunday in the trim, special-occasion look of such apparel as drifted into view here and there; there was Sunday in the dreamy lonesomeness that brooded over all things; and presently there came floating up out of the distance the muffled murmur of a bell. There was no need of an almanac.

I was the last man out of the sleeping-car. There was not a hack in sight nor an omnibus or any vehicle whatsoever, except a small boy. He volunteered to carry my valise to the hotel for the sum of thirty cents. I scrutinized him narrowly, for I was in a strange city, and he might be one of those plausible outlaws who lie in wait near depots and decoy the unsuspecting to obscure dens and murder them, for the sake of their teeth, which they sell to the dentists—and their hair, which they sell to the wig-makers—and their finger bones, which they sell to the ivory makers. I have often heard of such people, and I always try to avoid them, for I do not wish to be retailed when I am dead. This boy said his name was James—the ominous name of all the bad little boys in the Sunday School books. With many misgivings I placed myself in his power. I delivered to him my baggage, and began my reluctant march in his wake, oppressed by the knowledge that if this boy meant me harm he could easily accomplish his fell purpose, for of course there were no policemen abroad at that hour of the morning. But I tried to console myself with the reflection that I had been in situations of deadly peril before and had escaped unscathed. I trudged after him, keeping a vigilant watch upon him all the time. It was not long before my suspicions were aroused. I waited and watched, and soon I felt convinced that his actions savored of a hidden villainy of some kind. I said:

"Boy, why do you wind around in this way—why don't you go straight?"

"Sir?"

"Why do you poke in and out and wind around and about in this involved and sinuous way? Why don't you go straight?"

The boy turned and surveyed me impressively for many minutes, and then said, as if to himself:

"Go straight in Boston—ain't he innocent, though?"

He then marched on. But I had lost all confidence, and so I took refuge in the first hotel I came to and discharged James, satisfied that no virtue could abide in a boy whose ways were so crooked. In going from the depot to the hotel we passed one spot seven different times and approached it from a different direction every time.

Boston: A Modern Cretan Labyrinth

From *San Francisco Alta California*, July 25, 1869

New York, July, 1869

I found the gentleman whose guest I was to be—Rev. Petroleum V. Nasby—and thenceforward my two days' vacation had only pleasant experiences in it. Boston is just as delightful a city as there is in American, and one feels more tranquilly and satisfactorily at home in it in three hours than he could in New York in as many years. There is a comfortable air of good-will and good-fellowship in the aspect of the streets, the houses, the town in general, which it gets from the people, or imparts to them, I cannot tell which. One must keep a careful rein upon his "gushing" instincts, else he will shortly find himself loving Boston instead of merely admiring it—and such conduct as that would be undignified in a stranger. It only takes a little time to reconcile one to the awful crookedness of the streets—and only a little time longer to find in that crookedness a positive charm. The hard, straight, unrelenting lines one is used to in other cities, gives way, in Boston, to graceful curves that go sweeping in and out in a pleasant and undulating way that impels a man to assume a luxurious waltz-step in place of the driving, forward-march movement he has learned in unswerving and unbending Broadway. You cannot take in a whole Boston street with a single glance of the eye and then lose your interest because you have thus taken the edge off future discovery; on the contrary, every step reveals some portion of a building which you could not see before, some change in your vista, and some suggestion of pleasant variety yet to come, which not only keeps your interest alive but heightens it and persuades you to go on. And so your street continues to open before you and close behind you like a sure-enough panorama, and you are as well pleased with it as if you had paid fifty cents admission. Many of these bending and circling ranks of buildings are architecturally handsome, and there is a Venetian picturesqueness of effect in the unfolding of their pillared and sculptured graces as you drift around the curves and watch them swing into view.

Boston Antiquities

From *San Francisco Alta California,* July 25, 1869

New York, July, 1869

One of the most engaging peculiarities of Boston is her reverence for her tradition, her relics, her antiquities. She still purrs complacently over her "Boston Massacre," and thinks it the most gorgeous thing of the kind that ever happened, though Nasby says it only consisted in the crippling of three mulattoes and an Irishman—and they still point out three or four places where it occurred. I am not trying to detract from the subliminity of the Boston Massacre—though I do consider that for all Providence has been so partial, there are other places that are just as much entitled to a massacre as Boston is. But I find no fault. San Francisco has earthquakes, anyhow. Therefore let Boston make much of her massacre if she want to—who cares? I don't think anything of massacres. I scorn them.

And then there is that old church—the Old South, I believe, they call it—the one that has a British cannon ball sticking in it. Boston thinks the world of that. The people tell you about it, and point it out to you, and show off the moral advantages of it, till, in spite of your foreign prejudices, you are bound to confess that there is no happiness like having a church with a British cannon ball stuck in it. Boston values that relic, and cherishes it; and every time the Old South Church wears out they build another and stick the cannon ball in again, and go on overcoming the stranger with it as serenely as ever.

And next they trot out Benjamin Franklin. I am opposed to slang; but there isn't any other expression that is descriptive enough for this emergency. And how they do believe in that venerable adventurer! If it had not been for him, with his incendiary "Early to bed and early to rise," and all that sort of foolishness, I wouldn't have been so harried and worried and raked out of bed at such unseemly hours when I was young. The late Franklin was well enough in his way; but it would have looked more dignified in him to have gone on making candles and letting other people get up when they wanted to. I do not see why he ever made candles, though— as celebrated a man as he was. I would have turned my celebrity to better account. But Boston thinks a great deal of Franklin. He was born in two different places in Boston, simultaneously, and he came the nearest to being twins that he ever did in his life. Boston shows both of those places reverently to the stranger, and thinks just as much of one of them as she does of the other. Franklin was always fond of the sports of his boyhood, and until he was an old man he used to go out and fly his kite every Sunday. If he had ever read the Sunday School books he would have found out that it was dangerous to be tempting Providence in that way. He kept it up until at last, one beautiful Sabbath morning, he would have been struck by lightning and scattered all over the State but for a door-key that happened to be hanging on his kite-string. It was not a creditable adventure for an old person like him, but the Boston people got around it by saying that he was trying to attract the lightning on purpose, and therefore he was flying his kite in the interest of science. That cat won't fight, to use the language of metaphor. When General Washington chops down the cherry trees and Benjamin Franklin breaks the Sabbath, it is all right; but suppose I were to do such a thing? My parents would make it an interesting occasion for me.

And the Bostonians show you the ancient Capitol and Quincy market, and the residence of old John W. Hancock, the gentleman whose signature to the Declaration of Independence it is comfort to come back to and read, after you have got the blind-staggers trying to spell out the others. And they also show you old Fanueil Hall, the Cradle of Liberty. You must learn to pronounce Quincy as if it were Quinzy, and Fanueil as if it were Funnel. In this way you can palm yourself on the unsuspecting for a native, and so be respected. Presently they march you mysteriously to a pier, and standing uncovered, they point down at the water with impressive solemnity. That is where the Young Men's Christian Association, dressed as Mohawk Indians, threw the tea overboard in old Colonial times. It was one of the most spirited things that ever was, and is justly admired to this day. There was only one narrow-minded bigot in the whole commonwealth to refuse to swing his hat and say it was sublime. That was the gentleman who owned the tea. He never has collected a cent. When the Indians had finished their exploit their moccasins were full of tea. This was carefully preserved and distributed around to be kept always in remembrance of the incident. Nothing is now held in greater reverence in Boston, than these little parcels of tea. Nearly every family in New England is descended from those savages, and has some of the tea. It is estimated that there is as much as sixty tons of it in Boston alone. I shall always respect these Indians, for tea is a poor insipid beverage, and it is a pity the Indians could not have lived forever to indulge their fancy for emptying it into the sea.

But to the patriotic stranger, perhaps the most notable and interesting thing about Boston is the stately Bunker Hill Monument, which has been erected on the summit of Bunker Hill, to commemorate the battle of Bunker Hill, which was fought on another hill in a neighboring county. It is a very graceful and imposing structure, and is thirteen inches out of the perpendicular. This is the result of building it a little on the slant of the hill. One cannot stand on this sacred ground and feel no quickened impulse of the blood, no swelling of the heart, no exaltation. It was here that Warren fell. It was here that the angry tide of battle was to ebb and flow, and liberty flesh her maiden sword. It was here that Washington, careworn and anxious, leaned against the iron railing and prayed for night or Blucher. Drawn up behind the monument, his little patriot band stood in stern array awaiting the fateful onslaught of the British. At this juncture, when muscles and nerves were tense with expectancy, when every ear was listening, when every breath was clogged with restraint, and a dismal vague suspense brooded in the air, it was learned that the battle was to be fought on Breed's Hill, instead of here, by request of the British commander, whose relations resided in that neighborhood, and desired to witness it. It was thus that the battle of Bunker Hill came to be fought in another place. It was thus that this tranquil spot was spared those scenes of hell-ensanguined carnage which did not occur here.

The view from the top of the monument is one of the grandest the continent can afford. Toward the south the eye wanders over silvery glimpses of the bay, fringed with a long array of masts delicately pencilled against the sky; beyond, the blue hills of Canada lift their filmy outlines above the level world of tinted forest, and out of their midst Mount Washington thrusts its crown of ice and snow. Westward the bright grain fields of New Hampshire stretch their emerald undulations toward the rising sun; in the shadowy east the sullen furnaces glow among the cavernous glens of Pennsylvania and sadden the upper air with a sable pall of smoke; and in the distant north, beyond the swelling sea of vegetation flecked with white villages and threaded with sinuous brooks; beyond the dreamy belt where village and brook and forest melt together and lose their individuality; away beyond ranges of hazy mountains that lap their purple waves together under the clouds, one catches fitful glimpses of that mysterious ocean that heaves its sailless tides about the pole—and on a clear day one can see the pole itself. Such, I learn, is the view that one may obtain from Bunker Hill Monument. I did not go up.

Boston Politeness

From *San Francisco Alta California*, JULY 25, 1869

New York, July, 1869

One of the most winning features of Boston is the politeness of the people. I do not refer to any class particularly. One is civilly treated by all. You would not enjoy stopping New Yorkers to ask the way to places—you would not get in a habit of it, certainly, for you would get more curt answers than compliments. But you shortly learn in Boston to question whom you please on such matters. The native stops at once and maps your course out for you with a patience and a gentleness of speech that are as gratifying as they are unexpected and astonishing. Crooked streets are invaluable, if this is the effect they have—for I do not know what else to attribute Boston's patient affability to if it be not the schooling her citizens get in teaching lost strangers how to find themselves. We were inquiring the way pretty much all the time, but we did not get a crusty answer in a single instance. We made one inquiry of an Irishman, sitting on the ground with his back against a house. He got up to answer, and then it was plain that he was a distillery in disguise. He stretched out his hand to point, but it wavered and slewed around. He tried the other, and it slewed around also. He reeled magnificently at the same moment, and his cap slid off. In catching at his cap he tripped and fell in the gutter. He gathered himself up and apologized for the delay, and said he would tell us how to go, because he had the mumps and could not point good. Then he said:

"You go around that corner there, and turn to the right and go two blocks, and then turn to the left and go a block, and turn to the right and go two blocks to the left, and then go straight till you turn to the right, and then—"

He was tangled. He began over again, and got tangled again. He tried it all over, and checked it off on his fingers. But he got tangled in the same place. Then he reflected awhile in painful perplexity, but suddenly he said:

"Got it now! Might have thought of it before. I'll go along and show you myself." And he did.

I could not see much of Boston in a day and a half, of course, as we were simply idling about visiting people the greater part of the time, but what I did see of it has been very pleasant to remember. As it was early March that I was there, I cannot say anything about the great Peace Jubilee, for that enterprise had hardly been thought of at that time, in fact, I did not suggest it to Gilmore until about the first of April.

The Weather of New England

From the *New York Times*, December 23, 1876

The Oldest Inhabitant—The Weather—
Who hath lost and doth forget it?
Who hath it still and doth regret it?
"Interpose betwixt us Twain."

— Merchant of Venice

Gentlemen: I reverently believe that the Maker who made us all, makes everything in New England—but the weather. I don't know who makes that, but I think it must be raw apprentices in the Weather Clerk's factory, who experiment and learn how in New England, for board and clothes, and then are promoted to make weather for countries that require a good article, and will take their custom elsewhere if they don't get it. There is a sumptuous variety about the New England weather that compels the stranger's admiration—and regret. The weather is always doing something there; always attending strictly to business; always getting up new designs and trying them on the people to see how they will go. But it gets through more business in spring than in any other season. In the spring I have counted one hundred and thirty-six different kinds of weather inside of four and twenty hours. It was I that made the fame and fortune of that man that had that marvelous collection of weather on exhibition at the Centennial that so astounded the foreigners. He was going to travel all over the world and get specimens from all the climes. I said, "Don't you do it; you come to New England on a favorable spring day." I told him what we could do, in the way of style, variety, and quantity. Well, he came, and he made his collection in four days. As to variety—why, he confessed that he got hundreds of kinds of weather that he had never heard of before. And as to quantity—well, after he had picked out and discarded all that was blemished in any way, he not only had weather enough, but weather to spare; weather to hire out; weather to sell; to deposit; weather to invest; weather to give to the poor. The people of New England are by nature patient and forbearing; but there are some things which they will not stand. Every year they kill a lot of poets for writing about "Beautiful Spring." These are generally casual visitors, who bring their notions of spring from somewhere else, and cannot, of course, know how the natives feel about spring. And so, the first thing they know, the opportunity to inquire how they feel has permanently gone by.

Old Probabilities has a mighty reputation for accurate prophecy, and thoroughly well deserves it. You take up the papers and observe how crisply and confidently he checks off what today's weather is going to be on the Pacific, down South, in the Middle States, in the Wisconsin region; see him sail along in the joy and pride of his power till he gets to New England, and then—see his tail drop. He doesn't know what the weather is going to be like in New England. He can't any more tell than he can tell how many

Presidents of the United States there's going to be next year. Well, he mulls over it, and by and by he gets out something about like this: Probable nor'-east to sou'-west winds, varying to the southard and westard and eastard and points between; high and low barometer, swapping around from place to place; probable areas of rain, snow, hail, and drought, succeeded or preceded by earthquakes, with thunder and lightning. Then he jots down this postscript from his wandering mind, to cover accidents: "But it is possible that the program may be wholly changed in the meantime."

Yes, one of the brightest gems in the New England weather is the dazzling uncertainty of it. There is only one thing certain about it, you are certain there is going to be plenty of weather. A perfect grand review; but you never can tell which end of the procession is going to move first. You fix up for the drought; you leave your umbrella in the house and sally out with your sprinkling pot, and ten to one you get drowned. You make up your mind that the earthquake is due; you stand from under, and take hold of something to steady yourself, and the first thing you know, you get struck by lightning. These are great disappointments. But they can't be helped. The lightning there is peculiar; it is so convincing when it strikes a thing, it doesn't leave enough of that thing behind for you to tell whether—well, you'd think it was something valuable, and a Congressman had been there.

And the thunder. When the thunder commences to merely tune up, and scrape, and saw, and key up the instruments for the performance, strangers say, "Why, what awful thunder you have here!" But when the baton is raised and the real concert begins, you'll find that stranger down in the cellar, with his head in the ash barrel.

Now, as to the size of the weather in New England—lengthways, I mean. It is utterly disproportioned to the size of that little country. Half the time, when it is packed as full as it can stick, you will see that New England weather sticking out beyond the edges and projecting around hundreds and hundreds of miles over the neighboring states. She can't hold a tenth part of her weather. You can see cracks all about, where she has strained herself trying to do it.

I could speak volumes about the inhuman perversity of the New England weather, but I will give but a single specimen. I like to hear rain on a tin roof, so I covered part of my roof with tin, with an eye to that luxury. Well, sir, do you think it ever rains on the tin? No, sir; skips it every time.

Mind, in this speech I have been trying merely to do honor to the New England weather; no language could do it justice. But, after all, there are at least one of two things about that weather (or, if you please, effects produced by it) which we residents would not like to part with. If we hadn't our bewitching autumn foliage, we should still have to credit the weather with one feature which compensates for all its bullying vagaries—the ice storm—when a leafless tree is clothed with ice from the bottom to the top—ice that is as bright and clear as crystal; when every bough and twig is strung with ice beads, frozen dewdrops, and the whole tree sparkles, cold and white, like the Shah of Persia's diamond plume. Then the wind waves the branches, and the sun comes out and turns all those myriads of beads and drops to prisms, that glow and burn and flash with all manner of colored fires, which change and change again, with inconceivable rapidity, from blue to red, from red to green, and green to gold; the tree becomes a spraying fountain, a very explosion of dazzling jewels; and it stands there the acme, the climax, the supremest possibility in art or nature, of bewildering, intoxicating, intolerable magnificence! One cannot make the words too strong.

Month after month I lay up my hate and grudge against the New England weather; but when the ice storm comes at last, I say: "There, I forgive you, now; the books are square between us; you don't owe me a cent; go, and sin no more; your little faults and foibles count for nothing; you are the most enchanting weather in the world!"

Niagara

FROM *Sketches, New and Old*

Niagara Falls is a most enjoyable place of resort. The hotels are excellent, and the prices not at all exorbitant. The opportunities for fishing are not surpassed in the country; in fact, they are not even equaled elsewhere. Because, in other localities, certain places in the streams are much better than others; but at Niagara one place is just as good as another, for the reason that the fish do not bite anywhere, and so there is no use in your walking five miles to fish, when you can depend on being just as unsuccessful nearer home. The advantages of this state of things have never heretofore been properly placed before the public.

The weather is cool in summer, and the walks and drives are all pleasant and none of them fatiguing. When you start out to "do" the Falls you first drive down about a mile, and pay a small sum for the privilege of looking down from a precipice into the narrowest part of the Niagara River. A railway "cut" through a hill would be as comely if it had the angry river tumbling and foaming through its bottom. You can descend a staircase here a hundred and fifty feet down, and stand at the edge of the water. After you have done it, you will wonder why you did it; but you will then be too late.

The guide will explain to you, in his blood-curdling way, how he saw the little steamer, *Maid of the Mist,* descend the fearful rapids—how first one paddle-box was out of sight behind the raging billows and then the other, and at what point it was that her smokestack toppled overboard, and where her planking began to break and part asunder—and how she did finally live through the trip, after accomplishing the incredible feat of traveling seventeen miles in six minutes, or six miles in seventeen minutes, I have really forgotten which. But it was very extraordinary, anyhow. It is worth the price of admission to hear the guide tell the story nine times in succession to different parties, and never miss a word or alter a sentence or a gesture.

Then you drive over to Suspension Bridge, and divide your misery between the chances of smashing down two hundred feet into the river below, and the chances of having the railway-train overhead smashing down onto you. Either possibility is discomforting taken by itself, but, mixed together, they amount in the aggregate to positive unhappiness.

On the Canada side you drive along the chasm between long ranks of photographers standing guard behind their cameras, ready to make an ostentatious frontispiece of you and your decaying ambulance, and your solemn crate with a hide on it, which you are expected to regard in the light of a horse, and a diminished and unimportant background of sublime Niagara; and a great many people have the incredible effrontery or the native depravity to aid and abet this sort of crime.

Any day, in the hands of these photographers, you may see stately pictures of papa and mamma, Johnny and Bub and Sis or a couple of country cousins, all smiling vacantly, and all disposed in studied and uncomfortable attitudes in their carriage, and all looming up in their awe-inspiring imbecility before the snubbed and diminished presentment of that majestic presence whose ministering spirits are the rainbows, whose voice is the thunder, whose awful front is veiled in clouds, who was monarch here dead and forgotten ages before this hackful of small reptiles was deemed temporarily necessary to fill a crack in the world's unnoted myriads, and will still be monarch here ages and decades of ages after they shall have gathered themselves to their blood-relations, the other worms, and been mingled with the unremembering dust.

There is no actual harm in making Niagara a background whereon to display one's marvelous insignificance in a good strong light, but it requires a sort of superhuman self-complacency to enable one to do it.

When you have examined the stupendous Horseshoe Fall till you are satisfied you cannot improve on it, you return to America by the new Suspension Bridge, and follow up the bank to where they exhibit the Cave of the Winds.

Here I followed instructions, and divested myself of all my clothing, and put on a waterproof jacket and overalls. This costume is picturesque, but not beautiful. A guide, similarly dressed, led the way down a flight of winding stairs, which wound and wound, and still kept on winding long after the thing ceased to be a novelty, and then terminated long before it had begun to be a pleasure. We were then well down under the precipice, but still considerably above the level of the river.

We now began to creep along flimsy bridges of a single plank, our persons shielded from destruction by a crazy wooden railing, to which I clung with both hands—not because I was afraid, but because I wanted to. Presently the descent became steeper and the bridge flimsier, and sprays from the American Fall began to rain down on us in fast increasing sheets that soon became blinding, and after that our progress was mostly in the nature of groping. Now a furious wind began to rush out from behind the waterfall, which seemed determined to sweep us from the bridge, and scatter us on the rocks and among the torrents below. I remarked that I wanted to go home; but it was too late. We were almost under the monstrous wall of water thundering down from above, and speech was in vain in the midst of such a pitiless crash of sound.

In another moment the guide disappeared behind the deluge, and bewildered by the thunder, driven helplessly by the wind, and smitten by the arrowy tempest of rain, I followed. All was darkness. Such a mad storming, roaring, and bellowing of warring wind and water never crazed my ears before. I bent my head, and seemed to receive the Atlantic on my back. The world seemed going to destruction. I could not see anything, the flood poured down savagely. I raised my head, with open mouth, and the most of the American cataract went down my throat. If I had sprung a leak now I had been lost. And at this moment I discovered that the bridge had ceased, and we must trust for a foothold to the slippery and precipitous rocks. I never was so scared before and survived it. But we got through at last, and emerged into the open day, where we could stand in front of the laced and frothy and seething world of descending water, and look at it. When I saw how much of it there was, and how fearfully in earnest it was, I was sorry I had gone behind it.

The noble Red Man has always been a friend and darling of mine. I love to read about him in tales and legends and romances. I love to read of his inspired sagacity, and his love of the wild free life of mountain and forest, and his general nobility of character, and his stately metaphorical manner of speech, and his chivalrous love for the dusky maiden, and the picturesque pomp of his dress and accoutrements. Especially the picturesque pomp of his dress and accoutrements. When I found the shops at Niagara Falls full of dainty Indian beadwork, and stunning moccasins, and equally stunning toy figures representing human beings who carried their weapons in holes bored through their arms and bodies, and had feet shaped like a pie, I was filled with emotion. I knew that now, at last, I was going to come face to face with the noble Red Man.

A lady clerk in a shop told me, indeed, that all her grand array of curiosities were made by the Indians, and that they were plenty about the Falls, and that they were friendly, and it would not be dangerous to speak to them. And sure enough, as I approached the bridge leading over to Luna Island, I came upon a noble Son of the Forest sitting under a tree, diligently at work on a bead reticule. He wore a slouch hat and brogans, and had a short black pipe in his mouth. Thus does the baneful contact with our effeminate civilization dilute the picturesque pomp which is so natural to the Indian when far removed from us in his native haunts. I addressed the relic as follows:

"Is the Wawhoo-Wang-Wang of the Whack-a-Whack happy? Does the great Speckled Thunder sigh for the war-path, or is his heart contented with dreaming of the dusky maiden, the Pride of the Forest? Does the mighty Sachem yearn to drink the blood of his enemies, or is he satisfied to make bead reticules for the pappooses of the paleface? Speak, sublime relic of bygone grandeur—venerable ruin, speak!"

The relic said:

"An' is it mesilf, Dennis Hooligan, that ye'd be takon' for a dirty Injin, ye drawlin,' lantern-jawed, spider-legged divil! By the piper that played before Moses, I'll ate ye!"

I went away from there.

By and by, in the neighborhood of the Terrapin Tower, I came upon a

gentle daughter of the aborigines in fringed and beaded buckskin moccasins and leggins, seated on a bench with her pretty wares about her. She
had just carved out a wooden chief that had a strong family resemblance to
a clothes-pin, and was now boring a hole through his abdomen to put his
bow through. I hesitated a moment, and then addressed her:

"Is the heart of the forest maiden heavy? Is the Laughing Tadpole
lonely? Does she mourn over the extinguished council-fires of her race, and
the vanished glory of her ancestors? Or does her sad spirit wander afar
toward the hunting-grounds whither her brave Gobbler-of-the-Lightnings
is gone? Why is my daughter silent? Has she ought against the paleface
stranger?"

The maiden said:

"Faix, an' is it Biddy Malone ye dare to be callin' names? Lave this, or
I'll shy your lean carcass over the cataract, ye sniveling blaggard!"

I adjourned from there also.

"Confound these Indians!" I said. "They told me they were tame; but,
if appearances go for anything, I should say they were all on the warpath."

I made one more attempt to fraternize with them, and only one. I
came upon a camp of them gathered in the shade of a great tree, making
wampum and moccasins, and addressed them in the language of
friendship:

"Noble Red Men, Braves, Grand Sachems, War Chiefs, Squaws, and
High Muck-a-Mucks, the paleface from the land of the setting sun greets
you! You, Beneficent Polecat—you, Devourer of Mountains—you, Roaring
Thundergust—you, Bully Boy with a Glass eye—the paleface from beyond
the great waters greets you all! War and pestilence have thinned your ranks
and destroyed your once proud nation. Poker and seven-up, and a vain
modern expense for soap, unknown to your glorious ancestors, have
depleted your purses. Appropriating, in your simplicity, the property of
others has gotten you into trouble. Misrepresenting facts, in your simple
innocence, has damaged your reputation with the soulless usurper. Trading
for forty-rod whisky, to enable you to get drunk and happy and tomahawk
your families, has played the everlasting mischief with the picturesque

pomp of your dress, and here you are, in the broad light of the nineteenth century, gotten up like the ragtag and bobtail of the purlieus of New York. For shame! Remember your ancestors! Recall their mighty deeds! Remember Uncas!—and Red jacket! and Hole in the Day!—and Whoopdedoodledo! Emulate their achievements! Unfurl yourselves under my banner, noble savages, illustrious guttersnipes—"

"Down wid him!" "Scoop the blaggard!" "Burn him!" "Bang him!" "Dhround him!"

It was the quickest operation that ever was. I simply saw a sudden flash in the air of clubs, brickbats, fists, bead-baskets, and moccasins—a single flash, and they all appeared to hit me at once, and no two of them in the same place. In the next instant the entire tribe was upon me. They tore half the clothes off me; they broke my arms and legs; they gave me a thump that dented the top of my head till it would hold coffee like a saucer; and, to crown their disgraceful proceedings and add insult to injury, they threw me over the Niagara Falls, and I got wet.

About ninety or a hundred feet from the top, the remains of my vest caught on a projecting rock, and I was almost drowned before I could get loose. I finally fell, and brought up in a world of white foam at the foot of the Fall, whose celled and bubbly masses towered up several inches above my head. Of course I got into the eddy. I sailed round and round in it forty-four times—chasing a chip and gaining on it—each round trip a half-mile—reaching for the same bush on the bank forty-four times, and just exactly missing it by a hair's-breadth every time.

At last a man walked down and sat down close to that bush, and put a pipe in his mouth, and lit a match, and followed me with one eye and kept the other on the match, while he sheltered it in his hands from the wind. Presently a puff of wind blew it out. The next time I swept around he said:

"Got a match?"

"Yes; in my other vest. Help me out, please."

"Not for Joe."

When I came round again, I said:

"Excuse the seemingly impertinent curiosity of a drowning man, but will you explain this singular conduct of yours?"

"With pleasure. I am the coroner. Don't hurry on my account. I can wait for you. But I wish I had a match."

I said: "Take my place, and I'll go and get you one."

He declined. This lack of confidence on his part created a coldness between us, and from that time forward I avoided him. It was my idea, in case anything happened to me, to so time the occurrence as to throw my custom into the hands of the opposition coroner on the American side.

At last a policeman came along, and arrested me for disturbing the peace by yelling at people on shore for help. The judge fined me, but I had the advantage of him. My money was with my pantaloons, and my pantaloons were with the Indians.

Thus I escaped. I am now lying in a very critical condition. At least I am lying anyway—critical or not critical. I am hurt all over, but I cannot tell the full extent yet, because the doctor is not done taking inventory. He will make out my manifest this evening. However, thus far he thinks only sixteen of my wounds are fatal. I don't mind the others.

Upon regaining my right mind, I said:

"It is an awful savage tribe of Indians that do the beadwork and moccasins for Niagara Falls, doctor. Where are they from?"

"Limerick, my son."

Traveling with a Reformer

FROM *The Man Who Corrupted Hadleyburg and Other Stories*

Last spring I went out to Chicago to see the Fair, and although I did not see it my trip was not wholly lost—there were compensations. In New York I was introduced to a Major in the regular army who said he was going to the Fair, and we agreed to go together. I had to go to Boston first, but that did not interfere; he said he would go along and put in the time. He was a handsome man and built like a gladiator. But his ways were gentle, and his speech was soft and persuasive. He was companionable, but exceedingly reposeful. Yes, and wholly destitute of the sense of humour. He was full of interest in everything that went on around him, but his serenity was indestructible; nothing disturbed him, nothing excited him.

But before the day was done I found that deep down in him some-where he had a passion, quiet as he was—a passion for reforming petty public abuses. He stood for citizenship—it was his hobby. His idea was that every citizen of the republic ought to consider himself an unofficial policeman, and keep unsalaried watch and ward over the laws and their execution. He thought that the only effective way of preserving and pro-tecting public rights was for each citizen to do his share in preventing or punishing such infringements of them as came under his personal notice.

It was a good scheme, but I thought it would keep a body in trouble all the time; it seemed to me that one would be always trying to get offending little officials discharged, and perhaps getting laughed at for all reward. But he said no, I had the wrong idea: that there was no occasion to get anybody discharged; that in fact you mustn't get anybody discharged; that that would itself be a failure; no, one must reform the man—reform him and make him useful where he was.

"Must one report the offender and then beg his superior not to dis-charge him, but reprimand him and keep him?"

"No, that is not the idea; you don't report him at all, for then you risk his bread and butter. You can act as if you are going to report him—when nothing else will answer. But that's an extreme case. That is a sort of force, and force is bad. Diplomacy is the effective thing. Now if a man has tact—if a man will exercise diplomacy—"

For two minutes we had been standing at a telegraph wicket, and during all this time the Major had been trying to get the attention of one of the young operators, but they were all busy skylarking. The Major spoke now, and asked one of them to take his telegram. He got for reply:

"I reckon you can wait a minute, can't you?" And the skylarking went on.

The Major said yes, he was not in a hurry. Then he wrote another telegram:

"President Western Union Tel. Co.:

"Come and dine with me this evening. I can tell you how business is onducted in one of your branches."

Presently the young fellow who had spoken so pertly a little before reached out and took the telegram, and when he read it he lost colour and began to apologise and explain. He said he would lose his place if this deadly telegram was sent, and he might never get another. If he could be let off this time he would give no cause of complaint again. The compromise was accepted.

As we walked away, the Major said:

"Now, you see, that was diplomacy—and you see how it worked. It wouldn't do any good to bluster, the way people are always doing. That boy can always give you as good as you send, and you'll come out defeated and ashamed of yourself pretty nearly always. But you see he stands no chance against diplomacy. Gentle words and diplomacy—those are the tools to work with."

"Yes, I see: but everybody wouldn't have had your opportunity. It isn't everybody that is on those familiar terms with the President of the Western Union."

"Oh, you misunderstand. I don't know the President—I only use him diplomatically. It is for his good and for the public good. There's no harm in it."

I said with hesitation and diffidence:

"But is it ever right or noble to tell a lie?"

He took no note of the delicate self-righteousness of the question, but answered with undisturbed gravity and simplicity:

"Yes, sometimes. Lies told to injure a person and lies told to profit yourself are not justifiable, but lies told to help another person, and lies told in the public interest—oh, well, that is quite another matter. Anybody knows that. But never mind about the methods: you see the result. That youth is going to be useful now, and well-behaved. He had a good face. He was worth saving. Why, he was worth saving on his mother's account if not his own. Of course, he has a mother—sisters, too. Damn these people who are always forgetting that! Do you know, I've never fought a duel in my life—never once—and yet have been challenged, like other people. I could always see the other man's unoffending women folks or his little children standing between him and me. They hadn't done anything—I couldn't break their hearts, you know."

He corrected a good many little abuses in the course of the day, and always without friction—always with a fine and dainty "diplomacy" which left no sting behind; and he got such happiness and such contentment out of these performances that I was obliged to envy him his trade—and perhaps would have adopted it if I could have managed the necessary deflections from fact as confidently with my mouth as I believe I could with a pen, behind the shelter of print, after a little practice.

Away late that night we were coming up-town in a horse-car when three boisterous roughs got aboard, and began to fling hilarious obscenities and profanities right and left among the timid passengers, some of whom were women and children. Nobody resisted or retorted; the conductor tried soothing words and moral suasion, but the toughs only called him names and laughed at him. Very soon I saw that the Major realised that this was a matter which was in his line; evidently he was turning over his stock of diplomacy in his mind and getting ready. I felt that the first diplomatic remark he made in this place would bring down a landslide of ridicule upon him, and maybe something worse; but before I could whisper to him and check him he had begun, and it was too late. He said, in a level and dispassionate tone:

"Conductor, you must put these swine out. I will help you."

I was not looking for that. In a flash the three roughs plunged at him. But none of them arrived. He delivered three such blows as one could not expect to encounter outside the prize-ring, and neither of the men had life enough left in him to get up from where he fell. The Major dragged them out and threw them off the car, and we got under way again.

I was astonished: astonished to see a lamb act so; astonished at the strength displayed, and the clean and comprehensive result; astonished at the brisk and business-like style of the whole thing. The situation had a humorous side to it, considering how much I had been hearing about mild persuasion and gentle diplomacy all day from this pile-driver, and I would have liked to call his attention to that feature and do some sarcasms about it; but when I looked at him I saw that it would be of no use—his placid and contented face had no ray of humour in it; he would not have understood. When we left the car, I said:

"That was a good stroke of diplomacy—three good strokes of diplomacy, in fact."

"That? That wasn't diplomacy. You are quite in the wrong. Diplomacy is a wholly different thing. One cannot apply it to that sort; they would not understand it. No, that was not diplomacy; it was force."

"Now that you mention it, I—yes, I think perhaps you are right."

"Right? Of course I am right. It was just force."

"I think, myself, it had the outside aspect of it. Do you often have to reform people in that way?"

"Far from it. It hardly ever happens. Not oftener than once in half a year, at the outside."

"Those men will get well?"

"Get well? Why, certainly they will. They are not in any danger. I know how to hit and where to hit. You noticed that I did not hit them under the jaw. That would have killed them."

I believed that. I remarked—rather wittily, as I thought—that he had been a lamb all day, but now had all of a sudden developed into a ram— battering-ram; but with dulcet frankness and simplicity he said no, a battering-ram was quite a different thing, and not in use now. This was maddening, and I came near bursting out and saying he had no more appreciation of wit than a jackass—in fact, I had it right on my tongue, but did not say it, knowing there was no hurry and I could say it just as well some other time over the telephone.

We started to Boston the next afternoon. The smoking compartment in the parlour-car was full, and he went into the regular smoker. Across the aisle in the front seat sat a meek, farmer-looking old man with a sickly pallor in his face, and he was holding the door open with his foot to get the air. Presently a big brakeman came rushing through, and when he got to the door he stopped, gave the farmer an ugly scowl, then wrenched the door to with such energy as to almost snatch the old man's boot off. Then on he plunged about his business. Several passengers laughed, and the old gentleman looked pathetically shamed and grieved.

After a little the conductor passed along, and the Major stopped him and asked him a question in his habitually courteous way:

"Conductor, where does one report the misconduct of a brakeman? Does one report to you?"

"You can report him at New Haven if you want to. What has he been doing?"

The Major told the story. The conductor seemed amused. He said, with just a touch of sarcasm in his bland tones:

"As I understand you, the brakeman didn't say anything?"

"No, he didn't say anything."

"But he scowled, you say?"

"Yes."

"And snatched the door loose in a rough way?"

"Yes."

"That's the whole business, is it?"

"Yes, that is the whole of it."

The conductor smiled pleasantly, and said:

"Well, if you want to report him, all right, but I don't quite make out what it's going to amount to. You'll say—as I understand you—that the brakeman insulted this old gentleman. They'll ask you what he said. You'll say he didn't say anything at all. I reckon they'll say, How are you going to make out an insult when you acknowledge yourself that he didn't say a word?"

There was a murmur of applause at the conductor's compact reasoning, and it gave him pleasure—you could see it in his face. But the Major was not disturbed. He said:

"There—now you have touched upon a crying defect in the complaint system. The railway officials—as the public think and as you also seem to think—are not aware that there are any insults except spoken ones. So nobody goes to headquarters and reports insults of manner, insults of gesture, look, and so forth; and yet these are sometimes harder to bear than any words. They are bitter hard to bear because there is nothing tangible to take hold of; and the insulter can always say, if called before the railway officials, that he never dreamed of intending any offence. It seems to me that the officials ought to specially and urgently request the public to report unworded affronts and incivilities."

The conductor laughed, and said:

"Well, that would be trimming it pretty fine, sure!"

"But not too fine, I think. I will report this matter at New Haven, and I have an idea that I'll be thanked for it."

The conductor's face lost something of its complacency; in fact, it settled to a quite sober cast as the owner of it moved away. I said:

"You are not really going to bother with that trifle, are you?"

"It isn't a trifle. Such things ought always to be reported. It is a public duty and no citizen has a right to shirk it. But I sha'n't' have to report this case."

"Why?"

"It won't be necessary. Diplomacy will do the business. You'll see."

Presently the conductor came on his rounds again, and when he reached the Major he leaned over and said:

"That's all right. You needn't report him. He's responsible to me, and if he does it again I'll give him a talking to."

The Major's response was cordial:

"Now that is what I like! You mustn't think that I was moved by any vengeful spirit, for that wasn't the case. It was duty—just a sense of duty, that was all. My brother-in-law is one of the directors of the road, and when he learns that you are going to reason with your brakeman the very next time he brutally insults an unoffending old man it will please him, you may be sure of that."

The conductor did not look as joyous as one might have thought he would, but on the contrary looked sickly and uncomfortable. He stood around a little; then said:

"I think something ought to be done to him now. I'll discharge him."

"Discharge him! What good would that do? Don't you think it would be better wisdom to teach him better ways and keep him?"

"Well, there's something in that. What would you suggest?"

"He insulted the old gentleman in presence of all these people. How would it do to have him come and apologise in their presence?"

"I'll have him here right off. And I want to say this: If people would do as you've done, and report such things to me instead of keeping mum and going off and blackguarding the road, you'd see a different state of things pretty soon. I'm much obliged to you."

The brakeman came and apologised. After he was gone the Major said:

"Now you see how simple and easy that was. The ordinary citizen would have accomplished nothing—the brother-in-law of a directory can accomplish anything he wants to."

"But are you really the brother-in-law of a director?"

"Always. Always when the public interests require it. I have a brother-in-law on all the boards—everywhere. It saves me a world of trouble."

"It is a good wide relationship."

"Yes. I have over three hundred of them."

"Is the relationship never doubted by a conductor?"

"I have never met with a case. It is the honest truth—I never have."

"Why didn't you let him go ahead and discharge the brakeman, in spite of your favourite policy. You know he deserved it."

The Major answered with something which really had a sort of distant resemblance to impatience:

"If you would stop and think a moment you wouldn't ask such a question as that. Is a brakeman a dog, that nothing but dogs' methods will do for him? He is a man and has a man's fight for life. And he always has a sister, or a mother, or wife and children to support. Always—there are no exceptions. When you take his living away from him you take theirs away too— and what have they done to you? Nothing. And where is the profit in discharging an uncourteous brakeman and hiring another just like him? It's unwisdom. Don't you see that the rational thing to do is to reform the brakeman and keep him? Of course it is."

Then he quoted with admiration the conduct of a certain division superintendent of the Consolidated road, in a case where a switchman of two years' experience was negligent once and threw a train off the track and killed several people. Citizens came in a passion to urge the man's dismissal, but the superintendent said:

"No, you are wrong. He has learned his lesson, he will throw no more trains off the track. He is twice as valuable as he was before. I shall keep him."

We had only one more adventure on the train. Between Hartford and Springfield the train-boy came shouting with an armful of literature, and dropped a sample into a slumbering gentleman's lap, and the man woke up with a start. He was very angry, and he and a couple of friends discussed the outrage with much heat. They sent for the parlour-car conductor and described the matter, and were determined to have the boy expelled from his situation. The three complainants were wealthy Holyoke merchants, and it was evident that the conductor stood in some awe of them. He tried to pacify them, and explained that the boy was not under his authority, but under that of one of the news companies; but he accomplished nothing.

Then the Major volunteered some testimony for the defence. He said:

"I saw it all. You gentlemen have not meant to exaggerate the circumstances, but still that is what you have done. The boy has done nothing more than all train-boys do. If you want to get his ways softened down and his manners reformed, I am with you and ready to help, but it isn't fair to get him discharged without giving him a chance."

But they were angry, and would hear of no compromise. They were well acquainted with the President of the Boston and Albany, they said, and would put everything aside next day and go up to Boston and fix that boy.

The Major said he would be on hand too, and would do what he could to save the boy. One of the gentlemen looked him over and said:

"Apparently it is going to be a matter of who can wield the most influence with the President. Do you know Mr. Bliss personally?"

The Major said, with composure:

"Yes; he is my uncle."

The effect was satisfactory. There was an awkward silence for a minute or more; then the hedging and the half-confessions of over-haste and exaggerated resentment began, and soon everything was smooth and friendly and sociable, and it was resolved to drop the matter and leave the boy's bread and butter unmolested.

It turned out as I had expected: the President of the road was not the Major's uncle at all—except by adoption, and for this day and train only.

We got into no episodes on the return journey. Probably it was because we took a night train and slept all the way.

We left New York Saturday night by the Pennsylvania road. After breakfast the next morning we went into the parlour-car, but found it a dull place and dreary. There were but few people in it and nothing going on. Then we went into the little smoking compartment of the same car and found three gentlemen in there. Two of them were grumbling over one of the rules of the road—a rule which forbade card-playing on the trains on Sunday. They had started an innocent game of high-low-jack and had been stopped. The Major was interested. He said to the third gentleman:

"Did you object to the game?"

"Not at all. I am a Yale professor and a religious man, but my prejudices are not extensive."

Then the Major said to the others:

"You are at perfect liberty to resume your game, gentlemen; no one here objects."

One of them declined the risk, but the other one said he would like to begin again if the Major would join him. So they spread an overcoat over their knees and the game proceeded. Pretty soon the parlour-car conductor arrived, and said, brusquely:

"There, there, gentlemen, that won't do. Put up the cards—it's not allowed."

The Major was shuffling. He continued to shuffle, and said:

"By whose order is it forbidden?"

"It's my order. I forbid it."

The dealing began. The Major asked:

"Did you invent the idea?"

"What idea?"

"The idea of forbidding card-playing on Sunday."

"No—of course not."

"Who did?"

"The company."

"Then it isn't your order, after all, but the company's. Is that it?"

"Yes. But you don't stop playing! I have to require you to stop playing immediately."

"Nothing is gained by hurry, and often much is lost. Who authorised the company to issue such an order?"

"My dear sir, that is a matter of no consequence to me, and—"

"But you forget that you are not the only person concerned. It may be a matter of consequence to me. It is, indeed, a matter of very great importance to me. I cannot violate a legal requirement of my country without dishonouring myself; I cannot allow any man or corporation to hamper my liberties with illegal rules—a thing which railway companies are always trying to do—without dishonouring my citizenship. So I come back to that question: By whose authority has the company issued this order?"

"I don't know. That's their affair."

"Mine, too. I doubt if the company has any right to issue such a rule.

This road runs through several States. Do you know what State we are in now, and what its laws are in matters of this kind?"

"Its laws do not concern me, but the company's orders do. It is my duty to stop this game, gentlemen, and it must be stopped."

"Possibly; but still there is no hurry. In hotels they post certain rules in the rooms, but they always quote passages from the State law as authority for these requirements. I see nothing posted here of this sort. Please produce your authority and let us arrive at a decision, for you see yourself that you are marring the game."

"I have nothing of the kind, but I have my orders, and that is sufficient. They must be obeyed."

"Let us not jump to conclusions. It will be better all around to examine into the matter without heat or haste, and see just where we stand before either of us makes a mistake—for the curtailing of the liberties of a citizen of the United States is a much more serious matter than you and the railroads seem to think, and it cannot be done in my person until the curtailer proves his right to do so. Now—"

"My dear sir, will you put down those cards?"

"All in good time, perhaps. It depends. You say this order must be obeyed. Must. It is a strong word. You see yourself how strong it is. A wise company would not arm you with so drastic an order as this, of course, without appointing a penalty for its infringement. Otherwise it runs the risk of being a dead letter and a thing to laugh at. What is the appointed penalty for an infringement of this law?"

"Penalty? I never heard of any."

"Unquestionably you must be mistaken. Your company orders you to come here and rudely break up an innocent amusement, and furnishes you no way to enforce the order! Don't you see that that is nonsense? What do you do when people refuse to obey this order? Do you take the cards away from them?"

"No."

"Do you put the offender off at the next station?"

"Well, no—of course we couldn't if he had a ticket."

"Do you have him up before a court?"

The conductor was silent and apparently troubled. The Major started a new deal, and said:

"You see that you are helpless, and that the company has placed you in a foolish position. You are furnished with an arrogant order, and you deliver it in a blustering way, and when you come to look into the matter you find you haven't any way of enforcing obedience."

The conductor said, with chill dignity:

"Gentlemen, you have heard the order, and my duty is ended. As to obeying it or not, you will do as you think fit." And he turned to leave.

"But wait. The matter is not yet finished. I think you are mistaken about your duty being ended; but if it really is, I myself have a duty to perform yet."

"How do you mean?"

"Are you going to report my disobedience at headquarters in Pittsburg?"

"No. What good would that do?"

"You must report me, or I will report you."

"Report me for what?"

"For disobeying the company's orders in not stopping this game. As a citizen it is my duty to help the railway companies keep their servants to their work."

"Are you in earnest?"

"Yes, I am in earnest. I have nothing against you as a man, but I have this against you as an officer—that you have not carried out that order, and if you do not report me I must report you. And I will."

The conductor looked puzzled, and was thoughtful a moment; then he burst out with:

"I seem to be getting myself into a scrape! It's all a muddle; I can't make head or tail of it; it never happened before; they always knocked under and never said a word, and so I never saw how ridiculous that stupid order with no penalty is. I don't want to report anybody, and I don't want to be reported—why, it might do me no end of harm! No do go on with the game—play the whole day if you want to—and don't let's have any more trouble about it!"

"No, I only sat down here to establish this gentleman's rights—he can have his place now. But before won't you tell me what you think the company made this rule for? Can you imagine an excuse for it? I mean a rational one—an excuse that is not on its face silly, and the invention of an idiot?"

"Why, surely I can. The reason it was made is plain enough. It is to save the feelings of the other passengers—the religious ones among them, I mean. They would not like it to have the Sabbath desecrated by card-playing on the train."

"I just thought as much. They are willing to desecrate it themselves by travelling on Sunday, but they are not willing that other people—"

"By gracious, you've hit it! I never thought of that before. The fact is, it is a silly rule when you come to look into it."

At this point the train conductor arrived, and was going to shut down the game in a very high-handed fashion, but the parlour-car conductor stopped him, and took him aside to explain. Nothing more was heard of the matter.

I was ill in bed eleven days in Chicago and got no glimpse of the Fair, for I was obliged to return East as soon as I was able to travel. The Major secured and paid for a state-room in a sleeper the day before we left, so that I could have plenty of room and be comfortable; but when we arrived at the station a mistake had been made and our car had not been put on. The conductor had reserved a section for us—it was the best he could do, he said. But Major said we were not in a hurry, and would wait for the car to be put on. The conductor responded, with pleasant irony:

"It may be that you are not in a hurry, just as you say, but we are. Come, get aboard, gentlemen, get aboard—don't keep us waiting."

But the Major would not get aboard himself nor allow me to do it. He wanted his car, and said he must have it. This made the hurried and perspiring conductor impatient, and he said:

"It's the best we can do—we can't do impossibilities. You will take the section or go without. A mistake has been made and can't be rectified at this late hour. It's a thing that happens now and then, and there is nothing for it but to put up with it and make the best of it. Other people do."

"Ah, that is just it, you see. If they had stuck to their rights and enforced them you wouldn't be trying to trample mine underfoot in this bland way now. I haven't any disposition to give you unnecessary trouble, but it is my duty to protect the next man from this kind of imposition. So I must have my car. Otherwise I will wait in Chicago and sue the company for violating its contract."

"Sue the company?—for a thing like that!"

"Certainly."

"Do you really mean that?"

"Indeed, I do."

The conductor looked the Major over wonderingly, and then said:

"It beats me—it's bran-new—I've never struck the mate to it before. But I swear I think you'd do it. Look here, I'll send for the station-master."

When the station-master came he was a good deal annoyed—at the Major, not at the person who had made the mistake. He was rather brusque, and took the same position which the conductor had taken in the beginning; but he failed to move the soft-spoken artilleryman, who still insisted that he must have his car. However, it was plain that there was only one strong side in this case, and that that side was the Major's. The station-master banished his annoyed manner, and became pleasant and even half-apologetic. This made a good opening for a compromise, and the Major made a concession. He said he would give up the engaged state-room, but he must have a state-room. After a deal of ransacking, one was found whose owner was persuadable; he exchanged it for our section, and we got away at last. The conductor called on us in the evening, and was kind and courteous and obliging, and we had a long talk and got to be good friends. He said he wished the public would make trouble oftener—it would have a good effect. He said that the railroads could not be expected to do their whole duty by the traveller unless the traveller would take some interest in the matter himself.

I hoped that we were done reforming for the trip now, but it was not so. In the hotel car, in the morning, the Major called for broiled chicken. The waiter said:

"It's not in the bill of fare, sir; we do not serve anything but what is in the bill."

"That gentleman yonder is eating a broiled chicken."

"Yes, but that is different. He is one of the superintendents of the road."

"Then all the more must I have broiled chicken. I do not like these discriminations. Please hurry—bring me a broiled chicken."

The waiter brought the steward, who explained in a low and polite voice that the thing was impossible—it was against the rule, and the rule was rigid.

"Very well, then, you must either apply it impartially or break it impartially. You must take that gentleman's chicken away from him or bring me one."

The steward was puzzled, and did not quite know what to do. He began an incoherent argument, but the conductor came along just then, and asked what the difficulty was. The steward explained that here was a gentleman who was insisting on having a chicken when it was dead against the rule and not in the bill. The conductor said:

"Stick by your rules—you haven't any option. Wait a moment—is this the gentleman?" Then he laughed and said: "Never mind your rules—it's my advice, and sound: give him anything he wants—don't get him started on his rights. Give him whatever he asks for; and if you haven't got it, stop the train and get it."

The Major ate the chicken, but said he did it from a sense of duty and to establish a principle, for he did not like chicken.

I missed the Fair it is true, but I picked up some diplomatic tricks which I and the reader may find handy and useful as we go along.

PART IV

---•---

Travels in the Pacific

Our Fellow Citizens of the Sandwich Islands

FROM *Paul Fatout's Mark Twain Speaking*

Ladies and gentlemen: The next lecture in this course will be delivered this evening, by Samuel L. Clemens, a gentleman whose high character and unimpeachable integrity are only equalled by his comeliness of person and grace of manner. And I am the man! I was obliged to excuse the chairman from introducing me, because he never compliments anybody and I knew I could do it just as well.

The Sandwich Islands will be the subject of my lecture—when I get to it—and I shall endeavor to tell the truth as nearly as a newspaper man can. If I embellish it with a little nonsense, that makes no difference; it won't mar the truth; it is only as the barnacle ornaments the oyster by sticking to it. That figure is original with me! I was born back from tidewater and don't know as the barnacle does stick to the oyster.

Unfortunately, the first object I ever saw in the Sandwich Islands was a repulsive one. It was a case of Oriental leprosy, of so dreadful a nature that I have never been able to get it out of my mind since. I don't intend that it shall give a disagreeable complexion to this lecture at all, but inasmuch as it was the first thing I saw in those islands, it naturally suggested itself when I proposed to talk about the islands. It is a very hard matter to get a disagreeable object out of one's memory. I discovered that a good while ago. When I made that funeral excursion in the Quaker City they showed me some very interesting objects in a cathedral, and I expected to recollect every one of them—but I didn't.

I forgot every one of them—except one—and that I remembered because it was unpleasant. It was a curious piece of ancient sculpture. They don't know where they got it nor how long they have had it. It is a stone figure of a man without any skin—a freshly skinned man showing every vein, artery and tissue. It was the heaviest thing, and yet there was something fascinating about it. It looked so natural; it looked as if it was in pain, and you know a freshly skinned man would naturally look that way. He would unless his attention was occupied with some other matter. It was a dreadful object, and I have been sorry many a time since that I ever saw that man. Sometimes I dream of him, sometimes he is standing by my bedpost, sometimes he is stretched between the sheets, touching me—the most uncomfortable bedfellow I ever had.

I can't get rid of unpleasant recollections. Once when I ran away from school I was afraid to go home at night, so I crawled through a window and laid down on a lounge in my father's office. The moon shed a ghastly light in the room, and presently I descried a long, dark mysterious shape on the floor. I wanted to go and touch it—but I didn't—I restrained myself— I didn't do it. I had a good deal of presence of mind—tried to go to sleep— kept thinking of it. By and by when the moonlight fell upon it, I saw that it was a dead man lying there with his white face turned up in the moonlight. I never was so sick in all my life. I never wanted to take a walk so bad! I went away from there. I didn't hurry—simply went out of the window— and took the sash along with me. I didn't need the sash, but it was handier to take it than to leave it. I wasn't scared, but I was a good deal agitated. I have never forgotten that man. He had fallen dead in the street and they brought him in there to try him, and they brought him in guilty, too.

But I am losing time; what I have been saying don't bear strictly on the Sandwich Islands, but one reminiscence leads to another, and I am obliged to bring myself down in this way, on account of that unpleasant thing that I first saw there. It is not safe to come to any important matter in an entirely direct way. When a young gentleman is about to talk to a young lady about matrimony he don't go straight at it. He begins by talking about the weather. I have done that many a time.

My next remarks will refer to the Sandwich Islands. Now if an impression has gotten abroad in the land that the Sandwich Islands are in South America, that is the error I wish to attack; that is the error I wish to combat. To cut the matter short the Sandwich Isles are 2,000 miles southwest from

San Francisco, but why they were put away out there in the middle of the Pacific, so far away from any place and in such an inconvenient locality, is no business of ours—it was the work of providence and is not open to question. The subject is a good deal like many others we should like to inquire into, such as, what mosquitoes were made for, etc., but under the circumstances we naturally feel a delicacy about doing it.

The islands are a dozen in number and their entire area is not greater I suppose than that of Rhode Island and Connecticut combined. They are of volcanic origin, of volcanic construction I should say. There is not a spoonful of legitimate dirt in the whole group, unless it has been imported. Eight of the islands are inhabited, and four of them are entirely girdled with a belt of mountains comprising the most productive sugar lands in the world. The sugar lands in Louisiana are considered rich, and yield from 500 to 1,700 pounds per acre. A two-hundred-acre crop of wheat in the States is worth twenty or thirty thousand dollars; a two-hundred-acre crop of sugar in these islands is worth two hundred thousand dollars. You could not do that in this country unless you planted it with stamps and reaped it in bonds. I could go on talking about the sugar interest all night—and I have a notion to do it. But I will spare you. It is very interesting to those who are interested in it, but I'll drop it now. You will find it all in the Patent Office reports, and I can recommend them as the most placid literature in the world.

These islands were discovered some eighty or ninety years ago by Captain Cook, though another man came very near discovering them before, and he was diverted from his course by a manuscript found in a bottle. He wasn't the first man who has been diverted by suggestions got out of a bottle. When these islands were discovered the population was about 400,000, but the white man came and brought various complicated diseases, and education, and civilization, and all sorts of calamities, and consequently the population began to drop off with commendable activity. Forty years ago they were reduced to 200,000, and the educational and civilizing facilities being increased they dwindled down to 55,000, and it is proposed to send a few more missionaries and finish them. It isn't the education or civilization that has settled them; it is the imported diseases, and they have all got the consumption and other reliable distempers, and to speak figuratively, they are retiring from business pretty fast. When they pick up and leave we will take possession as lawful heirs.

There are about 3,000 white people in the islands; they are mostly Americans. In fact they are the kings of the Sandwich Islands; the monarchy is not much more than a mere name. These people stand as high in the scale of character as any people in the world, and some of them who were born and educated in those islands don't even know what vice is. A Kanaka or a native is nobody unless he has a princely income of $75 annually, or a splendid estate worth $100. The country is full of office-holders and office-seekers; there are plenty of such noble patriots. Of almost any party of three men, two would be office-holders and one an office-seeker. In a little island half the size of one of the wards of St. Louis, there are lots of noblemen, princes and men of high degree, with grand titles, holding big offices, receiving immense salaries—such as ministers of war, secretaries of the navy, secretaries of state and ministers of justice. They make a fine display of uniforms, and are very imposing at a funeral. That's the country for a petty hero to go to, he would soon have the conceit taken out of him. There are so many of them that a nobleman from any other country would be nobody. They only lionize their own people, and therefore they lionize everybody.

In color, the natives are a rich, dark brown—a sort of black and tan. A very pleasing tint. The tropical sun and the easy-going ways inherited from their ancestors, have made them rather idle, but they are not vicious at all, they are good people. The native women in the rural districts wear a loose, magnificent curtain calico garment, but the men don't. Upon great occasions the men wear an umbrella, or some little fancy article like that—further than this they have no inclination toward gorgeousness of attire.

In the old times the king was absolute, his person was sacred, and if even the shadow of a common Kanaka fell upon him the Kanaka had to die. There was no help for him. Whatever the king tabooed it was death to touch or speak of. After the king, came the high priests who sacrificed human victims; after them came the great feudal chiefs, and then the common Kanakas, who were the slaves of all, and wretchedly oppressed. Away down at the bottom of this pyramid were the women, the abject slaves of the whole party. They did all the work and were cruelly mistreated. It was death for a woman to sit at table with her husband, or to eat of the choice fruits of the islands at any time. They seemed to have had a sort of dim knowledge of what came of women eating fruit in the Garden of Eden and they didn't feel justified in taking any more chances. And it is wisdom—unquestionably it is wisdom. Adam wasn't strict enough. Eve broke the taboo, and hence comes all this trouble. Can't be too particular about fruit—with women.

They were a rusty set all round—those Kanakas. By and by the American missionaries came and they struck off the shackles from the whole race, breaking the power of the kings and chiefs. They set the common man free, elevated his wife to a position of equality, and gave a spot of land to each to hold forever. The missionaries taught the whole nation to read and write with facility, in the native tongue. I don't suppose there is today a single uneducated person above eight years of age in the Sandwich Islands. It is the best educated country in the world, I believe, not excepting portions of the United States. That has all been done by the American missionaries. And in a large degree it was paid for by the American Sunday school children with their pennies. We all took part in it. True, the system gave opportunities to bad boys. Many a bad boy acquired the habit of confiscating pennies of the missionary cause. But it is one of the proudest recollections of my life that I never did that—at least not more than once or twice. I know that I contributed. I have had nearly $2 invested there for thirty years. But I don't mind it. I don't care for the money if it has been doing good. I don't say this in order to show off, but just mention it as a gentle, humanizing fact that may possibly have a benevolent and beneficent effect upon some members of this audience.

These natives are very hospitable people indeed—very hospitable. If you want to stay a few days and nights in a native's cabin you can stay and welcome. They will do everything they possibly can to make you comfortable. They will feed you on baked dog, or poi, or raw fish, or raw salt pork, fricasseed cats—all the luxuries of the season. Everything the human heart can desire, they will set before you. Perhaps now, this isn't a captivating feast at first glance, but it is offered in all sincerity, and with the best motives in the world, and that makes any feast respectable whether it is palatable or not. But if you want to trade, that's quite another matter— that's business! And the Kanucker is ready for you. He is a born trader, and he will swindle you if he can. He will lie straight through, from the first word to the last. Not such lies as you and I tell, but gigantic lies, lies that awe you with their grandeur, lies that stun you with their imperial impossibility. He will sell you a molehill at the market price of a mountain, and will lie it up to an altitude that will make it cheap at the money. If he is caught, he slips out of it with an easy indifference that has an unmistakable charm about it.

One peculiarity of these Kanakas is that nearly every one of them has a dozen mothers—not natural ones—I haven't got down yet where I can make such a statement as that—but adopted mothers. They have a custom of calling any woman mother they take a liking to—no matter what her color or politics—and it is possible for one native to have a thousand mothers if his affections are liberal and stretchy, and most of them are. This custom breeds some curious incidents. A California man went down there and opened a sugar plantation. One of his hands came and said he wanted to bury his mother. He gave him permission. Shortly after he came again with the same request. "I thought you buried her last week," said the gentleman. "This is another one," said the native. "All right," said the gentleman, "go and plant her." Within a month the man wanted to bury some more mothers. "Look here," said the planter, "I don't want to be hard on you in your affliction, but it appears to me that your stock of mothers holds out pretty well. It interferes with business, so clear out, and never come back until you have buried every mother you have in the world."

They are an odd sort of people, too. They can die whenever they want to. That's a fact. They don't mind dying any more than a jilted Frenchman does. When they take a notion to die they die, and it don't make any difference whether there is anything the matter with them or not, and they can't be persuaded out of it. When one of them makes up his mind to die, he just lays down and is just as certain to die as though he had all the doctors in the world hold of him. A gentleman in Hawaii asked his servant if he wouldn't like to die and have a big funeral. He said yes, and looked happy, and the next morning the overseer came and said, "That boy of yours laid down and died last night and said you were going to give him a fine funeral."

They are very fond of funerals. Big funerals are their main weakness. Fine grave clothes, fine funeral appointments, and a long procession are things they take a generous delight in. Years ago a Kanaka and his wife were condemned to be hanged for murder. They received the sentence with manifest satisfaction because it gave an opening for a funeral, you know. It makes but little difference to them whose it is; they would as soon attend their own funeral as anybody else's. This couple were of consequence, and had landed estates. They sold every foot of ground they had and laid it out in fine clothes to be hanged in. And the woman appeared on the scaffold in a white satin dress and slippers and feathers of gaudy ribbon, and the man was arrayed in a gorgeous vest, blue clawhammer coat and brass buttons, and white kid gloves. As the noose was adjusted around his neck, he blew his nose with a grand theatrical flourish, so as to show his embroidered white handkerchief. I never, never knew of a couple who enjoyed hanging more than they did.

They are very fond of dogs, these people—not the great Newfoundland or the stately mastiff, but a species of little mean, contemptible cur that a white man would condemn to death on general principles. There is nothing attractive about these dogs—there is not a handsome feature about them, unless it is their bushy tails. A friend of mine said if he had one of these dogs he would cut off the tail and throw the rest of the dog away. They feed this dog, pet him, take ever so much care of him, and then cook and eat him. I couldn't do that. I would rather go hungry for two days than devour an old personal friend in that way; but many a white citizen of those islands throws aside his prejudices and takes his dinner off one of those puppies—and after all it is only our cherished American sausage with the mystery removed.

A Kanaka will eat anything he can bite—a live fish, scales and all, which must be rather annoying to the fish, but the Kanaka doesn't mind that. It used to be said that the Kanakas were cannibals, but that was a slander. They didn't eat Captain Cook—or if they did, it was only for fun. There was one instance of cannibalism. A foreigner, from the South Pacific Islands, set up an office and did eat a good many Kanakas. He was a useful citizen, but had strong political prejudices and used to save up a good appetite for just before election, so that he could thin out the Democratic vote.

At this point in my lecture, in other cities, I usually illustrate cannibalism, but I am a stranger here and don't feel like taking liberties. Still, if any one in the audience will lend me an infant, I will illustrate the matter. But it is of no consequence—it don't matter. I know children have become scarce and high, owing to the inattention they have received since the women's rights movement began. I will leave out that part of my program, though it is very neat and pleasant. Yet it is not necessary. I am not hungry.

Well, that foreign cannibal after a while got tired of Kanakas—as most anybody would—and thought he would like to try white man with onions. So he captured and devoured a tough old whaleship captain, but it was the worst thing he ever did. Of course, he could no more digest that old whaler than a keg of nails. There is no telling how much he suffered, with this sin on his conscience and the whaler on his stomach. He lingered for a few days and then died. Now I don't believe this story myself, and have only told it for its moral. You don't appear to see the moral; but I know there is a moral in it, because I have told it thirty or forty times, and never got a moral out of it yet!

With all these excellent and hospitable ways these Kanakers have some cruel instincts. They will put a live chicken in the fire just to see it hop about. In the olden times they used to be cruel to themselves. They used to tear their hair and burn their flesh, shave their heads, knock out an eye or a couple of front teeth, when a great person or a king died—just to testify to their sorrow, and if their grief was so sore that they couldn't possibly bear it, they would go out and scalp their neighbor, or burn his house down. It was an excellent custom, too, for it gave every one a good opportunity to square up old grudges. Pity we didn't have it here! They would also kill an infant now and then—bury him alive sometimes; but the missionaries have annihilated infanticide—for my part I can't see why.

The ladies of the Sandwich Islands have a great many pleasant customs which I don't know but we might practice with profit here. The women all ride like men. I wish to introduce that reform in this country. Our ladies ought, by all means to ride like men, these sidesaddles are so dangerous. When women meet each other in the road, they run and kiss and hug each other, and they don't blackguard each other behind each other's backs. I would like to introduce that reform, also. I don't suppose our ladies do it. But they might. But I believe I am getting on dangerous ground. I won't pursue that any further.

The chief glory of the Sandwich Islands is their great volcano. The volcano of Kee-law-ay-oh is 17,000 feet in diameter, and from 700 to 800 feet deep. Vesuvius is nowhere. It is the largest volcano in the world; shoots up flames tremendously high. You witness a scene of unrivaled sublimity, and witness the most astonishing sights. When the volcano of Kee-law-ay-oh broke through a few years ago, lava flowed out of it for twenty days and twenty nights, and made a stream forty miles in length, till it reached the sea, tearing up forests in its awful fiery path, swallowing up huts, destroying all vegetation, rioting through shady dells and sinuous canyons. Amidst this carnival of destruction, majestic columns of smoke ascended and formed a cloudy murky pall overhead. Sheets of green, blue, lambent flames were shot upward, and pierced the vast gloom, making all sublimely grand.

The natives are indifferent to volcanic terrors. During the progress of an eruption they ate, drank, bought, sold, planted, builded, apparently indifferent to the roar of consuming forests, the startling detonations, the hissing of escaping steam, the rending of the earth, the shivering and melting of gigantic rocks, the raging and dashing of the fiery waves, the bellowings and unearthly mutterings coming up from a burning deep. They went carelessly on, amid the rain of ashes, sand, and fiery scintillations, gazing vacantly at the ever-varying appearance of the atmosphere, murky, black, livid, blazing, the sudden rising of lofty pillars of flame, the upward curling of ten thousand columns of smoke, and their majestic roll in dense and lurid clouds. All these moving phenomena were regarded by them as the fall of a shower or the running of a brook; while to others they were as the tokens of a burning world, the departing heavens, and a coming judge. There! I'm glad I've got that volcano off my mind.

I once knew a great, tall gawky country editor, near Sacramento, to whom I sent an ode on the sea, starting it with "The long, green swell of the Pacific." The country editor sent back a letter and stated I couldn't fool him, and he didn't want any base insinuations from me. He knew who I meant when I wrote the "long, green swell of the Pacific."

There is one thing characteristic of the tropics that a stranger must have, whether he likes it or not, and that is the boo-hoo fever. Its symptoms are nausea of the stomach, severe headache, backache and bellyache, and a general utter indifference whether school keeps or not. You can't be a full citizen of the Sandwich Islands unless you have had the boo-hoo fever. You will never forget it. I remember a little boy who had it once there. A New Yorker asked him if he was afraid to die. He said, "No; I am not afraid to die of anything, except the boo-hoo fever."

The climate of these islands is delightful, it is beautiful. In Honolulu the thermometer stands at about 80 or 82 degrees pretty much all the year round—don't change more than 12 degrees in twelve months. In the sugar districts the thermometer stands at 70 and does not change at all. Any kind of thermometer will do—one without any quicksilver is just as good. Eighty degrees by the seashore, and 70 degrees farther inland, and 60 degrees as you ascend the slope of the mountain, and as you go higher 50 degrees, 40, 30, and ever decreasing in temperature, till you get to the top, where it's so cold that you can't speak the truth. I know, for I've been there! The climate is wonderfully healthy, for white people in particular, so healthy that white people venture on the most reckless imprudence. They get up too early:

you can see them as early as half-past seven in the morning, and they attend to all their business, and keep it up till sundown. It don't hurt 'em, don't kill 'em, and yet it ought to do so. I have seen it so hot in California that green-backs went up to 142 in the shade.

These Sandwichers believe in a superstition that the biggest liars in the world have got to visit the islands some time before they die. They believe that because it is a fact—you misunderstand—I mean that when liars get there they stay there. They have several specimens they boast of. They treasure up their little perfections, and they allude to them as if the man was inspired—from below. They had a man among them named Morgan. He never allowed anyone to tell a bigger lie than himself, and he always told the last one too. When someone was telling about the natural bridge in Virginia, he said he knew all about it, as his father had helped to build it. Someone was bragging of a wonderful horse he had. Morgan told them of one he had once. While out riding one day a thundershower came on and chased him for eighteen miles, and never caught him. Not a single drop of rain dropped onto his horse, but his dog was swimming behind the wagon the whole of the way.

Once, when the subject of mean men was being discussed, Morgan told them of an incorporated company of mean men. They hired a poor fellow to blast rock for them. He drilled a hole four feet deep, put in the powder, and began to tamp it down around the fuse. I know all about tamping, as I have worked in a mine myself. The crowbar struck a spark and caused a premature explosion and that man and his crowbar shot up into the air, and he went higher and higher, till he didn't look bigger than a boy, and he kept on going higher and higher, until he didn't look bigger than a dog, and he kept on going higher and higher, until he didn't look bigger than a bee, and then he went out of sight; and presently he came in sight again, looking no bigger than a bee, and he came further and further, until he was as big as a dog, and further and further and further, until he was as big as a boy, and he came further and further, until he assumed the full size and shape of a man, and he came down and fell right into the same old spot and went to tamping again. And would you believe it—concluded Morgan—although that poor fellow was not gone more than fifteen minutes, yet that mean company docked him for loss of time.

The land that I have tried to tell you about lies out there in the midst of the watery wilderness, in the very heart of the almost soilless solitudes of the Pacific. It is a dreamy, beautiful, charming land. I wish I could make you comprehend how beautiful it is. It is a land that seems ever so vague and fairy-like when one reads about it in books, peopled with a gentle, indolent, careless race.

It is Sunday land. The land of indolence and dreams, where the air is drowsy and things tend to repose and peace, and to emancipation from the labor, and turmoil, and weariness, and anxiety of life.

Letters from Hawaii

FROM *The Sacramento Daily Union,* APRIL 21, 1866

Honolulu, March, 1866

COMING HOME FROM PRISON

I am probably the most sensitive man in the kingdom of Hawaii to night—especially about sitting down in the presence of my betters. I have ridden fifteen or twenty miles on horseback since 5 P.M., and to tell the honest truth, I have a delicacy about sitting down at all. I am one of the poorest horsemen in the world, and I never mount a horse without experiencing a sort of dread that I may be setting out on that last mysterious journey which all of us must take sooner or later, and I never come back in safety from a horseback trip without thinking of my latter end for two or three days afterward. This same old regular devotional sentiment began just as soon as I sat down here five minutes ago. An excursion to Diamond Head and the King's Cocoanut Grove was planned to-day—time, 4:30 P.M.—the party to consist of half a dozen gentlemen and three ladies. They all started at the appointed hour except myself. I was at the Government Prison, and got so interested in its examination that I did not notice how quickly the time was passing. Somebody remarked that it was twenty minutes past five o'clock, and that woke me up. It was a fortunate circumstance that Captain Phillips was there with his "turn-out," as he calls a top-buggy that Captain Cook brought here in 1778, and a horse that was here when Captain Cook came. Captain Phillips takes a just pride in his driving and in the speed of his horse, and to his passion for displaying them I owe it that we were only sixteen minutes coming from the prison to the American Hotel—a distance which has been estimated to be over half a mile. But it took some awful driving. The Captain's whip came down fast, and the blows started so much dust out of the horse's hide that during the last half of the journey we rode through an impenetrable fog, and ran by a pocket compass in the hands of Captain Fish, a whaler Captain of twenty-six years experience, who sat there through that perilous voyage as self-possessed as if he had been on the euchre-deck of his own ship, and calmly said, "Port your helm—port," from time to time, and "Hold her a little free-steady—so-o," and "Luff—hard down to starboard!" and never once lost his presence of mind or betrayed the least anxiety by voice or manna. When we came to anchor at last, and Captain Phillips looked at his watch and said, "Sixteen minutes—I told you it was in her! That's over three miles an hour!" I could see he felt entitled to a compliment, and so I said I had never seen lightning go like that horse. And I never had.

THE STEED OAHU

The landlord of the American said the party had been gone nearly an hour, but that he could give me my choice of several horses that could easily overtake them. I said, never mind—I preferred a safe horse to a fast one—I would like to have an excessively gentle horse—a horse with no spirit what-ever—a lame one, if he had such a thing. Inside of five minutes I was mounted, and perfectly satisfied with my outfit. I had no time to label him "This is a horse," and so if the public took him for a sheep I cannot help it. I was satisfied, and that was the main thing. I could see that he had as many fine points as any man's horse, and I just hung my hat on one of them, behind the saddle, and swabbed the perspiration from my face and started. I named him after this island, "Oahu" (pronounced O-waw-hoo). The first gate he came to he started in; I had neither whip nor spur, and so I simply argued the case with him. He firmly resisted argument, but ultimately yielded to insult and abuse. He backed out of that gate and steered for another one on the other side of the street. I triumphed by my former process. Within the next six hundred yards he crossed the street fourteen times and attempted thirteen gates, and in the meantime the tropical sun was beating down and threatening to cave the top of my head in, and I was literally dripping with perspiration and profanity. (I am only human and I was sorely aggravated. I shall behave better next time.) He quit the gate business after that and went along peaceably enough, but absorbed in meditation. I noticed this latter circumstance, and it soon began to fill me with the gravest apprehension. I said to myself, this malignant brute is planning some new outrage, some fresh deviltry or other—no horse ever thought over a subject so profoundly as this one is doing just for nothing. The more this thing preyed upon my mind the more uneasy I became, until at last the suspense became unbeatable and I dismounted to see if there was anything wild in his eye—for I had heard that the eye of this noblest of our domestic animals is very expressive. I cannot describe what a load of anxiety was lifted from my mind when I found that he was only asleep. I woke him up and started him into a faster walk, and then the inborn villainy of his nature came out again. He tried to climb over a stone wall, five or six feet high. I saw that I must apply force to this horse, and that I might as well begin first as last. I plucked a stout switch from a tamarind tree, and the moment he saw it, he gave in. He broke into a convulsive sort of a canter, which had three short steps in it and one long one, and reminded me alternately of the clattering shake of the great earth quake, and the sweeping plunging of the Ajax in a storm.

OUT OF PRISON, BUT IN THE STOCKS

And now it occurs to me that there can be no fitter occasion than the present to pronounce a fervent curse upon the man who invented the American saddle. There is no seat to speak of about it—one might as well sit in a shovel—and the stirrups are nothing but an ornamental nuisance. If I were to write down here all the abuse I expended on those stirrups, it would make a large book, even without pictures. Sometimes I got one foot so far through, that the stirrup partook of the nature of an anklet— sometimes both feet were through and I was handcuffed by the legs and some times my feet got clear out and left the stirrups wildly dangling about my shins. Even when I was in proper position and carefully balanced upon the balls of my feet, there was no comfort in it, on account of my nervous dread that they were going to slip one way or the other in a moment. But the subject is too exasperating to write about.

RUINS OF AN ANCIENT HEATHEN TEMPLE

Near by is an interesting ruin—the meager remains of an ancient heathen temple—a place where human sacrifices were offered up in those old bygone days when the simple child of nature, yielding momentarily to sin when sorely tempted, acknowledged his error when calm reflection had shown it to him, and came forward with noble frankness and offered up his grandmother as an atoning sacrifice—in those old days when the luckless sinner could keep on cleansing his conscience and achieving periodical happiness as long as his relations held out; long, long before the missionaries braved a thousand privations to come and make them permanently miserable by telling them how beautiful and how blissful a place heaven is, and how nearly impossible it is to get there; and showed the poor native how dreary a place perdition is and what unnecessarily liberal facilities there are for going to it; showed him how, in his ignorance, he had gone and fooled away all his kinfolks to no purpose; showed him what rapture it is to work all day long for fifty cents to buy food for next day with, as compared with fishing for pastime and lolling in the shade through eternal Summer, and eating of the bounty that nobody labored to provide but Nature. How sad it is to think of the multitudes who have gone to their graves in this beautiful island and never knew there was a hell! And it inclines right thinking man to weep rather than to laugh when he reflects how surprised they must have been when they got there. This ancient temple was built of rough blocks of lava, and was simply a roofless inclosure, a hundred and thirty feet long and seventy wide—nothing but naked walls, very thick but not much higher than a man's head. They will last for, ages, no doubt, if left unmolested. Its three altars and other sacred appurtenances have crumbled and passed away years ago. It is said that in the old times thousands of human beings were slaughtered here, in the presence of multitudes of naked, whooping and howling savages. If these mute stones could speak, what tales they could tell, what pictures they could describe, of fettered victims, writhing and shrieking under the knife; of dense masses of dusky forms straining forward out of the gloom, with eager and ferocious faces lit up with the weird light of sacrificial fires—of the vague back ground of ghostly trees; of the mournful sea washing the dim shore—of the dark pyramid of Diamond Head standing sentinel over the dismal scene, and the peaceful moon looking calmly down upon it through rifts in the drifting clouds! When Kamehameha (pronounced Ka-may-ha-may-ah) the Great—who was a very Napoleon in military genius and uniform success—invaded this island of Oahu three-quarters of a century ago, and exterminated the army sent to oppose him, and took full and final possession of the country, he searched out the dead body of the king of Oahu, and those of the principal chiefs, and impaled their heads upon the walls of this temple. Those were savage times when this old slaughter-house was in its prime. The king and the chiefs ruled the common herd with a rod of iron; made them gather all the provisions the masters needed; build all the houses and temples; stand all the expenses, of whatever kind; take kicks and cuffs for thanks; drag out lives well flavored with misery, and then suffer death for trifling offenses or yield up their lives on the sacrificial alters to purchase favors from the gods for their hard rulers. The missionaries have clothed them, educated them, broken up the tyrannous authority of their chiefs, and given them freedom and the right to enjoy whatever the labor of their hand and brains produces, with equal laws for all and punishment for all alike who transgress them. The contrast is so strong—the wonderful benefit conferred upon this people by the missionaries is so prominent, so palpable and so unquestionable, that the frankest compliment I can pay them, and the best, is simply to point to the condition of the Sandwich Islanders of Captain Cook's time, and their condition today. Their work speaks for itself. The little collection of cottages (of which I was speaking a while ago) under the cocoanut trees is a historical point. It is the village of Waikiki (usually pronounced Wy-kee-ky), once the Capital of the kingdom and the abode of the great Kamehameha I. In 1801, while he lay encamped at this place with seven thousand men, preparing to invade the island of Kauai (he had previously captured and subdued the seven other inhabited islands of the group, one after another), a pestilence broke out in Oahu and raged with great virulence. It attacked the king's army and made great havoc in it. It is said that three hundred bodies were washed out to sea in one day. There is an opening in the coral reef at this point, and anchorage inside for a small number of vessels, though one accustomed to the great Bay of San Francisco would never take this little belt of smooth water, with its border of foaming surf, to be a harbor, save for Whitehall boats or something of that kind. But harbors are scarce in these islands—open roadsteads are the rule here. The harbor of Waikiki was discovered in 1786 (seven or eight years after Captain Cook's murder) by Captains Portlock and Dixon, in the ships *King George* and *Queen Charlotte*—the first English vessels that visited the islands after that unhappy occurrence. This little bathing tub of smooth water possesses some further historical interest as being the spot where the distinguished navigator Vancouver, landed when he came here in 1792. In a conversation with a gentleman today about the scarcity of harbors among the islands (and in all the islands of the South Pacific), he said the natives of Tahiti have a theory that the reason why there are harbors wherever fresh water streams empty into the sea, and none elsewhere, is that the fresh water kills the coral insect, or so discommodes or disgusts it that it will not build its stony wall in its vicinity, and instanced what is claimed as fact, viz., that the break in the reef is always found where the fresh water passes over it, in support of this theory. (This notable equestrian excursion will be concluded in my next, if nothing happens.)

THE EQUESTRIAN EXCURSION CONCLUDED

I wandered along the sea beach on my steed Oahu around the base of the extinct crater of Leahi, or Diamond Head, and a quarter of a mile beyond the point I overtook the party of ladies and gentlemen and assumed my proper place—that is, in the rear—for the horse I ride always persists in remaining in the rear in spite of kicks, cuffs and curses. I was satisfied as long as I could keep Oahu within hailing distance of the cavalcade—I knew I could accomplish nothing better even if Oahu were Norfolk himself. We went on—on—on—a great deal too far, I thought, for people who were unaccustomed to riding on horseback, and who must expect to suffer on the morrow if they indulged too freely in this sort of exercise. Finally we got to a point which we were expecting to go around in order to strike an easy road home; but we were too late; it was full tide and the sea had closed in on the shore. Young Henry McFarlane said he knew a nice, comfortable route over the hill—a short cut—and the crowd dropped into his wake. We climbed a hill a hundred and fifty feet high, and about as straight up and down as the side of a house, and as full of rough lava blocks as it could stick—not as wide, perhaps, as the broad road that leads to destruction, but nearly as dangerous to travel, and apparently leading in the same general direction. I felt for the ladies, but I had no time to speak any words of sympathy, by reason of my attention being so much occupied by Oahu. The place was so steep that at times he stood straight up on his tip-toes and clung by his forward toenails, with his back to the Pacific Ocean and his nose close to the moon—and thus situated we formed an equestrian picture which was as uncomfortable to me as it may have been picturesque to the spectators. You may think I was afraid, but I was not. I knew I could stay on him as long as his ears did not pull out. It was a great relief to me to know that we were all safe and sound on the summit at last, because the sun was just disappearing in the waves, night was abroad in the land, candles and lamps were already twinkling in the distant town, and we gratefully reflected that Henry had saved us from having to go back around the rocky, sandy beach. But a new trouble arose while the party were admiring the rising moon and the cool, balmy night breeze, with its odor of countless flowers, for it was discovered that we had got into a place we could not get out of—we were apparently surrounded by precipices—our pilot's chart was at fault, and he could not extricate us, and so we had the prospect before us of either spending the night in the admired night-breeze, under the admired moon, or of clambering down the way we came, in the dark. However, a Kanaka came along presently and found a first-rate road for us down an almost imperceptible decline, and the party set out on a cheerful gallop again, and Oahu struck up his miraculous canter once more. The moon rose up, and flooded mountain and valley and ocean with silvery light, and I was not sorry we had lately been in trouble, because the consciousness of being safe again raised our spirits and made us more capable of enjoying the beautiful scene than we would have been otherwise. I never breathed such a soft, delicious atmosphere before, nor one freighted with such rich fragrance. A barber shop is nothing to it.

LEGENDARY

Nothing whatever is known about this place—its story is a secret that will never be revealed. The oldest natives make no pretense of being possessed of its history. They say these bones were here when they were children. They were here when their grandfathers were children—but how they came here, they can only conjecture. Many people believe this spot to be an ancient battle-ground, and it is usual to call it so, and they believe that these skeletons have lain for ages just where their proprietors fell in the great fight. Other people believe that Kamehameha I fought his first battle here. On this point, I have heard a story, which may have been taken from one of the numerous books which have been written, concerning these

islands—I do not know where the narrator got it. He said that when Kamehameha (who was at first merely a subordinate chief on the island of
Hawaii), landed here, he brought a large army with him, and encamped at
Waikiki. The Oahuans marched against him, and so confident were they of
success that they readily acceded to a demand of their priests that they
should draw a line where these bones now lie, and take an oath that, if
forced to retreat at all, they would never retreat beyond this boundary. The
priests told them that death and everlasting punishment would over take
any who violated the oath, and the march was resumed. Kamehameha
drove them back step by step; the priests fought in the front rank and
exhorted them both by voice and inspiring example to remember their
oath—to die, if need be, but never cross the fatal line. The struggle was
manfully maintained, but at last the chief priest fell, pierced to the heart
with a spear, and the unlucky omen fell like a blight upon the brave souls
at his back; with a triumphant shout the invaders pressed forward—the
line was crossed—the offended gods deserted the despairing army, and
accepting the doom their perjury had brought upon them, they broke and
fled over the plain where Honolulu stands now—up the beautiful Nuuanu
Valley—paused a moment, hemmed in by precipitous mountains on either
hand and the frightful precipice of the Pari (pronounced Pally; intelligent
natives claim that there is no r in the Kanaka alphabet) in front, and then
were driven over—a sheer plunge of six hundred feet! The story is pretty
enough, but Mr. Jarves' excellent history says the Oahuans were intrenched
in Nuuanu Valley; that Kamehameha ousted them, routed them, pursued
them up the valley and drove them over the precipice. He makes no mention of our bone-yard at all in his book. There was a terrible pestilence here
in 1804, which killed great numbers of the inhabitants, and the natives have
legends of others that swept the islands long before that; and therefore
many persons now believe that these bones belonged to victims of one of
these epidemics who were hastily buried in a great pit. It is by far the most
reasonable conjecture, because Jarves says that the weapons of the Islanders
were so rude and inefficient that their battles were not often very bloody. If
this was a battle it was astonishingly deadly, for in spite of the depredations

of "skull hunters," we rode a considerable distance over ground so thickly strewn with human bones that the horses' feet crushed them, not occasionally, but at every step.

SENTIMENT

Impressed by the profound silence and repose that rested over the beautiful landscape, and being, as usual, in the rear, I gave voice to my thought. I said: "What a picture is here slumbering in the solemn glory of the moon! How strong the rugged outlines of the dead volcano stand out against the clear sky! What a snowy fringe marks the bursting of the surf over the long, curved reef! How calmly the dim city sleeps yonder in the plain! How soft the shadows lie upon the stately mountains that border the dream haunted Manoa Valley! What a grand pyramid of billowy clouds towers above the storied Pari! How the grim warriors of the past seem flocking in ghostly squadrons to their ancient battlefield again—how the wails of the dying well up from the—" At this point the horse called Oahu deliberately sat down in the sand. Sat down to listen, I suppose. Never mind what he heard. I stopped apostrophising and convinced him that I was not a man to allow contempt of Court on the part of a horse. I broke the back bone of a Chief over his rump and set out to join the cavalcade again. Very considerably fagged out we arrived in town at 9 o'clock at night, myself in the lead— for when my horse finally came to understand that he was homeward bound and hadn't far to go, he threw his legs wildly out before and behind him, depressed his head and laid his ears back, and flew by the admiring company like a telegram. In five minutes he was far away ahead of everybody. We stopped in front of a private residence—Brown and I did—to wait for the rest and see that none were lost. I soon saw that I had attracted the attention of a comely young girl and I felt duly flattered. Perhaps thought I, she admires my horsemanship—and I made a savage jerk at the bridle and said, "Ho! will you!" to show how fierce and unmanageable the beast was— though, to say truly, he was leaning up against a hitching post peaceably enough at the time. I stirred Oahu up and moved him about, and went up the street a short distance to look for the party, and "loped" gallantly back again, all the while making a pretense of being unconscious that I was an object of interest. I then addressed a few "peart" remarks to Brown, to give the young lady a chance to admire my style of conversation, and was gratified to see her step up and whisper to Brown and glance furtively at me at the same time. I could see that her gentle face bore an expression of the most kindly and earnest solicitude, and I was shocked and angered to hear Brown burst into a fit of brutal laughter. As soon as we started home, I asked with a fair show of indifference, what she had been saying. Brown laughed again and said: "She thought from the slouchy way you rode and the way you drawled out your words, that you was drunk! She said, 'Why don't you take the poor creature home, Mr. Brown? It makes me nervous to see him galloping that horse and just hanging on that way, and he so drunk.'" I laughed very loudly at the joke, but it was a sort of hollow, sepulchral laugh, after all. And then I took it out of Oahu.

Australians and Americans

From *Following the Equator,* CHAPTER XI

The Australians did not seem to me to differ noticeably from Americans, either in dress, carriage, ways, pronunciation, inflections, or general appearance. There were fleeting and subtle suggestions of their English origin, but these were not pronounced enough, as a rule, to catch one's attention. The people have easy and cordial manners from the beginning—from the moment that the introduction is completed. This is American. To put it in another way, it is English friendliness with the English shyness and self-consciousness left out.

Now and then—but this is rare—one hears such words as *piper* for paper, *lydy* for lady, and *tyble* for table fall from lips whence one would not expect such pronunciations to come. There is a superstition prevalent in Sydney that this pronunciation is an Australianism, but people who have been "home"—as the native reverently and lovingly calls England—know better. It is "costermonger." All over Australasia this pronunciation is nearly as common among servants as it is in London among the uneducated and the partially educated of all sorts and conditions of people. That mislaid "y" is rather striking when a person gets enough of it into a short sentence to enable it to show up. In the hotel in Sydney the chambermaid said, one morning:

"The tyble is set, and here is the piper; and if the lydy is ready I'll tell the wyter to bring up the breakfast."

I have made passing mention, a moment ago, of the native Australasian's custom of speaking of England as "home." It was always pretty to hear it, and often it was said in an unconsciously caressing way that made it touching; in a way which transmuted a sentiment into an embodiment, and made one seem to see Australasia as a young girl stroking mother England's old gray head.

In the Australasian home the table-talk is vivacious and unembarrassed; it is without stiffness or restraint. This does not remind one of England so much as it does of America. But Australasia is strictly democratic, and reserves and restraints are things that are bred by differences of rank.

English and colonial audiences are phenomenally alert and responsive. Where masses of people are gathered together in England, caste is submerged, and with it the English reserve; equality exists for the moment, and every individual is free; so free from any consciousness of fetters, indeed, that the Englishman's habit of watching himself and guarding himself against any injudicious exposure of his feelings is forgotten, and falls into abeyance—and to such a degree indeed, that he will bravely applaud all by himself if he wants to—an exhibition of daring which is unusual elsewhere in the world.

But it is hard to move a new English acquaintance when he is by himself, or when the company present is small and new to him. He is on his guard then, and his natural reserve is to the fore. This has given him the false reputation of being without humor and without the appreciation of humor.

Americans are not Englishmen, and American humor is not English humor; but both the American and his humor had their origin in England, and have merely undergone changes brought about by changed conditions and a new environment. About the best humorous speeches I have yet heard were a couple that were made in Australia at club suppers—one of them by an Englishman, the other by an Australian.

Entering Sydney

FROM *Following the Equator,* CHAPTER IX

It is your human environment that makes climate.

—PUDD'NHEAD WILSON'S NEW CALENDAR

Sept. 15—Night. Close to Australia now. Sydney 50 miles distant.

That note recalls an experience. The passengers were sent for, to come up in the bow and see a fine sight. It was very dark. One could not follow with the eye the surface of the sea more than fifty yards in any direction; it dimmed away and became lost to sight at about that distance from us. But if you patiently gazed into the darkness a little while, there was a sure reward for you. Presently, a quarter of a mile away you would see a blinding splash or explosion of light on the water—a flash so sudden and so astonishingly brilliant that it would make you catch your breath; then that blotch of light would instantly extend itself and take the corkscrew shape and imposing length of the fabled sea-serpent, with every curve of its body and the "break" spreading away from its head, and the wake following behind its tail clothed in a fierce splendor of living fire. And my, but it was coming at a lightning gait! Almost before you could think, this monster of light, fifty feet long, would go flaming and storming by, and suddenly disappear. And out in the distance whence he came you would see another flash; and another and another and another, and see them turn into sea-serpents on the instant; and once sixteen flashed up at the same time and came tearing towards us, a swarm of wiggling curves, a moving conflagration, a vision of bewildering beauty, a spectacle of fire and energy whose equal the most of those people will not see again until after they are dead.

It was porpoises—porpoises aglow with phosphorescent light. They presently collected in a wild and magnificent jumble under the bows, and there they played for an hour, leaping and frollicking and carrying on, turning summersaults in front of the stem or across it and never getting hit, never making a miscalculation, though the stem missed them only about an inch, as a rule. They were porpoises of the ordinary length—eight or ten feet—but every twist of their bodies sent a long procession of united and glowing curves astern. That fiery jumble was an enchanting thing to look at, and we stayed out the performance; one cannot have such a show as that twice in a lifetime. The porpoise is the kitten of the sea; he never has a serious thought, he cares for nothing but fun and play. But I think I never saw him at his winsomest until that night. It was near a center of civilization, and he could have been drinking.

By and by, when we had approached to somewhere within thirty miles of Sydney Heads the great electric light that is posted on one of those lofty ramparts began to show, and in time the little spark grew to a great sun and pierced the firmament of darkness with a far-reaching sword of light.

Sydney Harbor is shut in behind a precipice that extends some miles like a wall, and exhibits no break to the ignorant stranger. It has a break in the middle, but it makes so little show that even Captain Cook sailed by it without seeing it. Near by that break is a false break which resembles it, and which used to make trouble for the mariner at night, in the early days before the place was lighted. It caused the memorable disaster to the *Duncan Dunbar,* one of the most pathetic tragedies in the history of that pitiless ruffian, the sea. The ship was a sailing vessel; a fine and favorite passenger packet, commanded by a popular captain of high reputation. She was due from England, and Sydney was waiting, and counting the hours; counting the hours, and making ready to give her a heart-stirring welcome; for she was bringing back a great company of mothers and daughters, the long-missed light and bloom of life of Sydney homes; daughters that had been years absent at school, and mothers that had been with them all that time watching over them. Of all the world only India and Australasia have by custom freighted ships and fleets with their hearts, and know the tremendous meaning of that phrase; only they know what the waiting is like when this freightage is entrusted to the fickle winds, not steam, and what the joy is like when the ship that is returning this treasure comes safe to port and the long dread is over.

On board the *Duncan Dunbar,* flying toward Sydney Heads in the waning afternoon, the happy home-comers made busy preparation, for it was not doubted that they would be in the arms of their friends before the day was done; they put away their sea-going clothes and put on clothes meter for the meeting, their richest and their loveliest, these poor brides of the grave. But the wind lost force, or there was a miscalculation, and before the Heads were sighted the darkness came on. It was said that ordinarily the captain would have made a safe offing and waited for the morning; but this was no ordinary occasion; all about him were appealing faces, faces pathetic with disappointment. So his sympathy moved him to try the dangerous passage in the dark. He had entered the Heads seventeen times, and believed he knew the ground. So he steered straight for the false opening, mistaking it for the true one. He did not find out that he was wrong until it was too late. There was no saving the ship. The great seas swept her in and crushed her to splinters and rubbish upon the rock tushes at the base of the precipice. Not one of all that fair and gracious company was ever seen again alive. The tale is told to every stranger that passes the spot, and it will continue to be told to all that come, for generations; but it will never grow old, custom cannot stale it, the heart-break that is in it can never perish out of it.

There were two hundred persons in the ship, and but one survived the disaster. He was a sailor. A huge sea flung him up the face of the precipice and stretched him on a narrow shelf of rock midway between the top and the bottom, and there he lay all night. At any other time he would have lain there for the rest of his life, without chance of discovery; but the next morning the ghastly news swept through Sydney that the *Duncan Dunbar* had gone down in sight of home, and straightway the walls of the Heads were black with mourners; and one of these, stretching himself out over the precipice to spy out what might be seen below, discovered this miraculously preserved relic of the wreck. Ropes were brought and the nearly impossible feat of rescuing the man was accomplished. He was a person with a practical turn of mind, and he hired a hall in Sydney and exhibited himself at sixpence a head till he exhausted the output of the gold fields for that year.

We entered and cast anchor, and in the morning went oh-ing and ah-ing in admiration up through the crooks and turns of the spacious and beautiful harbor—a harbor which is the darling of Sydney and the wonder of the world. It is not surprising that the people are proud of it, nor that they put their enthusiasm into eloquent words. A returning citizen asked me what I thought of it, and I testified with a cordiality which I judged would be up to the market rate. I said it was beautiful—superbly beautiful. Then by a natural impulse I gave God the praise. The citizen did not seem altogether satisfied. He said:

"It is beautiful, of course it's beautiful—the Harbor; but that isn't all of it, it's only half of it; Sydney's the other half, and it takes both of them together to ring the supremacy-bell. God made the Harbor, and that's all right; but Satan made Sydney."

"Of course I made an apology; and asked him to convey it to his friend. He was right about Sydney being half of it. It would be beautiful without Sydney, but not above half as beautiful as it is now, with Sydney added. It is shaped somewhat like an oak-leaf—a roomy sheet of lovely blue water, with narrow off-shoots of water running up into the country on both sides between long fingers of land, high wooden ridges with sides sloped like graves. Handsome villas are perched here and there on these ridges, snuggling amongst the foliage, and one catches alluring glimpses of them as the ship swims by toward the city. The city clothes a cluster of hills and a ruffle of neighboring ridges with its undulating masses of masonry, and out of these masses spring towers and spires and other architectural dignities and grandeurs that break the flowing lines and give picturesqueness to the general effect.

The narrow inlets which I have mentioned go wandering out into the land everywhere and hiding themselves in it, and pleasure-launches are always exploring them with picnic parties on board. It is said by trustworthy people that if you explore them all you will find that you have covered 700 miles of water passage. But there are liars everywhere this year, and they will double that when their works are in good going order. October was close at hand, spring was come. It was really spring—everybody said so; but you could have sold it for summer in Canada, and nobody would have suspected. It was the very weather that makes our home summers the perfection of climatic luxury; I mean, when you are out in the wood or by the sea. But these people said it was cool, now—a person ought to see Sydney in the summer time if he wanted to know what warm weather is; and he ought to go north ten or fifteen hundred miles if he wanted to know what hot weather is. They said that away up there toward the equator the hens laid fried eggs. Sydney is the place to go to get information about other people's climates. It seems to me that the occupation of Unbiased Traveler Seeking Information is the pleasantest and most irresponsible trade there is. The traveler can always find out anything he wants to, merely by asking. He can get at all the facts, and more. Everybody helps him, nobody hinders him. Anybody who has an old fact in stock that is no longer negotiable in the domestic market will let him have it at his own price. An accumulation of such goods is easily and quickly made. They cost almost nothing and they bring par in the foreign market. Travelers who come to America always freight up with the same old nursery tales that their predecessors selected, and they carry them back and always work them off without any trouble in the home market.

If the climates of the world were determined by parallels of latitude, then we could know a place's climate by its position on the map; and so we should know that the climate of Sydney was the counterpart of the climate of Columbia, S.C., and of Little Rock, Arkansas, since Sydney is about the same distance south of the equator that those other towns are north-of-it-thirty-four degrees. But no, climate disregards the parallels of latitude. In Arkansas they have a winter; in Sydney they have the name of it, but not the thing itself. I have seen the ice in the Mississippi floating past the mouth of the Arkansas river; and at Memphis, but a little way above, the Mississippi has been frozen over, from bank to bank. But they have never had a cold spell in Sydney which brought the mercury down to freezing point. Once in a mid-winter day there, in the month of July, the mercury went down to 36 deg., and that remains the memorable "cold day" in the history of the town. No doubt Little Rock has seen it below zero. Once, in Sydney, in mid-summer, about New Year's Day, the mercury went up to 106 deg. in the shade, and that is Sydney's memorable hot day. That would about tally with Little Rock's hottest day also, I imagine. My Sydney figures are taken from a government report, and are trustworthy. In the matter of summer weather Arkansas has no advantage over Sydney, perhaps, but when it comes to winter weather, that is another affair. You could cut up an Arkansas winter into a hundred Sydney winters and have enough left for Arkansas and the poor.

The whole narrow, hilly belt of the Pacific side of New South Wales has the climate of its capital—a mean winter temperature of 54 deg. and a mean summer one of 71 deg. It is a climate which cannot be improved upon for healthfulness. But the experts say that 90 deg. in New South Wales is harder to bear than 112 deg. in the neighboring colony of Victoria, because the atmosphere of the former is humid, and of the latter dry. The mean temperature of the southernmost point of New South Wales is the same as that of Nice—60 deg.—yet Nice is further from the equator by 460 miles than is the former.

But Nature is always stingy of perfect climates; stingier in the case of Australia than usual. Apparently this vast continent has a really good climate nowhere but around the edges.

If we look at a map of the world we are surprised to see how big Australia is. It is about two-thirds as large as the United States was before we added Alaska.

But where as one finds a sufficiently good climate and fertile land almost everywhere in the United States, it seems settled that inside of the Australian border-belt one finds many deserts and in spots a climate which nothing can stand except a few of the hardier kinds of rocks. In effect, Australia is as yet unoccupied. If you take a map of the United States and leave the Atlantic sea-board States in their places; also the fringe of Southern States from Florida west to the Mouth of the Mississippi; also a narrow, inhabited streak up the Mississippi half-way to its head waters; also a narrow, inhabited border along the Pacific coast: then take a brushful of paint and obliterate the whole remaining mighty stretch of country that lies between the Atlantic States and the Pacific-coast strip, your map will look like the latest map of Australia.

This stupendous blank is hot, not to say torrid; a part of it is fertile, the rest is desert; it is not liberally watered; it has no towns. One has only to cross the mountains of New South Wales and descend into the westward-lying regions to find that he has left the choice climate behind him, and found a new one of a quite different character. In fact, he would not know by the thermometer that he was not in the blistering Plains of India. Captain Sturt, the great explorer, gives us a sample of the heat.

"The wind, which had been blowing all the morning from the N.E., increased to a heavy gale, and I shall never forget its withering effect. I sought shelter behind a large gum-tree, but the blasts of heat were so terrific that I wondered the very grass did not take fire. This really was nothing ideal: everything both animate and inanimate gave way before it; the horses stood with their backs to the wind and their noses to the ground, without the muscular strength to raise their heads; the birds were mute, and the leaves of the trees under which we were sitting fell like a snow shower around us. At noon I took a thermometer graded to 127 deg., out of my box, and observed that the mercury was up to 125. Thinking that it had been unduly influenced, I put it in the fork of a tree close to me, sheltered alike from the wind and the sun. I went to examine it about an hour afterwards, when I found the mercury had risen to the top of the instrument and had burst the bulb, a circumstance that I believe no traveler has ever before had to record. I cannot find language to convey to the reader's mind an idea of the intense and oppressive nature of the heat that prevailed."

That hot wind sweeps over Sydney sometimes, and brings with it what is called a "dust-storm." It is said that most Australian towns are acquainted with the dust-storm. I think I know what it is like, for the following description by Mr. Gape tallies very well with the alkali duststorm of Nevada, if you leave out the "shovel" part. Still the shovel part is a pretty important part, and seems to indicate that my Nevada storm is but a poor thing, after all.

"As we proceeded the altitude became less, and the heat proportionately greater until we reached Dubbo, which is only 600 feet above sea-level. It is a pretty town, built on an extensive plain . . . After the effects of a shower of rain have passed away the surface of the ground crumbles into a thick layer of dust, and occasionally, when the wind is in a particular quarter, it is lifted bodily from the ground in one long opaque cloud. In the midst of such a storm nothing can be seen a few yards ahead, and the unlucky person who happens to be out at the time is compelled to seek the nearest retreat at hand. When the thrifty housewife sees in the distance the dark column advancing in a steady whirl towards her house, she closes the doors and windows with all expedition. A drawing-room, the window of which has been carelessly left open during a dust-storm, is indeed an extraordinary sight. A lady who has resided in Dubbo for some years says that the dust lies so thick on the carpet that it is necessary to use a shovel to remove it."

And probably a wagon. I was mistaken; I have not seen a proper dust-storm. To my mind the exterior aspects and character of Australia are fascinating things to look at and think about, they are so strange, so weird, so new, so uncommonplace, such a startling and interesting contrast to the other sections of the planet, the sections that are known to us all, familiar to us all. In the matter of particulars—a detail here, a detail there—we have had the choice climate of New South Wales' seacoast; we have had the Australian heat as furnished by Captain Sturt; we have had the wonderful dust-storm; and we have considered the phenomenon of an almost empty hot wilderness half as big as the United States, with a narrow belt of civilization, population, and good climate around it.

Town of Wanganui

From *Following the Equator,* CHAPTER XXXV

December 8.

A couple of curious war-monuments here at Wanganui. One is in honor of white men "who fell in defense of law and order against fanaticism and barbarism." Fanaticism. We Americans are English in blood, English in speech, English in religion, English in the essentials of our governmental system, English in the essentials of our civilization; and so, let us hope, for the honor of the blend, for the honor of the blood, for the honor of the race, that that word got there through lack of heedfulness, and will not be suffered to remain. If you carve it at Thermopylae, or where Winkelried died, or upon Bunker Hill monument, and read it again "who fell in defence of law and order against fanaticism" you will perceive what the word means, and how mischosen it is. Patriotism is Patriotism. Calling it *Fanaticism* cannot degrade it; nothing can degrade it. Even though it be a political mistake, and a thousand times a political mistake, that does not affect it; it is honorable, always honorable, always noble—and privileged to hold its head up and look the nations in the face. It is right to praise these brave white men who fell in the Maori war—they deserve it; but the presence of that word detracts from the dignity of their cause and their deeds, and makes them appear to have spilt their blood in a conflict with ignoble men, men not worthy of that costly sacrifice. But the men were worthy. It was no shame to fight them. They fought for their homes, they fought for their country; they bravely fought and bravely fell; and it would take nothing from the honor of the brave Englishmen who lie under the monument, but add to it, to say that they died in defense of English laws and English homes against men worthy of the sacrifice—the Maori patriots.

The other monument cannot be rectified. Except with dynamite. It is a mistake all through, and a strangely thoughtless one. It is a monument erected by white men to Maoris who fell fighting with the whites and against their own people, in the Maori war. "Sacred to the memory of the brave men who fell on the 14th of May, 1864," etc. On one side are the names of about twenty Maoris. It is not a fancy of mine; the monument exists. I saw it. It is an object-lesson to the rising generation. It invites to treachery, disloyalty, unpatriotism. Its lesson, in frank terms is, "Desert your flag, slay your people, burn their homes, shame your nationality—we honor such."

The Weet-Weet

From *Following the Equator,* CHAPTER XXI

> *Man will do many things to get himself loved, he will do all things to get himself envied.*
>
> —PUDD'NHEAD WILSON'S NEW CALENDAR

Before I saw Australia I had never heard of the "weet-weet" at all. I met but few men who had seen it thrown—at least I met but few who mentioned having seen it thrown. Roughly described, it is a fat wooden cigar with its butt-end fastened to a flexible twig. The whole thing is only a couple of feet long, and weighs less than two ounces. This feather— so to call it—is not thrown through the air, but is flung with an under-handed throw and made to strike the ground a little way in front of the thrower; then it glances and makes a long skip; glances again, skips again, and again and again, like the flat stone which a boy sends skating over the water. The water is smooth, and the stone has a good chance; so a strong man may make it travel fifty or seventy-five yards; but the weet-weet has no such good chance, for it strikes sand, grass, and earth in its course. Yet an expert aboriginal has sent it a measured distance of two hundred and twenty yards. It would have gone even further but it encountered rank ferns and underwood on its passage and they damaged its speed. Two hundred and twenty yards; and so weightless a toy—a mouse on the end of a bit of wire, in effect; and not sailing through the accommodating air, but encountering grass and sand and stuff at every jump. It looks wholly impossible; but Mr. Brough Smyth saw the feat and did the measuring, and set down the facts in his book about aboriginal life, which he wrote by command of the Victorian Government.

What is the secret of the feat? No one explains. It cannot be physical strength, for that could not drive such a feather-weight any distance. It must be art. But no one explains what the art of it is; nor how it gets around that law of nature which says you shall not throw any two-ounce thing 220 yards, either through the air or bumping along the ground. Rev. J. G. Woods says:

"The distance to which the weet-weet or kangaroo-rat can be thrown is truly astonishing. I have seen an Australian stand at one side of Kennington Oval and throw the kangaroo rat completely across it." (Width of Kensington Oval not stated.) "It darts through the air with the sharp and menacing hiss of a rifle-ball, its greatest height from the ground being some seven or eight feet . . . When properly thrown it looks just like a living animal leaping along . . . Its movements have a wonderful resemblance to the long leaps of a kangaroo-rat fleeing in alarm, with its long tail trailing behind it."

The Old Settler said that he had seen distances made by the weet-weet, in the early days, which almost convinced him that it was as extraordinary an instrument as the boomerang.

There must have been a large distribution of acuteness among those naked skinny aboriginals, or they couldn't have been such unapproachable trackers and boomerangers and weet-weeters. It must have been race-aversion that put upon them a good deal of the low-rate intellectual reputation which they bear and have borne this long time in the world's estimate of them.

They were lazy—always lazy. Perhaps that was their trouble. It is a killing defect. Surely they could have invented and built a competent house, but they didn't. And they could have invented and developed the agricultural arts, but they didn't. They went naked and houseless, and lived on fish and grubs and worms and wild fruits, and were just plain savages, for all their smartness.

With a country as big as the United States to live and multiply in, and with no epidemic diseases among them till the white man came with those and his other appliances of civilization, it is quite probable that there was never a day in his history when he could muster 100,000 of his race in all Australia. He diligently and deliberately kept population down by infanticide—largely; but mainly by certain other methods. He did not need to practise these artificialities any more after the white man came. The white man knew ways of keeping down population which were worth several of his. The white man knew ways of reducing a native population 80 percent in 20 years. The native had never seen anything as fine as that before.

For example, there is the case of the country now called Victoria—a country eighty times as large as Rhode Island, as I have already said. By the best official guess there were 4,500 aboriginals in it when the whites came along in the middle of the 'Thirties. Of these, 1,000 lived in Gippsland, a patch of territory the size of fifteen or sixteen Rhode Islands: they did not diminish as fast as some of the other communities; indeed, at the end of forty years there were still 200 of them left. The Geelong tribe diminished more satisfactorily: from 173 persons it faded to 34 in twenty years; at the end of another twenty the tribe numbered one person altogether. The two Melbourne tribes could muster almost 300 when the white man came; they could muster but twenty, thirty-seven years later, in 1875. In that year there were still odds and ends of tribes scattered about the colony of Victoria, but I was told that natives of full blood are very scarce now. It is said that the aboriginals continue in some force in the huge territory called Queensland.

The early whites were not used to savages. They could not understand the primary law of savage life: that if a man do you a wrong, his whole tribe is responsible—each individual of it—and you may take your change out of any individual of it, without bothering to seek out the guilty one. When a white killed an aboriginal, the tribe applied the ancient law, and killed the first white they came across. To the whites this was a monstrous thing. Extermination seemed to be the proper medicine for such creatures as this. They did not kill all the blacks, but they promptly killed enough of them to make their own persons safe. From the dawn of civilization down to this day the white man has always used that very precaution. Mrs. Campbell Praed lived in Queensland, as a child, in the early days, and in her *Sketches and Impressions of Bush Life,* we get informing pictures of the early struggles of the white and the black to reform each other.

Speaking of pioneer days in the mighty wilderness of Queensland, Mrs. Praed says:

"At first the natives retreated before the whites; and, except that they every now and then speared a beast in one of the herds, gave little cause for uneasiness. But, as the number of squatters increased, each one taking up miles of country and bringing two or three men in his train, so that shepherds' huts and stockmen's camps lay far apart, and defenseless in the midst of hostile tribes, the Blacks' depredations became more frequent and murder was no unusual event.

"The loneliness of the Australian bush can hardly be painted in words. Here extends mile after mile of primeval forest where perhaps foot of white man has never trod—interminable vistas where the eucalyptus trees rear their lofty trunks and spread forth their lanky limbs, from which the red gum oozes and hangs in fantastic pendants like crimson stalactites; ravines along the sides of which the long-bladed grass grows rankly; level untimbered plains alternating with undulating tracts of pasture, here and there broken by a stony ridge, steep gully, or dried-up creek. All wild, vast and desolate; all the same monotonous gray coloring, except where the wattle, when in blossom, shows patches of feathery gold, or a belt of scrub lies green, glossy, and impenetrable as Indian jungle.

"The solitude seems intensified by the strange sounds of reptiles, birds, and insects, and by the absence of larger creatures; of which in the day-time, the only audible signs are the stampede of a herd of kangaroo, or the rustle of a wallabi, or a dingo stirring the grass as it creeps to its lair. But there are the whirring of locusts, the demoniac chuckle of the laughing jack-ass, the screeching of cockatoos and parrots, the hissing of the frilled lizard, and the buzzing of innumerable insects hidden under the dense undergrowth. And then at night, the melancholy wailing of the curlews, the dismal howling of dingoes, the discordant croaking of tree-frogs, might well shake the nerves of the solitary watcher."

That is the theater for the drama. When you comprehend one or two other details, you will perceive how well suited for trouble it was, and how loudly it invited it. The cattlemen's stations were scattered over that profound wilderness miles and miles apart—at each station half a dozen persons. There was a plenty of cattle, the black natives were always ill-nourished and hungry. The land belonged to them. The whites had not bought it, and couldn't buy it; for the tribes had no chiefs, nobody in authority, nobody competent to sell and convey; and the tribes themselves had no comprehension of the idea of transferable ownership of land. The ousted owners were despised by the white interlopers, and this opinion was not hidden under a bushel. More promising materials for a tragedy could not have been collated. Let Mrs. Praed speak:

"At Nie station, one dark night, the unsuspecting hut-keeper, having, as he believed, secured himself against assault, was lying wrapped in his blankets sleeping profoundly. The Blacks crept stealthily down the chimney and battered in his skull while he slept."

One could guess the whole drama from that little text. The curtain was up. It would not fall until the mastership of one party or the other was determined—and permanently:

"There was treachery on both sides. The Blacks killed the Whites when they found them defenseless, and the Whites slew the Blacks in a wholesale and promiscuous fashion which offended against my childish sense of justice.

"They were regarded as little above the level of brutes, and in some cases were destroyed like vermin.

"Here is an instance. A squatter, whose station was surrounded by Blacks, whom he suspected to be hostile and from whom he feared an attack, parleyed with them from his house-door. He told them it was Christmas-time—a time at which all men, black or white, feasted; that there were flour, sugar-plums, good things in plenty in the store, and that he would make for them such a pudding as they had never dreamed of—a great pudding of which all might eat and be filled. The Blacks listened and were lost. The pudding was made and distributed. Next morning there was howling in the camp, for it had been sweetened with sugar and arsenic!"

The white man's spirit was right, but his method was wrong. His spirit was the spirit which the civilized white has always exhibited toward the savage, but the use of poison was a departure from custom. True, it was merely a technical departure, not a real one; still, it was a departure, and therefore a mistake, in my opinion. It was better, kinder, swifter, and much more humane than a number of the methods which have been sanctified by custom, but that does not justify its employment. That is, it does not wholly justify it. Its unusual nature makes it stand out and attract an amount of attention which it is not entitled to. It takes hold upon morbid imaginations and they work it up into a sort of exhibition of cruelty, and this smirches the good name of our civilization, whereas one of the old harsher methods would have had no such effect because usage has made those methods familiar to us and innocent. In many countries we have chained the savage and starved him to death; and this we do not care for, because custom has inured us to it; yet a quick death by poison is loving-kindness to it. In many countries we have burned the savage at the stake; and this we do not care for, because custom has inured us to it; yet a quick death is loving-kindness to it. In more than one country we have hunted the savage and his little children and their mother with dogs and guns through the woods and swamps for an afternoon's sport, and filled the region with happy laughter over their sprawling and stumbling flight, and their wild supplications for mercy; but this method we do not mind, because custom has inured us to it; yet a quick death by poison is loving-kindness to it. In many countries we have taken the savage's land from him, and made him our slave, and lashed him every day, and broken his pride, and made death his only friend, and overworked him till he dropped in his tracks; and this we do not care for, because custom has inured us to it; yet a quick death by poison is loving-kindness to it. In the Matabeleland today—why, there we are confining ourselves to sanctified custom, we Rhodes-Beit millionaires in South Africa and Dukes in London; and nobody cares, because we are used to the old holy customs, and all we ask is that no notice-inviting new ones shall be intruded upon the attention of our comfortable consciences. Mrs. Praed says of the poisoner, "That squatter deserves to have his name handed down to the contempt of posterity."

I am sorry to hear her say that. I myself blame him for one thing, and severely, but I stop there. I blame him for, the indiscretion of introducing a novelty which was calculated to attract attention to our civilization. There was no occasion to do that. It was his duty, and it is every loyal man's duty to protect that heritage in every way he can; and the best way to do that is to attract attention elsewhere. The squatter's judgment was bad—that is plain; but his heart was right. He is almost the only pioneering representative of civilization in history who has risen above the prejudices of his caste and his heredity and tried to introduce the element of mercy into the superior race's dealings with the savage. His name is lost, and it is a pity; for it deserves to be handed down to posterity with homage and reverence.

This paragraph is from a London journal:

"To learn what France is doing to spread the blessings of civilization in her distant dependencies we may turn with advantage to New Caledonia. With a view to attracting free settlers to that penal colony, M. Feillet, the Governor, forcibly expropriated the Kanaka cultivators from the best of their plantations, with a derisory compensation, in spite of the protests of the Council General of the island. Such immigrants as could be induced to cross the seas thus found themselves in possession of thousands of coffee, cocoa, banana, and bread-fruit trees, the raising of which had cost the wretched natives years of toil whilst the latter had a few five-franc pieces to spend in the liquor stores of Noumea."

You observe the combination? It is robbery, humiliation, and slow, slow murder, through poverty and the white man's whisky. The savage's gentle friend, the savage's noble friend, the only magnanimous and unselfish friend the savage has ever had, was not there with the merciful swift release of his poisoned pudding.

There are many humorous things in the world; among them the white man's notion that he is less savage than the other savages.

PART V

Europe

The American Vandal Abroad

FROM *Mark Twain's Speeches*

I am to speak of the American Vandal this evening, but I wish to say in advance that I do not use this term in derision or apply it as a reproach, but I use it because it is convenient; and duly and properly modified, it best describes the roving, independent, free-and-easy character of that class of traveling Americans who are not elaborately educated, cultivated, and refined, and gilded and filigreed with the ineffable graces of the first society. The best class of our countrymen who go abroad keep us well posted about their doings in foreign lands, but their brethren vandals cannot sing their own praises or publish their adventures.

The American Vandal gallops over England, Scotland, Spain, and Switzerland, and finally brings up in Italy. He thinks it is the proper thing to visit Genoa, the stately old City of Palaces, whose vast marble edifices almost meet together over streets so narrow that three men can hardly walk abreast in them, and so crooked that a man generally comes out of them about the same place he went in. He only stays in Genoa long enough to see a few celebrated things and get some fragments of stone from the house Columbus was born in—for your genuine Vandal is an intolerable and incorrigible relic gatherer. It is estimated that if all the fragments of stone brought from Columbus's house by travelers were collected together they would suffice to build a house fourteen thousand feet high—and I suppose they would.

Next he hurries to Milan and takes notes of the Grand Cathedral (for he is always taking notes). Oh, I remember Milan and the noble cathedral well enough—that marble miracle of enchanting architecture. I remember how we entered and walked about its vast spaces and among its huge columns, gazing aloft at the monster windows all aglow with brilliantly colored scenes in the life of the Savior and his followers. And I remember the side-shows and curiosities there, too. The guide showed us a coffee-colored piece of sculpture which he said was supposed to have come from the hand of Phidias, since it was not possible that any other man, of any epoch, could have copied nature with such faultless accuracy. The figure was that of a man without a skin; with every vein, artery, muscle, every fiber and tendon and tissue of the human frame, represented in minute detail. It looked natural, because it looked somehow as if it were in pain. A skinned man would be likely to look that way—unless his attention were occupied by some other matter.

The Vandal goes to see the ancient and most celebrated painting in the world, *The Last Supper*. We all know it in engravings: the disciples all sitting on one side of a long, plain table and Christ with bowed head in the center—all the last suppers in the world are copied from this painting. It is so damaged now, by the wear and tear of three hundred years, that the figures can hardly be distinguished. The Vandal goes to see this picture— which all the world praises—looks at it with a critical eye, and says it's a perfect old nightmare of a picture and he wouldn't give forty dollars for a million like it (and I indorse his opinion), and then he is done with Milan.

He paddles around the Lake of Como for a few days, and then takes the cars. He is bound for Venice, the oldest and the proudest and the princeliest republic that ever graced the earth. We put on a good many airs with our little infant of a Republic of a century's growth, but we grow modest when we stand before this gray, old imperial city that used to laugh the armies and navies of half the world to scorn, and was a haughty, invin-cible, magnificent Republic for fourteen hundred years! The Vandal is bound for Venice! He has a long, long, weary ride of it; but just as the day is closing he hears some one shout, "Venice!" and puts his head out of a window, and sure enough, afloat on the placid sea, a league away, lies the great city with its towers and domes and steeples drowsing in a golden mist of sunset!

Have you been to Venice, and seen the winding canals, and the stately edifices that border them all along, ornamented with the quaint devices and sculptures of a former age? And have you seen the great Cathedral of St. Mark's—and the Giant's Staircase—and the famous Bridge of Sighs—and the great Square of St. Mark's—and the ancient pillar with the winged lion of St. Mark that stands on it, whose story and whose origin are a mystery—and the Rialto, where Shylock used to loan money on human flesh and other collateral?

I had begun to feel that the old Venice of song and story had departed forever. But I was too hasty. When we swept gracefully out into the Grand Canal and under the mellow moonlight the Venice of poetry and romance stood revealed. Right from the water's edge rose palaces of marble; gondolas were gliding swiftly hither and thither and disappearing suddenly through unsuspected gates and alleys; ponderous stone bridges threw their shadows athwart the glittering waves. There were life and motion everywhere, and yet everywhere there was a hush, a stealthy sort of stillness, that was suggestive of secret enterprises of bravos and of lovers; and clad half in moonbeams and half in mysterious shadows, the grim old mansions of the republic seemed to have an expression about them of having an eye out for just such enterprises as these. At that same moment music came stealing over the waters—Venice was complete.

Our Vandals hurried away from Venice and scattered abroad everywhere. You could find them breaking specimens from the dilapidated tomb of Romeo and Juliet at Padua—and infesting the picture galleries of Florence—and risking their necks on the Leaning Tower of Pisa—and snuffing sulphur fumes on the summit of Vesuvius—and burrowing among the exhumed wonders of Herculaneum and Pompeii—and you might see them with spectacles on, and blue cotton umbrellas under their arms, benignantly contemplating Rome from the venerable arches of the Coliseum.

And finally we sailed from Naples, and in due time anchored before the Piraeus, the seaport of Athens in Greece. But the quarantine was in force, and so they set a guard of soldiers to watch us and would not let us go ashore. However, I and three other Vandals took a boat, and muffled the oars, and slipped ashore at 11:30 at night, and dodged the guard successfully. Then we made a wide circuit around the slumbering town, avoiding all roads and houses—for they'd about as soon hang a body as not for violating the quarantine laws in those countries. We got around the town without any accident, and then struck out across the Attic Plain, steering straight for Athens—over rocks and hills and brambles and everything—with Mt. Helicon for a landmark. And so we tramped for five or six miles. The Attic Plain is a mighty uncomfortable plain to travel in, even if it is so historical. The armed guards got after us three times and flourished their gleaming gun barrels in the moonlight, because they thought we were stealing grapes occasionally—and the fact is we were— for we found by and by that the brambles that tripped us up so often were grape-vines—but these people in the country didn't know that we were quarantine-blockade runners, and so they only scared us and jawed Greek at us, and let us go, instead of arresting us.

We didn't care about Athens particularly, but we wanted to see the famous Acropolis and its ruined temples, and we did. We climbed the steep hill of the Acropolis about one in the morning and tried to storm that grand old fortress that had scorned the battles and sieges of three thousand years. We had the garrison out mighty quick—four Greeks—and we bribed them to betray the citadel and unlock the gates. In a moment we stood in the presence of the noblest ruins we had ever seen—the most elegant, the most graceful, the most imposing. The renowned Parthenon towered above us, and about us were the wreck of what were once the snowy marble Temples of Hercules and Minerva, and another whose name I have forgotten. Most of the Parthenon's grand columns are still standing, but the roof is gone.

As we wandered down the marble-paved length of this mighty temple, the scene was strangely impressive. Here and there in lavish profusion were gleaming white statues of men and women, propped against blocks of marble, some of them armless, some without legs, others headless, but all looking mournful and sentient and startlingly human! They rose up and confronted the midnight intruder on every side; they stared at him with stony eyes from unlooked-for nooks and recesses; they peered at him over fragmentary heaps far down the desolate corridors; they barred his way in the midst of the broad forum, and solemnly pointed with handless arms the way from the sacred fane; and through the roofless temple the moon looked down and banded the floor and darkened the scattered fragments and broken statues with the slanting shadows of the columns!

What a world of ruined sculpture was about us! Stood up in rows, stacked up in piles, scattered broadcast over the wide area of the Acropolis, were hundreds of crippled statues of all sizes and of the most exquisite worksmanship; and vast fragments of marble that once belonged to the entablatures, covered with bas-reliefs representing battles and sieges, ships of war with three and four tiers of oars, pageants and processions—everything one could think of.

We walked out into the grass-grown, fragment-strewn court beyond the Parthenon. It startled us every now and then, to see a stony white face stare suddenly up at us out of the grass, with its dead eyes. The place seemed alive with ghosts. We half expected to see the Athenian heroes of twenty centuries ago glide out of the shadows and steal into the old temple they knew so well and regarded with such boundless pride.

The full moon was riding high in the cloudless heavens now. We sauntered carelessly and unthinkingly to the edge of the lofty battlements of the citadel, and looked down, and, lo! a vision! And such a vision! Athens by moonlight! All the beauty in all the world could not rival it! The prophet that thought the splendors of the New Jerusalem were revealed to him, surely saw this instead. It lay in the level plain right under our feet—all spread abroad like a picture—and we looked down upon it as we might have looked from a balloon. We saw no semblance of a street, but every house, every window, every clinging vine, every projection, was as distinct and sharply marked as if the time were noonday; and yet there was no glare, no glitter, nothing harsh or repulsive—the silent city was flooded with the mellowest light that ever streamed from the moon, and seemed like some living creature wrapped in peaceful slumber. On its farther side was a little temple whose delicate pillars and ornate front glowed with a rich luster that chained the eye like a spell; and, nearer by, the palace of the king reared its creamy walls out of the midst of a great garden of shrubbery that was flecked all over with a random shower of amber lights—a spray of golden sparks that lost their brightness in the glory of the moon and glinted softly upon the sea of dark foliage like the pallid stars of the Milky Way! Overhead, the stately columns, majestic still in their ruin; underfoot, the dreaming city; in the distance the silver sea—not on the broad earth is there another picture half so beautiful!

We got back to the ship safely, just as the day was dawning. We had walked upon pavements that had been pressed by Plato, Aristotle, Demosthenes, Socrates, Phocion, Euclid, Xenophon, Herodotus, Diogenes, and a hundred others of deathless fame, and were satisfied. We got to stealing grapes again on the way back, and half a dozen rascally guards with muskets and pistols captured us and marched us in the center of a hollow square nearly to the sea—till we were beyond all the graperies. Military escort—ah, I never travelled in so much state in all my life.

I leave the Vandal here. I have not time to follow him farther—not our Vandals to Constantinople and Smyrna and the Holy Land, Egypt, the islands of the sea, and to Russia and his visit to the emperor. But I wish I could tell of that visit of our gang of Quaker City Vandals to the grandest monarch of the age, American's stanch, old steadfast friend, Alexander II, Autocrat of Russia!

IN CLOSING these remarks I will observe that I could have said more about the American Vandal abroad, and less about other things, but I found that he had too many disagreeable points about him, and so I thought I would touch him lightly and let him go.

If there is a moral to this lecture it is an injunction to all Vandals to travel. I am glad the American Vandal goes abroad. It does him good. It makes a better man of him. It rubs out a multitude of his old unworthy biases and prejudices. It aids his religion, for it enlarges his charity and his benevolence, it broadens his views of men and things; it deepens his generosity and his compassion for the failings and shortcomings of his fellow creatures. Contact with men of various nations and many creeds teaches him that there are other people in the world besides his own little clique, and other opinions as worthy of attention and respect as his own. He finds that he and his are not the most momentous matters in the universe. Cast into trouble and misfortune in strange lands and being mercifully cared for by those he never saw before, he begins to learn that best lesson of all— that one which culminates in the conviction that God puts something good and something lovable in every man his hands create—that the world is not a cold, harsh, cruel, prison-house, stocked with all manner of selfishness and hate and wickedness. It liberalizes the Vandal to travel. You never saw a bigoted, opinionated, stubborn, narrow-minded, self-conceited, almighty mean man in your life but he had stuck in one place ever since he was born and thought God made the world and dyspepsia and bile for his especial comfort and satisfaction. So I say, by all means let the American Vandal go on traveling, and let no man discourage him.

Old-Master Worshippers

FROM *Daily Alta California*, OCTOBER 23, 1867

ALTA LETTER 18

Constantinople, August 23rd, 1867

I understand it, I think. The people who go into ecstasies over St. Sophia get them out of the guide book (where every church is spoken of as being "considered by good judges to be the most marvelous structure, in many respects, that the world has ever seen"). Or else they are these old-master worshippers from the wilds of New Jersey, who can't tell a fresco from lath-and-plaster, and don't know any more about pictures than a kangaroo does about astronomy. And so you always hear them carrying on about wonderful pictures, wonderful statuary and wonderful architecture, the shameless lunatics! as if they had always been used to palaces and studios, extensive travel and the company of the elegant and accomplished, instead of being raised in a cow-lot, educated in a saw-mill, and their minds enlarged and stored with precious knowledge by travel down a creek on a shingle raft.

Now there was that wretched woman in the Vatican in Rome. She overheard Brown say something outrageous about the old masters, and she permitted him to overhear her say something rather savage about "people who had no appreciation of the divine works of the great masters." It was not a gentlemanly thing for a lady to do, but she did not know that, perhaps. However, she went into hysterics, pretty soon, over a picture marked "Angelo," and called it a miracle of art, and a heavenly conception and a work such as none but inspired hands could have wrought, and a lot more of sickening nonsense like that, but finally an officer of the institution came along and set her back. He said that that particular "Angelo" was not Mike, but a certain other Angelo who used to be a butcher in Pisa—and that after painting until he found out it was not his best hold, he went back into the butchering business again. I just had an idea that may be that woman had had more experience in tending babies on a salary than in setting in judgment on the inspired fire-screens of the old masters.

Old Saint Paul's

FROM *Mark Twain's Sketches. Number One*

Who can look upon this venerable edifice, with its clustering memories and old traditions, without emotion! Who can contemplate its scarred and blackened walls without drifting insensibly into dreams of the historic past! Who can hold to be trivial even the least detail or appurtenance of this stately national altar! It is with diffidence that I approach the work of description, it is with humility that I offer the thoughts that crowd upon me.

Upon arriving at Saint Paul's; the first thing that bursts upon the beholder/attracts the beholder's attention is the back yard. This fine work of art is forty-three feet long by thirty-four and a half feet wide—and all enclosed with real iron railings. The pavement is of fine oolite, or skylight, or some other stone of that geologic period, and is laid almost flat on the ground, in places. The stones are exactly square, and it is thought that they were made so by design; though of course, as in all matters of antiquarian science, there are wide differences of opinion about this. The architect of the pavement was Morgan Jones, of No. 4, Piccadilly, Cheapside, Islington. He died in the reign of Richard III, of the prevailing disorder. An axe fell on his neck. The coloring of the pavement is very beautiful, and will immediately attract the notice of the visitor. Part of it is white and the other part black. The part that is white, has been washed. This was done upon the occasion of the coronation of George II, and the person who did it was knighted, as the reader will already have opined. The iron railings cannot be too much admired. They were designed and constructed by Ralph Benson, of No. 9, Gracechurch-street, Fenchurch-street, Upper-Terrace, Tottenham-court-road, Felter-lane, London, C.E., by special appointment blacksmith to his royal Majesty, George III, of gracious memory, and were done at his own shop, by his own hands, and under his own personal supervision. Specimens/Relics of this great artist's inspiration are exceedingly rare, and are valued at enormous sums; however, two shovels and a horseshoe made by him are on file at the British Museum, and no stranger should go away from London without seeing them. One of the shovels is undoubtedly genuine, but all authorities agree that the other one is spurious. It is not known which is the spurious one, and this is unfortunate, for nothing connected with this great man can be deemed of trifling importance. It is said that he was buried at Westminster Abbey, but was taken up and hanged in chains at Tyburn, at the time of the restoration under the impression that he was Cromwell. But this is considered doubtful, by some, because he was not yet born at the time of the restoration. The railings are nine feet three inches high, from the top of the stone pediment to the spear-heads that form the apex, and twelve feet four inches high from the ground to the apex, the stone pediment being three feet one inch high, all of solid stone. The railings are not merely stood up on the pediment, but are mortised in, in the most ravishing manner. It was originally intended to make the railings two inches higher than they are, but the idea was finally abandoned, for some reason or other. This is greatly to be regretted, because it makes the fence out of proportion to the rest of St. Paul's, and seriously mars the general effect. The spear-heads upon the tops of the railings were gilded upon the death of Henry VIII, out of respect for the memory of that truly great king. The artist who performed the work was knighted by the regency, and hanged by Queen Mary when she came into power. No charge is made for contemplating the railings, or looking through them or climbing over them—which is in marked and generous contrast to some of the other sights of London. All you have to do is to apply to a member of the Common Council and get a letter to the Lord Mayor, who will give you a note to the Lord High Chamberlain of the Exchequer, who will grant you a pass, good for two days, together with a return ticket. This is much simpler than the system observed by the custodians of some of the other sights of London. You can walk, but it is best to go in a cab, for there is no place in London which is less than two miles and a half from any other place. I am not speaking heedlessly, but from experience. At all the other public buildings and parks in London, there is an arched and prodigious gateway which is special and sacred to the queen, who is either sixty feet high or the gateways don't fit—but at St. Paul's the case is different. There is no special gate for the queen, and so I do not know how she gets in there. It must be very inconvenient to go through a common highway when one is not used to it.

The stone pediment upon which the iron railings stand was designed and erected by William Marlow, of 14, Threadneedle-street, Paternoster Row, St. Giles's, Belgravia, W. C., and is composed of alternate layers of rock, one above the other, and all cemented together in the most compact and impressive manner. The style of its architecture is a combination of the pre-raphaelite and the renaissance,—just enough of the pre-raphaelite to make it firm and substantial, and just enough of the renaissance to impart to the whole a calm and gracious expression. There is nothing like this stone wall in England. We have no such artists now-a-days. To find true art, we must go back to the past. Let the visitor note the tone of this wall, and the feeling. No work of art can be intelligently and enjoyably contemplated unless you know about tone and feeling; unless you know *all* about tone and feeling, and can tell at a glance which is the tone and which is the feeling—and can talk about it with the guide-book shut up. I will venture to say that there is more tone in that stone wall than was ever hurled into a stone wall before; and as for feeling, it is just suffocated with it. As a whole, this fence is absolutely without its equal. If Michael Angelo could have seen this fence, would he have wasted his years sitting on a stone worshiping the cathedral of Florence? No; he would have spent his life gazing at this fence, and he would have taken a wax impression of it with him when he died. Michael Angelo and I may be considered extravagant, but as for me, if you simply mention art, I cannot be calm. I can go down on my knees before one of those decayed and venerable old Masters that you have to put a sign on to tell which side of it you are looking at, and I do not want any bread, I do not want any meat, I do not want any air to breathe—I can *live*, in the tone and the feeling of it. Expression—expression is the thing—in art. I do not care what it expresses, and I cannot most always sometimes tell, generally, but expression is what I worship, it is what I glory in, with all my impetuous nature. All the traveling world are just like me.

Marlow, the architect and builder of the stone pediment I was speaking of, was the favorite pupil of the lamented Hugh Miller, and worked in the same quarry with him. Specimens of the stone, for the cabinet, can be easily chipped off by the tourist with his hammer, in the customary way. I will observe that the stone was brought from a quarry on the Surrey side, near London. You can go either by Blackfriars bridge, or Westminster bridge or the Thames tunnel—fare, two shillings in a cab. It is best seen at sunrise, though many prefer moonlight.

The front yard of St Paul's is just like the back yard, except that it is adorned with a very noble and imposing statue of a black woman which is said to have resembled queen Anne, in some respects. It is five feet four inches high from the top of the figure to the pedestal, and nine feet seven inches from the top of the figure to the ground, the pedestal being four feet three inches high—all of solid stone. The figure measures eleven inches around the arm, and fifty three inches around the body. The rigidity of the drapery has been much admired.

I will not make any description of the rest of Old Saint Paul's, for that has already been done in every book upon London that has thus far been written, and therefore the reader must be measurably familiar with it. My only object is to instruct the reader upon matters which have been strangely neglected by other tourists; and if I have supplied a vacuum which must often have been painfully felt, my reward is sufficient. I have endeavored to furnish the exact dimensions of everything in feet and inches, in the customary exciting way, and likewise to supply names and dates and gushings upon art which will instruct the future tourist how to feel, and what to think, and how to tell it when he gets home.

Concerning Chambermaids

FROM *The Celebrated Jumping Frog of Calaveras County, and Other Sketches*

Against all chambermaids, of whatsoever age or nationality, I launch the curse of bachelordom! Because:

They always put the pillows at the opposite end of the bed from the gas-burner, so that while you read and smoke before sleeping, (as is the ancient and honored custom of bachelors), you have to hold your book aloft, in an uncomfortable position, to keep the light from dazzling your eyes.

When they find the pillows removed to the other end of the bed in the morning, they receive not the suggestion in a friendly spirit; but, glorying in their absolute sovereignty, and unpitying your helplessness, they make the bed just as it was originally, and gloat in secret over the pang their tyranny will cause you.

Always after that, when they find you have transposed the pillows, they undo your work, and thus defy and seek to embitter the life that God has given you.

If they cannot get the light in an inconvenient position any other way, they move the bed.

If you pull your trunk out six inches from the wall, so that the lid will stay up when you open it, they always shove that trunk back again. They do it on purpose.

If you want the spittoon in a certain spot, where it will be handy, they don't, and so they move it.

They always put your other boots into inaccessible places. They chiefly enjoy depositing them as far under the bed as the wall will permit. It is because this compels you to get down in an undignified attitude and make wild sweeps for them in the dark with the boot-jack, and swear.

They always put the match-box in some other place. They hunt up a new place for it every day, and put up a bottle, or other perishable glass thing, where the box stood before. This is to cause you to break that glass thing, groping in the dark, and get yourself into trouble.

They are forever and ever moving the furniture. When you come in, in the night, you can calculate on finding the bureau where the wardrobe was in the morning. And when you go out in the morning, if you leave the slop-bucket by the door and rocking-chair by the window, when you come in at midnight, or thereabouts, you will fall over that rocking chair, and you will proceed toward the window and sit down in that slop-tub. This will disgust you. They like that.

No matter where you put any thing, they are not going to let it stay there. They will take it and move it the first chance they get. It is their nature. And, besides, it gives them pleasure to be mean and contrary this way. They would die if they couldn't be villains.

They always save up all the old scraps of printed rubbish you throw on the floor, and stack them up carefully on the table, and start the fire with your valuable manuscripts. If there is any one particular old scrap that you are more down on than any other, and which you are gradually wearing your life out trying to get rid of, you may take all the pains you possibly can in that direction, but it won't be of any use, because they will always fetch that old scrap back and put it in the same old place again every time. It does them good.

And they use up more hair-oil than any six men. If charged with purloining the same, they lie about it. What do they care about a hereafter? Absolutely nothing.

If you leave your key in the door for convenience sake, they will carry it down to the office and give it to the clerk. They do this under the vile pretense of trying to protect your property from thieves; but actually they do it because they want to make you tramp back down-stairs after it when you come home tired, or put you to the trouble of sending a waiter for it, which waiter will expect you to pay him something. In which case I suppose the degraded creatures divide.

They keep always trying to make your bed before you get up, thus destroying your rest and inflicting agony upon you; but after you get up, they don't come any more till next day.

They do all the mean things they can think of, and they do them just out of pure cussedness, and nothing else.

Chambermaids are dead to every human instinct.

I have cursed them in behalf of outraged bachelordom. They deserve it. If I can get a bill through the Legislature abolishing chambermaids, I mean to do it.

Mark Twain's Map of Paris

FROM *Tales, Speeches, Essays, and Sketches*

The Galaxy, NOVEMBER 1870

Ipublished my "Map of the Fortifications of Paris" in my own paper a
fortnight ago, but am obliged to reproduce it in *The Galaxy*, to satisfy
the extraordinary demand for it which has arisen in military circles
throughout the country. General Grant's outspoken commendation originated this demand, and General Sherman's fervent endorsement added
fuel to it. The result is that tons of these maps have been fed to the suffering soldiers of our land, but without avail. They hunger still. We will cast
The Galaxy into the breach and stand by and await the effect.

The next Atlantic mail will doubtless bring news of a European frenzy
for the map. It is reasonable to expect that the siege of Paris will be suspended till a German translation of it can be forwarded (it is now in preparation), and that the defense of Paris will likewise be suspended to await
the reception of the French translation (now progressing under my own
hands, and likely to be unique). King William's high praise of the map and
Napoleon's frank enthusiasm concerning its execution will ensure its
prompt adoption in Europe as the only authoritative and legitimate exposi-
tion of the present military situation. It is plain that if the Prussians cannot
get into Paris with the facilities afforded by this production of mine they
ought to deliver the enterprise into abler hands.

Strangers to me keep insisting that this map does not "explain itself."
One person came to me with bloodshot eyes and a harassed look about
him, and shook the map in my face and said he believed I was some new
kind of idiot. I have been 'bused a good deal by other quick-tempered
people like him, who came with similar complaints. Now, therefore, I
yield willingly, and for the information of the ignorant will briefly explain
the present military situation as illustrated by the map. Part of the Prussian
forces, under Prince Frederick William, are now boarding at the

"farm-house" in the margin of the map. There is nothing between them and Vincennes but a rail fence in bad repair. Any corporal can see at a glance that they have only to burn it, pull it down, crawl under, climb over, or walk around it, just as the commander-in-chief shall elect. Another portion of the Prussian forces are at Podunk, under Von Moltke. They have nothing to do but float down the river Seine on a raft and scale the walls of Paris. Let the worshippers of that overrated soldier believe in him still, and abide the result—for me, I do not believe he will ever think of a raft. At Omaha and the High Bridge are vast masses of Prussian infantry, and it is only fair to say that they are likely to stay there, as that figure of a window-sash between them stands for a brewery. Away up out of sight over the top of the map is the fleet of the Prussian navy, ready at any moment to come cavorting down the Erie Canal (unless some new iniquity of an unprincipled Legislature shall put up the tolls and so render it cheaper to walk). To me it looks as if Paris is in a singularly close place. She never was situated before as she is in this map.

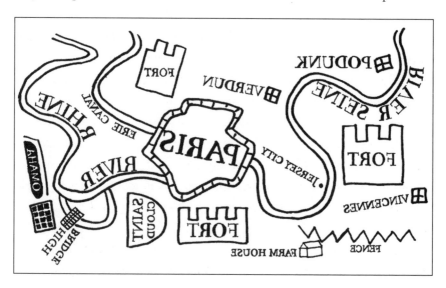

TO THE READER

The accompanying map explains itself.

The idea of this map is not original with me, but is borrowed from the *Tribune* and the other great metropolitan journals.

I claim no other merit for this production (if I may so call it) than that it is accurate. The main blemish of the city-paper maps of which it is an imitation, is, that in them more attention seems paid to artistic picturesqueness than geographical reliability.

Inasmuch as this is the first time I ever tried to draft and engrave a map, or attempt anything in the line of art at all, the commendations the work has received and the admiration it has excited among the people, have been very grateful to my feelings. And it is touching to reflect that by far the most enthusiastic of these praises have come from people who know nothing at all about art.

By an unimportant oversight I have engraved the map so that it reads wrong end first, except to left-handed people. I forgot that in order to make it right in print it should be drawn and engraved upside down. However, let the student who desires to contemplate the map stand on his head or hold it before her looking-glass. That will bring it right.

The reader will comprehend at a glance that that piece of river with the "High Bridge" over it got left out to one side by reason of a slip of the graving-tool, which rendered it necessary to change the entire course of the river Rhine or else spoil the map. After having spent two days in digging and gouging at the map, I would have changed the course of the Atlantic ocean before I would have lost so much work.

I never had so much trouble with anything in my life as I did with this map. I had heaps of little fortifications scattered all around Paris, at first, but every now and then my instruments would slip and fetch away whole miles of batteries and leave the vicinity as clean as if the Prussians had been there.

The reader will find it well to frame this map for future reference, so that it may aid in extending popular intelligence and dispelling the widespread ignorance of the day.

OFFICIAL COMMENDATIONS

"It is the only map of the kind I ever saw."

—U. S. GRANT

"It places the situation in an entirely new light."
— BISMARCK

"I cannot look upon it without shedding tears."
— BRIGHAM YOUNG

"It is very nice, large print."
— NAPOLEON

"My wife was for years afflicted with freckles, and though everything was done for her relief that could be done, all was in vain. But, sir, since her first glance at your map, they have entirely left her. She has nothing but convulsions now."
— J. SMITH

"If I had had this map I could have got out of Metz without any trouble."
— BAZAINE

"I have seen a great many maps in my time, but none that this one reminds me of."
— TROCHU

"It is but fair to say that in some respects it is a truly remarkable map."
— W. T. SHERMAN

"I said to my son Frederick William, 'If you could only make a map like that, I would be perfectly willing to see you die—even anxious.'"
— WILLIAM III.

The Chicago of Europe

From Mark Twain's Travel Letters from 1891–92

Chicago Daily Tribune, April 3, 1892

[Often titled "The German Chicago"]

I feel lost in Berlin. It has no resemblance to the city I had supposed it was. There was once a Berlin which I would have known, from descriptions in books—the Berlin of the last century and the beginning of the present one: a dingy city in a marsh, with rough streets, muddy and lantern-lighted, dividing straight rows of ugly houses all alike, compacted into blocks as square and plain and uniform and monotonous and serious as so many dry-goods boxes. But that Berlin has disappeared. It seems to have disappeared totally, and left no sign. The bulk of the Berlin of today has about it no suggestion of a former period. The site it stands on has traditions and a history, but the city itself has no traditions and no history. It is a new city; the newest I have ever seen. Chicago would seem venerable beside it; for there are many old-looking districts in Chicago, but not many in Berlin. The main mass of the city looks as if it had been built last week, the rest of it has a just perceptibly graver tone, and looks as if it might be six or even eight months old.

The next feature that strikes one is the spaciousness, the roominess of the city. There is no other city, in any country, whose streets are so generally wide. Berlin is not merely a city of wide streets, it is *the* city of wide streets. As a wide-street city it has never had its equal, in any age of the world. "Unter den Linden" is three streets in one; the Potsdamerstrasse is bordered on both sides by sidewalks which are themselves wider than some of the historic thoroughfares of the old European capitals; there seem to be no lanes or alleys; there are no short cuts; here and there, where several important streets empty into a common center, that center's circumference is of a magnitude calculated to bring that word *spaciousness* into your mind again. The park in the middle of the city is so huge that it calls up that expression once more.

The next feature that strikes one is the straightness of the streets. The short ones haven't so much as a waver in them; the long ones stretch out to prodigious distances and then tilt a little to the right or left, then stretch out on another immense reach as straight as a ray of light. A result of this arrangement is that at night Berlin is an inspiring sight to see. Gas and the electric light are employed with a wasteful liberality, and so, wherever one goes, he has always double ranks of brilliant lights stretching far down into the night on every hand, with here and there a wide and splendid constellation of them spread out over an intervening "platz," and between the interminable double procession of street lamps one has the swarming and darting cab lamps, a lively and pretty addition to the fine spectacle, for they counterfeit the rush and confusion and sparkle of an invasion of fireflies.

There is one other noticeable feature—the absolutely level surface of the site of Berlin. Berlin, to recapitulate, is newer to the eye than is any other city, and also blonder of complexion and tidier; no other city has such an air of roominess, freedom from crowding; no other city has so many straight streets; and with Chicago it contests the chromo for flatness of surface and for phenomenal swiftness of growth. Berlin is the European Chicago. The two cities have about the same population—say a million and a half. I cannot speak in exact terms, because I only know what Chicago's population was week before last; but at that time it was about a million and a half. Fifteen years ago Berlin and Chicago were large cities, of course, but neither of them was the giant it now is.

But now the parallels fail. Only parts of Chicago are stately and beautiful, whereas all of Berlin is stately and substantial, and it is not merely in parts but uniformly beautiful. There are buildings in Chicago that are architecturally finer than any in Berlin, I think, but what I have just said above is still true. These two flat cities would lead the world for phenomenal good health if London were out of the way. As it is, London leads by a point or two. Berlin's death rate is only nineteen in the thousand. Fourteen years ago the rate was a third higher.

Berlin is a surprise in a great many ways—in a multitude of ways, to speak strongly and be exact. It seems to be the most governed city in the world, but one must admit that it also seems to be the best governed. Method and system are observable on every hand—in great things, in little things, in all details, of whatsoever size. And it is not method and system on paper, and there an end—it is method and system in practice. It has a rule for everything, and puts the rule in force; puts it in force against the poor and powerful alike, without favor or prejudice. It deals with great matters and minute particulars with equal faithfulness, and with a plodding and painstaking diligence and persistency which compel admiration—and sometimes regret. There are several taxes, and they are collected quarterly. Collected is the word; they are not merely levied, they are collected—every time. This makes light taxes. It is in cities and countries where a consider-able part of the community shirks payment that taxes have to be lifted to a burdensome rate. Here the police keep coming, calmly and patiently, until you pay your tax. They charge you 5 or 10 cents per visit after the first call. By experiment you will find that they will presently collect that money.

In one respect the 1,500,000 of Berlin's population are like a family: the head of this large family knows the names of its several members, and where the said members are located, and when and where they were born, and what they do for a living, and what their religious brand is. Whoever comes to Berlin must furnish these particulars to the police immediately; moreover, if he knows how long he is going to stay, he must say so. If he takes a house he will be taxed on the rent and taxed also on his income. He will not be asked what his income is, and so he may save some lies for home consumption. The police will estimate his income from the house rent he pays, and tax him on that basis.

Duties on imported articles are collected with inflexible fidelity, be the sum large or little; but the methods are gentle, prompt, and full of the spirit of accommodation. The postman attends to the whole matter for you, in cases where the article comes by mail, and you have no trouble and suffer no inconvenience. The other day a friend of mine was informed that there was a package in the post-office for him, containing a lady's silk belt with gold clasp, and a gold chain to hang a bunch of keys on. In his first agitation he was going to try to bribe the postman to chalk it through, but acted upon his sober second thought and allowed the matter to take its proper and regular course. In a little while the postman brought the package and made these several collections: duty on the silk belt, 7½ cents; duty on the gold chain, 10 cents; charge for fetching the package, 5 cents. These devastating imposts are exacted for the protection of German home industries.

The calm, quiet, courteous, cussed persistence of the police is the most admirable thing I have encountered on this side. They undertook to persuade me to send and get a passport for a Swiss maid whom we had brought with us, and at the end of six weeks of patient, tranquil, angelic daily effort they succeeded. I was not intending to give them trouble, but I was lazy and I thought they would get tired. Meanwhile they probably thought I would be the one. It turned out just so.

One is not allowed to build unstable, unsafe, or unsightly houses in Berlin; the result is this comely and conspicuously stately city, with its security from conflagrations and breakdowns. It is built of architectural Gibraltars. The building commissioners inspect while the building is going up. It has been found that this is better than to wait till it falls down. These people are full of whims.

One is not allowed to cram poor folk into cramped and dirty tenement houses. Each individual must have just so many cubic feet of room-space, and sanitary inspections are systematic and frequent.

Everything is orderly. The fire brigade march in rank, curiously uniformed, and so grave is their demeanor that they look like a Salvation Army under conviction of sin. People tell me that when a fire alarm is sounded, the firemen assemble calmly, answer to their names when the roll is called, then proceed to the fire. There they are ranked up, military fashion, and told off in detachments by the chief, who parcels out to the detachments the several parts of the work which they are to undertake in putting out that fire. This is all done with low-voiced propriety, and strangers think these people are working a funeral. As a rule, the fire is confined to a single floor in these great masses of bricks and masonry, and consequently there is little or no interest attaching to a fire here for the rest of the occupants of the house.

There is an abundance of newspapers in Berlin, and there was also a newsboy, but he died. At intervals of half a mile on the thoroughfares there are booths, and it is at these that you buy your papers. There are plenty of theaters, but they do not advertise in a loud way. There are no big posters of any kind, and the display of vast type and of pictures of actors and performance framed on a big scale and done in rainbow colors is a thing unknown. If the big show bills existed there would be no place to exhibit them; for there are no poster fences, and one would not be allowed to disfigure dead walls with them. Unsightly things are forbidden here; Berlin is a rest to the eye.

And yet the saunterer can easily find out what is going on at the theaters. All over the city, at short distances apart, there are neat round pillars eighteen feet high and about as thick as a hogshead, and on these the little black and white theater bills and other notices are posted. One generally finds a group around each pillar reading these things. There are plenty of things in Berlin worth importing to America. It is these that I have particularly wished to make a note of. When Buffalo Bill was here his biggest poster was probably not larger than the top of an ordinary trunk.

There is a multiplicity of clean and comfortable horse-cars, but whenever you think you know where a car is going to you would better stop ashore, because that car is not going to that place at all. The car routes are marvelously intricate, and often the drivers get lost and are not heard of for years. The signs on the cars furnish no details as to the course of the journey; they name the end of it, and then experiment around to see how much territory they can cover before they get there. The conductor will collect your fare over again every few miles, and give you a ticket which he hasn't apparently kept any record of, and you keep it till an inspector comes aboard by and by and tears a corner off it (which he does not keep), then you throw the ticket away and get ready to buy another. Brains are of no value when you are trying to navigate Berlin in a horse-car. When the ablest of Brooklyn's editors was here on a visit he took a horse-car in the early morning, and wore it out trying to go to a point in the center of the city. He was on board all day and spent many dollars in fares, and then did not arrive at the place which he had started to go to. This is the most thorough way to see Berlin, but it is also the most expensive.

But there are excellent features about the car system, nevertheless. The car will not stop for you to get on or off, except at certain places a block or two apart where there is a sign to indicate that that is a halting-station. This system saves many bones. There are twenty places inside the car; when these seats are filled, no more can enter. Four or five persons may stand on each platform—the law decrees the number—and when these standing places are all occupied the next applicant is refused. As there is no crowding, and as no rowdyism is allowed, women stand on the platforms as well as the men; they often stand there when there are vacant seats inside, for these places are comfortable, there being little or no jolting. A native tells me that when the first car was put on, thirty or forty years ago, the public had such a terror of it that they didn't feel safe inside of it, or outside either. They made the company keep a man at every crossing with a red flag in his hand. Nobody would travel in the car except convicts on the way to the gallows. This made business in only one direction, and the car had to go back light. To save the company, the city government transferred the convict cemetery to the other end of the line. This made traffic in both directions and kept the company from going under. This sounds like some of the information which traveling foreigners are furnished with in America. To my mind it has a doubtful ring about it.

The first-class cab is neat and trim, and has leather-cushion seats and a swift horse. The second-class cab is an ugly and lubberly vehicle, and is always old. It seems a strange thing that they have never built any new ones. Still, if such a thing were done everybody that had time to flock would flock to see it, and that would make a crowd, and the police do not like crowds and disorder here. If there were an earthquake in Berlin the police would take charge of it and conduct it in that sort of orderly way that would make you think it was a prayer meeting. That is what an earthquake generally ends in, but this one would be different from those others; it would be kind of soft and self-contained, like a Republican praying for a mugwump.

For a course (a quarter of an hour or less), one pays 25 cents in a first-class cab, and 15 cents in a second-class. The first-class will take you along faster, for the second-class horse is old—always old—as old as his cab, some authorities say—and ill-fed and weak. He has been a first-class once, but has been degraded to second class for long and faithful service.

The streets are very clean. They are kept so—not by prayer and talk and the other New York methods, but by daily and hourly work with scrapers and brooms; and when an asphalted street has been tidily scraped after a rain or a light snowfall, they scatter clean sand over it. This saves some of the horses from falling down. In fact, this is a city government which seems to stop at no expense where the public convenience, comfort, and health are concerned—except in one detail. That is the naming of the streets and the numbering of the houses. Sometimes the name of a street will change in the middle of a block. You will not find it out till you get to the next corner and discover the new name on the wall, and of course you don't know just when the change happened.

The names are plainly marked on the corners—on all the corners— there are no exceptions. But the numbering of the houses—there has never been anything like it since original chaos. It is not possible that it was done by this wise city government. At first one thinks it was done by an idiot; but there is too much variety about it for that; an idiot could not think of so many different ways of making confusion and propagating blasphemy. The numbers run up one side the street and down the other. That is endurable, but the rest isn't. They often use one number for three or four houses—and sometimes they put the number on only one of the houses and let you guess at the others. Sometimes they put a number on a house—4, for instance—then put 4a, 4b, 4c, on the succeeding houses, and one becomes old and decrepit before he finally arrives at 5. A result of this systemless system is that when you are at No. 1 in a street you haven't any idea how far it may be to No. 150; it may be only six or eight blocks, it may be a couple of miles. Frederick Street is long, and is one of the great thoroughfares. The other day a man put up his money behind the assertion that there were more refreshment places in that street than numbers on the houses—and he won. There were 254 numbers and 257 refreshment places. Yet as I have said, it is a long street.

But the worst feature of all this complex business is that in Berlin the numbers do not travel in any one direction; no, they travel along until they get to 50 or 60, perhaps, then suddenly you find yourself up in the hundreds—140, maybe; the next will be 139—then you perceive by that sign that the numbers are now traveling toward you from the opposite direction. They will keep that sort of insanity up as long as you travel that street; every now and then the numbers will turn and run the other way. As a rule, there is an arrow under the number, to show by the direction of its flight which way the numbers are proceeding. There are a good many suicides in Berlin; I have seen six reported in one day. There is always a deal of learned and laborious arguing and ciphering going on as to the cause of this state of things. If they will set to work and number their houses in a rational way perhaps they will find out what was the matter.

More than a month ago Berlin began to prepare to celebrate Professor Virchow's seventieth birthday. When the birthday arrived, the middle of October, it seemed to me that all the world of science arrived with it; deputation after deputation came, bringing the homage and reverence of far cities and centers of learning, and during the whole of a long day the hero of it sat and received such witness of his greatness as has seldom been vouchsafed to any man in any walk of life in any time, ancient or modern. These demonstrations were continued in one form or another day after day, and were presently merged in similar demonstrations to his twin in science and achievement, Professor Helmholtz, whose seventieth birthday is separated from Virchow's by only about three weeks; so nearly as this did these two extraordinary men come to being born together. Two such births have seldom signalized a single year in human history.

But perhaps the final and closing demonstration was peculiarly grateful to them. This was a commers given in their honor the other night by 1,000 students. It was held in a huge hall, very long and very lofty, which had five galleries, far above everybody's head, which were crowded with ladies— 400 or 500, I judged. It was beautifully decorated with clustered flags and various ornamental devices, and was brilliantly lighted. On the spacious floor of this place were ranged, in files, innumerable tables, seating twenty-four persons each, extending from one end of the great hall clear to the other, and with narrow aisles between the files. In the center on one side was a high and tastefully decorated platform twenty or thirty feet long, with a long table on it, behind which sat the half-dozen chiefs of the choir of the commers in the rich medieval costumes of as many different college corps. Behind these youths a band of musicians was concealed. On the floor directly in front of this platform were half a dozen tables which were distinguished from the outlying continent of tables by being covered instead of left naked. Of these the central table was reserved for the two heroes of the occasion and twenty particularly eminent professors of the Berlin University, and the other covered tables were for the occupancy of a hundred less distinguished professors.

I was glad to be honored with a place at the table of the two heroes of the occasion, although I was not really learned enough to deserve it. Indeed, there was a pleasant strangeness in being in such company; to be thus associated with twenty-three men who forget more every day than I ever knew. Yet there was nothing embarrassing about it, because loaded men and empty ones look about alike. I knew that to that multitude there I was a professor. It required but little art to catch the ways and attitude of those men and imitate them, and I had no difficulty in looking as much like a professor as anybody there.

We arrived early; so early that only Professors Virchow and Helmholtz and a dozen guests of the special tables were ahead of us, and 300 or 400 students. But people were arriving in floods now, and within fifteen minutes all but the special tables were occupied, and the great house was crammed, the aisles included. It was said that there were 4,000 men present. It was a most animated scene, there is no doubt about that; it was a stupendous beehive. At each end of each table stood a corps student in the uniform of his corps. These quaint costumes are of brilliant colored silks and velvets, with sometimes a high plumed hat, sometimes a broad Scotch cap, with a great plume wound about it, sometimes—oftenest— a little shallow silk cap on the tip of the crown, like an inverted saucer; sometimes the pantaloons are snow-white, sometimes of other colors; the boots in all cases come up well above the knee; and in all cases also white gauntlets are worn; the sword is a rapier with a bowl-shaped guard for the hand, painted in several colors. Each corps has a uniform of its own, and all are of rich material, brilliant in color, and exceedingly picturesque; for they are survivals of the vanished costumes of the Middle Ages, and they reproduce for us the time when men were beautiful to look at. The student who stood guard at our end of the table was of grave countenance and great frame and grace of form, and he was doubtless an accurate reproduction, clothes and all, of some ancestor of his of two or three centuries ago—a reproduction as far as the outside, the animal man, goes, I mean.

As I say, the place was now crowded. The nearest aisle was packed with students standing up, and they made a fence which shut off the rest of the house from view. As far down this fence as you could see all these wholesome young faces were turned in one direction, all these intent and worshiping eyes were centered upon one spot—the place where Virchow and Helmholtz sat. The boys seemed lost to everything, unconscious of their own existence; they devoured these two intellectual giants with their eyes, they feasted upon them, and the worship that was in their hearts shone in their faces. It seemed to me that I would rather be flooded with a glory like that—instinct with sincerity, innocent of self-seeking—than win a hundred battles and break a million hearts.

There was a big mug of beer in front of each of us, and more to come when wanted. There was also a quarto pamphlet containing the words of the songs to be sung. After the names of the officers of the feast were these words in large type:

Wahrend des Kommerses herrscht allgemeiner Burgfriede.

I was not able to translate this to my satisfaction, but a professor helped me out. This was his explanation: The students in uniform belong to different college corps; not all students belong to corps; none join the corps except those who enjoy fighting. The corps students fight duels with swords every week, one corps challenging another corps to furnish a certain number of duelists for the occasion, and it is only on this battlefield that students of different corps exchange courtesies. In common life they do not drink with each other or speak. The above line now translates itself: "There is truce during the Commers; war is laid aside and fellowship takes its place."

Now the performance began. The concealed band played a piece of martial music; then there was a pause. The students on the platform rose to their feet, the middle one gave a toast to the Emperor, then all the house rose, mugs in hand. At the call "One, two, three!" all glasses were drained and then brought down with a slam on the tables in unison. The result was as good an imitation of thunder as I have ever heard. From now on, during an hour, there was singing, in mighty chorus. During each interval between songs a number of the special guests—the professors—arrived. There seemed to be some signal whereby the students on the platform were made aware that a professor had arrived at the remote door of entrance; for you would see them suddenly rise to their feet, strike an erect military attitude, then draw their swords; the swords of all their brethren standing guard at the innumerable tables would flash from their scabbards and be held aloft—a handsome spectacle. Three clear bugle notes would ring out, then all these swords would come down with a crash, twice repeated, on the tables, and be uplifted and held aloft again; then in the distance you would see the gay uniforms and uplifted swords of a guard of honor clearing the way and conducting the guest down to his place. The songs were stirring, the immense out-pour from young life and young lungs, the crash of swords and the thunder of the beer-mugs gradually worked a body up to what seemed the last possible summit of excitement. It surely seemed to me that I had reached that summit, that I had reached my limit, and that there was no higher lift desirable for me. When apparently the last eminent guest had long ago taken his place, again those three bugle blasts rang out and once more the swords leaped from their scabbards. Who might this late comer be? Nobody was interested to inquire. Still, indolent eyes were turned toward the distant entrance; we saw the silken gleam and the lifted swords of a guard of honor plowing through the remote crowds. Then we saw that end of the house rising to its feet; saw it rise abreast the advancing guard all along, like a wave. This supreme honor had been offered to no one before. Then there was an excited whisper at our table—"Mommsen!"—and the whole house rose. Rose and shouted and stamped and clapped, and banged the beer-mugs. Just simply a storm! Then the little man with his long hair and Emersonian face edged his way past us and took his seat. I could have touched him with my hand—Mommsen!—think of it!

This was one of those immense surprises that can happen only a few times in one's life. I was not dreaming of him; he was to me only a giant myth, a world-shadowing specter, not a reality. The surprise of it all can be only comparable to a man's suddenly coming upon Mont Blanc, with its awful form towering into the sky, when he didn't suspect he was in its neighborhood. I would have walked a great many miles to get a sight of him, and here he was, without trouble or tramp or cost of any kind. Here he was, clothed in a Titanic deceptive modesty which made him look like other men. Here he was, carrying the Roman world and all the Caesars in his hospitable skull, and doing it as easily as that other luminous vault, the skull of the universe, carries the Milky Way and the constellations.

One of the professors said that once upon a time an American young lady was introduced to Mommsen, and found herself badly scared and speechless. She dreaded to see his mouth unclose, for she was expecting him to choose a subject several miles above her comprehension, and didn't suppose he could get down to the world that other people lived in; but when his remark came, her terrors disappeared.

"Well, how do you do? Have you read Howells's last book? I think it's his best."

The active ceremonies of the evening closed with the speeches of welcome delivered by two students and the replies made by Professors Virchow and Helmholtz.

Virchow has long been a member of the city government of Berlin. He works as hard for the city as does any other Berlin Alderman, and gets the same pay—nothing. I don't know that we in America could venture to ask our most illustrious citizen to serve in a Board of Aldermen, and if we might venture it I am not positively sure that we could elect him. But here the municipal system is such that the best men in the city consider it an honor to serve gratis as Aldermen, and the people have the good sense to prefer these men and to elect them year after year. As a result Berlin is a thoroughly well-governed city. It is a free city; its affairs are not meddled with by the state; they are managed by its own citizens, and after methods of their own devising.

The Awful German Language

FROM APPENDIX D TO *A Tramp Abroad*. 1880.

A little learning makes the whole world kin.
—PROVERBS XXXII, 7

I went often to look at the collection of curiosities in Heidelberg Castle, and one day I surprised the keeper of it with my German. I spoke entirely in that language. He was greatly interested; and after I had talked a while he said my German was very rare, possibly a "unique"; and wanted to add it to his museum.

If he had known what it had cost me to acquire my art, he would also have known that it would break any collector to buy it. Harris and I had been hard at work on our German during several weeks at that time, and although we had made good progress, it had been accomplished under great difficulty and annoyance, for three of our teachers had died in the mean time. A person who has not studied German can form no idea of what a perplexing language it is.

Surely there is not another language that is so slipshod and system-less, and so slippery and elusive to the grasp. One is washed about in it, hither and thither, in the most helpless way; and when at last he thinks he has captured a rule which offers firm ground to take a rest on amid the general rage and turmoil of the ten parts of speech, he turns over the page and reads, "Let the pupil make careful note of the following **exceptions**." He runs his eye down and finds that there are more exceptions to the rule than instances of it. So overboard he goes again, to hunt for another Ararat and find another quicksand. Such has been, and continues to be, my experience. Every time I think I have got one of these four confusing "cases" where I am master of it, a seemingly insignificant preposition intrudes itself into my sentence, clothed with an awful and unsuspected power, and crumbles the ground from under me. For instance, my book inquires after a certain bird—(it is always inquiring after things which are of no sort of consequence to anybody): "Where is the bird?" Now the answer to this question—according to the book—is that the bird is waiting in the black-smith shop on account of the rain. Of course no bird would do that, but then you must stick to the book. Very well, I begin to cipher out the German for that answer. I begin at the wrong end, necessarily, for that is the German idea. I say to myself, "*Regen* (rain) is masculine—or maybe it is feminine—or possibly neuter—it is too much trouble to look now. Therefore, it is either *der* (the) *Regen*, or *die* (the) *Regen*, or *das* (the) Regen, according to which gender it may turn out to be when I look. In the interest of science, I will cipher it out on the hypothesis that it is masculine. Very well—then **the** rain is *der Regen*, if it is simply in the quiescent state of being **mentioned**, without enlargement or discussion—Nominative case; but if this rain is lying around, in a kind of a general way on the ground, it is then definitely located, it is **doing something**—that is, **resting** (which is one of the German grammar's ideas of doing something), and this throws the rain into the Dative case, and makes it *dem Regen*. However, this rain is not resting, but is doing something **actively**,—it is falling—to interfere with the bird, likely—and this indicates **movement**, which has the effect of sliding it into the Accusative case and changing *dem Regen* into *den Regen*." Having completed the grammatical horoscope of this matter, I answer up confidently and state in German that the bird is staying in the blacksmith shop "*wegen* (on account of) *den Regen*." Then the teacher lets me softly down with the remark that whenever the word "*wegen*" drops into a sentence, it **always** throws that subject into the **Genitive** case, regardless of consequences—and that therefore this bird stayed in the blacksmith shop "*wegen des Regens*."

N.B.—I was informed, later, by a higher authority, that there was an "exception" which permits one to say "*wegen den Regen*" in certain peculiar and complex circumstances, but that this exception is not extended to anything **but** rain.

There are ten parts of speech, and they are all troublesome. An average sentence, in a German newspaper, is a sublime and impressive curiosity; it occupies a quarter of a column; it contains all the ten parts of speech—not in regular order, but mixed; it is built mainly of compound words constructed by the writer on the spot, and not to be found in any dictionary—six or seven words compacted into one, without joint or seam—that is, without hyphens; it treats of fourteen or fifteen different subjects, each inclosed in a parenthesis of its own, with here and there extra parentheses which reinclose three or four of the minor parentheses, making pens within pens: finally, all the parentheses and reparentheses are massed together between a couple of king-parentheses, one of which is placed in the first line of the majestic sentence and the other in the middle of the last line of it—**after which comes the VERB**, and you find out for the first time what the man has been talking about; and after the verb—merely by way of ornament, as far as I can make out—the writer shovels in "*haben sind gewesen gehabt haben geworden sein*," or words to that effect, and the monument is finished. I suppose that this closing hurrah is in the nature of the flourish to a man's signature—not necessary, but pretty. German books are easy enough to read when you hold them before the looking-glass or stand on your head—so as to reverse the construction—but I think that to learn to read and understand a German newspaper is a thing which must always remain an impossibility to a foreigner.

Yet even the German books are not entirely free from attacks of the Parenthesis distemper—though they are usually so mild as to cover only a few lines, and therefore when you at last get down to the verb it carries some meaning to your mind because you are able to remember a good deal of what has gone before. Now here is a sentence from a popular and excellent German novel—which has a slight parenthesis in it. I will make a perfectly literal translation, and throw in the parenthesis-marks and some hyphens for the assistance of the reader—though in the original there are no parenthesis-marks or hyphens, and the reader is left to flounder through to the remote verb the best way he can:

> But when he, upon the street, the (in-satin-and-silk-covered-now-very-unconstrained-after-the-newest-fashioned-dressed) government counselor's wife **met**, etc., etc.

That is from *The Old Mamselle's Secret*, by Mrs. Marlitt. And that sentence is constructed upon the most approved German model. You observe how far that verb is from the reader's base of operations; well, in a German newspaper they put their verb away over on the next page; and I have heard that sometimes after stringing along the exciting preliminaries and parentheses for a column or two, they get in a hurry and have to go to press without getting to the verb at all. Of course, then, the reader is left in a very exhausted and ignorant state.

We have the Parenthesis disease in our literature, too; and one may see cases of it every day in our books and newspapers: but with us it is the mark and sign of an unpracticed writer or a cloudy intellect, whereas with the Germans it is doubtless the mark and sign of a practiced pen and of the presence of that sort of luminous intellectual fog which stands for clearness among these people. For surely it is **not** clearness—it necessarily can't be clearness. Even a jury would have penetration enough to discover that. A writer's ideas must be a good deal confused, a good deal out of line and sequence, when he starts out to say that a man met a counselor's wife in the street, and then right in the midst of this so simple undertaking halts these approaching people and makes them stand still until he jots down an inventory of the woman's dress. That is manifestly absurd. It reminds a person of those dentists who secure your instant and breathless interest in a tooth by taking a grip on it with the forceps, and then stand there and drawl through a tedious anecdote before they give the dreaded jerk. Parentheses in literature and dentistry are in bad taste.

The Germans have another kind of parenthesis, which they make by splitting a verb in two and putting half of it at the beginning of an exciting chapter and the **other half** at the end of it. Can any one conceive of anything more confusing than that? These things are called *separable verbs*. The German grammar is blistered all over with separable verbs; and the wider the two portions of one of them are spread apart, the better the author of the crime is pleased with his performance. A favorite one is **reiste ab**—which means departed. Here is an example which I culled from a novel and reduced to English:

> "The trunks being now ready, he **DE-** after kissing his mother and sisters, and once more pressing to his bosom his adored Gretchen, who, dressed in simple white muslin, with a single tuberose in the ample folds of her rich brown hair, had tottered feebly down the stairs, still pale from the terror and excitement of the past evening, but longing to lay her poor aching head yet once again upon the breast of him whom she loved more dearly than life itself, **PARTED**."

However, it is not well to dwell too much on the separable verbs. One is sure to lose his temper early; and if he sticks to the subject, and will not be warned, it will at last either soften his brain or petrify it. Personal pronouns and adjectives are a fruitful nuisance in this language, and should have been left out. For instance, the same sound, *sie,* means **you**, and it means **she**, and it means **her**, and it means **it**, and it means **they**, and it means **them**. Think of the ragged poverty of a language which has to make one word do the work of six—and a poor little weak thing of only three letters at that. But mainly, think of the exasperation of never knowing which of these meanings the speaker is trying to convey. This explains why, whenever a person says *sie* to me, I generally try to kill him, if a stranger.

Now observe the Adjective. Here was a case where simplicity would have been an advantage; therefore, for no other reason, the inventor of this language complicated it all he could. When we wish to speak of our "good friend or friends," in our enlightened tongue, we stick to the one form and have no trouble or hard feeling about it; but with the German tongue it is different. When a German gets his hands on an adjective, he declines it, and keeps on declining it until the common sense is all declined out of it. It is as bad as Latin. He says, for instance:

SINGULAR

Nominative—*Mein guter Freund*, my good friend.
Genitive—*Meines guten Freundes*, of my good friend.
Dative—*Meinem guten Freund*, to my good friend.
Accusative—*Meinen guten Freund*, my good friend.

PLURAL

N.—*Meine guten Freunde*, my good friends.
G.—*Meiner guten Freunde*, of my good friends.
D.—*Meinen guten Freunden*, to my good friends.
A.—*Meine guten Freunde*, my good friends.

Now let the candidate for the asylum try to memorize those variations, and see how soon he will be elected. One might better go without friends in Germany than take all this trouble about them. I have shown what a bother it is to decline a good (male) friend; well this is only a third of the work, for there is a variety of new distortions of the adjective to be learned when the object is feminine, and still another when the object is neuter. Now there are more adjectives in this language than there are black cats in Switzerland, and they must all be as elaborately declined as the examples above suggested. Difficult?—troublesome?—these words cannot describe it. I heard a Californian student in Heidelberg say, in one of his calmest moods, that he would rather decline two drinks than one German adjective.

In German, all the Nouns begin with a capital letter. Now that is a good idea; and a good idea, in this language, is necessarily conspicuous from its lonesomeness. I consider this capitalizing of nouns a good idea, because by reason of it you are almost always able to tell a noun the minute you see it. You fall into error occasionally, because you mistake the name of a person for the name of a thing, and waste a good deal of time trying to dig a meaning out of it. German names almost always do mean something, and this helps to deceive the student. I translated a passage one day, which said that "the infuriated tigress broke loose and utterly ate up the unfortunate fir forest" (**Tannenwald**). When I was girding up my loins to doubt this, I found out that *Tannenwald* in this instance was a man's name.

Every noun has a gender, and there is no sense or system in the distribution; so the gender of each must be learned separately and by heart. There is no other way. To do this one has to have a memory like a memorandum-book. In German, a young lady has no sex, while a turnip has. Think what overwrought reverence that shows for the turnip, and what callous disrespect for the girl. See how it looks in print—I translate this from a conversation in one of the best of the German Sunday-school books:

Gretchen.
Wilhelm, where is the turnip?
Wilhelm.
She has gone to the kitchen.
Gretchen.
Where is the accomplished and beautiful English maiden?
Wilhelm.
It has gone to the opera.

To continue with the German genders: a tree is male, its buds are female, its leaves are neuter; horses are sexless, dogs are male, cats are female—tomcats included, of course; a person's mouth, neck, bosom, elbows, fingers, nails, feet, and body are of the male sex, and his head is male or neuter according to the word selected to signify it, and **not** according to the sex of the individual who wears it—for in Germany all the women have either male heads or sexless ones; a person's nose, lips, shoulders, breast, hands, and toes are of the female sex; and his hair, ears, eyes, chin, legs, knees, heart, and conscience haven't any sex at all. The inventor of the language probably got what he knew about a conscience from hearsay.

Now, by the above dissection, the reader will see that in Germany a man may **think** he is a man, but when he comes to look into the matter closely, he is bound to have his doubts; he finds that in sober truth he is a most ridiculous mixture; and if he ends by trying to comfort himself with the thought that he can at least depend on a third of this mess as being manly and masculine, the humiliating second thought will quickly remind him that in this respect he is no better off than any woman or cow in the land.

In the German it is true that by some oversight of the inventor of the language, a Woman is a female; but a Wife (**Weib**) is not—which is unfortunate. A Wife, here, has no sex; she is neuter; so, according to the grammar, a fish is **he**, his scales are **she**, but a fishwife is neither. To describe a wife as sexless may be called under-description; that is bad enough, but over-description is surely worse. A German speaks of an Englishman as the **Engländer**; to change the sex, he adds **inn**, and that stands for Englishwoman—**Engländerinn**. That seems descriptive enough, but still it is not exact enough for a German; so he precedes the word with that article which indicates that the creature to follow is feminine, and writes it down thus: "**die** Engländer**inn**,"—which means "the **she-Englishwoman**." I consider that that person is over-described.

WELL, AFTER THE STUDENT has learned the sex of a great number of nouns, he is still in a difficulty, because he finds it impossible to persuade his tongue to refer to things as "**he**" and "**she**," and "**him**" and "**her**," which it has been always accustomed to refer to it as "**it**." When he even frames a German sentence in his mind, with the hims and hers in the right places, and then works up his courage to the utterance-point, it is no use—the moment he begins to speak his tongue flies the track and all those labored males and females come out as "**its**." And even when he is reading German to himself, he always calls those things "**it**," where as he ought to read in this way:

TALE OF THE FISHWIFE AND ITS SAD FATE*

It is a bleak Day. Hear the Rain, how he pours, and the Hail, how he rattles; and see the Snow, how he drifts along, and of the Mud, how deep he is! Ah the poor Fishwife, it is stuck fast in the Mire; it has dropped its Basket of Fishes; and its Hands have been cut by the Scales as it seized some of the falling Creatures; and one Scale has even got into its Eye, and it cannot get her out. It opens its Mouth to cry for Help; but if any Sound comes out of him, alas he is drowned by the raging of the Storm. And now a Tomcat has got one of the Fishes and she will surely escape with him. No, she bites off a Fin, she holds her in her Mouth—will she swallow her? No, the Fishwife's brave Mother-dog deserts his Puppies and rescues the Fin—which he eats, himself, as his Reward. O, horror, the Lightning has struck the Fish-basket; he sets him on Fire; see the Flame, how she licks the doomed Utensil with her red and angry Tongue; now she attacks the helpless Fishwife's Foot—she burns him up, all but the big Toe, and even she is partly consumed; and still she spreads, still she waves her fiery Tongues; she attacks the Fishwife's Leg and destroys it; she attacks its Hand and destroys her also; she attacks the Fishwife's Leg and destroys her also; she attacks its Body and consumes him; she wreathes herself about its Heart and it is consumed; next about its Breast, and in a Moment she is a Cinder; now she reaches its Neck— he goes; now its Chin—it goes; now its Nose—she goes. In another Moment, except Help come, the Fishwife will be no more. Time presses—is there none to succor and save? Yes! Joy, joy, with flying Feet the she-Englishwoman comes! But alas, the generous she-Female is too late: where now is the fated Fishwife? It has ceased from its

*I capitalize the nouns, in the German (and ancient English) fashion.

Sufferings, it has gone to a better Land; all that is left of it for its loved Ones to lament over, is this poor smoldering Ash-heap. Ah, woeful, woeful Ash-heap! Let us take him up tenderly, reverently, upon the lowly Shovel, and bear him to his long Rest, with the Prayer that when he rises again it will be a Realm where he will have one good square responsible Sex, and have it all to himself, instead of having a mangy lot of assorted Sexes scattered all over him in Spots.

There, now, the reader can see for himself that this pronoun business is a very awkward thing for the unaccustomed tongue. I suppose that in all languages the similarities of look and sound between words which have no similarity in meaning are a fruitful source of perplexity to the foreigner. It is so in our tongue, and it is notably the case in the German. Now there is that troublesome word **vermählt**: to me it has so close a resemblance—either real or fancied—to three or four other words, that I never know whether it means despised, painted, suspected, or married; until I look in the dictionary, and then I find it means the latter. There are lots of such words and they are a great torment. To increase the difficulty there are words which **seem** to resemble each other, and yet do not; but they make just as much trouble as if they did. For instance, there is the word **vermiethen** (to let, to lease, to hire); and the word **verheirathen** (another way of saying to marry). I heard of an Englishman who knocked at a man's door in Heidelberg and proposed, in the best German he could command, to "*verheirathen*" that house. Then there are some words which mean one thing when you emphasize the first syllable, but mean something very different if you throw the emphasis on the last syllable. For instance, there is a word which means a runaway, or the act of glancing through a book, according to the placing of the emphasis; and another word which signifies to **associate** with a man, or to **avoid** him, according to where you put the emphasis—and you can generally depend on putting it in the wrong place and getting into trouble.

There are some exceedingly useful words in this language. **Schlag**, for example; and **Zug**. There are three-quarters of a column of **Schlag**s in the dictionary, and a column and a half of **Zug**s. The word **Schlag** means Blow, Stroke, Dash, Hit, Shock, Clap, Slap, Time, Bar, Coin, Stamp, Kind, Sort, Manner, Way, Apoplexy, Wood-cutting, Enclosure, Field, Forest-clearing. This is its simple and **exact** meaning—that is to say, its restricted, its fettered meaning; but there are ways by which you can set it free, so that it can soar away, as on the wings of the morning, and never be at rest. You can hang any word you please to its tail, and make it mean anything you want to. You can begin with **Schlag-ader**, which means artery, and you can hang on the whole dictionary, word by word, clear through the alphabet to **Schlag-wasser**, which means bilge-water—and including **Schlag-mutter**, which means mother-in-law.

Just the same with **Zug**. Strictly speaking, **Zug** means Pull, Tug, Draught, Procession, March, Progress, Flight, Direction, Expedition, Train, Caravan, Passage, Stroke, Touch, Line, Flourish, Trait of Character, Feature, Lineament, Chess-move, Organ-stop, Team, Whiff, Bias, Drawer, Propensity, Inhalation, Disposition: but that thing which it does **not** mean—when all its legitimate pennants have been hung on, has not been discovered yet.

One cannot overestimate the usefulness of **Schlag** and **Zug**. Armed just with these two, and the word **also**, what cannot the foreigner on German soil accomplish? The German word **also** is the equivalent of the English phrase "You know," and does not mean anything at all—in **talk**, though it sometimes does in print. Every time a German opens his mouth an **also** falls out; and every time he shuts it he bites one in two that was trying to **get** out.

Now, the foreigner, equipped with these three noble words, is master of the situation. Let him talk right along, fearlessly; let him pour his indifferent German forth, and when he lacks for a word, let him heave a **Schlag** into the vacuum; all the chances are that it fits it like a plug, but if it doesn't let him promptly heave a **Zug** after it; the two together can hardly fail to bung the hole; but if, by a miracle, they **should** fail, let him simply say **also**! and this will give him a moment's chance to think of the needful word.

In my note-book I find this entry:

JULY 1.—In the hospital yesterday, a word of thirteen syllables was successfully removed from a patient—a North German from near Hamburg; but as most unfortunately the surgeons had opened him in the wrong place, under the impression that he contained a panorama, he died. The sad event has cast a gloom over the whole community.

That paragraph furnishes a text for a few remarks about one of the most curious and notable features of my subject—the length of German words. Some German words are so long that they have a perspective. Observe these examples:

Freundschaftsbezeigungen.
Dilettantenaufdringlichkeiten.
Stadtverordnetenversammlungen.

These things are not words, they are alphabetical processions. And they are not rare; one can open a German newspaper at any time and see them marching majestically across the page—and if he has any imagination he can see the banners and hear the music, too. They impart a martial thrill to the meekest subject. I take a great interest in these curiosities. Whenever I come across a good one, I stuff it and put it in my museum. In this way I have made quite a valuable collection. When I get duplicates, I exchange with other collectors, and thus increase the variety of my stock. Here are some specimens which I lately bought at an auction sale of the effects of a bankrupt bric-a-brac hunter:

Generalstaatsverordnetenversammlungen.
Alterthumswissenschaften.
Kinderbewahrungsanstalten.
Unabhaengigkeitserklaerungen.

Europe

Wiedererstellungbestrebungen.
Waffenstillstandsunterhandlungen.

Of course when one of these grand mountain ranges goes stretching across the printed page, it adorns and ennobles that literary landscape— but at the same time it is a great distress to the new student, for it blocks up his way; he cannot crawl under it, or climb over it, or tunnel through it. So he resorts to the dictionary for help, but there is no help there. The dictionary must draw the line somewhere—so it leaves this sort of words out. And it is right, because these long things are hardly legitimate words, but are rather combinations of words, and the inventor of them ought to have been killed. They are compound words with the hyphens left out. The various words used in building them are in the dictionary, but in a very scattered condition; so you can hunt the materials out, one by one, and get at the meaning at last, but it is a tedious and harassing business. We used to have a good deal of this sort of crime in our literature, but it has gone out now. We used to speak of a thing as a "never-to-be-forgotten" circumstance, instead of cramping it into the simple and sufficient word "memorable" and then going calmly about our business as if nothing had happened. In those days we were not content to embalm the thing and bury it decently, we wanted to build a monument over it.

But in our newspapers the compounding-disease lingers a little to the present day, but with the hyphens left out, in the German fashion. This is the shape it takes: instead of saying "Mr. Simmons, clerk of the county and district courts, was in town yesterday," the new form put it thus: "Clerk of the County and District Courts Simmons was in town yesterday." This saves neither time nor ink, and has an awkward sound besides I wish to submit the following local item, from a Mannheim journal, by way of illustration:

In the daybeforeyesterdayshortlyaftereleveno'clock Night, the inthis-townstandingtavern called "The Wagoner" was downburnt. When the fire to the onthedownburninghouseresting Stork's Nest reached, flew the parent Storks away. But when the bytheraging, firesurrounded Nest **itself** caught Fire, straightway plunged the quickreturning Mother-stork into the Flames and died, her Wings over her young ones outspread.

Even the cumbersome German construction is not able to take the pathos out of that picture—indeed, it somehow seems to strengthen it. This item is dated away back yonder months ago. I could have used it sooner, but I was waiting to hear from the Father-stork. I am still waiting.

"**Also**!" If I had not shown that the German is a difficult language, I have at least intended to do so. I have heard of an American student who was asked how he was getting along with his German, and who answered promptly: "I am not getting along at all. I have worked at it hard for three level months, and all I have got to show for it is one solitary German phrase—'**Zwei Glas**'" (two glasses of beer). He paused for a moment, reflectively; then added with feeling: "But I've got that **solid**!"

And if I have not also shown that German is a harassing and infuriating study, my execution has been at fault, and not my intent. I heard lately of a worn and sorely tried American student who used to fly to a certain German word for relief when he could bear up under his aggravations no longer—the only word whose sound was sweet and precious to his ear and healing to his lacerated spirit. This was the word **Damit**. It was only the **sound** that helped him, not the meaning;* and so, at last, when he learned that the emphasis was not on the first syllable, his only stay and support was gone, and he faded away and died.

I think that a description of any loud, stirring, tumultuous episode must be tamer in German than in English. Our descriptive words of this character have such a deep, strong, resonant sound, while their German equivalents do seem so thin and mild and energyless. Boom, burst, crash, roar, storm, bellow, blow, thunder, explosion; howl, cry, shout, yell, groan;

*It merely means, in its general sense, "herewith."

battle, hell. These are magnificent words; they have a force and magnitude of sound befitting the things which they describe. But their German equivalents would be ever so nice to sing the children to sleep with, or else my awe-inspiring ears were made for display and not for superior usefulness in analyzing sounds. Would any man want to die in a battle which was called by so tame a term as a **Schlacht**? Or would not a consumptive feel too much bundled up, who was about to go out, in a shirt-collar and a seal-ring, into a storm which the bird-song word **Gewitter** was employed to describe? And observe the strongest of the several German equivalents for explosion—**Ausbruch**. Our word Toothbrush is more powerful than that. It seems to me that the Germans could do worse than import it into their language to describe particularly tremendous explosions with. The German word for hell—*Hölle*—sounds more like **helly** than anything else; therefore, how necessarily chipper, frivolous, and unimpressive it is. If a man were told in German to go there, could he really rise to thee dignity of feeling insulted?

Having pointed out, in detail, the several vices of this language, I now come to the brief and pleasant task of pointing out its virtues. The capitalizing of the nouns I have already mentioned. But far before this virtue stands another—that of spelling a word according to the sound of it. After one short lesson in the alphabet, the student can tell how any German word is pronounced without having to ask; whereas in our language if a student should inquire of us, "What does B, O, W, spell?" we should be obliged to reply, "Nobody can tell what it spells when you set if off by itself; you can only tell by referring to the context and finding out what it signifies—whether it is a thing to shoot arrows with, or a nod of one's head, or the forward end of a boat."

There are some German words which are singularly and powerfully effective. For instance, those which describe lowly, peaceful, and affectionate home life; those which deal with love, in any and all forms, from mere kindly feeling and honest good will toward the passing stranger, clear up to courtship; those which deal with outdoor Nature, in its softest and loveliest aspects—with meadows and forests, and birds and flowers, the fragrance and sunshine of summer, and the moonlight of peaceful winter nights; in a word, those which deal with any and all forms of rest, repose, and peace; those also which deal with the creatures and marvels of fairyland; and lastly and chiefly, in those words which express pathos, is the language surpassingly rich and affective. There are German songs which can make a stranger to the language cry. That shows that the **sound** of the words is correct—it interprets the meanings with truth and with exactness; and so the ear is informed, and through the ear, the heart.

The Germans do not seem to be afraid to repeat a word when it is the right one. They repeat it several times, if they choose. That is wise. But in English, when we have used a word a couple of times in a paragraph, we imagine we are growing tautological, and so we are weak enough to exchange it for some other word which only approximates exactness, to escape what we wrongly fancy is a greater blemish. Repetition may be bad, but surely inexactness is worse.

There are people in the world who will take a great deal of trouble to point out the faults in a religion or a language, and then go blandly about their business without suggesting any remedy. I am not that kind of person. I have shown that the German language needs reforming. Very well, I am ready to reform it. At least I am ready to make the proper suggestions. Such a course as this might be immodest in another; but I have devoted upward of nine full weeks, first and last, to a careful and critical study of this tongue, and thus have acquired a confidence in my ability to reform it which no mere superficial culture could have conferred upon me.

In the first place, I would leave out the Dative case. It confuses the plurals; and, besides, nobody ever knows when he is in the Dative case, except he discover it by accident—and then he does not know when or where it was that he got into it, or how long he has been in it, or how he is going to get out of it again. The Dative case is but an ornamental folly—it is better to discard it.

In the next place, I would move the Verb further up to the front. You may load up with ever so good a Verb, but I notice that you never really bring down a subject with it at the present German range—you only cripple it. So I insist that this important part of speech should be brought forward to a position where it may be easily seen with the naked eye.

Thirdly, I would import some strong words from the English tongue— to swear with, and also to use in describing all sorts of vigorous things in vigorous ways.[*]

Fourthly, I would reorganize the sexes, and distribute them accordingly to the will of the creator. This as a tribute of respect, if nothing else.

Fifthly, I would do away with those great long compounded words; or require the speaker to deliver them in sections, with intermissions for refreshments. To wholly do away with them would be best, for ideas are more easily received and digested when they come one at a time than when they come in bulk. Intellectual food is like any other; it is pleasanter and more beneficial to take it with a spoon than with a shovel.

Sixthly, I would require a speaker to stop when he is done, and not hang a string of those useless "**haben sind gewesen gehabt haben geworden seins**" to the end of his oration. This sort of gewgaws undignify a speech, instead of adding a grace. They are, therefore, an offense, and should be discarded.

Seventhly, I would discard the Parenthesis. Also the reparenthesis, the re-reparenthesis, and the re-re-re-re-re-reparentheses, and likewise the final wide-reaching all-inclosing king-parenthesis. I would require every

---

*"*Verdammt*," and its variations and enlargements, are words which have plenty of meaning, but the **sounds** are so mild and ineffectual that German ladies can use them without sin. German ladies who could not be induced to commit a sin by any persuasion or compulsion, promptly rip out one of these harmless little words when they tear their dresses or don't like the soup. It sounds about as wicked as our "My gracious." German ladies are constantly saying, "*Ach! Gott!*" "*Mein Gott!*" "*Gott in Himmel!*" "*Herr Gott*" "*Der Herr Jesus!*" etc. They think our ladies have the same custom, perhaps; for I once heard a gentle and lovely old German lady say to a sweet young American girl: "The two languages are so alike—how pleasant that is; we say '*Ach! Gott!*' you say 'Goddamn.'"

individual, be he high or low, to unfold a plain straightforward tale, or else coil it and sit on it and hold his peace. Infractions of this law should be punishable with death.

And eighthly, and last, I would retain **Zug** and **Schlag**, with their pendants, and discard the rest of the vocabulary. This would simplify the language.

I have now named what I regard as the most necessary and important changes. These are perhaps all I could be expected to name for nothing; but there are other suggestions which I can and will make in case my proposed application shall result in my being formally employed by the government in the work of reforming the language.

My philological studies have satisfied me that a gifted person ought to learn English (barring spelling and pronouncing) in thirty hours, French in thirty days, and German in thirty years. It seems manifest, then, that the latter tongue ought to be trimmed down and repaired. If it is to remain as it is, it ought to be gently and reverently set aside among the dead languages, for only the dead have time to learn it.

An Austrian Health Factory

From Mark Twain's Travel Letters from 1891–92

Chicago Daily Tribune, February 7, 1892

[Often retitled as "Marienbad—A Health Factory"]

This place is the village of Marienbad, Bohemia. It seems no very great distance from Annecy, in Haute-Savoie, to this place—you make it in less than thirty hours by these continental express trains—but the changes in the scenery are great; they are quite out of proportion to the distance covered. From Annecy by Aix to Geneva, you have blue lakes, with bold mountains springing from their borders, and far glimpses of snowy wastes lifted against the horizon beyond, while all about you is a garden cultivated to the last possibility of grace and beauty—a cultivation which doesn't stop with the handy lower levels, but is carried right up the sheer steeps and propped there with ribs of masonry, and made to stay there in spite of Newton's law. Beyond Geneva—beyond Lausanne, at any rate—you have for a while a country which noticeably resembles New England, and seems out of place and like an intruder—an intruder who is wearing his every-day clothes at a fancy-dress ball. But presently on your right, huge green mountain ramparts rise up, after that for hours you are absorbed in watching the rich shadow effects which they furnish, and are only dully aware that New England is gone and that you are flying past quaint and unspeakable old towns and towers. Next day you have the lake of Zurich, and presently the Rhine is swinging by you. How clean it is! How clear it is! How blue it is! How green it is! How swift and rollicking and insolent are its gait and style! How vivid and splendid its colors—beautiful wreck and chaos of all the soap bubbles in the universe! A person born on the Rhine must worship it.

I saw the blue Rhine sweep along; I heard, or seemed to hear, the German songs we used to sing in chorus sweet and clear.

Yes, that is where his heart would be, that is where his last thoughts would be, the "soldier of the legion" who "lay dying in Algiers."

And by and by you are in a German region, which you discover to be quite different from the recent Swiss lands behind you. You have a sea before you, that is to say; the green land goes rolling away, in ocean swells, to the horizon. And there is another new feature. Here and there at wide intervals you have islands, hills 200 and 300 feet high, of a haystack form, that rise abruptly out of the green plain, and are wooded solidly to the top. On the top there is just room for a ruined castle, and there it is, every time; above the summit you see the crumbling arches and broken towers projecting.

Beyond Stuttgart, next day, you find other changes still. By and by, approaching and leaving Nuremberg and down by Newhaus, your landscape is humped everywhere with scattered knobs of rock, unsociable crags of a rude, towerlike look, and thatched with grass and vines and bushes. And now and then you have gorges, too, of a modest pattern as to size, with precipice walls curiously carved and honeycombed by—I don't know what—but water, no doubt.

The changes are not done yet, for the instant the country finds it is out of Wurtemberg and into Bavaria it discards one more thickness of soil to go with previous disrobings, and then nothing remains over the bones but the shift. There may be a poorer soil somewhere, but it is not likely.

A couple of hours from Bayreuth you cross into Bohemia, and before long you reach this Marienbad, and recognize another sharp change, the change from the long ago to to-day; that is to say from the very old to the spick and span new; from an architecture totally without shapeliness or ornament to an architecture attractively equipped with both; from universal dismalness as to color to universal brightness and beauty as to tint; from a town which seems made up of prisons to a town which is made up of gracious and graceful mansions proper to the light of heart and crimeless. It is like jumping out of Jerusalem into Chicago.

The more I think of these many changes, the more surprising the thing seems. I have never made so picturesque a journey before, and there cannot be another trip of like length in the world that can furnish so much variety and of so charming and interesting a sort.

There are only two or three streets here in this snug pocket in the hemlock hills, but they are handsome. When you stand at the foot of a street and look up at the slant of it you see only block fronts of graceful pattern, with happily broken lines and the pleasant accent of bay projections and balconies in orderly disorder and harmonious confusion, and always the color is fresh and cheery, various shades of cream, with softly contrasting trimmings of white, and now and then a touch of dim red. These blocks are all thick walled, solid, massive, tall for this Europe; but it is the brightest and newest looking town on the Continent, and as pretty as anybody could require. The steep hills spring high aloft from their very back doors and are clothed densely to their tops with hemlocks.

In Bavaria everybody is in uniform, and you wonder where the private citizens are, but here in Bohemia the uniforms are very rare. Occasionally one catches a glimpse of an Austrian officer, but it is only occasionally. Uniforms are so scarce that we seem to be in a republic. Almost the only striking figure is the Polish Jew. He is very frequent. He is tall and of grave countenance and wears a coat that reaches to his ankle bones, and he has a little wee curl or two in front of each ear. He has a prosperous look, and seems to be as much respected as anybody.

The crowds that drift along the promenade at music time twice a day are fashionably dressed after the Parisian pattern, and they look a good deal alike, but they speak a lot of languages which you have not encountered before, and no ignorant person can spell their names, and they can't pronounce them themselves.

Marienbad—Mary's Bath. The Mary is the Virgin. She is the patroness of these curative springs. They try to cure everything—gout, rheumatism, leanness, fatness, dyspepsia, and all the rest. The whole thing is the property of a convent, and has been for six or seven hundred years. However, there was never a boom here until a quarter of a century ago.

If a person has the gout, this is what they do with him: they have him out at 5:30 in the morning, and give him an egg and let him look at a cup of tea. At 6 he must be at his particular spring, with his tumbler hanging at his belt—and he will have plenty of company there. At the first note of the orchestra he must lift his tumbler and begin to sip his dreadful water with the rest. He must sip slowly and be a long time at it. Then he must tramp about the hills for an hour or so, and get all the exercise and fresh air possible. Then he takes his tub or wallows in his mud, if mud baths are his sort. By noon he has a fine appetite, and the rules allow him to turn himself loose and satisfy it, so long as he is careful and eats only such things as he doesn't want. He puts in the afternoon walking the hills and filling up with fresh air. At night he is allowed to take three ounces of any kind of food he doesn't like and drink one glass of any kind of liquor that he has a prejudice against; he may also smoke one pipe if he isn't used to it. At 9:30 sharp he must be in bed and his candle out. Repeat the whole thing the next day. I don't see any advantage in this over having the gout.

In the case of most diseases that is about what one is required to undergo, and if you have any pleasant habit that you value, they want that. They want that the first thing. They make you drop everything that gives an interest to life. Their idea is to reverse your whole system of existence and make a regenerating revolution. If you are a Republican, they make you talk free trade. If you are a Democrat they make you talk protection; if you are a Prohibitionist, you have got to go to bed drunk every night till you get well. They spare nothing, they spare nobody. Reform, reform, that is the whole song. If a person is an orator, they gag him; if he likes to read, they won't let him; if he wants to sing, they make him whistle. They say they can cure any ailment, and they do seem to do it; but why should a patient come all the way here? Why shouldn't he do these things at home and save the money? No disease would stay with a person who treated it like that.

I didn't come here to take baths, I only came to look around. But first one person, then another began to throw out hints, and pretty soon I was a good deal concerned about myself. One of these goutees here said I had a gouty look about the eye; next a person who has catarrh of the intestines asked me if I didn't notice a dim sort of stomach ache when I sneezed. I hadn't before, but I did seem to notice it then. A man that's here for heart disease said he wouldn't come downstairs so fast if he had my build and aspect. A person with an old gold complexion said a man died here in the mud bath last week that had a petrified liver—good deal such a looking man as I am, and the same initials, and so on, and so on.

Of course, there was nothing to be uneasy about, and I wasn't what you may call really uneasy; but I was not feeling very well—that is, not brisk—and I went to bed. I suppose that that was not a good idea, because then they had me. I started in at the upper end of the mill and went through. I am said to be all right now, and free from disease, but this does not surprise me. What I have been through in these two weeks would free a person of pretty much everything in him that wasn't nailed there—any loose thing, any unattached fragment of bone, or meat or morals, or disease or propensities or accomplishments, or what not. And I don't say but that I feel well enough, I feel better than I would if I was dead, I reckon. And, besides, they say I am going to build up now and come right along and be all right. I am not saying anything, but I wish I had enough of my diseases back to make me aware of myself, and enough of my habits to make it worth while to live. To have nothing the matter with you and no habits is pretty tame, pretty colorless. It is just the way a saint feels, I reckon; it is at least the way he looks. I never could stand a saint. That reminds me that you see very few priests around here, and yet, as I have already said, this whole big enterprise is owned and managed by a convent. The few priests one does see here are dressed like human beings, and so there may be more of them than I imagine. Fifteen priests dressed like these could not attract as much of your attention as would one priest at Aix-les-Bains. You cannot pull your eye loose from the French priest as long as he is in sight, his dress is so fascinatingly ugly.

I seem to be wandering from the subject, but I am not. This is about the coldest place I ever saw, and the wettest, too. This August seems like an English November to me. Rain? Why, it seems to like to rain here. It seems to rain every time there is a chance. You are strictly required to be out airing and exercising whenever the sun is shining, so I hate to see the sun shining because I hate air and exercise—duty air and duty exercise taken for medicine. It seems ungenuine, out of season, degraded to sordid utilities, a subtle spiritual something gone from it which one can't describe in words, but—don't you understand? With that gone what is left but canned air, canned exercise, and you don't want it.

When the sun does shine for a few moments or a few hours these people swarm out and flock through the streets and over the hills and through the pine woods, and make the most of the chance, and I have flocked out, too, on some of these occasions, but as a rule I stay in and try to get warm.

And what is there for means, besides heavy clothing and rugs, and the polished white tomb that stands lofty and heartless in the corner and thinks it is a stove? Of all the creations of human insanity this thing is the most forbidding. Whether it is heating the room or isn't, the impression is the same—cold indifference. You can't tell which it is doing without going and putting your hand on it. They burn little handfuls of kindlings in it, no substantial wood, and no coal.

The fire burns out every fifteen minutes, and there is no way to tell when this has happened. On these dismal days, with the rain steadily falling, it is no better company than a corpse. A roaring hickory fire, with the cordial flames leaping up the chimney—but I must not think of such things, they make a person homesick. This is a most strange place to come to get rid of disease.

That is what you think most of the time. But in the intervals, when the sun shines and you are tramping the hills and are comparatively warm, you get to be neutral, maybe even friendly. I went up to the Aussichtthurm the other day. This is a tower which stands on the summit of a steep hemlock mountain here; a tower which there isn't the least use for, because the view is as good at the base of it as it is at the top of it. But Germanic people are just mad for views—they never get enough of a view—if they owned Mount Blanc, they would build a tower on top of it.

The roads up that mountain through that hemlock forest are hard packed and smooth, and the grades are easy and comfortable. They are for walkers, not for carriages. You move through deep silence and twilight, and you seem to be in a million-columned temple; whether you look up the hill or down it you catch glimpses of distant figures flitting without sound, appearing and disappearing in the dim distances, among the stems of the trees, and it is all very spectral, and solemn and impressive. Now and then the gloom is accented and sized up to your comprehension in a striking way; a ray of sunshine finds its way down through and suddenly calls your attention, for where it falls, far up the hillslope in the brown duskiness, it lays a stripe that has a glare like lightning. The utter stillness of the forest depths, the soundless hush, the total absence of stir or motion of any kind in leaf or branch, are things which we have no experience of at home, and consequently no name for in our language. At home there would be the plaint of insects and the twittering of birds and vagrant breezes would quiver the foliage. Here it is the stillness of death. This is what the Germans are forever talking about, dreaming about, and despairingly trying to catch and imprison in a poem, or a picture, or a song—they adored *Waldeinsamkeit*, loneliness of the woods. But how catch it? It has not a body; it is a spirit. We don't talk about it in America, or dream of it, or sing about it, because we haven't it. Certainly there is something wonderfully alluring about it, beguiling, dreamy, unworldly. Where the gloom is softest and richest, and the peace and stillness deepest, far up on the side of that hemlock mountain, a spot where Goethe used to sit and dream, is marked by a granite obelisk, and on its side is carved this famous poem, which is the master's idea of *Waldeinsamkeit*:

Ueber allen Gipfeln ist Ruh, In allen Wipfeln spurest du Kaum einen Hauch: Die Vögelein schweigen im Walde, Warte nur—Balde Ruhest du auch.

It is raining again now. However, it was doing that before. I have been over to the establishment and had a tub bath with two kinds of pine juice in it. These fill the room with a pungent and most pleasant perfume; they also turn the water to a color of ink and cover it with a snowy suds, two or three inches deep. The bath is cool—about 75° or 80° F., and there is a cooler shower bath after it. While waiting in the reception room all by myself two men came in and began to talk. Politics, literature, religion? No, their ailments. There is no other subject here, apparently. Wherever two or three of these people are gathered together, there you have it, every time. The first that can get his mouth open contributes his disease and the condition of it, and the others follow with theirs. The two men just referred to were acquaintances, and they followed the custom. One of them was built like a gasometer and is here to reduce his girth; the other was built like a derrick and is here to fat up, as they express it, at this resort. They were well satisfied with the progress they were making. The gasometer had lost a quarter of a ton in ten days, and showed the record on his belt with pride, and he walked briskly across the room, smiling in a vast and luminous way, like a harvest moon, and said he couldn't have done that when he arrived here. He buttoned his coat around his equator and showed how loose it was. It was pretty to see his happiness, it was so childlike and honest. He set his feet together and leaned out over his person and proved that he could see them. He said he hadn't seen them from that point before for fifteen years. He had a hand like a boxing glove. And on one of his fingers he had just found a diamond ring which he had missed eleven years ago.

The minute the derrick got a chance he broke in and began to tell how he was piling on blubber right along three-quarters of an ounce every four days; and he was still piping away when I was sent for. I left the fat man standing there panting and blowing, and swelling and collapsing like a balloon, his next speech all ready and urgent for delivery.

The patients are always at that sort of thing, trying to talk one another to death. The fat ones and the lean ones are nearly the worse at it, but not quite; the dyspeptics are the worst. They are at it all day and all night, and all along. They have more symptoms than all the others put together and so there is more variety of experience, more change of condition, more adventure, and consequently more play for the imagination, more scope for lying, and in every way a bigger field to talk. Go where you will, hide where you may, you cannot escape that word *liver*; you overhear it constantly—in the street, in the shop, in the theater, in the music grounds. Wherever you see two or a dozen people of ordinary bulk talking together, you know they are talking about their livers. When you first arrive here your new acquaintances seem sad and hard to talk to, but pretty soon you get the lay of the land and the hand of things, and after that you haven't any more trouble. You look into the dreary dull eye and softly say:

"Well, how's your liver?"

You will see that dim eye flash up with a grateful flame, and you will see that jaw begin to work, and you will recognize that nothing is required of you from this out but to listen as long as you remain conscious. After a few days you will begin to notice that out of these people's talk a gospel is framing itself and next you will find yourself believing it. It is this—that a man is not what his rearing, his schooling, his beliefs, his principles make him, he is what his liver makes him; that with a healthy liver he will have the clear-seeing eye, the honest heart, the sincere mind, the loving spirit, the loyal soul, the truth and trust and faith that are based as Gibraltar is based, and that with an unhealthy liver he must and will have the opposite of all these, he will see nothing as it really is, he cannot trust anybody, or believe in anything, his moral foundations are gone from under him. Now, isn't that interesting? I think it is.

Two days ago, perceiving that there was something unusual the matter with me, I went around from doctor to doctor, but without avail; they said they had never seen this kind of symptoms before—at least not all of them. They had seen some of them, but differently arranged. It was a new disease, as far as they could see. Apparently it was scrofulous, but a new kind. That was as much as they felt able to say. Then they made a stethescopic examination and decided that if anything would dislodge it a mud bath was the thing. It was a very ingenious idea. I took the mud bath, and it did dislodge it. Here it is—A Love Song:

I ask not, "Is thy heart still sure,
Thy love still warm, thy faith secure?"
I ask not, "Dream'st thou still of me?
Long'st away to fly with me?"

Ah, no—but as the sun includeth all
The good gifts of the giver,
I sum all these in asking thee.
"O, sweetheart, how's your liver?"
For if thy liver worketh right,
Thy faith stands sure, thy hope is bright,
Their dreams are sweet and I their god.
Doubt threats in vain—thou scorn'st his rod.
Keep only thy digestion clear,
No other foe my love doth fear.
But indigestion hath the power
To mar the soul's serenest hour—
To crumble adamantine trust,
And turn its certainties to dust,
To dim the eye with the nameless grief,
To chill the heart with unbelief,
To banish hope, and faith, and love,
Place heaven below and hell above.
Then list—details are naught to me
So thou'st the sum-gift of the giver—
I ask thee all in asking thee,
"O darling, how's your liver?"

Yes, it is easy to say it is scrofulous, but I don't see the signs of it. In my opinion it is as good poetry as I have ever written. Experts say it isn't poetry at all, because it lacks the element of fiction, but that is the voice of envy, I reckon. I call it good medical poetry, and I consider that I am a judge.

One of the most curious things in these countries is the street manners of the men and women. In meeting you they come straight on without swerving a hair's breadth from the direct line and wholly ignoring your right to any part of the road. At the last moment you must yield up your share of it and step aside, or there will be a collision. I noticed this strange barbarism first in Geneva twelve years ago.

In Aix-les-Bains, where sidewalks are scarce and everybody walks in the streets, there is plenty of room, but that is no matter; you are always escaping collisions by mere quarter inches. A man or woman who is headed in such a way as to cross your course presently without a collision will actually alter his direction shade by shade and compel a collision unless at the last instant you jump out of the way. Those folks are not dressed as ladies and gentlemen. And they do not seem to be consciously crowding you out of the road; they seem to be innocently and stupidly unaware that they are doing it. But not so in Geneva. There this class, especially the men, crowd out men, women, and girls of all rank and raiment consciously and intentionally—crowd them off the sidewalk and into the gutter.

There was nothing of this sort in Bayreuth. But here—well, here the thing is astonishing. Collisions are unavoidable unless you do all the yielding yourself. Another odd thing—here this savagery is confined to the folk who wear the fine clothes; the others are courteous and considerate. A big burly Comanche, with all the signs about him of wealth and education, will tranquilly force young ladies to step off into the gutter to avoid being run down by him. It is a mistake that there is no bath that will cure people's manners. But drowning would help.

However, perhaps one can't look for any real showy amount of delicacy of feeling in a country where a person is brought up to contemplate without a shudder the spectacle of women harnessed up with dogs and hauling carts. The woman is on one side of the pole, the dog on the other, and they bend to the work and tug and pant and strain—and the man tramps leisurely alongside and smokes his pipe. Often the woman is old and gray, and the man is her grandson. The Austrian national ornithological device ought to be replaced by a grandmother harnessed to a slush cart with a dog. This merely in the interest of fact. Heraldic fancy has been a little too much overworked in these countries, anyway.

Lately one of those curious things happened here which justify the felicitous extravagances of the stage and help us to accept them. A despondent man, bankrupt, friendless, and desperate, dropped a dose of strychnia into a bottle of whisky and went out in the dusk to find a handy place for his purpose, which was suicide. In a lonely spot he was stopped by a tramp, who said he would kill him if he didn't give up his money. Instead of jumping at the chance of getting himself killed and thus saving himself the impropriety and annoyance of suicide, he forgot all about his late project and attacked the tramp in a most sturdy and valiant fashion. He made a good fight, but failed to win. The night passed, the morning came, and he woke out of unconsciousness to find that he had been clubbed half to death and left to perish at his leisure. Then he reached for his bottle to add the finishing touch, but it was gone. He pulled himself together and went limping away, and presently came upon the tramp stretched out stone dead with the empty bottle beside him. He had drunk the whisky and committed suicide innocently. Now, while the man who had been cheated out of his suicide stood there bemoaning his hard luck and wondering how he might manage to raise money enough to buy some more whisky and poison, some people of the neighborhood came by and he told them about his curious adventure. They said that this tramp had been the scourge of the neighborhood and the dread of the constabulary. The inquest passed off quietly and to everybody's satisfaction, and then the people, to testify their gratitude to the hero of the occasion, put him on the police, on a good-enough salary, and he is all right now and is not meditating suicide any more. Here are all the elements of the naivest Arabian tale; a man who resists robbery when he hasn't anything to be robbed of does the very best to save his life when he has come out purposely to throw it away; and finally is victorious in defeat, killing his adversary in an effectual and poetic fashion after being already *hors de combat* himself. Now if you let him rise in the service and marry the chief of police's daughter it has the requisite elements of the Oriental romance, lacking not a detail so far as I can see.

Bayreuth

From Mark Twain's Travel Letters from 1891–92

Chicago Daily Tribune, December 6, 1891

[Often retitled "At the Shrine of St. Wagner"]

It was at Nuremberg that we struck the inundation of music-mad strangers that was rolling down upon Bayreuth. It had been long since we had seen such multitudes of excited and struggling people. It took a good half-hour to pack them and pair them into the train—and it was the longest train we have yet seen in Europe. Nuremberg had been witnessing this sort of experience a couple of times a day for about two weeks. It gives one an impressive sense of the magnitude of this biennial pilgrimage. For a pilgrimage is what it is. The devotees come from the very ends of the earth to worship their prophet in his own Kaaba in his own Mecca.

If you are living in New York or San Francisco or Chicago or anywhere else in America, and you conclude, by the middle of May, that you would like to attend the Bayreuth opera two months and a half later, you must use the cable and get about it immediately or you will get no seats, and you must cable for lodgings, too. Then if you are lucky you will get seats in the last row and lodgings in the fringe of the town. If you stop to write you will get nothing. There were plenty of people in Nuremberg when we passed through who had come on pilgrimage without first securing seats and lodgings. They had found neither in Bayreuth; they had walked Bayreuth streets a while in sorrow, then had gone to Nuremberg and found neither beds nor standing room, and had walked those quaint streets all night, waiting for the hotels to open and empty their guests into trains, and so make room for these, their defeated brethren and sisters in the faith. They had endured from thirty to forty hours' railroading on the continent of Europe—with all which that implies of worry, fatigue, and financial impoverishment—and all they had got and all they were to get for it was handiness and accuracy in kicking themselves, acquired by practice in the back streets of the two towns when other people were in bed; for back they must go over that unspeakable journey with their pious mission unfulfilled. These humiliated outcasts had the frowsy and unbrushed and apologetic look of wet cats, and their eyes were glazed with drowsiness, their bodies were adroop from crown to sole, and all kind-hearted people refrained from asking them if they had been to Bayreuth and failed to connect, as knowing they would lie.

We reached Bayreuth about mid-afternoon of a rainy Saturday. We were of the wise, and had secured lodgings and opera seats months in advance.

I am not a musical critic, and did not come here to write essays about the operas and deliver judgment upon their merits. The little children of Bayreuth could do that with a finer sympathy and a broader intelligence than I. I only care to bring four or five pilgrims to the operas, pilgrims able to appreciate them and enjoy them. What I write about the performance to put in my odd time would be offered to the public as merely a cat's view of a king, and not of didactic value.

Next day, which was Sunday, we left for the opera-house—that is to say, the Wagner temple—a little after the middle of the afternoon. The great building stands all by itself, grand and lonely, on a high ground outside the town. We were warned that if we arrived after 4 o'clock we should be obliged to pay $2.50 apiece by way of fine. We saved that; and it may be remarked here that this is the only opportunity that Europe offers of saving money. There was a big crowd in the grounds about the building, and the ladies' dresses took the sun with fine effect. I do not mean to intimate that the ladies were in full dress, for that was not so. The dresses were pretty, but neither sex was in evening dress.

The interior of the building is simple—severely so; but there is no occasion for color and decoration, since the people sit in the dark. The auditorium has the shape of a keystone, with the stage at the narrow end. There is an aisle on each side, but no aisle in the body of the house. Each row of seats extends in an unbroken curve from one side of the house to the other. There are seven entrance doors on each side of the theater and four at the butt end—eighteen doors to admit and emit 1,650 persons. The number of the particular door by which you are to enter the house or leave it is printed on your ticket, and you can use no door but that one. Thus, crowding and confusion are impossible. Not so many as a hundred people use any one door. This is better than having the usual (and useless) elaborate fireproof arrangements. It is the model theater of the world. It can be emptied while the second hand of a watch makes its circuit. It would be entirely safe, even if it were built of Lucifer Matches.

If your seat is near the center of a row and you enter late you must work your way along a rank of about twenty-five ladies and gentlemen to get to it. Yet this causes no trouble, for everybody stands up until all the seats are full, and the filling is accomplished in a very few minutes. Then all sit down, and you have a solid mass of fifteen hundred heads, making a steep cellar-door slant from the rear of the house down to the stage.

All the lights were turned low, so low that the congregation sat in a deep and solemn gloom. The funereal rustling of dresses and the low buzz of conversation began to die swiftly down, and presently not the ghost of a sound was left. This profound and increasingly impressive stillness endured for some time—the best preparation for music, spectacle, or speech conceivable. I should think our show people would have invented or imported that simple and impressive device for securing and solidifying the attention of an audience long ago; instead of which there continue to this day to open a performance against a deadly competition in the form of noise, confusion, and a scattered interest.

Finally, out of darkness and distance and mystery soft rich notes rose upon the stillness, and from his grave the dead magician began to weave his spells about his disciples and steep their souls in his enchantments. There was something strangely impressive in the fancy which kept intruding itself that the composer was conscious in his grave of what was going on here, and that these divine souls were the clothing of thoughts which were at this moment passing through his brain, and not recognized and familiar ones which had issued from it at some former time.

The entire overture, long as it was, was played to a dark house with the curtain down. It was exquisite; it was delicious. But straightway thereafter, or course, came the singing, and it does seem to me that nothing can make a Wagner opera absolutely perfect and satisfactory to the untutored but to leave out the vocal parts. I wish I could see a Wagner opera done in pantomime once. Then one would have the lovely orchestration unvexed to listen to and bathe his spirit in, and the bewildering beautiful scenery to intoxicate his eyes with, and the dumb acting couldn't mar these pleasures, because there isn't often anything in the Wagner opera that one would call by such a violent name as acting; as a rule all you would see would be a couple of silent people, one of them standing still, the other catching flies. Of course I do not really mean that he would be catching flies; I only mean that the usual operatic gestures which consist in reaching first one hand out into the air and then the other might suggest the sport I speak of if the operator attended strictly to business and uttered no sound.

This present opera was *Parsifal*. Madame Wagner does not permit its representation anywhere but in Bayreuth. The first act of the three occupied two hours, and I enjoyed that in spite of the singing.

I trust that I know as well as anybody that singing is one of the most entrancing and bewitching and moving and eloquent of all the vehicles invented by man for the conveying of feeling; but it seems to me that the chief virtue in song is melody, air, tune, rhythm, or what you please to call it, and that when this feature is absent what remains is a picture with the color left out. I was not able to detect in the vocal parts of *Parsifal* anything that might with confidence be called rhythm or tune or melody; one person performed at a time—and a long time, too—often in a noble, and always in a high-toned, voice; but he only pulled out long notes, then some short ones, then another long one, then a sharp, quick, peremptory bark or two— and so on and so on; and when he was done you saw that the information which he had conveyed had not compensated for the disturbance. Not always, but pretty often. If two of them would but put in a duet occasionally and blend the voices; but no, they don't do that. The great master, who knew so well how to make a hundred instruments rejoice in unison and pour out their souls in mingled and melodious tides of delicious sound, deals only in barren solos when he puts in the vocal parts. It may be that he was deep, and only added the singing to his operas for the sake of the contrast it would make with the music. Singing! It does seem the wrong name to apply to it. Strictly described, it is a practicing of difficult and unpleasant intervals, mainly. An ignorant person gets tired of listening to gymnastic intervals in the long run, no matter how pleasant they may be. In *Parsifal* there is a hermit named Gurnemanz who stands on the stage in one spot and practices by the hour, while first one and then another character of the cast endures what he can of it and then retires to die.

During the evening there was an intermission of three-quarters of an hour after the first act and one an hour long after the second. In both instances the theater was totally emptied. People who had previously engaged tables in the one sole eating-house were able to put in their time very satisfactorily; the other thousand went hungry. The opera was concluded at ten in the evening or a little later. When we reached home we had been gone more than seven hours. Seven hours at $5 a ticket is almost too much for the money.

While browsing about the front yard among the crowd between the acts I encountered twelve or fifteen friends from different parts of America, and those of them who were most familiar with Wagner said that *Parsifal* seldom pleased at first, but that after one had heard it several times it was almost sure to become a favorite. It seemed impossible, but it was true, for the statement came from people whose word was not to be doubted.

And I gathered some further information. On the ground I found part of a German musical magazine, and in it a letter written by Uhlic thirty-three years ago, in which he defends the scorned and abused Wagner against people like me, who found fault with the comprehensive absence of what our kind regards as singing. Uhlic says Wagner despised "*jene plapperude musik,*" and therefore "runs, trills, and schnörkel are discarded by him." I don't know what a schnörkel is, but now that I know it has been left out of these operas I never have missed so much in my life. And Uhlic further says that Wagner's song is true: that it is "simply emphasized intoned speech." That certainly describes it—in *Parsifal* and some of the operas; and if I understand Uhlic's elaborate German he apologizes for the beautiful airs in *Tannhäuser*. Very well; now that Wagner and I understand each other, perhaps we shall get along better, and I shall stop calling him Waggner, on the American plan, and hereafter call him Voggner as per German custom, for I feel entirely friendly now. The minute we get reconciled to a person, how willing we are to throw aside little needless punctilios and pronounce his name right!

Of course I came home wondering why people should come from all corners of America to hear these operas, when we have lately had a season or two of them in New York with these same singers in the several parts, and possibly this same orchestra. I resolved to think that out at all hazards.

Tuesday.—Yesterday they played the only operatic favorite I have ever had—an opera which has always driven me mad with ignorant delight whenever I have heard it—*Tannhäuser*. I heard it first when I was a youth; I heard it last in the last German season in New York. I was busy yesterday and I did not intend to go, knowing I should have another *Tannhäuser* opportunity in a few days; but after five o'clock I found myself free and walked out to the opera-house and arrived about the beginning of the second act. My opera ticket admitted me to the grounds in front, past the policeman and the chain, and I thought I would take a rest on a bench for an hour or two and wait for the third act.

In the opera-house there is a long loft back of the audience, a kind of open gallery, in which Princes are displayed. It is sacred to them; it is the holy of holies. As soon as the filling of the house is about complete the standing multitude turn and fix their eyes upon the princely layout and gaze mutely and longingly and adoringly and regretfully like sinners looking into heaven. They become rapt, unconscious, steeped in worship. There is no spectacle anywhere that is more pathetic than this worth crossing many oceans to see. It is somehow not the same gaze that people rivet upon a Victor Hugo, or Niagara, or the bones of the mastodon, or the guillotine of the revolution, or the great pyramid, or distant Vesuvius smoking in the sky, or any man long celebrated to you by his genius and achievements, or thing long celebrated to you by the praises of books and pictures—no, that gaze is only the gaze of intense curiosity, interest, wonder, engaged in drinking delicious deep draughts that taste good all the way down and appease and satisfy the thirst of a lifetime. Satisfy it—that is the word. Hugo and the mastodon will still have a degree of intense interest thereafter when encountered, but never anything approaching the ecstasy of that first view. The interest of a Prince is different. It may be envy, it may be worship, doubtless it is a mixture of both—and it does not satisfy its thirst with one view, or even noticeably diminish it. Perhaps the essence of the thing is the value which men attach to a valuable something which has come by luck and not been earned. A dollar picked up in the road is more satisfaction to you than the ninety and nine which you had to work for, and money won at faro or in stocks snuggles into your heart in the same way. A Prince picks up grandeur, power, and a permanent holiday and gratis support by a pure accident, the accident of birth, and he stands always before the grieved eye of poverty and obscurity a monumental representative of luck. And then— supremest value of all—his is the only high fortune on the earth which is secure. The commercial millionaire may become a beggar; the illustrious statesman can make a vital mistake and be dropped and forgotten; the illustrious general can lose a decisive battle and with it the consideration of men; but once a Prince always a Prince—that is to say, an imitation god, and neither hard fortune nor an infamous character nor an addled brain nor the speech of an ass can undeify him. By common consent of all the nations and all the ages the most valuable thing in this world is the homage of men, whether deserved or undeserved. It follows without doubt or question, then, that the most desirable position possible is that of a Prince. And I think it also follows that the so-called usurpations with which history is littered are the most excusable misdemeanors which men have committed. To usurp a usurpation—that is all it amounts to, isn't it?

A Prince is not to us what he is to a European, of course. We have not been taught to regard him as a god, and so one good look at him is likely to so nearly appease our curiosity as to make him an object of no greater interest the next time. We want a fresh one. But it is not so with the European. I am quite sure of it. The same old one will answer; he never stales. Eighteen years ago I was in London and I called at an Englishman's house on a bleak and foggy and dismal December afternoon to visit his wife and married daughter by appointment. I waited half an hour and then they arrived, frozen. They explained that they had been delayed by an unlooked-for circumstance: while passing in the neighborhood of Marlborough House they saw a crowd gathering and were told that the Prince of Wales was about to drive out, so they stopped to get a sight of him. They had waited half an hour on the sidewalk, freezing with the crowd, but were disappointed at last—the Prince had changed his mind. I said, with a good deal of surprise:

"Is it possible that you two have lived in London all your lives and have never seen the Prince of Wales?"

Apparently it was their turn to be surprised, for they exclaimed:

"What an idea! Why, we have seen him hundreds of times."

They had seem him hundreds of times, yet they had waited half an hour in the gloom and the bitter cold, in the midst of a jam of patients from the same asylum, on the chance of seeing him again. It was a stupefying statement, but one is obliged to believe the English, even when they say a thing like that. I fumbled around for a remark, and got out this one: "I can't understand it at all. If I had never seen General Grant I doubt if I would do that even to get a sight of him," with a slight emphasis on the last word.

Their blank faces showed that they wondered where the parallel came in. Then they said, blankly:

"Of course not. He is only a President."

It is doubtless a fact that a Prince is a permanent interest, an interest not subject to deterioration. The general who was never defeated, the general who never held a council of war, the only general who ever commanded a connected battle-front 1,200 miles long, the smith who welded together the broken parts of a great republic and re-established it where it is quite likely to outlast all the monarchies present and to come, was really a person of no serious consequence to these people. To them, with their training, my

General was only a man, after all, while their Prince was clearly much more than that—a being of a wholly unsimilar construction and constitution, and being of no more blood and kinship with men than are the serene eternal lights of the firmament with the poor dull tallow candles of commerce that sputter and die and leave nothing behind but a pinch of ashes and a stink.

I saw the last act of *Tannhäuser*. I sat in the gloom and the deep stillness, waiting—one minute, two minutes, I do not know exactly how long—then the soft music of the hidden orchestra began to breathe its rich, long sighs out from under the distant stage, and by and by the drop-curtain parted in the middle and was drawn softly aside, disclosing the twilighted wood and a wayside shrine, with a white-robed girl praying and a man standing near. Presently that noble chorus of men's voices was heard approaching, and from that moment until the closing of the curtain it was music, just music—music to make one drunk with pleasure, music to make one take scrip and staff and beg his way round the globe to hear it.

To such as are intending to come here in the Wagner season next year I wish to say, bring your dinner-pail with you. If you do, you will never cease to be thankful. If you do not, you will find it a hard fight to save yourself from famishing in Bayreuth. Bayreuth is merely a large village, and has no very large hotels or eating-houses. The principal inns are the Golden Anchor and the Sun. At either of these places you can get an excellent meal—no, I mean you can go there and see other people get it. There is no charge for this. The town is littered with restaurants, but they are small and bad, and they are overdriven with custom. You must secure a table hours beforehand, and often when you arrive you will find somebody occupying it. We have had this experience. We have had a daily scramble for life; and when I say we, I include shoals of people. I have the impression that the only people who do not have to scramble are the veterans—the disciples who have been here before and know the ropes. I think they arrive about a week before the first opera, and engage all the tables for the season. My tribe had tried all kinds of places—some outside of the town, a mile or two—and have captured only nibblings and odds and ends, never in any instance a complete and satisfying meal. Digestible? No, the reverse. These odds and ends are going to serve as souvenirs of Bayreuth, and in that regard their value is not to be overestimated. Photographs fade, bric-a-brac gets lost, busts of Wagner get broken, but once you absorb a Bayreuth restaurant meal it is your possession and your property until the time comes to embalm the rest of you. Some of these pilgrims here become, in effect, cabinets; cabinets of souvenirs of Bayreuth. It is believed among scientists that you could examine the crop of a dead Bayreuth pilgrim anywhere in the earth and tell where he came from. But I like this ballast. I think a "Hermitage" scrape-up at 8 in the evening, when all the famine-breeders have been there and laid in their mementoes and gone, is the quietest thing you can lay on your keelson except gravel.

Thursday.—They keep two teams of singers in stock for the chief roles, and one of these is composed of the most renowned artists in the world, with Materna and Alvary in the lead. I suppose a double team is necessary; doubtless a single team would die of exhaustion in a week, for all the plays last from 4 in the afternoon till 10 at night. Nearly all the labor falls upon the half dozen head singers, and apparently they are required to furnish all the noise they can for the money. If they feel a soft, whispery, mysterious feeling they are required to open out and let the public know it. Operas are given only on Sundays, Mondays, Wednesdays, and Thursdays, with three days of ostensible rest per week, and two teams to do the four operas; but the ostensible rest is devoted largely to rehearsing. It is said that the off days are devoted to rehearsing from some time in the morning till 10 at night. Are there two orchestras also? It is quite likely, since there are a hundred and ten names in the orchestra list.

Yesterday the opera was *Tristan and Isolde*. I have seen all sorts of audiences—at theaters, operas, concerts, lectures, sermons, funerals—but none which was twin to the Wagner audience of Bayreuth for fixed and reverential attention, absolute attention and petrified retention to the end of an act of the attitude assumed at the beginning of it. You detect no movement in the solid mass of heads and shoulders. You seem to sit with the dead in the gloom of a tomb. You know that they are being stirred to their profoundest depths; that there are times when they want to rise and wave handkerchiefs and shout their approbation, and times when tears are running down their faces, and it would be a relief to free their pent emotions in sobs or screams; yet you hear not one utterance till the curtain swings together and the closing strains have slowly faded out and died; then the dead rise with one impulse and shake the building with their applause. Every seat is full in the first act; there is not a vacant one in the last. If a man would be conspicuous, let him come here and retire from the house in the midst of an act. It would make him celebrated.

This audience reminds me of nothing I have ever seen and of nothing I have read about except the city in the Arabian tale where all the inhabitants have been turned to brass and the traveler finds them after centuries mute, motionless, and still retaining the attitudes which they last knew in life. Here the Wagner audience dress as they please, and sit in the dark and worship in silence. At the Metropolitan in New York they sit in a glare, and wear their showiest harness; they hum airs, they squeak fans, they titter, and they gabble all the time. In some of the boxes the conversation and laughter are so loud as to divide the attention of the house with the stage. In large measure the Metropolitan is a show-case for rich fashionables who are not trained in Wagnerian music and have no reverence for it, but who like to promote art and show their clothes.

Can that be an agreeable atmosphere to persons in whom this music produces a sort of divine ecstasy and to whom its creator is a very deity, his stage a temple, the works of his brain and hands consecrated things, and the partaking of them with eye and ear a sacred solemnity? Manifestly, no. Then, perhaps the temporary expatriation, the tedious traversing of seas and continents, the pilgrimage to Bayreuth stands explained. These devotees would worship in an atmosphere of devotion. It is only here that they can find it without fleck or blemish or any worldly pollution. In this remote village there are no sights to see, there is no newspaper to intrude the worries of the distant world, there is nothing going on, it is always Sunday. The pilgrim wends to his temple out of town, sits out his moving service, returns to his bed with his heart and soul and his body exhausted by long hours of tremendous emotion, and he is in no fit condition to do anything but to lie torpid and slowly gather back life and strength for the next service. This opera of *Tristan and Isolde* last night broke the hearts of all witnesses who were of the faith, and I know of some who have heard of many who could not sleep after it, but cried the night away. I feel strongly out of place here. Sometimes I feel like the sane person in a community of the mad; sometimes I feel like the one blind man where all others see; the one groping savage in the college of the learned, and always, during service, I feel like a heretic in heaven.

But by no means do I ever overlook or minify the fact that this is one of the most extraordinary experiences of my life. I have never seen anything like this before. I have never seen anything so great and fine and real as this devotion.

Friday.—Yesterday's opera was *Parsifal* again. The others went and they show marked advance in appreciation; but I went hunting for relics and reminders of the Margravine Wilhelmina, she of the imperishable *Memoirs*. I am properly grateful to her for her (unconscious) satire upon monarchy and nobility, and therefore nothing which her hand touched or her eye looked upon is indifferent to me. I am her pilgrim; the rest of this multitude here are Wagner's.

Tuesday.—I have seen my last two operas; my season is ended, and we cross over into Bohemia this afternoon. I was supposing that my musical regeneration was accomplished and perfected, because I enjoyed both of these operas, singing and all, and, moreover, one of them was *Parsifal,* but the experts have disenchanted me. They say:

"Singing! That wasn't singing; that was the wailing, screeching of third-rate obscurities, palmed off on us in the interest of economy."

Well, I ought to have recognized the sign—the old, sure sign that has never failed me in matters of art. Whenever I enjoy anything in art it means that it is mighty poor. The private knowledge of this fact has saved me from going to pieces with enthusiasm in front of many and many a chromo. However, my base instinct does bring me profit sometimes; I was the only man out of 3,200 who got his money back on those two operas.

The Knighted Knave of Bergen

FROM *A Tramp Abroad,* CHAPTER I

One day it occurred to me that it had been many years since the world had been afforded the spectacle of a man adventurous enough to undertake a journey through Europe on foot. After much thought, I decided that I was a person fitted to furnish to mankind this spectacle. So I determined to do it. This was in March, 1878.

I looked about me for the right sort of person to accompany me in the capacity of agent, and finally hired a Mr. Harris for this service.

It was also my purpose to study art while in Europe. Mr. Harris was in sympathy with me in this. He was as much of an enthusiast in art as I was, and not less anxious to learn to paint. I desired to learn the German language; so did Harris.

Toward the middle of April we sailed in the *Holsatia,* Captain Brandt, and had a very pleasant trip, indeed.

After a brief rest at Hamburg, we made preparations for a long pedestrian trip southward in the soft spring weather, but at the last moment we changed the program, for private reasons, and took the express-train.

We made a short halt at Frankfort-on-the-Main, and found it an interesting city. I would have liked to visit the birthplace of Gutenburg, but it could not be done, as no memorandum of the site of the house has been kept. So we spent an hour in the Goethe mansion instead. The city permits this house to belong to private parties, instead of gracing and dignifying herself with the honor of possessing and protecting it.

Frankfort is one of the sixteen cities which have the distinction of being the place where the following incident occurred. Charlemagne, while chasing the Saxons (as *he* said), or being chased by them (as *they* said), arrived at the bank of the river at dawn, in a fog. The enemy were either before him or behind him; but in any case he wanted to get across, very badly. He would have given anything for a guide, but none was to be had.

Presently he saw a deer, followed by her young, approach the water. He watched her, judging that she would seek a ford, and he was right. She waded over, and the army followed. So a great Frankish victory or defeat was gained or avoided; and in order to commemorate the episode, Charlemagne commanded a city to be built there, which he named Frankfort—the ford of the Franks. None of the other cities where this event happened were named for it. This is good evidence that Frankfort was the first place it occurred at.

Frankfort has another distinction—it is the birthplace of the German alphabet; or at least of the German word for alphabet—*Buchstaben*. They say that the first movable types were made on birch sticks—*Buchstabe*—hence the name.

I was taught a lesson in political economy in Frankfort. I had brought from home a box containing a thousand very cheap cigars. By way of experiment, I stepped into a little shop in a queer old back street, took four gaily decorated boxes of wax matches and three cigars, and laid down a silver piece worth 48 cents. The man gave me 43 cents change.

The Matterhorn and the Glacier

FROM *A Tramp Abroad,* CHAPTERS XXXVIII–XXXIX

We followed the mule-road, a zigzag course, now to the right, now to the left, but always up, and always crowded and incommoded by going and coming files of reckless tourists who were never, in a single instance, tied together. I was obliged to exert the utmost care and caution, for in many places the road was not two yards wide, and often the lower side of it sloped away in slanting precipices eight and even nine feet deep. I had to encourage the men constantly, to keep them from giving way to their unmanly fears.

We might have made the summit before night, but for a delay caused by the loss of an umbrella. I was allowing the umbrella to remain lost, but the men murmured, and with reason, for in this exposed region we stood in peculiar need of protection against avalanches; so I went into camp and detached a strong party to go after the missing article.

The difficulties of the next morning were severe, but our courage was high, for our goal was near. At noon we conquered the last impediment— we stood at last upon the summit, and without the loss of a single man except the mule that ate the glycerin. Our great achievement was achieved— the possibility of the impossible was demonstrated, and Harris and I walked proudly into the great dining-room of the Riffelberg Hotel and stood our alpenstocks up in the corner.

. . . I had a magnificent view of Monte Rosa, and apparently all the rest of the Alpine world, from that high place. All the circling horizon was piled high with a mighty tumult of snowy crests. One might have imagined he saw before him the tented camps of a beleaguering host of Brobdingnagians.

But lonely, conspicuous, and superb, rose that wonderful upright wedge, the Matterhorn. Its precipitous sides were powdered over with snow, and the upper half hidden in thick clouds which now and then dissolved to cobweb films and gave brief glimpses of the imposing tower as through a veil.[*] A little later the Matterhorn took to himself the semblance of a volcano; he was stripped naked to his apex—around this circled vast wreaths of white cloud which strung slowly out and streamed away slant-wise toward the sun, a twenty-mile stretch of rolling and tumbling vapor, and looking just as if it were pouring out of a crater. Later again, one of the

---

*NOTE—I had the very unusual luck to catch one little momentary glimpse of the Matterhorn wholly unencumbered by clouds. I leveled my photographic apparatus at it without the loss of an instant, and should have got an elegant picture if my donkey had not interfered. It was my purpose to draw this photograph all by myself for my book, but was obliged to put the mountain part of it into the hands of the professional artist because I found I could not do landscape well.

mountain's sides was clean and clear, and another side densely clothed from base to summit in a thick smokelike cloud which feathered off and flew around the shaft's sharp edge like the smoke around the corners of a burning building. The Matterhorn is always experimenting, and always gets up fine effects, too. In the sunset, when all the lower world is palled in gloom, it points toward heaven out of the pervading blackness like a finger of fire. In the sunrise—well, they say it is very fine in the sunrise.

Authorities agree that there is no such tremendous "layout" of snowy Alpine magnitude, grandeur, and sublimity to be seen from any other accessible point as the tourist may see from the summit of the Riffelberg. Therefore, let the tourist rope himself up and go there; for I have shown that with nerve, caution, and judgment, the thing can be done…

A guide-book is a queer thing. The reader has just seen what a man who undertakes the great ascent from Zermatt to the Riffelberg Hotel must experience. Yet Baedeker makes these strange statements concerning this matter:

1. Distance—3 hours.
2. The road cannot be mistaken.
3. Guide unnecessary.
4. Distance from Riffelberg Hotel to the Gorner Grat, one hour and a half.
5. Ascent simple and easy. Guide unnecessary.
6. Elevation of Zermatt above sea-level, 5,315 feet.
7. Elevation of Riffelberg Hotel above sea-level, 8,429 feet.
8. Elevation of the Gorner Grat above sea-level, 10,289 feet.

I have pretty effectually throttled these errors by sending him the following demonstrated facts:

1. Distance from Zermatt to Riffelberg Hotel, 7 days.
2. The road CAN be mistaken. If I am the first that did it, I want the credit of it, too.

3. Guides ARE necessary, for none but a native can read those finger-boards.
4. The estimate of the elevation of the several localities above sea-level is pretty correct—for Baedeker. He only misses it about a hundred and eighty or ninety thousand feet.

I found my arnica invaluable. My men were suffering excruciatingly, from the friction of sitting down so much. During two or three days, not one of them was able to do more than lie down or walk about; yet so effective was the arnica, that on the fourth all were able to sit up. I consider that, more than to anything else, I owe the success of our great undertaking to arnica and paregoric.

My men are being restored to health and strength, my main perplexity, now, was how to get them down the mountain again. I was not willing to expose the brave fellows to the perils, fatigues, and hardships of that fearful route again if it could be helped. First I thought of balloons; but, of course, I had to give that idea up, for balloons were not procurable. I thought of several other expedients, but upon consideration discarded them, for cause. But at last I hit it. I was aware that the movement of glaciers is an established fact, for I had read it in Baedeker; so I resolved to take passage for Zermatt on the great Gorner Glacier.

Very good. The next thing was, how to get down the glacier comfortably—for the mule-road to it was long, and winding, and wearisome. I set my mind at work, and soon thought out a plan. One looks straight down upon the vast frozen river called the Gorner Glacier, from the Gorner Grat, a sheer precipice twelve hundred feet high. We had one hundred and fifty-four umbrellas—and what is an umbrella but a parachute?

I mentioned this noble idea to Harris, with enthusiasm, and was about to order the Expedition to form on the Gorner Grat, with their umbrellas, and prepare for flight by platoons, each platoon in command of a guide, when Harris stopped me and urged me not to be too hasty. He asked me if this method of descending the Alps had ever been tried before. I said no, I had not heard of an instance. Then, in his opinion, it was a matter of considerable gravity; in his opinion it would not be well to send the whole command over the cliff at once; a better way would be to send down a single individual, first, and see how he fared.

I saw the wisdom in this idea instantly. I said as much, and thanked my agent cordially, and told him to take his umbrella and try the thing right away, and wave his hat when he got down, if he struck in a soft place, and then I would ship the rest right along.

Harris was greatly touched with this mark of confidence, and said so, in a voice that had a perceptible tremble in it; but at the same time he said he did not feel himself worthy of so conspicuous a favor; that it might cause jealousy in the command, for there were plenty who would not hesitate to say he had used underhanded means to get the appointment, whereas his conscience would bear him witness that he had not sought it at all, nor even, in his secret heart, desired it.

I said these words did him extreme credit, but that he must not throw away the imperishable distinction of being the first man to descend an Alp per parachute, simply to save the feelings of some envious underlings. No, I said, he MUST accept the appointment—it was no longer an invitation, it was a command.

He thanked me with effusion, and said that putting the thing in this form removed every objection. He retired, and soon returned with his umbrella, his eye flaming with gratitude and his cheeks pallid with joy. Just then the head guide passed along. Harris's expression changed to one of infinite tenderness, and he said:

"That man did me a cruel injury four days ago, and I said in my heart he should live to perceive and confess that the only noble revenge a man can take upon his enemy is to return good for evil. I resign in his favor. Appoint him."

I threw my arms around the generous fellow and said:

"Harris, you are the noblest soul that lives. You shall not regret this sublime act, neither shall the world fail to know of it. You shall have opportunity far transcending this one, too, if I live—remember that."

I called the head guide to me and appointed him on the spot. But the thing aroused no enthusiasm in him. He did not take to the idea at all.

He said:

"Tie myself to an umbrella and jump over the Gorner Grat! Excuse me, there are a great many pleasanter roads to the devil than that."

Upon a discussion of the subject with him, it appeared that he considered the project distinctly and decidedly dangerous. I was not convinced, yet I was not willing to try the experiment in any risky way—that is, in a way that might cripple the strength and efficiency of the Expedition. I was about at my wits' end when it occurred to me to try it on the Latinist.

He was called in. But he declined, on the plea of inexperience, diffidence in public, lack of curiosity, and I didn't know what all. Another man declined on account of a cold in the head; thought he ought to avoid exposure. Another could not jump well—never COULD jump well—did not believe he could jump so far without long and patient practice. Another was afraid it was going to rain, and his umbrella had a hole in it. Everybody had an excuse. The result was what the reader has by this time guessed: the most magnificent idea that was ever conceived had to be abandoned, from sheer lack of a person with enterprise enough to carry it out. Yes, I actually had to give that thing up—while doubtless I should live to see somebody use it and take all the credit from me.

Well, I had to go overland—there was no other way. I marched the Expedition down the steep and tedious mule-path and took up as good a position as I could upon the middle of the glacier—because Baedeker said the middle part travels the fastest. As a measure of economy, however, I put some of the heavier baggage on the shoreward parts, to go as slow freight. I waited and waited, but the glacier did not move. Night was coming on, the darkness began to gather—still we did not budge. It occurred to me then, that there might be a time-table in Baedeker; it would be well to find out the hours of starting. I called for the book—it could not be found. Bradshaw would certainly contain a time-table; but no Bradshaw could be found.

Very well, I must make the best of the situation. So I pitched the tents, picketed the animals, milked the cows, had supper, paregoricked the men, established the watch, and went to bed—with orders to call me as soon as we came in sight of Zermatt.

I awoke about half past ten next morning, and looked around. We hadn't budged a peg! At first I could not understand it; then it occurred to me that the old thing must be aground. So I cut down some trees and rigged a spar on the starboard and another on the port side, and fooled away upward of three hours trying to spar her off. But it was no use. She was half a mile wide and fifteen or twenty miles long, and there was no telling just whereabouts she WAS aground. The men began to show uneasiness, too, and presently they came flying to me with ashy faces, saying she had sprung a leak.

Nothing but my cool behavior at this critical time saved us from another panic. I ordered them to show me the place. They led me to a spot where a huge boulder lay in a deep pool of clear and brilliant water. It did look like a pretty bad leak, but I kept that to myself. I made a pump and set the men to work to pump out the glacier. We made a success of it. I perceived, then, that it was not a leak at all. This boulder had descended from a precipice and stopped on the ice in the middle of the glacier, and the sun had warmed it up, every day, and consequently it had melted its way deeper and deeper into the ice, until at last it reposed, as we had found it, in a deep pool of the clearest and coldest water.

Presently Baedeker was found again, and I hunted eagerly for the time-table. There was none. The book simply said the glacier was moving all the time. This was satisfactory, so I shut up the book and chose a good position to view the scenery as we passed along. I stood there some time enjoying the trip, but at last it occurred to me that we did not seem to be gaining any on the scenery. I said to myself, "This confounded old thing's aground again, sure"—and opened Baedeker to see if I could run across any remedy for these annoying interruptions. I soon found a sentence which threw a dazzling light upon the matter. It said, "The Gorner Glacier travels at an average rate of a little less than an inch a day." I have seldom felt so outraged. I have seldom had my confidence so wantonly betrayed. I made a small calculation: One inch a day, say thirty feet a year; estimated distance to Zermatt, three and one-eighteenth miles. Time required to go by glacier, A LITTLE OVER FIVE HUNDRED YEARS! I said to myself, "I can WALK it quicker—and before I will patronize such a fraud as this, I will do it."

When I revealed to Harris the fact that the passenger part of this glacier—the central part—the lightning-express part, so to speak—was not due in Zermatt till the summer of 2378, and that the baggage, coming along the slow edge, would not arrive until some generations later, he burst out with:

"That is European management, all over! An inch a day—think of that! Five hundred years to go a trifle over three miles! But I am not a bit surprised. It's a Catholic glacier. You can tell by the look of it. And the management."

I said, no, I believed nothing but the extreme end of it was in a Catholic canton.

"Well, then, it's a government glacier," said Harris. "It's all the same. Over here the government runs everything—so everything's slow; slow, and ill-managed. But with us, everything's done by private enterprise—and then there ain't much lolling around, you can depend on it. I wish Tom Scott could get his hands on this torpid old slab once—you'd see it take a different gait from this."

I said I was sure he would increase the speed, if there was trade enough to justify it.

"He'd MAKE trade," said Harris. "That's the difference between governments and individuals. Governments don't care, individuals do. Tom Scott would take all the trade; in two years Gorner stock would go to two hundred, and inside of two more you would see all the other glaciers under the hammer for taxes." After a reflective pause, Harris added, "A little less than an inch a day; a little less than an INCH, mind you. Well, I'm losing my reverence for glaciers."

I was feeling much the same way myself. I have traveled by

canal-boat, ox-wagon, raft, and by the Ephesus and Smyrna railway; but when it comes down to good solid honest slow motion, I bet my money on the glacier. As a means of passenger transportation, I consider the glacier a failure; but as a vehicle of slow freight, I think she fills the bill. In the matter of putting the fine shades on that line of business, I judge she could teach the Germans something.

I ordered the men to break camp and prepare for the land journey to Zermatt. At this moment a most interesting find was made; a dark object, bedded in the glacial ice, was cut out with the ice-axes, and it proved to be a piece of the undressed skin of some animal—a hair trunk, perhaps; but a close inspection disabled the hair-trunk theory, and further discussion and examination exploded it entirely—that is, in the opinion of all the scientists except the one who had advanced it. This one clung to his theory with affectionate fidelity characteristic of originators of scientific theories, and afterward won many of the first scientists of the age to his view, by a very able pamphlet which he wrote, entitled, "Evidences going to show that the hair trunk, in a wild state, belonged to the early glacial period, and roamed the wastes of chaos in the company with the cave-bear, primeval man, and the other Ooelitics of the Old Silurian family."

Each of our scientists had a theory of his own, and put forward an animal of his own as a candidate for the skin. I sided with the geologist of the Expedition in the belief that this patch of skin had once helped to cover a Siberian elephant, in some old forgotten age—but we divided there, the geologist believing that this discovery proved that Siberia had formerly been located where Switzerland is now, whereas I held the opinion that it merely proved that the primeval Swiss was not the dull savage he is represented to have been, but was a being of high intellectual development, who liked to go to the menagerie.

We arrived that evening, after many hardships and adventures, in some fields close to the great ice-arch where the mad Visp boils and surges out from under the foot of the great Gorner Glacier, and here we camped, our perils over and our magnificent undertaking successfully completed.

We marched into Zermatt the next day, and were received with the most lavish honors and applause. A document, signed and sealed by the authorities, was given to me which established and endorsed the fact that I had made the ascent of the Riffelberg. This I wear around my neck, and it will be buried with me when I am no more.

Rafting Down the Neckar

FROM *A Tramp Abroad*, CHAPTER XIV

When the landlord learned that I and my agents were artists, our party rose perceptibly in his esteem; we rose still higher when he learned that we were making a pedestrian tour of Europe.

He told us all about the Heidelberg road, and which were the best places to avoid and which the best ones to tarry at; he charged me less than cost for the things I broke in the night; he put up a fine luncheon for us and added to it a quantity of great light-green plums, the pleasantest fruit in Germany; he was so anxious to do us honor that he would not allow us to walk out of Heilbronn, but called up Goetz von Berlichingen's horse and cab and made us ride.

I made a sketch of the turnout. It is not a Work, it is only what artists call a "study"—a thing to make a finished picture from. This sketch has several blemishes in it; for instance, the wagon is not traveling as fast as the horse is. This is wrong. Again, the person trying to get out of the way is too small; he is out of perspective, as we say. The two upper lines are not the horse's back, they are the reins; there seems to be a wheel missing—this would be corrected in a finished Work, of course. This thing flying out behind is not a flag, it is a curtain. That other thing up there is the sun, but I didn't get enough distance on it. I do not remember, now, what that thing is that is in front of the man who is running, but I think it is a haystack or a woman. This study was exhibited in the Paris Salon of 1879, but did not take any medal; they do not give medals for studies.

We discharged the carriage at the bridge. The river was full of logs— long, slender, barkless pine logs—and we leaned on the rails of the bridge, and watched the men put them together into rafts. These rafts were of a shape and construction to suit the crookedness and extreme narrowness of the Neckar. They were from fifty to one hundred yards long, and they gradually tapered from a nine-log breadth at their sterns, to a three-log breadth at their bow-ends. The main part of the steering is done at the bow, with a pole; the three-log breadth there furnishes room for only the steersman, for these little logs are not larger around than an average young lady's waist. The connections of the several sections of the raft are slack and pliant, so that the raft may be readily bent into any sort of curve required by the shape of the river.

The Neckar is in many places so narrow that a person can throw a dog across it, if he has one; when it is also sharply curved in such places, the raftsman has to do some pretty nice snug piloting to make the turns. The river is not always allowed to spread over its whole bed—which is as much as thirty, and sometimes forty yards wide—but is split into three equal bodies of water, by stone dikes which throw the main volume, depth, and current into the central one. In low water these neat narrow-edged dikes project four or five inches above the surface, like the comb of a submerged roof, but in high water they are overflowed. A hatful of rain makes high water in the Neckar, and a basketful produces an overflow.

There are dikes abreast the Schloss Hotel, and the current is violently swift at that point. I used to sit for hours in my glass cage, watching the long, narrow rafts slip along through the central channel, grazing the right-bank dike and aiming carefully for the middle arch of the stone bridge below; I watched them in this way, and lost all this time hoping to see one of them hit the bridge-pier and wreck itself sometime or other, but was always disappointed. One was smashed there one morning, but I had just stepped into my room a moment to light a pipe, so I lost it.

While I was looking down upon the rafts that morning in Heilbronn, the daredevil spirit of adventure came suddenly upon me, and I said to my comrades:

"I am going to Heidelberg on a raft. Will you venture with me?"

Their faces paled a little, but they assented with as good a grace as they could. Harris wanted to cable his mother—thought it his duty to do that, as he was all she had in this world—so, while he attended to this, I went down to the longest and finest raft and hailed the captain with a hearty "Ahoy, shipmate!" which put us upon pleasant terms at once, and we entered upon business. I said we were on a pedestrian tour to Heidelberg, and would like to take passage with him. I said this partly through young Z, who spoke German very well, and partly through Mr. X, who spoke it peculiarly. I can *understand* German as well as the maniac that invented it, but I *talk* it best through an interpreter.

The captain hitched up his trousers, then shifted his quid thoughtfully. Presently he said just what I was expecting he would say—that he had no license to carry passengers, and therefore was afraid the law would be after him in case the matter got noised about or any accident happened. So I *chartered* the raft and the crew and took all the responsibilities on myself.

With a rattling song the starboard watch bent to their work and hove the cable short, then got the anchor home, and our bark moved off with a stately stride, and soon was bowling along at about two knots an hour.

Our party were grouped amidships. At first the talk was a little gloomy, and ran mainly upon the shortness of life, the uncertainty of it, the perils which beset it, and the need and wisdom of being always prepared for the worst; this shaded off into low-voiced references to the dangers of the deep, and kindred matters; but as the gray east began to redden and the mysterious solemnity and silence of the dawn to give place to the joy-songs of the birds, the talk took a cheerier tone, and our spirits began to rise steadily.

Germany, in the summer, is the perfection of the beautiful, but nobody has understood, and realized, and enjoyed the utmost possibilities of this soft and peaceful beauty unless he has voyaged down the Neckar on a raft. The motion of a raft is the needful motion; it is gentle, and gliding, and smooth, and noiseless; it calms down all feverish activities, it soothes to sleep all nervous hurry and impatience; under its restful influence all the troubles and vexations and sorrows that harass the mind vanish away, and existence becomes a dream, a charm, a deep and tranquil ecstasy. How it contrasts with hot and perspiring pedestrianism, and dusty and deafening railroad rush, and tedious jolting behind tired horses over blinding white roads!

We went slipping silently along, between the green and fragrant banks, with a sense of pleasure and contentment that grew, and grew, all the time. Sometimes the banks were overhung with thick masses of willows that wholly hid the ground behind; sometimes we had noble hills on one hand, clothed densely with foliage to their tops, and on the other hand open levels blazing with poppies, or clothed in the rich blue of the corn-flower; sometimes we drifted in the shadow of forests, and sometimes along the margin of long stretches of velvety grass, fresh and green and bright, a tireless charm to the eye. And the birds!—they were everywhere; they swept back and forth across the river constantly, and their jubilant music was never stilled.

It was a deep and satisfying pleasure to see the sun create the new morning, and gradually, patiently, lovingly, clothe it on with splendor after splendor, and glory after glory, till the miracle was complete. How different is this marvel observed from a raft, from what it is when one observes it through the dingy windows of a railway-station in some wretched village while he munches a petrified sandwich and waits for the train.

The Cave of the Specter

From *A Tramp Abroad,* CHAPTER XV

Two miles below Hornberg castle is a cave in a low cliff, which the captain of the raft said had once been occupied by a beautiful heiress of Hornberg—the Lady Gertrude—in the old times. It was seven hundred years ago. She had a number of rich and noble lovers and one poor and obscure one, Sir Wendel Lobenfeld. With the native chuckleheadedness of the heroine of romance, she preferred the poor and obscure lover. With the native sound judgment of the father of a heroine of romance, the von Berlichingen of that day shut his daughter up in his donjon keep, or his oubliette, or his culverin, or some such place, and resolved that she should stay there until she selected a husband from among her rich and noble lovers. The latter visited her and persecuted her with their supplications, but without effect, for her heart was true to her poor despised Crusader, who was fighting in the Holy Land. Finally, she resolved that she would endure the attentions of the rich lovers no longer; so one stormy night she escaped and went down the river and hid herself in the cave on the other side. Her father ransacked the country for her, but found not a trace of her. As the days went by, and still no tidings of her came, his conscience began to torture him, and he caused proclamation to be made that if she were yet living and would return, he would oppose her no longer, she might marry whom she would. The months dragged on, all hope forsook the old man, he ceased from his customary pursuits and pleasures, he devoted himself to pious works, and longed for the deliverance of death.

Now just at midnight, every night, the lost heiress stood in the mouth of her cave, arrayed in white robes, and sang a little love ballad which her Crusader had made for her. She judged that if he came home alive the superstitious peasants would tell him about the ghost that sang in the cave, and that as soon as they described the ballad he would know that none but he and she knew that song, therefore he would suspect that she was alive, and would come and find her. As time went on, the people of the region became sorely distressed about the Specter of the Haunted Cave. It was said that ill luck of one kind or another always overtook any one who had the misfortune to hear that song. Eventually, every calamity that happened thereabouts was laid at the door of that music. Consequently, no boatmen would consent to pass the cave at night; the peasants shunned the place, even in the daytime.

But the faithful girl sang on, night after night, month after month, and patiently waited; her reward must come at last. Five years dragged by, and still, every night at midnight, the plaintive tones floated out over the silent land, while the distant boatmen and peasants thrust their fingers into their ears and shuddered out a prayer.

And now came the Crusader home, bronzed and battle-scarred, but bringing a great and splendid fame to lay at the feet of his bride. The old lord of Hornberg received him as his son, and wanted him to stay by him and be the comfort and blessing of his age; but the tale of that young girl's devotion to him and its pathetic consequences made a changed man of the knight. He could not enjoy his well-earned rest. He said his heart was broken, he would give the remnant of his life to high deeds in the cause of humanity, and so find a worthy death and a blessed reunion with the brave true heart whose love had more honored him than all his victories in war.

When the people heard this resolve of his, they came and told him there was a pitiless dragon in human disguise in the Haunted Cave, a dread creature which no knight had yet been bold enough to face, and begged him to rid the land of its desolating presence. He said he would do it. They told him about the song, and when he asked what song it was, they said the memory of it was gone, for nobody had been hardy enough to listen to it for the past four years and more.

Toward midnight the Crusader came floating down the river in a boat, with his trusty cross-bow in his hands. He drifted silently through the dim reflections of the crags and trees, with his intent eyes fixed upon the low cliff which he was approaching. As he drew nearer, he discerned the black mouth of the cave. Now—is that a white figure? Yes. The plaintive song begins to well forth and float away over meadow and river—the cross-bow is slowly raised to position, a steady aim is taken, the bolt flies straight to the mark—the figure sinks down, still singing, the knight takes the wool out of his ears, and recognizes the old ballad—too late! Ah, if he had only not put the wool in his ears!

The Crusader went away to the wars again, and presently fell in battle, fighting for the Cross. Tradition says that during several centuries the spirit of the unfortunate girl sang nightly from the cave at midnight, but the music carried no curse with it; and although many listened for the mysterious sounds, few were favored, since only those could hear them who had never failed in a trust. It is believed that the singing still continues, but it is known that nobody has heard it during the present century.

The Belated Russian Passport

From *The Man Who Corrupted Hadleyburg and Other Stories*

One fly makes a summer.

—Pudd'nhead Wilson's Calendar

I.

A great beer-saloon in the Friedrichstrasse, Berlin, towards midafternoon. At a hundred round tables gentlemen sat smoking and drinking; flitting here and there and everywhere were white-aproned waiters bearing foaming mugs to the thirsty. At a table near the main entrance were grouped half a dozen lively young fellows—American students—drinking good-bye to a visiting Yale youth on his travels, who had been spending a few days in the German capital.

"But why do you cut your tour short in the middle, Parrish?" asked one of the students. "I wish I had your chance. What do you want to go home for?"

"Yes," said another, "what is the idea? You want to explain, you know, because it looks like insanity. Homesick?"

A girlish blush rose in Parrish's fresh young face, and after a little hesitation he confessed that that was his trouble.

"I was never away from home before," he said, "and every day I get more and more lonesome. I have not seen a friend for weeks, and it's been horrible. I meant to stick the trip through, for pride's sake, but seeing you boys has finished me. It's been heaven to me, and I can't take up that companionless dreariness again. If I had company—but I haven't, you know, so it's no use. They used to call me Miss Nancy when I was a small chap, and I reckon I'm that yet—girlish and timorous, and all that. I ought to have been a girl! I can't stand it; I'm going home."

The boys rallied him good-naturedly, and said he was making the mistake of his life; and one of them added that he ought at least to see St. Petersburg before turning back.

"Don't!" said Parrish, appealingly. "It was my dearest dream, and I'm throwing it away. Don't say a word more on that head, for I'm made of water, and can't stand out against anybody's persuasion. I can't go alone; I think I should die." He slapped his breast-pocket, and added: "Here is my protection against a change of mind; I've bought ticket and sleeper for Paris, and I leave to-night. Drink, now—this is on me—bumpers—this is for home!"

The good-byes were said, and Alfred Parrish was left to his thoughts and his loneliness. But for a moment only. A sturdy, middle-aged man with a brisk and business-like bearing, and an air of decision and confidence suggestive of military training, came bustling from the next table, and seated himself at Parrish's side, and began to speak, with concentrated interest and earnestness. His eyes, his face, his person, his whole system, seemed to exude energy. He was full of steam—racing pressure—one could almost hear his gauge-cocks sing. He extended a frank hand, shook Parrish cordially, and said, with a most convincing air of strenuous conviction:

"Ah, but you mustn't; really you mustn't; it would be the greatest mistake; you would always regret it. Be persuaded, I beg you; don't do it—don't!"

There was such a friendly note in it, and such a seeming of genuineness, that it brought a sort of uplift to the youth's despondent spirits, and a telltale moisture betrayed itself in his eyes, an unintentional confession that he was touched and grateful. The alert stranger noted that sign, was quite content with that response, and followed up his advantage without waiting for a spoken one:

"No, don't do it; it would be a mistake. I have heard everything that was said—you will pardon that—I was so close by that I couldn't help it. And it troubled me to think that you would cut your travels short when you really want to see St. Petersburg, and are right here almost in sight of it! Reconsider it—ah, you must reconsider it. It is such a short distance—it is very soon done and very soon over—and think what a memory it will be!"

Then he went on and made a picture of the Russian capital and its wonders, which made Alfred Parrish's mouth water and his roused spirits cry out with longing. Then—

"Of course you must see St. Petersburg—you must! Why, it will be a joy to you—a joy! I know, because I know the place as familiarly as I know my own birthplace in America. Ten years—I've known it ten years. Ask anybody there; they'll tell you; they all know me—Major Jackson. The very dogs know me. Do go; oh, you must go; you must, indeed."

Alfred Parrish was quivering with eagerness now. He would go. His face said it as plainly as his tongue could have done it. Then—the old shadow fell, and he said, sorrowfully:

"Oh no—no, it's no use; I can't. I should die of the loneliness."

The Major said, with astonishment: "The—loneliness! Why, I'm going with you!"

It was startlingly unexpected. And not quite pleasant. Things were moving too rapidly. Was this a trap? Was this stranger a sharper? Whence all this gratuitous interest in a wandering and unknown lad? Then he glanced at the Major's frank and winning and beaming face, and was ashamed; and wished he knew how to get out of this scrape without hurting the feelings of its contriver. But he was not handy in matters of diplomacy, and went at the difficulty with conscious awkwardness and small confidence. He said, with a quite overdone show of unselfishness:

"Oh no, no, you are too kind; I couldn't—I couldn't allow you to put yourself to such an inconvenience on my—"

"Inconvenience? None in the world, my boy; I was going to-night, anyway; I leave in the express at nine. Come! We'll go together. You sha'n't be lonely a single minute. Come along—say the word!"

So that excuse had failed. What to do now? Parrish was disheartened; it seemed to him that no subterfuge which his poor invention could contrive would ever rescue him from these toils. Still, he must make another effort, and he did; and before he had finished his new excuse he thought he recognized that it was unanswerable:

"Ah, but most unfortunately luck is against me, and it is impossible. Look at these"—and he took out his tickets and laid them on the table. "I am booked through to Paris, and I couldn't get these tickets and baggage coupons changed for St. Petersburg, of course, and would have to lose the money; and if I could afford to lose the money I should be rather short after I bought the new tickets—for there is all the cash I've got about me"—and he laid a five-hundred-mark bank-note on the table.

In a moment the Major had the tickets and coupons and was on his feet, and saying, with enthusiasm:

"Good! It's all right, and everything safe. They'll change the tickets and baggage pasters for me; they all know me—everybody knows me. Sit right where you are; I'll be back right away." Then he reached for the bank-note, and added, "I'll take this along, for there will be a little extra pay on the new tickets, maybe"—and the next moment he was flying out at the door.

II.

Alfred Parrish was paralyzed. It was all so sudden. So sudden, so daring, so incredible, so impossible. His mouth was open, but his tongue wouldn't work; he tried to shout "Stop him," but his lungs were empty; he wanted to pursue, but his legs refused to do anything but tremble; then they gave way under him and let him down into his chair. His throat was dry, he was gasping and swallowing with dismay, his head was in a whirl. What must he do? He did not know. One thing seemed plain, however—he must pull himself together, and try to overtake that man. Of course the man could not get back the ticket money, but would he throw the tickets away on that account? No; he would certainly go to the station and sell them to some one at half-price; and to-day, too, for they would be worthless to-morrow, by German custom. These reflections gave him hope and strength, and he rose and started. But he took only a couple of steps, then he felt a sudden sickness, and tottered back to his chair again, weak with a dread that his movement had been noticed—for the last round of beer was at his expense; it had not been paid for, and he hadn't a pfennig. He was a prisoner— Heaven only could know what might happen if he tried to leave the place. He was timid, scared, crushed; and he had not German enough to state his case and beg for help and indulgence.

Then his thoughts began to persecute him. How could he have been such a fool? What possessed him to listen to such a manifest adventurer? And here comes the waiter! He buried himself in the newspaper—trembling. The waiter passed by. It filled him with thankfulness. The hands of the clock seemed to stand still, yet he could not keep his eyes from them.

Ten minutes dragged by. The waiter again! Again he hid behind the paper. The waiter paused—apparently a week—then passed on.

Another ten minutes of misery—once more the waiter; this time he wiped off the table, and seemed to be a month at it; then paused two months, and went away.

Parrish felt that he could not endure another visit; he must take the chances: he must run the gantlet; he must escape. But the waiter stayed around about the neighborhood for five minutes—months and months seemingly, Parrish watching him with a despairing eye, and feeling the infirmities of age creeping upon him and his hair gradually turning gray.

At last the waiter wandered away—stopped at a table, collected a bill, wandered farther, collected another bill, wandered farther—Parrish's praying eye riveted on him all the time, his heart thumping, his breath coming and going in quick little gasps of anxiety mixed with hope.

The waiter stopped again to collect, and Parrish said to himself, it is now or never! and started for the door. One step—two steps—three—four—he was nearing the door—five—his legs shaking under him—was that a swift step behind him?—the thought shrivelled his heart—six steps—seven, and he was out!—eight—nine—ten—eleven—twelve—there is a pursuing step!—he turned the corner, and picked up his heels to fly—a heavy hand fell on his shoulder, and the strength went out of his body!

It was the Major. He asked no question. He showed no surprise. He said, in his breezy and exhilarating fashion:

"Confound those people, they delayed me; that's why I was gone so long. New man in the ticket-office, and he didn't know me, and wouldn't make the exchange because it was irregular; so I had to hunt up my old friend, the great mogul—the station-master, you know—hi, there, cab! cab!—jump in, Parrish!—Russian consulate, cabby, and let them fly!—so, as I say, that all cost time. But it's all right now, and everything straight; your luggage reweighed, rechecked, fare-ticket and sleeper changed, and I've got the documents for it in my pocket; also the change—I'll keep it for you. Whoop along, cabby, whoop along; don't let them go to sleep!"

Poor Parrish was trying his best to get in a word edgeways, as the cab flew farther and farther from the bilked beer-hall, and now at last he succeeded, and wanted to return at once and pay his little bill.

"Oh, never mind about that," said the Major, placidly; "that's all right, they know me, everybody knows me—I'll square it next time I'm in Berlin—push along, cabby, push along—no great lot of time to spare, now."

They arrived at the Russian consulate, a moment after hours, and hurried in. No one there but a clerk. The Major laid his card on the desk, and said, in the Russian tongue, "Now, then, if you'll visé this young man's passport for Petersburg as quickly as—"

"But, dear sir, I'm not authorized, and the consul has just gone." "Gone where?" "Out in the country, where he lives." "And he'll be back—" "Not till morning."

"Thunder! Oh, well, look here, I'm Major Jackson—he knows me, everybody knows me. You visé it yourself; tell him Major Jackson asked you; it'll be all right."

But it would be desperately and fatally irregular; the clerk could not be persuaded; he almost fainted at the idea.

"Well, then, I'll tell you what to do," said the Major. "Here's stamps and the fee—visé it in the morning, and start it along by mail."

The clerk said, dubiously, "He—well, he may perhaps do it, and so—"

"May? He will! He knows me—everybody knows me."

"Very well," said the clerk, "I will tell him what you say." He looked bewildered, and in a measure subjugated; and added, timidly: "But—but—you know you will beat it to the frontier twenty-four hours. There are no accommodations there for so long a wait."

"Who's going to wait? Not I, if the court knows herself."

The clerk was temporarily paralyzed, and said, "Surely, sir, you don't wish it sent to Petersburg!"

"And why not?"

"And the owner of it tarrying at the frontier, twenty-five miles away? It couldn't do him any good, in those circumstances."

"Tarry—the mischief! Who said he was going to do any tarrying?"

"Why, you know, of course, they'll stop him at the frontier if he has no passport."

"Indeed they won't! The Chief Inspector knows me—everybody does. I'll be responsible for the young man. You send it straight through to Petersburg—Hôtel de l'Europe, care Major Jackson: tell the consul not to worry; I'm taking all the risks myself."

The clerk hesitated, then chanced one more appeal:

"You must bear in mind, sir, that the risks are peculiarly serious, just now. The new edict is in force."

"What is it?"

"Ten years in Siberia for being in Russia without a passport."

"Mm—damnation!" He said it in English, for the Russian tongue is but a poor stand-by in spiritual emergencies. He mused a moment, then brisked up and resumed in Russian: "Oh, it's all right—label her St. Petersburg and let her sail! I'll fix it. They all know me there—all the authorities—everybody."

III.

The Major turned out to be an adorable travelling companion, and young Parrish was charmed with him. His talk was sunshine and rainbows, and lit up the whole region around, and kept it gay and happy and cheerful; and he was full of accommodating ways, and knew all about how to do things, and when to do them, and the best way. So the long journey was a fairy dream for that young lad who had been so lonely and forlorn and friendless so many homesick weeks. At last, when the two travellers were approaching the frontier, Parrish said something about passports; then started, as if recollecting something, and added:

"Why, come to think, I don't remember your bringing my passport away from the consulate. But you did, didn't you?"

"No; it's coming by mail," said the Major, comfortably.

"K—coming—by—mail!" gasped the lad; and all the dreadful things he had heard about the terrors and disasters of passportless visitors to Russia rose in his frightened mind and turned him white to the lips. "Oh, Major—oh, my goodness, what will become of me! How could you do such a thing?"

The Major laid a soothing hand upon the youth's shoulder and said:

"Now don't you worry, my boy, don't you worry a bit. I'm taking care of you, and I'm not going to let any harm come to you. The Chief Inspector knows me, and I'll explain to him, and it'll be all right—you'll see. Now don't you give yourself the least discomfort—I'll fix it all up, easy as nothing."

Alfred trembled, and felt a great sinking inside, but he did what he could to conceal his misery, and to respond with some show of heart to the Major's kindly pettings and reassurings.

At the frontier he got out and stood on the edge of the great crowd, and waited in deep anxiety while the Major ploughed his way through the mass to "explain to the Chief Inspector." It seemed a cruelly long wait, but at last the Major reappeared. He said, cheerfully, "Damnation, it's a new inspector, and I don't know him!"

Alfred fell up against a pile of trunks, with a despairing, "Oh, dear, dear, I might have known it!" and was slumping limp and helpless to the ground, but the Major gathered him up and seated him on a box, and sat down by him, with a supporting arm around him, and whispered in his ear:

"Don't worry, laddie, don't—it's going to be all right; you just trust to me. The sub-inspector's as near-sighted as a shad. I watched him, and I know it's so. Now I'll tell you how to do. I'll go and get my passport chalked, then I'll stop right yonder inside the grille where you see those peasants with their packs. You be there, and I'll back up against the grille, and slip my passport to you through the bars, then you tag along after the crowd and hand it in, and trust to Providence and that shad. Mainly the shad. You'll pull through all right—now don't you be afraid."

"But, oh dear, dear, your description and mine don't tally any more than—"

"Oh, that's all right—difference between fifty-one and nineteen—just entirely imperceptible to that shad—don't you fret, it's going to come out as right as nails."

Ten minutes later Alfred was tottering towards the train, pale, and in a collapse, but he had played the shad successfully, and was as grateful as an untaxed dog that has evaded the police.

"I told you so," said the Major, in splendid spirits. "I knew it would come out all right if you trusted in Providence like a little, trusting child and didn't try to improve on His ideas—it always does."

Between the frontier and Petersburg the Major laid himself out to restore his young comrade's life, and work up his circulation, and pull him out of his despondency, and make him feel again that life was a joy and worth living. And so, as a consequence, the young fellow entered the city in high feather and marched into the hotel in fine form, and registered his name. But instead of naming a room, the clerk glanced at him inquiringly, and waited. The Major came promptly to the rescue, and said, cordially:

"It's all right—you know me—set him down, I'm responsible." The clerk looked grave, and shook his head. The Major added: "It's all right, it'll be here in twenty-four hours—it's coming by mail. Here's mine, and his is coming right along."

The clerk was full of politeness, full of deference, but he was firm. He said, in English:

"Indeed, I wish I could accommodate you, Major, and certainly I would if I could; but I have no choice, I must ask him to go; I cannot allow him to remain in the house a moment."

Parrish began to totter, and emitted a moan; the Major caught him and stayed him with an arm, and said to the clerk, appealingly:

"Come, you know me—everybody does—just let him stay here the one night, and I give you my word—"

The clerk shook his head, and said:

"But, Major, you are endangering me, you are endangering the house. I—I hate to do such a thing, but I—I must call the police."

"Hold on, don't do that. Come along, my boy, and don't you fret—it's going to come out all right. Hi, there, cabby! Jump in, Parrish. Palace of the General of the Secret Police—turn them loose, cabby! Let them go! Make them whiz! Now we're off, and don't you give yourself any uneasiness. Prince Bossloffsky knows me, knows me like a book; he'll soon fix things all right for us."

They tore through the gay streets and arrived at the palace, which was brilliantly lighted. But it was half-past eight; the Prince was about going in to dinner, the sentinel said, and couldn't receive any one.

"But he'll receive me," said the Major, robustly, and handed his card. "I'm Major Jackson. Send it in; it'll be all right."

The card was sent in, under protest, and the Major and his waif waited in a reception-room for some time. At length they were sent for, and conducted to a sumptuous private office and confronted with the Prince, who stood there gorgeously arrayed and frowning like a thunder-cloud. The Major stated his case, and begged for a twenty-four-hour stay of proceedings until the passport should be forthcoming.

"Oh, impossible!" said the Prince, in faultless English. "I marvel that you should have done so insane a thing as to bring the lad into the country without a passport, Major, I marvel at it; why, it's ten years in Siberia, and no help for it—catch him! support him!" for poor Parrish was making another trip to the floor. "Here—quick, give him this. There—take another draught; brandy's the thing, don't you find it so, lad? Now you feel better, poor fellow. Lie down on the sofa. How stupid it was of you, Major, to get him into such a horrible scrape."

The Major eased the boy down with his strong arms, put a cushion under his head, and whispered in his ear:

"Look as damned sick as you can! Play it for all it's worth; he's touched, you see; got a tender heart under there somewhere; fetch a groan, and say, 'Oh, mamma, mamma'; it'll knock him out, sure as guns."

Parrish was going to do these things anyway, from native impulse, so they came from him promptly, with great and moving sincerity, and the Major whispered: "Splendid! Do it again; Bernhardt couldn't beat it."

What with the Major's eloquence and the boy's misery, the point was gained at last; the Prince struck his colors, and said:

"Have it your way; though you deserve a sharp lesson and you ought to get it. I give you exactly twenty-four hours. If the passport is not here then, don't come near me; it's Siberia without hope of pardon."

While the Major and the lad poured out their thanks, the Prince rang in a couple of soldiers, and in their own language he ordered them to go with these two people, and not lose sight of the younger one a moment for the next twenty-four hours; and if, at the end of that term, the boy could not show a passport, impound him in the dungeons of St. Peter and St. Paul, and report.

The unfortunates arrived at the hotel with their guards, dined under their eyes, remained in Parrish's room until the Major went off to bed, after cheering up the said Parrish, then one of the soldiers locked himself and Parrish in, and the other one stretched himself across the door outside and soon went off to sleep.

So also did not Alfred Parrish. The moment he was alone with the solemn soldier and the voiceless silence his machine-made cheerfulness began to waste away, his medicated courage began to give off its supporting gases and shrink towards normal, and his poor little heart to shrivel like a raisin. Within thirty minutes he struck bottom; grief, misery, fright, despair, could go no lower. Bed? Bed was not for such as he; bed was not for the doomed, the lost! Sleep? He was not the Hebrew children, he could not sleep in the fire! He could only walk the floor. And not only could, but must. And did, by the hour. And mourned, and wept, and shuddered, and prayed.

Then all-sorrowfully he made his last dispositions, and prepared himself, as well as in him lay, to meet his fate. As a final act, he wrote a letter:

"My darling Mother,—When these sad lines shall have reached you your poor Alfred will be no more. No; worse than that, far worse! Through my own fault and foolishness I have fallen into the hands of a sharper or a lunatic; I do not know which, but in either case I feel that I am lost. Sometimes I think he is a sharper, but most of the time I think he is only mad, for he has a kind, good heart, I know, and he certainly seems to try the hardest that ever a person tried to get me out of the fatal difficulties he has gotten me into.

"In a few hours I shall be one of a nameless horde plodding the snowy solitudes of Russia, under the lash, and bound for that land of mystery and misery and termless oblivion, Siberia! I shall not live to see it; my heart is broken and I shall die. Give my picture to her, and ask her to keep it in memory of me, and to so live that in the appointed time she may join me in that better world where there is no marriage nor giving in marriage, and where there are no more separations, and troubles never come. Give my yellow dog to Archy Hale, and the other one to Henry Taylor; my blazer I give to brother Will, and my fishing things and Bible.

"There is no hope for me. I cannot escape; the soldier stands there with his gun and never takes his eyes off me, just blinks; there is no other movement, any more than if he was dead. I cannot bribe him, the maniac has my money. My letter of credit is in my trunk, and may never come— will never come, I know. Oh, what is to become of me! Pray for me, darling mother, pray for your poor Alfred. But it will do no good."

IV.

In the morning Alfred came out looking scraggy and worn when the Major summoned him to an early breakfast. They fed their guards, they lit cigars, the Major loosened his tongue and set it going, and under its magic influence Alfred gradually and gratefully became hopeful, measurably cheerful, and almost happy once more.

But he would not leave the house. Siberia hung over him black and threatening, his appetite for sights was all gone, he could not have borne the shame of inspecting streets and galleries and churches with a soldier at each elbow and all the world stopping and staring and commenting—no, he would stay within and wait for the Berlin mail and his fate. So, all day long the Major stood gallantly by him in his room, with one soldier standing stiff and motionless against the door with his musket at his shoulder, and the other one drowsing in a chair outside; and all day long the faithful veteran spun campaign yarns, described battles, reeled off explosive anecdotes, with unconquerable energy and sparkle and resolution, and kept the scared student alive and his pulses functioning. The long day wore to a close, and the pair, followed by their guards, went down to the great dining-room and took their seats.

"The suspense will be over before long, now," sighed poor Alfred.

Just then a pair of Englishmen passed by, and one of them said, "So we'll get no letters from Berlin to-night."

Parrish's breath began to fail him. The Englishmen seated themselves at a near-by table, and the other one said:

"No, it isn't as bad as that." Parrish's breathing improved. "There is later telegraphic news. The accident did detain the train formidably, but that is all. It will arrive here three hours late to-night."

Parrish did not get to the floor this time, for the Major jumped for him in time. He had been listening, and foresaw what would happen. He patted Parrish on the back, hoisted him out of his chair, and said, cheerfully:

"Come along, my boy, cheer up, there's absolutely nothing to worry about. I know a way out. Bother the passport; let it lag a week if it wants to, we can do without it."

Parrish was too sick to hear him; hope was gone, Siberia present; he moved off on legs of lead, upheld by the Major, who walked him to the American legation, heartening him on the way with assurances that on his recommendation the minister wouldn't hesitate a moment to grant him a new passport.

"I had that card up my sleeve all the time," he said. "The minister knows me—knows me familiarly—chummed together hours and hours under a pile of other wounded at Cold Harbor; been chummies ever since, in spirit, though we haven't met much in the body. Cheer up, laddie, every-thing's looking splendid! By gracious! I feel as cocky as a buck angel. Here we are, and our troubles are at an end! If we ever really had any."

There, alongside the door, was the trade-mark of the richest and freest and mightiest republic of all the ages: the pine disk, with the planked eagle spread upon it, his head and shoulders among the stars, and his claws full of out-of-date war material; and at that sight the tears came into Alfred's eyes, the pride of country rose in his heart, "Hail Columbia" boomed up in his breast, and all his fears and sorrows vanished away; for here he was safe,

safe! Not all the powers of the earth would venture to cross that threshold to lay a hand upon him!

For economy's sake the mightiest republic's legations in Europe consist of a room and a half on the ninth floor, when the tenth is occupied, and the legation furniture consists of a minister or an ambassador with a brakeman's salary, a secretary of legation who sells matches and mends crockery for a living, hired girl for interpreter and general utility, pictures of the American liners, a chromo of the reigning President, a desk, three chairs, kerosene-lamp, a cat, a clock, and a cuspidor with motto, "In God We Trust."

The party climbed up there, followed by the escort. A man sat at the desk writing official things on wrapping-paper with a nail. He rose and faced about; the cat climbed down and got under the desk; the hired girl squeezed herself up into the corner by the vodka-jug to make room; the soldiers squeezed themselves up against the wall alongside of her, with muskets at shoulder arms. Alfred was radiant with happiness and the sense of rescue. The Major cordially shook hands with the official, rattled off his case in easy and fluent style, and asked for the desired passport.

The official seated his guests, then said: "Well, I am only the secretary of legation, you know, and I wouldn't like to grant a passport while the minister is on Russian soil. There is far too much responsibility."

"All right, send for him."

The secretary smiled, and said: "That's easier said than done. He's away up in the wilds, somewhere, on his vacation."

"Ger-reat Scott!" ejaculated the Major.

Alfred groaned; the color went out of his face, and he began to slowly collapse in his clothes. The secretary said, wonderingly:

"Why, what are you Great-Scotting about, Major? The Prince gave you twenty-four hours. Look at the clock; you're all right; you've half an hour left; the train is just due; the passport will arrive in time."

"Man, there's news! The train is three hours behind time! This boy's life and liberty are wasting away by minutes, and only thirty of them left! In half an hour he's the same as dead and damned to all eternity! By God, we must have the passport!"

"Oh, I am dying, I know it!" wailed the lad, and buried his face in his arms on the desk. A quick change came over the secretary, his placidity vanished away, excitement flamed up in his face and eyes, and he exclaimed:

"I see the whole ghastliness of the situation, but, Lord help us, what can I do? What can you suggest?"

"Why, hang it, give him the passport!"

"Impossible! Totally impossible! You know nothing about him; three days ago you had never heard of him; there's no way in the world to identify him. He is lost, lost—there's no possibility of saving him!"

The boy groaned again, and sobbed out, "Lord, Lord, it's the last of earth for Alfred Parrish!"

Another change came over the secretary.

In the midst of a passionate outburst of pity, vexation, and hopelessness, he stopped short, his manner calmed down, and he asked, in the indifferent voice which one uses in introducing the subject of the weather when there is nothing to talk about, "Is that your name?"

The youth sobbed out a yes.

"Where are you from?"

"Bridgeport."

The secretary shook his head—shook it again—and muttered to himself. After a moment:

"Born there?"

"No; New Haven."

"Ah-h." The secretary glanced at the Major, who was listening intently, with blank and unenlightened face, and indicated rather than said, "There is vodka there, in case the soldiers are thirsty. The Major sprang up, poured for them, and received their gratitude. The questioning went on.

"How long did you live in New Haven?"

"Till I was fourteen. Came back two years ago to enter Yale."

"When you lived there, what street did you live on?"

"Parker Street."

With a vague half-light of comprehension dawning in his eye, the

Major glanced an inquiry at the secretary. The secretary nodded, the Major poured vodka again.

"What number?"

"It hadn't any."

The boy sat up and gave the secretary a pathetic look which said, "Why do you want to torture me with these foolish things, when I am miserable enough without it?"

The secretary went on, unheeding: "What kind of a house was it?"

"Brick—two-story."

"Flush with the sidewalk?"

"No, small yard in front."

"Iron fence?"

"No, palings."

The Major poured vodka again—without instructions—poured brimmers this time; and his face had cleared and was alive now.

"What do you see when you enter the door?"

"A narrow hall; door at the end of it, and a door at your right."

"Anything else?"

"Hat-rack."

"Room at the right?"

"Parlor."

"Carpet?"

"Yes."

"Kind of carpet?"

"Old-fashioned Wilton."

"Figures?"

"Yes—hawking-party, horseback."

The Major cast an eye at the clock—only six minutes left! He faced about with the jug, and as he poured he glanced at the secretary, then at the clock—inquiringly. The secretary nodded; the Major covered the clock from view with his body a moment, and set the hands back half an hour; then he refreshed the men—double rations.

"Room beyond the hall and hat-rack?"

"Dining-room."

"Stove?"

"Grate."

"Did your people own the house?"

"Yes."

"Do they own it yet?"

"No; sold it when we moved to Bridgeport."

The secretary paused a little, then said, "Did you have a nickname among your playmates?"

The color slowly rose in the youth's pale cheeks, and he dropped his eyes. He seemed to struggle with himself a moment or two, then he said, plaintively, "They called me Miss Nancy."

The secretary mused awhile, then he dug up another question:

"Any ornaments in the dining-room?"

"Well, y—no."

"None? None at all?"

"No."

"The mischief! Isn't that a little odd? Think!"

The youth thought and thought; the secretary waited, slightly panting. At last the imperilled waif looked up sadly and shook his head.

"Think—think!" cried the Major, in anxious solicitude; and poured again.

"Come!" said the secretary, "not even a picture?"

"Oh, certainly! But you said ornament."

"Ah! What did your father think of it?"

The color rose again. The boy was silent.

"Speak," said the secretary.

"Speak," cried the Major, and his trembling hand poured more vodka outside the glasses than inside.

"I—I can't tell you what he said," murmured the boy.

"Quick! quick!" said the secretary; "out with it; there's no time to lose—home and liberty or Siberia and death depend upon the answer."

"Oh, have pity! He is a clergyman, and—"

"No matter; out with it, or—"

"He said it was the hellfiredest nightmare he ever struck!"

"Saved!" shouted the secretary, and seized his nail and a blank passport. "I identify you; I've lived in the house, and I painted the picture myself!"

"Oh, come to my arms, my poor rescued boy!" cried the Major. "We will always be grateful to God that He made this artist!—if He did."

Nude Bathers

FROM *Daily Alta California*, NOVEMBER 3, 1867

ALTA LETTER 22

Odessa, Russia, August 22d.

If there is one thing that is really cheerful in the world, it is cheerfulness. I have noticed it often. And I have noticed that when a man is right down cheerful, he is seldom unhappy for the time being. Such is the nature of man. Now I have often thought that our style of bathing was rather reserved than otherwise, and lacked many elements of cheerfulness. But you cannot say that of the Russian style. I watched a party of them at it this afternoon in the harbor, and it is really nice. The men and women, and boys and girls, all go in together, along about noon, and the men don't wear anything at all, the boys don't, the little girls don't, and the young women and the old women usually wear a single white thin garment with ruffles around the top of it and short sleeves (which I have forgotten the name of it), but this would be a very good apology for a bathing dress, if it would only stay down. But it don't do it. It will float up around their necks in the most scandalous way, and the water is clear, and yet they don't seem to know enough to kick up the mud on the bottom. I never was so outraged in my life. At least a hundred times, in the seven hours I stayed there, I would just have got up and gone away from there disgusted, if I had had any place to go to. Several times I had a mind to go anyhow. Why, those young ladies thought no more of turning somersaults, when I was not looking, than nothing in the world. Incensed as I was, I was compelled to look, most of the time, during this barbarous exhibition, because it forced them to make a show of modesty, at least. Yet it wouldn't even have accomplished that, if they hadn't been so fond of show naturally.

Well, you can't conceive of it. It was awful. But sometimes my outraged feelings were crowded down by my fears for the safety of those girls. They were so reckless. One splendid-looking young woman went in with nothing on but a shawl, and she kept it wrapped around her so that I was afraid all the time that she would tangle her feet in its long fringes and drown herself. My solicitude became so unbearable at last that I went and signified to her that if she wanted to take off her shawl I would hold it for her. But she only kicked up her heels and dived out of sight. I just took her to be one of your high-flyer, mock-modest kind, and left her to her fate. But she was the handsomest girl in the party, and it was a pity to see her endangering her life in that way.

I said to Brown: "It makes my heart bleed to look upon this unhallowed scene."

"We better go, then," he said. "If you stay here seven more hours you might bleed to death."

So we went away. But it was marvellously cheerful bathing.

Mark Twain in the Cradle of Liberty

FROM MARK TWAIN'S TRAVEL LETTERS FROM 1891–92

***Chicago Daily Tribune*, March 6, 1892**

It is a good many years since I was in Switzerland last. In that remote time there was only one ladder railway in the country. That state of things is all changed. There isn't a mountain in Switzerland now that hasn't a ladder railroad or two up its back like suspenders; indeed, some mountains are latticed with them, and two years hence all will be. In that day the peasant of the high altitudes will have to carry a lantern when he goes visiting in the night to keep from stumbling over railroads that have been built since his last round. And also in that day, if there shall remain a high-altitude peasant whose potato-patch hasn't a railroad through it, it will make him as conspicuous as William Tell.

However, there are only two best ways to travel through Switzerland. The first best is afoot. The second best is by open two-horse carriage. One can come from Lucerne to Interlaken over the Brunig by ladder railroad in an hour or so now, but you can glide smoothly in a carriage in ten, and have two hours for luncheon at noon. For luncheon, not for rest. There is no fatigue connected with the trip. One arrives fresh in spirit and in person in the evening—no fret in his heart, no grime on his face, no grit in his hair, not a cinder in his eye. This is the right condition of mind and body, the right and due preparation for the solemn event which closed the day— stepping with metaphorically uncovered head into the presence of the most impressive mountain mass that the globe can show—the Jungfrau.

The stranger's first feeling, when suddenly confronted by that towering and awful apparition wrapped in its shroud of snow, is breath-taking astonishment. It is as if heaven's gates had swung open and exposed the throne.

It is peaceful here and pleasant at Interlaken. Nothing going on—at least nothing but brilliant life-giving sunshine. There are floods and floods of that. One may properly speak of it as "going on," for it is full of the suggestion of activity; the light pours down with energy, with visible enthusiasm. This is a good atmosphere to be in, morally as well as physically. After trying the political atmosphere of the neighboring monarchies, it is healing and refreshing to breathe in air that has known no taint of slavery for six hundred years, and to come among a people whose political history is great and fine, and worthy to be taught in all schools and studied by all races and peoples. For the struggle here throughout the centuries has not been in the interest of any private family, or any church, but in the interest of the whole body of the nation, and for shelter and protection of all forms of belief. This fact is colossal. If one would realize how colossal it is, and of what dignity and majesty, let him contrast it with the purposes and objects of the Crusades, the siege of York, the War of the Roses, and other historic comedies of that sort and size.

Last week I was beating around the Lake of Four Cantons, and I saw Rütli and Altorf. Rütli is a remote little patch of a meadow, but I do not know how any piece of ground could be holier or better worth crossing oceans and continents to see, since it was there that the great trinity of Switzerland joined hands six centuries ago and swore the oath which set their enslaved and insulted country forever free; and Altorf is also honorable ground and worshipful, since it was there that William, surnamed Tell (which interpreted means "The foolish talker," that is to say, the too daring talker), refused to bow to Gessler's hat. Of late years the prying student of history has been delighting himself beyond measure over a wonderful find which he has made—to wit, that Tell did not shoot the apple from his son's head. To hear the students jubilate, one would suppose that the question of whether Tell shot the apple or didn't was an important matter; whereas it ranks in importance exactly with the question of whether Washington chopped down the cherry tree or didn't. The deeds of Washington, the patriot, are the essential thing; the cherry tree incident is of no consequence. To prove that Tell did shoot the apple from his son's head would merely prove that he had better nerve than most men and was as skilful with a bow as a million others who preceded and followed him, but not one whit more so. But Tell was more and better than a mere marksman, more and better than a mere cool head; he was a type; he stands for Swiss patriotism; in his person was represented a whole people; his spirit was their spirit—the spirit which would bow to none but God, the spirit which said this in words and confirmed it with deeds. There have always been Tells in Switzerland—people who would not bow. There was a sufficiency of them at Rütli; there were plenty of them at Murten; plenty at Grandson; there are plenty to-day. And the first of them all—the very first, earliest banner-bearer of human freedom in this world—was not a man, but a woman—Stauffacher's wife. There she looms dim and great, through the haze of the centuries, delivering into her husband's ear that gospel of revolt which was to bear fruit in the conspiracy of Rütli and the birth of the first free government the world had ever seen.

THURSDAY, Sept. 10.—

From this Victoria Hotel one looks straight across a flat of trifling width to a lofty mountain barrier, which has a gateway in it shaped like an inverted pyramid. Beyond this gateway arises the vast bulk of the Jungfrau, a spotless mass of gleaming snow, into the sky. The gateway, in the dark-colored barrier, makes a strong frame for the great picture. The somber frame and the glowing snow-pile are startlingly contrasted. It is this frame which concentrates and emphasizes the glory of the Jungfrau and makes it the most engaging and beguiling and fascinating spectacle that exists on the earth. There are many mountains of snow that are as lofty as the Jungfrau and as nobly proportioned, but they lack the fame. They stand at large; they are intruded upon and elbowed by neighboring domes and summits, and their grandeur is diminished and fails of effect.

It is a good name, Jungfrau—Virgin. Nothing could be whiter; nothing could be purer; nothing could be saintlier of aspect. At 6 yesterday evening the great intervening barrier seen through a faint bluish haze seemed made of air and substanceless, so soft and rich it was, so shimmering where the wandering lights touched it and so dim where the shadows lay. Apparently it was a dream stuff, a work of the imagination, nothing real about it. The tint was green, slightly varying shades of it, but mainly very dark. The sun was down—as far as that barrier was concerned, but not for the Jungfrau, towering into the heavens beyond the gateway. She was a roaring conflagration of blinding white.

It is said that Fridolin (the holy Fridolin), a new saint, but formerly a missionary, gave the mountain its gracious name. He was an Irishman, son of an Irish king—there were 30,000 kings reigning in County Cork alone in his time, 1,500 years ago. It got so that they could not make a living, there was so much competition and wages got cut so. Some of them were out of work months at a time, with wife and little children to feed, and not a crust in the place. At last a particularly severe winter fell upon the country, and hundreds of them were reduced to mendicancy and were to be seen day after day in the bitterest weather, standing barefoot in the snow, holding out their crowns for alms.

Indeed, they would have been obliged to emigrate or starve but for a fortunate idea of Prince Fridolin's, who started a labor-union, the first one in history, and got the great bulk of them to join it. He thus won the general gratitude, and they wanted to make him emperor—emperor over them all—emperor of County Cork, but he said no, walking delegate was good enough for him. For behold, he was modest beyond his years, and keen as a whip. To this day in Germany and Switzerland, where St. Fridolin is deeply revered and honored, the peasantry speak of him affectionately as the first walking delegate.

The first walk he took was into France and Germany, missionarying— for missionarying was a better thing in those days than it is in ours. All you had to do was to cure the head savage's sick daughter by a "miracle"— a miracle like the miracle of Lourdes in our day, for instance—and immediately that head savage was your convert; he was your convert and filled to the eyes with a new convert's enthusiasm. You could sit down and make yourself easy, now. He would take the ax and convert the rest of the nation himself. Charlemagne was that kind of a walking delegate.

Yes, there were great missionaries in those days, for the methods were sure and the rewards great. We have no such missionaries now, and no such methods.

But to continue the history of the first walking delegate, if you are interested. I am interested myself because I have seen his relics at Sackingen, and also the very spot where he worked his great miracle—the one which won him his saintship in the Papal C Court a few centuries later. To have seen these things makes me feel very near to him, almost like a member of the family, in fact. While wandering about the continent he arrived at the spot on the Rhine which is now occupied by Sackingen, and proposed to settle there, but the people warned him off. He appealed to the King of the Franks, who made him a present of the whole region, people and all. He built a great cloister there for women and proceeded to teach in it and accumulate more land. There were two wealthy brothers in the neighborhood, Urso and Landulph. Urso died and Fridolin claimed his estates. Landulph asked for documents and papers. Fridolin had none to show. He said the bequest had been made to him by word of mouth. Landulph suggested that he produce a witness and said it in a way which he thought was very witty, very sarcastic. This shows that he did not know the walking delegate. Fridolin was not disturbed. He said:

"Appoint your court. I will bring a witness."

The court thus created consisted of fifteen Counts and Barons. A day was appointed for the trial of the case. On that day the Judges took their seats in state, and proclamation was made that the court was ready for business. Five minutes, ten minutes, fifteen minutes passed, and yet no Fridolin appeared. Landulph rose, and was in the act of claiming judgment by default when a strange clacking sound was heard coming up the stairs. In another moment Fridolin entered at the door and came walking in a deep hush down the middle aisle, with a tall skeleton stalking in his rear.

Amazement and terror sat upon every countenance, for everybody suspected that the skeleton was Urso's. It stopped before the chief judge and raised its bony arm aloft and began to speak, while all the assembly shuddered, for they could see the words leak out between its ribs. It said:

"Brother, why dost thou disturb my blessed rest and withhold by robbery the gift which I gave thee for the honor of God?"

It seems a strange thing and most irregular, but the verdict was actually given against Landulph on the testimony of this wandering rack-heap of unidentified bones. In our day a skeleton would not be allowed to testify at all, for a skeleton has no moral responsibility, and its word could not be rationally trusted. Most skeletons are not to be believed on oath, and this was probably one of them. However, the incident is valuable as preserving to us a curious sample of the quaint laws of evidence of that remote time—a time so remote, so far back toward the beginning of original idiocy, that the difference between a bench of judges and a basket of vegetables was as yet so slight that we may say with all confidence that it didn't really exist.

Sunday—During several afternoons I have been engaged in an interesting, maybe useful, piece of work—that is to say, I have been trying to make the mighty Jungfrau earn her living—earn it in a most humble sphere, but on a prodigious scale, on a prodigious scale of necessity, for she couldn't do anything in a small way with her size and style. I have been trying to make her do service on a stupendous dial and check off the hours as they glide along her pallid face up there against the sky, and tell the time of day to the populations lying within fifty miles of her and to the people in the moon, if they have a good telescope there.

Until late in the afternoon the Jungfrau's aspect is that of a spotless desert of snow set upon edge against the sky. But by mid-afternoon some elevations which rise out of the western border of the desert, whose presence you perhaps had not detected or suspected up to that time, begin to cast black shadows eastward across the gleaming surface. At first there is only one shadow; later there are two. Toward 4 p.m. the other day I was gazing and worshiping as usual when I chanced to notice that shadow No. 1 was beginning to take itself something of the shape of the human profile. By 4 the back of the head was good, the military cap was pretty good, the nose was bold and strong, the upper lip sharp, but not pretty, and there was a great goatee that shot straight aggressively forward from the chin.

At 4:30 the nose had changed its shape considerably, and the altered slant of the sun had revealed and made conspicuous a huge buttress or barrier of naked rock which was so located as to answer very well for a shoulder or coat collar to this swarthy and indiscreet sweetheart who had stolen out there right before everybody to pillow his head on the Virgin's white breast and whisper soft sentimentalities to her to the sensuous music of crashing ice domes and the boom and thunder of the passing avalanche—music very familiar to his ear, for he has heard it every afternoon at this hour since the day he first came courting this child of the earth, who lives in the sky, and that day is far, yes—for he was at this pleasant sport before the Middle Ages drifted by him in the valley; before the Romans marched past, and before the antique and recordless barbarians fished and hunted here and wondered who he might be, and were probably afraid of him; and before primeval man himself, just emerged from his four-footed estate, stepped out upon this plain, first sample of his race, a thousand centuries ago, and cast a glad eye up there, judging he had found a brother human being and consequently something to kill; and before the big saurians wallowed here, still some eons earlier. O, yes, a day so far back that the eternal son was present to see that first visit; a day so far back that neither tradition nor history was born yet and a whole weary eternity must come and go before the restless little creature, of whose face this stupendous Shadow-Face was the prophecy, would arrive in the earth and begin his shabby career and think it a big thing. O, indeed yes; when you talk about your poor Roman and Egyptian day-before-yesterday antiquities, you should choose a time when the hoary Shadow-Face of the Jungfrau is not by. It antedates all antiquities known or imaginable; for it was here the world itself created the theater of future antiquities. And it is the only witness with a human face that was there to see the marvel, and remains to us a memorial of it.

By 4:40 P.M. the nose of the shadow is perfect and is beautiful. It is black and is powerfully marked against the upright canvas of glowing snow, and covers hundreds of acres of that resplendent surface.

Meantime shadow No. 2 has been creeping out well to the rear of the face west of it—and at 5 o'clock has assumed a shape that has rather a poor and rude semblance of a shoe.

Meantime, also, the great Shadow-Face has been gradually changing for twenty minutes, and now, 5 p.m., it is becoming a quite fair portrait of Roscoe Conkling. The likeness is there, and is unmistakable. The goatee is shortened, now, and has an end; formerly it hadn't any, but ran off eastward and arrived nowhere.

By 6 P.M. the Face has dissolved and gone, and the goatee has become what looks like the shadow of a tower with a pointed roof, and the shoe had turned into what the printers call a "fist" with a finger pointing.

If I were now imprisoned on a mountain summit a hundred miles northward of this point, and was denied a timepiece, I could get along well enough from 4 till 6 on clear days, for I could keep trace of the time by the changing shapes of these mighty shadows on the Virgin's front, the most stupendous dial I am acquainted with, the oldest clock in the world by a couple of million years.

I suppose I should not have noticed the forms of the shadows if I hadn't the habit of hunting for faces in the clouds and in mountain crags— a sort of amusement which is very entertaining even when you don't find any, and brilliantly satisfying when you do. I have searched through several bushels of photographs of the Jungfrau here, but found only one with the Face in it, and in this case it was not strictly recognizable as a face, which was evidence that the picture was taken before 4 in the afternoon, and also evidence that all the photographers have persistently overlooked one of the most fascinating features of the Jungfrau show. I say fascinating, because if you once detect a human face produced on a great plan by unconscious nature, you never get tired of watching it. At first you can't make another person see it at all, but after he has made it out once he can't see anything else afterward.

The King of Greece is a man who goes around quietly enough when off duty. One day this summer he was traveling in an ordinary first-class compartment, just in his other suit, the one which he works the realm in when he is at home, and so he was not looking like anybody in particular, but a good deal like everybody in general. By and by a hearty and healthy German-American got in and opened up a frank and interesting and sympathetic conversation with him, and asked him a couple of thousand questions about himself, which the king answered good-naturedly, but in a more or less indefinite way as to private particulars.

"Where do you live when you are at home?"

"In Greece."

"Greece! Well, now, that is just astonishing! Born there?"

"Yes."

"Do you speak Greek?"

"Yes."

"Now, ain't that strange! I never expected to live to see that. What is your trade? I mean how do you get your living? What is your line of business?"

"Well, I hardly know how to answer. I am only a kind of foreman, on a salary; and the business—well, is a very general kind of business."

"Yes, I understand—general jobbing—little of everything—anything that there's money in."

"That's about it, yes."

"Are you traveling for the house now?"

"Well, partly; but not entirely. Of course I do a stroke of business if it falls in the way—"

"Good! I like that in you! That's me every time. Go on."

"I was only going to say I am off on my vacation now."

"Well, that's all right. No harm in that. A man works all the better for a little let-up now and then. Not that I've been used to having it myself; for I haven't. I reckon this is my first. I was born in Germany, and when I was a couple of weeks old shipped for America, and I've been there ever since, and that's sixty-four years by the watch. I'm an American in principle and a German at heart, and it's the boss combination. Well, how do you get along, as a rule—pretty fair?"

"I've a rather large family—"

"There, that's it—big family and trying to raise them on a salary. Now, what did you go to do that for?"

"Well, I thought—"

"Of course you did. You were young and confident and thought you could branch out and make things go with a whirl, and here you are, you see! But never mind about that. I'm not trying to discourage you. Dear me, I've been just where you are myself. You've got good grit; there's good stuff in you, I can see that. You got a wrong start, that's the whole trouble. But you hold your grip, and we'll see what can be done. Your case ain't half as bad as it might be. You are going to come out all right—I'm bail for that. Boys and girls?"

"My family? Yes, some of them are boys—"

"And the rest girls. It's just as I expected. But that's all right, and it's better so, anyway. What are the boys doing—learning a trade?"

"Well, no—I thought—"

"It's a great mistake. It's the biggest mistake you ever made. You see that in your own case. A man ought always to have a trade to fall back on. Now, I was harness-maker at first. Did that prevent me from becoming one of the biggest brewers in America? Oh no. I always had the harness trick to fall back on in rough weather. Now, if you had learned how to make a harness—however, it's too late now; too late; and it's no good plan to cry over spilt milk. But as to the boys, you see—what's to become of them if anything happens to you?"

"It has been my idea to let the eldest one succeed me—"

"O, come! Suppose the firm don't want him?"

"I hadn't thought of that, but—"

"Now, look here; you want to get right down to business and stop dreaming. You are capable of immense things—man. You can make a perfect success in life; all you want is somebody to steady you and boost you along on the right road. Do you own anything in the business?"

"No—not exactly; but if I continue to give satisfaction, I suppose I can keep my—"

"Keep your place—yes. Well, don't you depend on anything of the kind. They'll bounce you the minute you get a little old and worked out; they'll do it sure. Can't you manage somehow to get into the firm? That's the great thing, you know."

"I think it is doubtful, very doubtful."

"Um—that's bad—yes, and unfair, too. Do you suppose that if I should go there and have a talk with your people—Look here—do you think you could run a brewery?"

"I have never tried, but I think I could do it after I got a little familiarity with the business."

The German was silent for some time. He did a good deal of thinking, and the king waited with curiosity to see what the result was going to be. Finally the German said:

"My mind's made up. You leave that crowd—you'll never amount to anything there. In these old countries they never give a fellow a show. Yes, you come over to America—come to my place in Rochester; bring the family along. You shall have a show in the business and the foremanship, besides. George—you said your name was George?—I'll make a man of you. I give you my word. You've never had a chance here, but that's all going to change. By gracious! I'll give you a lift that'll make your hair curl!"

A Holiday Flight through France

FROM *The Innocents Abroad,* CHAPTER XII

We have come five hundred miles by rail through the heart of France. What a bewitching land it is! What a garden! Surely the leagues of bright green lawns are swept and brushed and watered every day and their grasses trimmed by the barber. Surely the hedges are shaped and measured and their symmetry preserved by the most architectural of gardeners. Surely the long straight rows of stately poplars that divide the beautiful landscape like the squares of a checker-board are set with line and plummet, and their uniform height determined with a spirit level. Surely the straight, smooth, pure white turnpikes are jack-planed and sand-papered every day. How else are these marvels of symmetry, cleanliness, and order attained? It is wonderful. There are no unsightly stone walls and never a fence of any kind. There is no dirt, no decay, no rubbish anywhere—nothing that even hints at untidiness—nothing that ever suggests neglect. All is orderly and beautiful—every thing is charming to the eye.

We had such glimpses of the Rhone gliding along between its grassy banks; of cosy cottages buried in flowers and shrubbery; of quaint old red-tiled villages with mossy medieval cathedrals looming out of their midst; of wooded hills with ivy-grown towers and turrets of feudal castles projecting above the foliage; such glimpses of Paradise, it seemed to us, such visions of fabled fairyland!

We knew then what the poet meant when he sang of: "—thy cornfields green, and sunny vines, O pleasant land of France!"

And it is a pleasant land. No word describes it so felicitously as that one. They say there is no word for "home" in the French language. Well, considering that they have the article itself in such an attractive aspect, they ought to manage to get along without the word. Let us not waste too much pity on "homeless" France. I have observed that Frenchmen abroad seldom wholly give up the idea of going back to France some time or other. I am not surprised at it now.

We are not infatuated with these French railway cars, though. We took first-class passage, not because we wished to attract attention by doing a thing which is uncommon in Europe but because we could make our journey quicker by so doing. It is hard to make railroading pleasant in any country. It is too tedious. Stagecoaching is infinitely more delightful. Once I crossed the plains and deserts and mountains of the West in a stagecoach, from the Missouri line to California, and since then all my pleasure trips must be measured to that rare holiday frolic. Two thousand miles of cease-less rush and rattle and clatter, by night and by day, and never a weary moment, never a lapse of interest! The first seven hundred miles a level continent, its grassy carpet greener and softer and smoother than any sea and figured with designs fitted to its magnitude—the shadows of the clouds. Here were no scenes but summer scenes, and no disposition inspired by them but to lie at full length on the mail sacks in the grateful breeze and dreamily smoke the pipe of peace—what other, where all was repose and contentment? In cool mornings, before the sun was fairly up, it was worth a lifetime of city toiling and moiling to perch in the foretop with the driver and see the six mustangs scamper under the sharp snapping of the whip that never touched them; to scan the blue distances of a world that knew no lords but us; to cleave the wind with uncovered head and feel the sluggish pulses rousing to the spirit of a speed that pretended to the resistless rush of a typhoon! Then thirteen hundred miles of desert solitudes; of limitless panoramas of bewildering perspective; of mimic cities, of pinnacled cathedrals, of massive fortresses, counterfeited in the eternal rocks and splendid with the crimson and gold of the setting sun; of dizzy altitudes among fog-wreathed peaks and never-melting snows, where thunders and lightnings and tempests warred magnificently at our feet and the storm clouds above swung their shredded banners in our very faces! But I forgot. I am in elegant France now, and not scurrying through the great South Pass and the Wind River Mountains, among antelopes and buffaloes and painted Indians on the warpath. It is not meet that I should make too disparaging comparisons between humdrum travel on a railway and that royal summer flight across a continent in a stagecoach. I meant in the beginning to say that railway journeying is tedious and tiresome, and so it is—though at the time I was thinking particularly of a dismal fifty-hour pilgrimage between New York and St. Louis. Of course our trip through France was not really tedious because all its scenes and experiences were new and strange; but as Dan says, it had its "discrepancies."

The cars are built in compartments that hold eight persons each. Each compartment is partially subdivided, and so there are two tolerably distinct parties of four in it. Four face the other four. The seats and backs are thickly padded and cushioned and are very comfortable; you can smoke if you wish; there are no bothersome peddlers; you are saved the infliction of a multitude of disagreeable fellow passengers. So far, so well. But then the conductor locks you in when the train starts; there is no water to drink in the car; there is no heating apparatus for night travel; if a drunken rowdy should get in, you could not remove a matter of twenty seats from him or enter another car; but above all, if you are worn out and must sleep, you must sit up and do it in naps, with cramped legs and in a torturing misery that leaves you withered and lifeless the next day—for behold they have not that culmination of all charity and human kindness, a sleeping car, in all France. I prefer the American system. It has not so many grievous "discrepancies."

In France, all is clockwork, all is order. They make no mistakes. Every third man wears a uniform, and whether he be a marshal of the empire or a brakeman, he is ready and perfectly willing to answer all your questions with tireless politeness, ready to tell you which car to take, yea, and ready to go and put you into it to make sure that you shall not go astray. You cannot pass into the waiting room of the depot till you have secured your ticket, and you cannot pass from its only exit till the train is at its threshold to receive you. Once on board, the train will not start till your ticket has been examined—till every passenger's ticket has been inspected. This is chiefly for your own good. If by any possibility you have managed to take the wrong train, you will be handed over to a polite official who will take you whither you belong and bestow you with many an affable bow. Your ticket will be inspected every now and then along the route, and when it is time to change cars you will know it. You are in the hands of officials who zealously study your welfare and your interest, instead of turning their talents to the invention of new methods of discommoding and snubbing you, as is very often the main employment of that exceedingly self-satisfied monarch, the railroad conductor of America.

But the happiest regulation in French railway government is—thirty minutes to dinner! No five-minute boltings of flabby rolls, muddy coffee, questionable eggs, gutta-percha beef, and pies whose conception and execution are a dark and bloody mystery to all save the cook that created them! No, we sat calmly down—it was in old Dijon, which is so easy to spell and so impossible to pronounce except when you civilize it and call it Demijohn—and poured out rich Burgundian wines and munched calmly through a long *table d'hôte* bill of fare, snail patties, delicious fruits and all, then paid the trifle it cost and stepped happily aboard the train again, without once cursing the railroad company. A rare experience and one to be treasured forever.

Versailles

FROM *The Innocents Abroad,* CHAPTER XVI

Versailles! It is wonderfully beautiful! You gaze and stare and try to understand that it is real, that it is on the earth, that it is not the Garden of Eden—but your brain grows giddy, stupefied by the world of beauty around you, and you half believe you are the dupe of an exquisite dream. The scene thrills one like military music! A noble palace, stretching its ornamented front, block upon block away, till it seemed that it would never end; a grand promenade before it, whereon the armies of an empire might parade; all about it rainbows of flowers, and colossal statues that were almost numberless and yet seemed only scattered over the ample space; broad flights of stone steps leading down from the promenade to lower grounds of the park—stairways that whole regiments might stand to arms upon and have room to spare; vast fountains whose great bronze effigies discharged rivers of sparkling water into the air and mingled a hundred curving jets together in forms of matchless beauty; wide grass-carpeted avenues that branched hither and thither in every direction and wandered to seemingly interminable distances, walled all the way on either side with compact ranks of leafy trees whose branches met above and formed arches as faultless and as symmetrical as ever were carved in stone; and here and there were glimpses of sylvan lakes with miniature ships glassed in their surfaces. And every where—on the palace steps, and the great promenade, around the fountains, among the trees, and far under the arches of the endless avenues—hundreds and hundreds of people in gay costumes walked or ran or danced, and gave to the fairy picture the life and animation which was all of perfection it could have lacked.

It was worth a pilgrimage to see. Everything is on so gigantic a scale. Nothing is small—nothing is cheap. The statues are all large; the palace is grand; the park covers a fair-sized county; the avenues are interminable. All the distances and all the dimensions about Versailles are vast. I used to think the pictures exaggerated these distances and these dimensions beyond all reason, and that they made Versailles more beautiful than it was possible for any place in the world to be. I know now that the pictures never came up to the subject in any respect, and that no painter could represent Versailles on canvas as beautiful as it is in reality. I used to abuse Louis XIV for spending two hundred millions of dollars in creating this marvelous park, when bread was so scarce with some of his subjects; but I have forgiven him now. He took a tract of land sixty miles in circumference and set to work to make this park and build this palace and a road to it from Paris. He kept 36,000 men employed daily on it, and the labor was so unhealthy that they used to die and be hauled off by cartloads every night. The wife of a nobleman of the time speaks of this as an "inconvenience," but naively remarks that "it does not seem worthy of attention in the happy state of tranquillity we now enjoy."

I always thought ill of people at home who trimmed their shrubbery into pyramids and squares and spires and all manner of unnatural shapes, and when I saw the same thing being practiced in this great park I began to feel dissatisfied. But I soon saw the idea of the thing and the wisdom of it. They seek the general effect. We distort a dozen sickly trees into unaccustomed shapes in a little yard no bigger than a dining room, and then surely they look absurd enough. But here they take two hundred thousand tall forest trees and set them in a double row; allow no sign of leaf or branch to grow on the trunk lower down than six feet above the ground; from that point the boughs begin to project, and very gradually they extend outward further and further till they meet overhead, and a faultless tunnel of foliage is formed. The arch is mathematically precise. The effect is then very fine. They make trees take fifty different shapes, and so these quaint effects are infinitely varied and picturesque. The trees in no two avenues are shaped alike, and consequently the eye is not fatigued with anything in the nature of monotonous uniformity. I will drop this subject now, leaving it to others to determine how these people manage to make endless ranks of lofty forest trees grow to just a certain thickness of trunk (say a foot and two-thirds); how they make them spring to precisely the same height for miles; how they make them grow so close together; how they compel one huge limb to spring from the same identical spot on each tree and form the main sweep of the arch; and how all these things are kept exactly in the same condition and in the same exquisite shapeliness and symmetry month after month and year after year—for I have tried to reason out the problem and have failed.

We walked through the great hall of sculpture and the one hundred and fifty galleries of paintings in the palace of Versailles, and felt that to be in such a place was useless unless one had a whole year at his disposal. These pictures are all battle scenes, and only one solitary little canvas among them all treats of anything but great French victories. We wandered, also, through the Grand Trianon and the Petit Trianon, those monuments of royal prodigality, and with histories so mournful—filled, as it is, with souvenirs of Napoleon the First, and three dead kings and as many queens. In one sumptuous bed they had all slept in succession, but no one occupies it now. In a large dining room stood the table at which Louis XIV and his mistress Madame Maintenon, and after them Louis XV, and Pompadour, had sat at their meals naked and unattended—for the table stood upon a trapdoor, which descended with it to regions below when it was necessary to replenish its dishes. In a room of the Petit Trianon stood the furniture, just as poor Marie Antoinette left it when the mob came and dragged her and the King to Paris, never to return. Near at hand, in the stables, were prodigious carriages that showed no color but gold—carriages used by former kings of France on state occasions, and never used now save when a kingly head is to be crowned or an imperial infant christened. And with them were some curious sleighs, whose bodies were shaped like lions, swans, tigers, etc.—vehicles that had once been handsome with pictured designs and fine workmanship, but were dusty and decaying now. They had their history. When Louis XIV had finished the Grand Trianon, he told Maintenon he had created a Paradise for her, and asked if she could think of anything now to wish for. He said he wished the Trianon to be perfection—nothing less. She said she could think of but one thing—it was summer, and it was balmy France—yet she would like well to sleigh ride in the leafy avenues of Versailles! The next morning found miles and miles of grassy avenues spread thick with snowy salt and sugar, and a procession of those quaint sleighs waiting to receive the chief concubine of the gaiest and most unprincipled court that France has ever seen!

The Story of Abelard and Heloise

FROM *The Innocents Abroad,* CHAPTER XV

But among the thousands and thousands of tombs in Père la Chaise, there is one that no man, no woman, no youth of either sex, ever passes by without stopping to examine. Every visitor has a sort of indistinct idea of the history of its dead and comprehends that homage is due there, but not one in twenty thousand clearly remembers the story of that tomb and its romantic occupants. This is the grave of Abelard and Heloise—a grave which has been more revered, more widely known, more written and sung about and wept over, for seven hundred years, than any other in Christendom save only that of the Saviour. All visitors linger pensively about it; all young people capture and carry away keepsakes and mementoes of it; all Parisian youths and maidens who are disappointed in love come there to bail out when they are full of tears; yea, many stricken lovers make pilgrimages to this shrine from distant provinces to weep and wail and "grit" their teeth over their heavy sorrows, and to purchase the sympathies of the chastened spirits of that tomb with offerings of immortelles and budding flowers.

Go when you will, you find somebody snuffling over that tomb. Go when you will, you find it furnished with those bouquets and immortelles. Go when you will, you find a gravel-train from Marseilles arriving to supply the deficiencies caused by memento-cabbaging vandals whose affections have miscarried.

Yet who really knows the story of Abelard and Heloise? Precious few people. The names are perfectly familiar to every body, and that is about all. With infinite pains I have acquired a knowledge of that history, and I propose to narrate it here, partly for the honest information of the public and partly to show that public that they have been wasting a good deal of marketable sentiment very unnecessarily.

THE STORY OF ABELARD AND HELOISE

Heloise was born seven hundred and sixty-six years ago. She may have had parents. There is no telling. She lived with her uncle Fulbert, a canon of the cathedral of Paris. I do not know what a canon of a cathedral is, but that is what he was. He was nothing more than a sort of a mountain howitzer, likely, because they had no heavy artillery in those days. Suffice it, then, that Heloise lived with her uncle the howitzer and was happy. She spent the most of her childhood in the convent of Argenteuil—never heard of Argenteuil before, but suppose there was really such a place. She then returned to her uncle, the old gun, or son of a gun, as the case may be, and he taught her to write and speak Latin, which was the language of literature and polite society at that period.

Just at this time, Pierre Abelard, who had already made himself widely famous as a rhetorician, came to found a school of rhetoric in Paris. The originality of his principles, his eloquence, and his great physical strength and beauty created a profound sensation. He saw Heloise, and was captivated by her blooming youth, her beauty, and her charming disposition. He wrote to her; she answered. He wrote again; she answered again. He was now in love. He longed to know her—to speak to her face to face.

His school was near Fulbert's house. He asked Fulbert to allow him to call. The good old swivel saw here a rare opportunity: his niece, whom he so much loved, would absorb knowledge from this man, and it would not cost him a cent. Such was Fulbert—penurious.

Fulbert's first name is not mentioned by any author, which is unfortunate. However, George W. Fulbert will answer for him as well as any other. We will let him go at that. He asked Abelard to teach her.

Abelard was glad enough of the opportunity. He came often and staid long. A letter of his shows in its very first sentence that he came under that friendly roof like a cold-hearted villain as he was, with the deliberate intention of debauching a confiding, innocent girl. This is the letter:

"I cannot cease to be astonished at the simplicity of Fulbert; I was as much surprised as if he had placed a lamb in the power of a hungry wolf. Heloise and I, under pretext of study, gave ourselves up wholly to love, and the solitude that love seeks our studies procured for us. Books were open before us, but we spoke oftener of love than philosophy, and kisses came more readily from our lips than words."

And so, exulting over an honorable confidence which to his degraded instinct was a ludicrous "simplicity," this unmanly Abelard seduced the niece of the man whose guest he was. Paris found it out. Fulbert was told of it—told often—but refused to believe it. He could not comprehend how a man could be so depraved as to use the sacred protection and security of hospitality as a means for the commission of such a crime as that. But when he heard the rowdies in the streets singing the love-songs of Abelard to Heloise, the case was too plain—love-songs come not properly within the teachings of rhetoric and philosophy.

He drove Abelard from his house. Abelard returned secretly and carried Heloise away to Palais, in Brittany, his native country. Here, shortly afterward, she bore a son, who, from his rare beauty, was surnamed Astrolabe—William G. The girl's flight enraged Fulbert, and he longed for vengeance, but feared to strike lest retaliation visit Heloise—for he still loved her tenderly. At length Abelard offered to marry Heloise—but on a shameful condition: that the marriage should be kept secret from the world, to the end that (while her good name remained a wreck, as before) his priestly reputation might be kept untarnished. It was like that miscreant. Fulbert saw his opportunity and consented. He would see the parties married, and then violate the confidence of the man who had taught him that trick; he would divulge the secret and so remove somewhat of the obloquy that attached to his niece's fame. But the niece suspected his scheme. She refused the marriage at first; she said Fulbert would betray the secret to save her, and besides, she did not wish to drag down a lover who was so gifted, so honored by the world, and who had such a splendid career before him. It was noble, self-sacrificing love, and characteristic of the pure-souled Heloise, but it was not good sense.

But she was overruled, and the private marriage took place. Now for Fulbert! The heart so wounded should be healed at last; the proud spirit so tortured should find rest again; the humbled head should be lifted up once more. He proclaimed the marriage in the high places of the city and rejoiced that dishonor had departed from his house. But lo! Abelard denied the marriage! Heloise denied it! The people, knowing the former circumstances, might have believed Fulbert had only Abelard denied it, but when the person chiefly interested—the girl herself—denied it, they laughed, despairing Fulbert to scorn.

The poor canon of the cathedral of Paris was spiked again. The last hope of repairing the wrong that had been done his house was gone. What next? Human nature suggested revenge. He compassed it. The historian says:

"Ruffians, hired by Fulbert, fell upon Abelard by night, and inflicted upon him a terrible and nameless mutilation."

I am seeking the last resting place of those "ruffians." When I find it I shall shed some tears on it, and stack up some bouquets and immortelles, and cart away from it some gravel whereby to remember that howsoever blotted by crime their lives may have been, these ruffians did one just deed, at any rate, albeit it was not warranted by the strict letter of the law.

Heloise entered a convent and gave good-bye to the world and its pleasures for all time. For twelve years she never heard of Abelard—never even heard his name mentioned. She had become prioress of Argenteuil and led a life of complete seclusion. She happened one day to see a letter written by him, in which he narrated his own history. She cried over it and wrote him. He answered, addressing her as his "sister in Christ." They continued to correspond, she in the unweighed language of unwavering affection, he in the chilly phraseology of the polished rhetorician. She poured out her heart in passionate, disjointed sentences; he replied with finished essays, divided deliberately into heads and sub-heads, premises and argument. She showered upon him the tenderest epithets that love could devise, he addressed her from the North Pole of his frozen heart as the "Spouse of Christ!" The abandoned villain!

On account of her too easy government of her nuns, some disreputable irregularities were discovered among them, and the Abbot of St. Denis broke up her establishment. Abelard was the official head of the monastery of St. Gildas de Ruys, at that time, and when he heard of her homeless condition a sentiment of pity was aroused in his breast (it is a wonder the unfamiliar emotion did not blow his head off) and he placed her and her troop in the little oratory of the Paraclete, a religious establishment which he had founded. She had many privations and sufferings to undergo at first, but her worth and her gentle disposition won influential friends for her, and she built up a wealthy and flourishing nunnery. She became a great favorite with the heads of the church, and also the people, though she seldom appeared in public. She rapidly advanced in esteem, in good report, and in usefulness, and Abelard as rapidly lost ground. The Pope so honored her that he made her the head of her order. Abelard, a man of splendid talents, and ranking as the first debater of his time, became timid, irresolute, and distrustful of his powers. He only needed a great misfortune to topple him from the high position he held in the world of intellectual excellence, and it came. Urged by kings and princes to meet the subtle St. Bernard in debate and crush him, he stood up in the presence of a royal and illustrious assemblage, and when his antagonist had finished he looked about him and stammered a commencement; but his courage failed him, the cunning of his tongue was gone: with his speech unspoken, he trembled and sat down, a disgraced and vanquished champion.

He died a nobody, and was buried at Cluny, A.D., 1144. They removed his body to the Paraclete afterward, and when Heloise died, twenty years later, they buried her with him, in accordance with her last wish. He died at the ripe age of 64, and she at 63. After the bodies had remained entombed three hundred years, they were removed once more. They were removed again in 1800, and finally, seventeen years afterward, they were taken up and transferred to Père la Chaise, where they will remain in peace and quiet until it comes time for them to get up and move again.

History is silent concerning the last acts of the mountain howitzer. Let the world say what it will about him, I, at least, shall always respect the memory and sorrow for the abused trust and the broken heart and the troubled spirit of the old smooth-bore. Rest and repose be his!

Such is the story of Abelard and Heloise. Such is the history that Lamartine has shed such cataracts of tears over. But that man never could come within the influence of a subject in the least pathetic without overflowing his banks. He ought to be dammed—or leveed, I should more properly say. Such is the history—not as it is usually told, but as it is when stripped of the nauseous sentimentality that would enshrine for our loving worship a dastardly seducer like Pierre Abelard. I have not a word to say against the misused, faithful girl, and would not withhold from her grave a single one of those simple tributes which blighted youths and maidens offer to her memory, but I am sorry enough that I have not time and opportunity to write four or five volumes of my opinion of her friend the founder of the Parachute, or the Paraclete, or whatever it was.

The tons of sentiment I have wasted on that unprincipled humbug in my ignorance! I shall throttle down my emotions hereafter, about this sort of people, until I have read them up and know whether they are entitled to any tearful attentions or not. I wish I had my immortelles back, now, and that bunch of radishes.

The Famous Gondola

FROM *The Innocents Abroad,* CHAPTER XXIII

The Venetian gondola is as free and graceful, in its gliding movement, as a serpent. It is twenty or thirty feet long, and is narrow and deep, like a canoe; its sharp bow and stern sweep upward from the water like the horns of a crescent with the abruptness of the curve slightly modified.

The bow is ornamented with a steel comb with a battle-ax attachment which threatens to cut passing boats in two occasionally, but never does. The gondola is painted black because in the zenith of Venetian magnificence the gondolas became too gorgeous altogether, and the Senate decreed that all such display must cease, and a solemn, unembellished black be substituted. If the truth were known, it would doubtless appear that rich plebeians grew too prominent in their affectation of patrician show on the Grand Canal, and required a wholesome snubbing. Reverence for the hallowed Past and its traditions keeps the dismal fashion in force now that the compulsion exists no longer. So let it remain. It is the color of mourning. Venice mourns. The stern of the boat is decked over and the gondolier stands there. He uses a single oar—a long blade, of course, for he stands nearly erect. A wooden peg, a foot and a half high, with two slight crooks or curves in one side of it and one in the other, projects above the starboard gunwale. Against that peg the gondolier takes a purchase with his oar, changing it at intervals to the other side of the peg or dropping it into another of the crooks, as the steering of the craft may demand—and how in the world he can back and fill, shoot straight ahead, or flirt suddenly around a corner, and make the oar stay in those insignificant notches, is a problem to me and a never diminishing matter of interest. I am afraid I study the gondolier's marvelous skill more than I do the sculptured palaces we glide among. He cuts a corner so closely, now and then, or misses another gondola by such an imperceptible hair-breadth that I feel myself "scrooching," as the children say, just as one does when a buggy wheel grazes his elbow. But he makes all his calculations with the nicest precision, and goes darting in and out among a Broadway confusion of busy craft with the easy confidence of the educated hackman. He never makes a mistake.

Sometimes we go flying down the great canals at such a gait that we can get only the merest glimpses into front doors, and again, in obscure alleys in the suburbs, we put on a solemnity suited to the silence, the mildew, the stagnant waters, the clinging weeds, the deserted houses and the general lifelessness of the place, and move to the spirit of grave meditation.

The gondolier is a picturesque rascal for all he wears no satin harness, no plumed bonnet, no silken tights. His attitude is stately; he is lithe and supple; all his movements are full of grace. When his long canoe, and his fine figure, towering from its high perch on the stern, are cut against the evening sky, they make a picture that is very novel and striking to a foreign eye.

We sit in the cushioned carriage-body of a cabin, with the curtains drawn, and smoke, or read, or look out upon the passing boats, the houses, the bridges, the people, and enjoy ourselves much more than we could in a buggy jolting over our cobble-stone pavements at home. This is the gentlest, pleasantest locomotion we have ever known.

But it seems queer—ever so queer—to see a boat doing duty as a private carriage. We see business men come to the front door, step into a gondola, instead of a street car, and go off down town to the counting-room.

We see visiting young ladies stand on the stoop, and laugh, and kiss good-bye, and flirt their fans and say "Come soon—now do—you've been just as mean as ever you can be—mother's dying to see you—and we've moved into the new house, O such a love of a place!—so convenient to the post office and the church, and the Young Men's Christian Association; and we do have such fishing, and such carrying on, and such swimming-matches in the back yard—Oh, you must come—no distance at all, and if you go down through by St. Mark's and the Bridge of Sighs, and cut through the alley and come up by the church of Santa Maria dei Frari, and into the Grand Canal, there isn't a bit of current—now do come, Sally Maria—by-bye!" and then the little humbug trips down the steps, jumps into the gondola, says, under her breath, "Disagreeable old thing, I hope she won't!" goes skimming away, round the corner; and the other girl slams the street door and says, "Well, that infliction's over, any way,—but I suppose I've got to go and see her—tiresome stuck-up thing!" Human nature appears to be just the same, all over the world. We see the diffident young man, mild of moustache, affluent of hair, indigent of brain, elegant of costume, drive up to her father's mansion, tell his hackman to bail out and wait, start fearfully up the steps and meet "the old gentleman" right on the threshold!—hear him ask what street the new British Bank is in—as if that were what he came for—and then bounce into his boat and skurry away with his coward heart in his boots!—see him come sneaking around the corner again, directly, with a crack of the curtain open toward the old gentleman's disappearing gondola, and out scampers his Susan with a flock of little Italian endearments fluttering from her lips, and goes to drive with him in the watery avenues down toward the Rialto.

We see the ladies go out shopping, in the most natural way, and flit from street to street and from store to store, just in the good old fashion, except that they leave the gondola, instead of a private carriage, waiting at the curbstone a couple of hours for them,—waiting while they make the nice young clerks pull down tons and tons of silks and velvets and moire antiques and those things; and then they buy a paper of pins and go paddling away to confer the rest of their disastrous patronage on some other firm. And they always have their purchases sent home just in the good old way. Human nature is very much the same all over the world; and it is so like my dear native home to see a Venetian lady go into a store and buy ten cents' worth of blue ribbon and have it sent home in a scow. Ah, it is these little touches of nature that move one to tears in these far-off foreign lands.

We see little girls and boys go out in gondolas with their nurses, for an airing. We see staid families, with prayer-book and beads, enter the gondola dressed in their Sunday best, and float away to church. And at midnight we see the theatre break up and discharge its swarm of hilarious youth and beauty; we hear the cries of the hackman-gondoliers, and behold the struggling crowd jump aboard, and the black multitude of boats go skimming down the moonlit avenues; we see them separate here and there, and disappear up divergent streets; we hear the faint sounds of laughter and of shouted farewells floating up out of the distance; and then, the strange pageant being gone, we have lonely stretches of glittering water—of stately buildings—of blotting shadows—of weird stone faces creeping into the moonlight—of deserted bridges—of motionless boats at anchor. And over all broods that mysterious stillness, that stealthy quiet, that befits so well this old dreaming Venice.

We have been pretty much every where in our gondola. We have bought beads and photographs in the stores, and wax matches in the Great Square of St. Mark. The last remark suggests a digression. Every body goes to this vast square in the evening. The military bands play in the centre of it and countless couples of ladies and gentlemen promenade up and down on either side, and platoons of them are constantly drifting away toward the old Cathedral, and by the venerable column with the Winged Lion of St. Mark on its top, and out to where the boats lie moored; and other platoons are as constantly arriving from the gondolas and joining the great throng. Between the promenaders and the side-walks are seated hundreds and hundreds of people at small tables, smoking and taking granita (a first cousin to ice-cream); on the side-walks are more employing themselves in the same way. The shops in the first floor of the tall rows of buildings that wall in three sides of the square are brilliantly lighted, the air is filled with music and merry voices, and altogether the scene is as bright and spirited and full of cheerfulness as any man could desire. We enjoy it thoroughly. Very many of the young women are exceedingly pretty and dress with rare good taste. We are gradually and laboriously learning the ill-manners of staring them unflinchingly in the face—not because such conduct is agreeable to us, but because it is the custom of the country and they say the girls like it. We wish to learn all the curious, outlandish ways of all the different countries, so that we can "show off" and astonish people when we get home. We wish to excite the envy of our untraveled friends with our strange foreign fashions which we can't shake off. All our passengers are paying strict attention to this thing, with the end in view which I have mentioned. The gentle reader will never, never know what a consummate ass he can become, until he goes abroad. I speak now, of course, in the supposition that the gentle reader has not been abroad, and therefore is not already a consummate ass. If the case be otherwise, I beg his pardon and extend to him the cordial hand of fellowship and call him brother. I shall always delight to meet an ass after my own heart when I shall have finished my travels.

Italian without a Master

FROM *The $30,000 Bequest and Other Stories*

It is almost a fortnight now that I am domiciled in a medieval villa in the country, a mile or two from Florence. I cannot speak the language; I am too old not to learn how, also too busy when I am busy, and too indolent when I am not; wherefore some will imagine that I am having a dull time of it. But it is not so. The "help" are all natives; they talk Italian to me, I answer in English; I do not understand them, they do not understand me, consequently no harm is done, and everybody is satisfied. In order to be just and fair, I throw in an Italian word when I have one, and this has a good influence. I get the word out of the morning paper. I have to use it while it is fresh, for I find that Italian words do not keep in this climate. They fade toward night, and next morning they are gone. But it is no matter; I get a new one out of the paper before breakfast, and thrill the domestics with it while it lasts. I have no dictionary, and I do not want one; I can select words by the sound, or by orthographic aspect. Many of them have

French or German or English look, and these are the ones I enslave for the day's service. That is, as a rule. Not always. If I find a learnable phrase that has an imposing look and warbles musically along I do not care to know the meaning of it; I pay it out to the first applicant, knowing that if I pronounce it carefully he will understand it, and that's enough.

Yesterday's word was *avanti*. It sounds Shakespearian, and probably means Avaunt and quit my sight. Today I have a whole phrase: *Sono dispia-centissimo*. I do not know what it means, but it seems to fit in everywhere and give satisfaction. Although as a rule my words and phrases are good for one day and train only, I have several that stay by me all the time, for some unknown reason, and these come very handy when I get into a long conversation and need things to fire up with in monotonous stretches. One of the best ones is *dov'è il gatto*. It nearly always produces a pleasant surprise; therefore I save it up for places where I want to express applause or admiration. The fourth word has a French sound, and I think the phrase means "that takes the cake."

During my first week in the deep and dreamy stillness of this woodsy and flowery place I was without news of the outside world, and was well content without it. It has been four weeks since I had seen a newspaper, and this lack seemed to give life a new charm and grace, and to saturate it with a feeling verging upon actual delight. Then came a change that was to be expected: the appetite for news began to rise again, after this invigorating rest. I had to feed it, but I was not willing to let it make me its helpless slave again; I determined to put it on a diet, and a strict and limited one. So I examined an Italian paper, with the idea of feeding it on that, and on that exclusively. On that exclusively, and without help of a dictionary. In this way I should surely be well protected against overloading and indigestion.

A glance at the telegraphic page filled me with encouragement. There were no scare-heads. That was good—supremely good. But there were headings—one-liners and two-liners—and that was good too; for without these, one must do as one does with a German paper—pay our precious time in finding out what an article is about, only to discover, in many cases, that there is nothing in it of interest to you. The headline is a valuable thing.

Necessarily we are all fond of murders, scandals, swindles, robberies, explosions, collisions, and all such things, when we knew the people, and when they are neighbors and friends, but when they are strangers we do not get any great pleasure out of them, as a rule. Now the trouble with an American paper is that it has no discrimination; it rakes the whole earth for blood and garbage, and the result is that you are daily overfed and suffer a surfeit. By habit you stow this muck every day, but you come by and by to take no vital interest in it—indeed, you almost get tired of it. As a rule, forty-nine-fiftieths of it concerns strangers only—people away off yonder, a thousand miles, two thousand miles, ten thousand miles from where you are. Why, when you come to think of it, who cares what becomes of those people? I would not give the assassination of one personal friend for a whole massacre of those others. And, to my mind, one relative or neighbor mixed up in a scandal is more interesting than a whole Sodom and Gomorrah of outlanders gone rotten. Give me the home product every time.

Very well. I saw at a glance that the Florentine paper would suit me: five out of six of its scandals and tragedies were local; they were adventures of one's very neighbors, one might almost say one's friends. In the matter of world news there was not too much, but just about enough. I subscribed. I have had no occasion to regret it. Every morning I get all the news I need for the day; sometimes from the headlines, sometimes from the text. I have never had to call for a dictionary yet. I read the paper with ease. Often I do not quite understand, often some of the details escape me, but no matter, I get the idea. I will cut out a passage or two; then you see how limpid the language is:

Il ritorno dei Beati d'Italia

Elargizione del Re all' Ospedale italiano

The first line means that the Italian sovereigns are coming back—they have been to England. The second line seems to mean that they enlarged the King at the Italian hospital. With a banquet, I suppose. An English banquet has that effect. Further:

Il ritorno dei Sovrani

a Roma

ROMA, 24, ore 22,50.—I Sovrani e le Principessine Reali si attendono a Roma domani alle ore 15,51.

Return of the sovereigns to Rome, you see. Date of the telegram, Rome, November 24, ten minutes before twenty-three o'clock. The telegram seems to say, "The Sovereigns and the Royal Children expect themselves at Rome tomorrow at fifty-one minutes after fifteen o'clock."

I do not know about Italian time, but I judge it begins at midnight and runs through the twenty-four hours without breaking bulk. In the following ad, the theaters open at half-past twenty. If these are not matinees, 20.30 must mean 8.30 P.M., by my reckoning.

This is a four-page paper; and as it is set in long primer leaded and has a page of advertisements, there is no room for the crimes, disasters, and general sweepings of the outside world—thanks be! Today I find only a single importation of the off-color sort:

Una Principessa

che fugge con un cocchiere

Parigi, 24.—Il Matin ha da Berlino che la principessa Schovenbare-Waldenbure scomparve il 9 novembre. Sarebbe partita col suo cocchiere.

La Principassa ha 27 anni.

Twenty-seven years old, and *scomparve*—scampered—on the 9th November. You see by the added detail that she departed with her coachman. I hope Sarebbe has not made a mistake, but I am afraid the chances are that she has. *Sono Dispiacentissimo.*

There are several fires: also a couple of accidents. This is one of them:

Grave disgrazia sul Ponte Vecchio

Stammattina, circe le 7,30, mentre Giuseppe Sciatti, di anni 55, di Casellina e Torri, passava dal Ponte Vecchio, stando seduto sopra un barroccio carico di verdura, perse l' equilibrio e cadde al suolo, rimanendo con la gamba destra sotto una ruota del veicolo.

Lo Sciatti fu subito raccolto da alcuni cittadini, che, per mezzo della pubblica vettura n. 365, lo transporto a San Giovanni di Dio.

Ivi il medico di guardia gli riscontro la frattura della gamba destra e alcune lievi escoriazioni giudicandolo guaribile in 50 giorni salvo complicazioni.

What it seems to say is this: "Serious Disgrace on the Old Old Bridge. This morning about 7.30, Mr. Joseph Sciatti, aged 55, of Casellina and Torri, while standing up in a sitting posture on top of a *carico* barrow of vedure (foliage? hay? vegetables?), lost his equilibrium and fell on himself, arriving with his left leg under one of the wheels of the vehicle.

"Said Sciatti was suddenly harvested (gathered in?) by several citizens, who by means of public cab No. 365 transported to St. John of God."

Paragraph No. 3 is a little obscure, but I think it says that the medico set the broken left leg—right enough, since there was nothing the matter with the other one—and that several are encouraged to hope that fifty days will fetch him around in quite *giudicandolo-guaribile* way, if no complications intervene.

I am sure I hope so myself.

There is a great and peculiar charm about reading news-scraps in a language which you are not acquainted with—the charm that always goes with the mysterious and the uncertain. You can never be absolutely sure of the meaning of anything you read in such circumstances; you are chasing an alert and gamy riddle all the time, and the baffling turns and dodges of the prey make the life of the hunt. A dictionary would spoil it. Sometimes a single word of doubtful purport will cast a veil of dreamy and golden uncertainty over a whole paragraph of cold and practical certainties, and leave steeped in a haunting and adorable mystery an incident which had been vulgar and commonplace but for that benefaction. Would you be wise to draw a dictionary on that gracious word? would you be properly grateful?

After a couple of days' rest I now come back to my subject and seek a case in point. I find it without trouble, in the morning paper; a cablegram from Chicago and Indiana by way of Paris. All the words save one are guessable by a person ignorant of Italian:

Revolverate in teatro

Parigi, 27.—La Patrie ha da Chicago:

Il guardiano del teatro dell'opera di Walace (Indiana), avendo voluto espellare uno spettatore che continuava a fumare malgrado il diviety, questo spalleggiato dai suoi amici tir'o diversi colpi di rivoltella. Il guardiano ripose. Nacque una scarica generale. Grande panico tra gli spettatori. Nessun ferito.

Translation.—"Revolveration in Theater. Paris, 27th. La Patrie has from Chicago: The cop of the theater of the opera of Wallace, Indiana, had willed to expel a spectator which continued to smoke in spite of the prohibition, who, *spalleggiato* by his friends, *tir'o* (Fr. *Tir'e, Anglice* pulled) manifold revolver-shots; great panic among the spectators. Nobody hurt."

It is bettable that that harmless cataclysm in the theater of the opera of Wallace, Indiana, excited not a person in Europe but me, and so came near to not being worth cabling to Florence by way of France. But it does excite me. It excites me because I cannot make out, for sure, what it was that moved the spectator to resist the officer. I was gliding along smoothly and without obstruction or accident, until I came to that word *spalleggiato;* then the bottom fell out. You notice what a rich gloom, what a somber and pervading mystery, that word sheds all over the whole Wallachian tragedy.

That is the charm of the thing, that is the delight of it. This is where you begin, this is where you revel. You can guess and guess, and have all the fun you like; you need not be afraid there will be an end to it; none is possible, for no amount of guessing will ever furnish you a meaning for that word that you can be sure is the right one. All the other words give you hints, by their form, their sound, or their spelling—this one doesn't, this one throws out no hints, this one keeps its secret. If there is even the slightest slight shadow of a hint anywhere, it lies in the very meagerly suggestive fact that *spalleggiato* carries our word "egg" in its stomach. Well, make the most out of it, and then where are you at? You conjecture that the spectator which was smoking in spite of the prohibition and become reprohibited by the guardians, was "egged on" by his friends, and that was owing to that evil influence that he initiated the revolveration in theater that has galloped under the sea and come crashing through the European press without exciting anybody but me. But are you sure, are you dead sure, that that was the way of it? No. Then the uncertainty remains, the mystery abides, and with it the charm. Guess again.

The Chief Charm of European Life

FROM *The Innocents Abroad,* CHAPTER XIX

Do you wis zo haut can be?"
That was what the guide asked when we were looking up at the bronze horses on the Arch of Peace. It meant, "Do you wish to go up there?" I give it as a specimen of guide-English. These are the people that make life a burthen to the tourist. Their tongues are never still. They talk forever and forever, and that is the kind of billingsgate they use. Inspiration itself could hardly comprehend them. If they would only show you a

masterpiece of art, or a venerable tomb, or a prison-house, or a battle-field, hallowed by touching memories or historical reminiscences, or grand traditions, and then step aside and hold still for ten minutes and let you think, it would not be so bad. But they interrupt every dream, every pleasant train of thought, with their tiresome cackling. Sometimes when I have been standing before some cherished old idol of mine that I remembered years and years ago in pictures in the geography at school, I have thought I would give a whole world if the human parrot at my side would suddenly perish where he stood and leave me to gaze, and ponder, and worship.

No, we did not "wis zo haut can be." We wished to go to La Scala, the largest theater in the world, I think they call it. We did so. It was a large place. Seven separate and distinct masses of humanity—six great circles and a monster parquette.

We wished to go to the Ambrosian Library, and we did that also. We saw a manuscript of Virgil, with annotations in the handwriting of Petrarch, the gentleman who loved another man's Laura, and lavished upon her all through life a love which was a clear waste of the raw material. It was sound sentiment, but bad judgment. It brought both parties fame, and created a fountain of commiseration for them in sentimental breasts that is running yet. But who says a word in behalf of poor Mr. Laura? (I do not know his other name.) Who glorifies him? Who bedews him with tears? Who writes poetry about him? Nobody. How do you suppose he liked the state of things that has given the world so much pleasure? How did he enjoy having another man following his wife every where and making her name a familiar word in every garlic-exterminating mouth in Italy with his sonnets to her pre-empted eyebrows? They got fame and sympathy—he got neither. This is a peculiarly felicitous instance of what is called poetical justice. It is all very fine; but it does not chime with my notions of right. It is too one-sided—too ungenerous.

Let the world go on fretting about Laura and Petrarch if it will; but as for me, my tears and my lamentations shall be lavished upon the unsung defendant.

We saw also an autograph letter of Lucrezia Borgia, a lady for whom I have always entertained the highest respect, on account of her rare histrionic capabilities, her opulence in solid gold goblets made of gilded wood, her high distinction as an operatic screamer, and the facility with which she could order a sextuple funeral and get the corpses ready for it. We saw one single coarse yellow hair from Lucrezia's head, likewise. It awoke emotions, but we still live. In this same library we saw some drawings by Michael Angelo (these Italians call him Mickel Angelo) and Leonardo da Vinci. (They spell it Vinci and pronounce it Vinchy; foreigners always spell better than they pronounce.) We reserve our opinion of these sketches.

In another building they showed us a fresco representing some lions and other beasts drawing chariots; and they seemed to project so far from the wall that we took them to be sculptures. The artist had shrewdly heightened the delusion by painting dust on the creatures' backs, as if it had fallen there naturally and properly. Smart fellow—if it be smart to deceive strangers.

Elsewhere we saw a huge Roman amphitheatre, with its stone seats still in good preservation. Modernized, it is now the scene of more peaceful recreations than the exhibition of a party of wild beasts with Christians for dinner. Part of the time, the Milanese use it for a race track, and at other seasons they flood it with water and have spirited yachting regattas there. The guide told us these things, and he would hardly try so hazardous an experiment as the telling of a falsehood, when it is all he can do to speak the truth in English without getting the lock-jaw.

In another place we were shown a sort of summer arbor, with a fence before it. We said that was nothing. We looked again, and saw, through the arbor, an endless stretch of garden, and shrubbery, and grassy lawn. We were perfectly willing to go in there and rest, but it could not be done. It was only another delusion—a painting by some ingenious artist with little charity in his heart for tired folk. The deception was perfect. No one could have imagined the park was not real. We even thought we smelled the flowers at first.

We got a carriage at twilight and drove in the shaded avenues with the other nobility, and after dinner we took wine and ices in a fine garden with the great public. The music was excellent, the flowers and shrubbery were pleasant to the eye, the scene was vivacious, everybody was genteel and well-behaved, and the ladies were slightly moustached, and handsomely dressed, but very homely.

We adjourned to a cafe and played billiards an hour, and I made six or seven points by the doctor pocketing his ball, and he made as many by my pocketing my ball. We came near making a carom sometimes, but not the one we were trying to make. The table was of the usual European style—cushions dead and twice as high as the balls; the cues in bad repair. The natives play only a sort of pool on them. We have never seen any body playing the French three-ball game yet, and I doubt if there is any such game known in France, or that there lives any man mad enough to try to play it on one of these European tables. We had to stop playing finally because Dan got to sleeping fifteen minutes between the counts and paying no attention to his marking.

Afterward we walked up and down one of the most popular streets for some time, enjoying other people's comfort and wishing we could export some of it to our restless, driving, vitality-consuming marts at home. Just in this one matter lies the main charm of life in Europe—comfort. In America, we hurry—which is well; but when the day's work is done, we go on thinking of losses and gains, we plan for the morrow, we even carry our business cares to bed with us, and toss and worry over them when we ought to be restoring our racked bodies and brains with sleep. We burn up our energies with these excitements, and either die early or drop into a lean and mean old age at a time of life which they call a man's prime in Europe. When an acre of ground has produced long and well, we let it lie fallow and rest for a season; we take no man clear across the continent in the same coach he started in—the coach is stabled somewhere on the plains and its heated machinery allowed to cool for a few days; when a razor has seen long service and refuses to hold an edge, the barber lays it away for a few weeks, and the edge comes back of its own accord. We bestow thoughtful care upon inanimate objects, but none upon ourselves. What a robust people, what a nation of thinkers we might be, if we would only lay ourselves on the shelf occasionally and renew our edges!

I do envy these Europeans the comfort they take. When the work of the day is done, they forget it. Some of them go, with wife and children, to a beer hall and sit quietly and genteelly drinking a mug or two of ale and listening to music; others walk the streets, others drive in the avenues; others assemble in the great ornamental squares in the early evening to enjoy the sight and the fragrance of flowers and to hear the military bands play—no European city being without its fine military music at eventide; and yet others of the populace sit in the open air in front of the refreshment houses and eat ices and drink mild beverages that could not harm a child. They go to bed moderately early, and sleep well. They are always quiet, always orderly, always cheerful, comfortable, and appreciative of life and its manifold blessings. One never sees a drunken man among them. The change that has come over our little party is surprising. Day by day we lose some of our restlessness and absorb some of the spirit of quietude and ease that is in the tranquil atmosphere about us and in the demeanor of the people. We grow wise apace. We begin to comprehend what life is for.

We have had a bath in Milan, in a public bath-house. They were going to put all three of us in one bath-tub, but we objected. Each of us had an Italian farm on his back. We could have felt affluent if we had been officially surveyed and fenced in. We chose to have three bathtubs, and large ones—tubs suited to the dignity of aristocrats who had real estate, and brought it with them. After we were stripped and had taken the first chilly dash, we discovered that haunting atrocity that has embittered our lives in so many cities and villages of Italy and France—there was no soap. I called. A woman answered, and I barely had time to throw myself against the door—she would have been in, in another second. I said:

"Beware, woman! Go away from here—go away, now, or it will be the worse for you. I am an unprotected male, but I will preserve my honor at the peril of my life!"

These words must have frightened her, for she skurried away very fast.

Dan's voice rose on the air:

"Oh, bring some soap, why don't you!"

The reply was Italian. Dan resumed:

"Soap, you know—soap. That is what I want—soap. S-o-a-p, soap; s-o-p-e, soap; s-o-u-p, soap. Hurry up! I don't know how you Irish spell it, but I want it. Spell it to suit yourself, but fetch it. I'm freezing."

I heard the doctor say impressively:

"Dan, how often have we told you that these foreigners cannot understand English? Why will you not depend upon us? Why will you not tell us what you want, and let us ask for it in the language of the country? It would save us a great deal of the humiliation your reprehensible ignorance causes us. I will address this person in his mother tongue: 'Here, *cospetto! corpo di Bacco! Sacramento! Solferino!*—Soap, you son of a gun!' Dan, if you would let us talk for you, you would never expose your ignorant vulgarity."

Even this fluent discharge of Italian did not bring the soap at once, but there was a good reason for it. There was not such an article about the establishment. It is my belief that there never had been. They had to send far up town, and to several different places before they finally got it, so they said. We had to wait twenty or thirty minutes. The same thing had occurred the evening before, at the hotel. I think I have divined the reason for this state of things at last. The English know how to travel comfortably, and they carry soap with them; other foreigners do not use the article.

PART VI

Africa, India, and the Holy Land

The Taj Mahal

FROM *Following the Equator,* CHAPTER LIX

In Agra and its neighborhood, and afterwards at Delhi, we saw forts, mosques, and tombs, which were built in the great days of the Mohammedan emperors, and which are marvels of cost, magnitude, and richness of materials and ornamentation, creations of surpassing grandeur, wonders which do indeed make the like things in the rest of the world seem tame and inconsequential by comparison. I am not purposing to describe them. By good fortune I had not read too much about them, and therefore was able to get a natural and rational focus upon them, with the result that they thrilled, blessed, and exalted me. But if I had previously overheated my imagination by drinking too much pestilential literary hot Scotch, I should have suffered disappointment and sorrow.

I mean to speak of only one of these many world-renowned buildings, the Taj Mahal, the most celebrated construction in the earth. I had read a great deal too much about it. I saw it in the daytime, I saw it in the moonlight, I saw it near at hand, I saw it from a distance; and I knew all the time, that of its kind it was the wonder of the world, with no competitor now and no possible future competitor; and yet, it was not my Taj. My Taj had been built by excitable literary people; it was solidly lodged in my head, and I could not blast it out.

I wish to place before the reader some of the usual descriptions of the Taj, and ask him to take note of the impressions left in his mind. These descriptions do really state the truth—as nearly as the limitations of language will allow. But language is a treacherous thing, a most unsure vehicle, and it can seldom arrange descriptive words in such a way that they will not inflate the facts—by help of the reader's imagination, which is always ready to take a hand, and work for nothing, and do the bulk of it at that.

I will begin with a few sentences from the excellent little local guide-book of Mr. Satya Chandra Mukerji. I take them from here and there in his description:

"The inlaid work of the Taj and the flowers and petals that are to be found on all sides on the surface of the marble evince a most delicate touch."

That is true.

"The inlaid work, the marble, the flowers, the buds, the leaves, the petals, and the lotus stems are almost without a rival in the whole of the civilized world."

"The work of inlaying with stones and gems is found in the highest perfection in the Taj."

Gems, inlaid flowers, buds, and leaves to be found on all sides. What do you see before you? Is the fairy structure growing? Is it becoming a jewel casket?

"The whole of the Taj produces a wonderful effect that is equally sublime and beautiful."

Then Sir William Wilson Hunter:

"The Taj Mahal with its beautiful domes, 'a dream of marble,' rises on the river bank."

"The materials are white marble and red sandstone."

"The complexity of its design and the delicate intricacy of the workmanship baffle description."

Sir William continues. I will italicize some of his words:

"The mausoleum stands on a raised marble platform at each of whose corners rises a tall and slender minaret of graceful proportions and of exquisite beauty. Beyond the platform stretch the two wings, one of which is itself a mosque of great architectural merit. In the center of the whole design the mausoleum occupies a square of 186 feet, with the angles deeply truncated to also form an unequal octagon. The main feature in this central pile is the great dome, which swells upward to nearly two-thirds of a sphere and tapers at its extremity into a pointed spire crowned by a crescent. Beneath it an enclosure of marble trellis-work surrounds the tomb of the princess and of her husband, the Emperor. Each corner of the mausoleum is covered by a similar though much smaller dome erected on a pediment pierced with graceful Saracenic arches. Light is admitted into the interior through a double screen of pierced marble, which tempers the glare of an Indian sky while its whiteness prevents the mellow effect from degenerating into gloom. The internal decorations consist of inlaid work in *precious stones, such as agate, jasper, etc., with which every squandril or salient point in the architecture is richly fretted.* Brown and violet marble is also freely employed in wreaths, scrolls, and lintels to relieve the monotony of white wall. *In regard to color and design, the interior of the Taj may rank first in the world for purely decorative work-manship*; while the perfect symmetry of its exterior, once seen can never be forgotten, nor the aerial grace of its domes, rising like marble bubbles into the clear sky. The Taj represents the most highly elaborated stage of ornamentation reached by the Indo-Mohammedan builders, the stage in which the architect ends and the *jeweler* begins. In its magnificent gateway the diagonal ornamentation at the corners, which satisfied the designers of the gateways of Itimad-ud-doulah and Sikandra mausoleums is superseded by fine marble cables, in bold twists, strong and handsome. The triangular insertions of white marble and large flowers have in like manner given place to *fine inlaid work.* Firm perpendicular lines in black marble with well proportioned panels of the same material are effectively used in the interior of the gateway. On its top the Hindu brackets and monolithic architraves of Sikandra are replaced by Moorish carped arches, usually single blocks of red sandstone, in the Kiosks and pavilions which adorn the roof. From the pillared pavilions a magnificent view is obtained of the Taj gardens below, with the noble Jumna river at their farther end, and the city and fort of Agra in the distance. From this beautiful and splendid gateway one passes up a straight alley shaded by evergreen trees cooled by a broad shallow piece of water running along the middle of the path to the Taj itself. *The Taj is entirely of marble and gems.* The red sand-stone of the other Mohammedan buildings has entirely disappeared, or rather the red sandstone which used to form the thickness of the walls, is in the Taj itself overlaid completely with white marble, and the white marble is itself *inlaid with precious stones arranged in lovely patterns of flowers*. A feeling of purity impresses itself on the eye and the mind from the absence of the coarser material which forms so invariable a material in Agra architecture. The lower wall and panels are covered with tulips, oleanders, and fullblown lilies, in flat carving on the white marble; and *although the inlaid work of flowers done in gems is very brilliant* when looked at closely, there is on the whole but little color, and the all-prevailing sentiment is one of whiteness, silence, and calm. The whiteness is broken only by the fine color of the inlaid gems, by lines in black marble, and by delicately written inscriptions, also in black, from the Koran. Under the dome of *the vast mausoleum* a high and beautiful screen of open tracery in white marble rises around the two tombs, or rather cenotaphs of the emperor and his princess; and in this *marvel of marble* the carving has advanced from the old geometrical patterns to a trellis-work of flowers and foliage, handled with great freedom and spirit. The two cenotaphs in the center of the *exquisite* enclosure have no carving except the plain *Kalamdan* or oblong pen-box on the tomb of Emperor Shah Jehan. But both cenotaphs are *inlaid with flowers made of costly gems*, and with the ever graceful oleander scroll."

Bayard Taylor, after describing the details of the Taj, goes on to say:

"On both sides the palm, the banyan, and the feathery bamboo mingle their foliage; the song of birds meets your ears, and the odor of roses and lemon flowers sweetens the air. Down such a vista and over such a fore-ground rises the Taj. There is no mystery, no sense of partial failure about the Taj. A *thing of perfect beauty and of absolute finish* in every detail, it might pass for the work of genii who knew naught of the weaknesses and ills with which mankind are beset."

All of these details are true. But, taken together, they state a falsehood—to you. You cannot add them up correctly. Those writers know the values of their words and phrases, but to you the words and phrases convey other and uncertain values. To those writers their phrases have values which I think I am now acquainted with; and for the help of the reader I will here repeat certain of those words and phrases, and follow them with numerals which shall represent those values—then we shall see the difference between a writer's ciphering and a mistaken reader's—

Precious stones, such as agate, jasper, etc.—5.

With which every salient point is richly fretted—5.

First in the world for purely decorative workmanship—9.

The Taj represents the stage where the architect ends and the jeweler begins—5.

The Taj is entirely of marble and gems—7.

Inlaid with precious stones in lovely patterns of flowers—5.

The inlaid work of flowers done in gems is very brilliant (followed by a most important modification which the reader is sure to read too carelessly)—2.

The vast mausoleum—5.

This marvel of marble—5.

The exquisite enclosure—5.

Inlaid with flowers made of costly gems—5.

A thing of perfect beauty and absolute finish—5.

Those details are correct; the figures which I have placed after them represent quite fairly their individual values. Then why, as a whole, do they convey a false impression to the reader? It is because the reader—beguiled by his heated imagination—masses them in the wrong way. The writer would mass the first three figures in the following way, and they would speak the truth:

$$
\begin{array}{r}
5 \\
5 \\
\underline{9} \\
\text{Total—19}
\end{array}
$$

But the reader masses them thus—and then they tell a lie—559.

The writer would add all of his twelve numerals together, and then the sum would express the whole truth about the Taj, and the truth only—63.

But the reader—always helped by his imagination—would put the figures in a row one after the other, and get this sum, which would tell him a noble big lie:

559575255555.

You must put in the commas yourself; I have to go on with my work.

The reader will always be sure to put the figures together in that wrong way, and then as surely before him will stand, sparkling in the sun, a gem-crusted Taj tall as the Matterhorn.

I had to visit Niagara fifteen times before I succeeded in getting my imaginary Falls gauged to the actuality and could begin to sanely and whole-somely wonder at them for what they were, not what I had expected them to be. When I first approached them it was with my face lifted toward the sky, for I thought I was going to see an Atlantic ocean pouring down thence over cloud-vexed Himalayan heights, a sea-green wall of water sixty miles front and six miles high, and so, when the toy reality came suddenly into view—that beruiled little wet apron hanging out to dry—the shock was too much for me, and I fell with a dull thud.

Yet slowly, surely, steadily, in the course of my fifteen visits, the propor-tions adjusted themselves to the facts, and I came at last to realize that a waterfall a hundred and sixty-five feet high and a quarter of a mile wide was an impressive thing. It was not a dipperful to my vanished great vision, but it would answer.

I know that I ought to do with the Taj as I was obliged to do with Niagara—see it fifteen times, and let my mind gradually get rid of the Taj built in it by its describers, by help of my imagination, and substitute for it the Taj of fact. It would be noble and fine, then, and a marvel; not the marvel which it replaced, but still a marvel, and fine enough. I am a care-less reader, I suppose—an impressionist reader; an impressionist reader of what is not an impressionist picture; a reader who overlooks the informing details or masses their sum improperly, and gets only a large splashy, general effect—an effect which is not correct, and which is not warranted by the particulars placed before me, particulars which I did not examine, and whose meanings I did not cautiously and carefully estimate. It is an effect which is some thirty-five or forty times finer than the reality, and is therefore a great deal better and more valuable than the reality; and so, I ought never to hunt up the reality, but stay miles away from it, and thus preserve undamaged my own private mighty Niagara tumbling out of the vault of heaven, and my own ineffable Taj, built of tinted mists upon jeweled arches of rainbows supported by colonnades of moonlight. It is a mistake for a person with an unregulated imagination to go and look at an illustrious world's wonder.

I suppose that many, many years ago I gathered the idea that the Taj's place in the achievements of man was exactly the place of the ice-storm in the achievements of Nature; that the Taj represented man's supremest possibility in the creation of grace and beauty and exquisiteness and splendor, just as the ice-storm represents Nature's supremest possibility in the combination of those same qualities. I do not know how long ago that idea was bred in me, but I know that I cannot remember back to a time when the thought of either of these symbols of gracious and unapproachable perfection did not at once suggest the other. If I thought of the ice-storm, the Taj rose before me divinely beautiful; if I thought of the Taj, with its encrustings and inlayings of jewels, the vision of the ice-storm rose. And so, to me, all these years, the Taj has had no rival among the temples and palaces of men, none that even remotely approached it—it was man's architectural ice-storm.

Here in London the other night I was talking with some Scotch and English friends, and I mentioned the ice-storm, using it as a figure—a figure which failed, for none of them had heard of the ice-storm. One gentleman, who was very familiar with American literature, said he had never seen it mentioned in any book. That is strange. And I, myself, was not able to say that I had seen it mentioned in a book; and yet the autumn foliage, with all other American scenery, has received full and competent attention.

The oversight is strange, for in America the ice-storm is an event. And it is not an event which one is careless about. When it comes, the news flies from room to room in the house, there are bangings on the doors, and shoutings, "The ice-storm! the ice-storm!" and even the laziest sleepers throw off the covers and join the rush for the windows. The ice-storm occurs in midwinter, and usually its enchantments are wrought in the silence and the darkness of the night. A fine drizzling rain falls hour after hour upon the naked twigs and branches of the trees, and as it falls it freezes. In time the trunk and every branch and twig are incased in hard pure ice; so that the tree looks like a skeleton tree made all of glass—glass that is crystal-clear. All along the underside of every branch and twig is a comb of little icicles—the frozen drip. Sometimes these pendants do not quite amount to icicles, but are round beads—frozen tears.

The weather clears, toward dawn, and leaves a brisk pure atmosphere and a sky without a shred of cloud in it—and everything is still, there is not a breath of wind. The dawn breaks and spreads, the news of the storm goes about the house, and the little and the big, in wraps and blankets, flock to the window and press together there, and gaze intently out upon the great white ghost in the grounds, and nobody says a word, nobody stirs. All are waiting; they know what is coming, and they are waiting, waiting for the miracle. The minutes drift on and on and on, with not a sound but the ticking of the clock; at last the sun fires a sudden sheaf of rays into the ghostly tree and turns it into a white splendor of glittering diamonds. Everybody catches his breath, and feels a swelling in his throat and a moisture in his eyes—but waits again; for he knows what is coming; there is more yet. The sun climbs higher, and still higher, flooding the tree from its loftiest spread of branches to its lowest, turning it to a glory of white fire; then in a moment, without warning, comes the great miracle, the supreme miracle, the miracle without its fellow in the earth; a gust of wind sets every branch and twig to swaying, and in an instant turns the whole white tree into a spouting and spraying explosion of flashing gems of every conceivable color; and there it stands and sways this way and that, flash! flash! flash! a dancing and glancing world of rubies, emeralds, diamonds, sapphires, the most radiant spectacle, the most blinding spectacle, the divinest, the most exquisite, the most intoxicating vision of fire and color and intolerable and unimaginable splendor that ever any eye has rested upon in this world, or will ever rest upon outside of the gates of heaven.

By all my senses, all my faculties, I know that the icestorm is Nature's supremest achievement in the domain of the superb and the beautiful; and by my reason, at least, I know that the Taj is man's ice-storm.

In the ice-storm every one of the myriad ice-beads pendant from twig and branch is an individual gem, and changes color with every motion caused by the wind; each tree carries a million, and a forest-front exhibits the splendors of the single tree multiplied by a thousand.

It occurs to me now that I have never seen the ice-storm put upon canvas, and have not heard that any painter has tried to do it. I wonder why that is. Is it that paint cannot counterfeit the intense blaze of a sun-flooded jewel? There should be, and must be, a reason, and a good one, why the most enchanting sight that Nature has created has been neglected by the brush.

Often, the surest way to convey misinformation is to tell the strict truth. The describers of the Taj have used the word *gem* in its strictest sense—its scientific sense. In that sense it is a mild word, and promises but little to the eye—nothing bright, nothing brilliant, nothing sparkling, nothing splendid in the way of color. It accurately describes the sober and unobtrusive gem-work of the Taj; that is, to the very highly-educated one person in a thousand; but it most falsely describes it to the 999. But the 999 are the people who ought to be especially taken care of, and to them it does not mean quiet-colored designs wrought in carnelians, or agates, or such things; they know the word in its wide and ordinary sense only, and so to them it means diamonds and rubies and opals and their kindred, and the moment their eyes fall upon it in print they see a vision of glorious colors clothed in fire.

These describers are writing for the "general," and so, in order to make sure of being understood, they ought to use words in their ordinary sense, or else explain. The word *fountain* means one thing in Syria, where there is but a handful of people; it means quite another thing in North America, where there are 75,000,000. If I were describing some Syrian scenery, and should exclaim, "Within the narrow space of a quarter of a mile square I saw, in the glory of the flooding moonlight, two hundred noble fountains—imagine the spectacle!" the North American would have a vision of clustering columns of water soaring aloft, bending over in graceful arches, bursting in beaded spray and raining white fire in the moonlight—and he would be deceived. But the Syrian would not be deceived; he would merely see two hundred fresh-water springs—two hundred drowsing puddles, as level and unpretentious and unexcited as so many door-mats, and even with the help of the moonlight he would not lose his grip in the presence of the exhibition. My word *fountain* would be correct; it would speak the strict truth; and it would convey the strict truth to the handful of Syrians, and the strictest misinformation to the North American millions. With their gems—and gems—and more gems—and gems again—and still other gems—the describers of the Taj are within their legal but not their moral rights; they are dealing in the strictest scientific truth; and in doing it they succeed to admiration in telling "what ain't so."

Another Living God

FROM *Following the Equator,* CHAPTER LIII

> *True irreverence is disrespect for another man's god.*
> —PUDD'NHEAD WILSON'S NEW CALENDAR

It was in Benares that I saw another living god. That makes two. I believe I have seen most of the greater and lesser wonders of the world, but I do not remember that any of them interested me so overwhelmingly as did that pair of gods.

When I try to account for this effect I find no difficulty about it. I find that, as a rule, when a thing is a wonder to us it is not because of what we see in it, but because of what others have seen in it. We get almost all our wonders at second hand. We are eager to see any celebrated thing—and we never fail of our reward; just the deep privilege of gazing upon an object which has stirred the enthusiasm or evoked the reverence or affection or admiration of multitudes of our race is a thing which we value; we are profoundly glad that we have seen it, we are permanently enriched from having seen it, we would not part with the memory of that experience for a great price. And yet that very spectacle may be the Taj. You cannot keep your enthusiasms down, you cannot keep your emotions within bounds when that soaring bubble of marble breaks upon your view. But these are not your enthusiasms and emotions—they are the accumulated emotions and enthusiasms of a thousand fervid writers, who have been slowly and steadily storing them up in your heart day by day and year by year all your life; and now they burst out in a flood and overwhelm you; and you could not be a whit happier if they were your very own. By and by you sober down, and then you perceive that you have been drunk on the smell of somebody else's cork. For ever and ever the memory of my distant first glimpse of the Taj will compensate me for creeping around the globe to have that great privilege.

But the Taj—with all your inflation of delusive emotions, acquired at second-hand from people to whom in the majority of cases they were also delusions acquired at second-hand—a thing which you fortunately did not think of or it might have made you doubtful of what you imagined were your own—what is the Taj as a marvel, a spectacle and an uplifting and overpowering wonder, compared with a living, breathing, speaking personage whom several millions of human beings devoutly and sincerely and unquestioningly believe to be a God, and humbly and gratefully worship as a God?

He was sixty years old when I saw him. He is called Sri 108 Swami Bhaskarananda Saraswati. That is one form of it. I think that that is what you would call him in speaking to him—because it is short. But you would use more of his name in addressing a letter to him; courtesy would require this. Even then you would not have to use all of it, but only this much:

Sri 108 Matparamahansrzpairivrajakacharyaswamibhaskaranandasaraswati.

You do not put "Esq." after it, for that is not necessary. The word which opens the volley is itself a title of honor "Sri." The "108" stands for the rest of his names, I believe. Vishnu has 108 names which he does not use in business, and no doubt it is a custom of gods and a privilege sacred to their order to keep 108 extra ones in stock. Just the restricted name set down above is a handsome property, without the 108. By my count it has 58 letters in it. This removes the long German words from competition; they are permanently out of the race.

Sri 108 S. B. Saraswati has attained to what among the Hindoos is called the "state of perfection." It is a state which other Hindoos reach by being born again and again, and over and over again into this world, through one re-incarnation after another—a tiresome long job covering centuries and decades of centuries, and one that is full of risks, too, like the accident of dying on the wrong side of the Ganges some time or other and waking up in the form of an ass, with a fresh start necessary and the numerous trips to be made all over again. But in reaching perfection, Sri 108 S. B. S. has escaped all that. He is no longer a part or a feature of this world; his substance has changed, all earthiness has departed out of it; he is utterly holy, utterly pure; nothing can desecrate this holiness or stain this purity; he is no longer of the earth, its concerns are matters foreign to him, its pains and griefs and troubles cannot reach him. When he dies, Nirvana is his; he will be absorbed into the substance of the Supreme Deity and be at peace forever.

The Hindoo Scriptures point out how this state is to be reached, but it is only once in a thousand years, perhaps, that candidate accomplishes it. This one has traversed the course required, stage by stage, from the beginning to the end, and now has nothing left to do but wait for the call which shall release him from a world in which he has now no part nor lot. First, he passed through the student stage, and became learned in the holy books.

Next he became citizen, householder, husband, and father. That was the required second stage. Then—like John Bunyan's Christian he bade perpetual good-bye to his family, as required, and went wandering away. He went far into the desert and served a term as hermit. Next, he became a beggar, "in accordance with the rites laid down in the Scriptures," and wandered about India eating the bread of mendicancy. A quarter of a century ago he reached the stage of purity. This needs no garment; its symbol is nudity; he discarded the waist-cloth which he had previously worn. He could resume it now if he chose, for neither that nor any other contact can defile him; but he does not choose.

There are several other stages, I believe, but I do not remember what they are. But he has been through them. Throughout the long course he was perfecting himself in holy learning, and writing commentaries upon the sacred books. He was also meditating upon Brahma, and he does that now.

White marble relief-portraits of him are sold all about India. He lives in a good house in a noble great garden in Benares, all meet and proper to his stupendous rank. Necessarily he does not go abroad in the streets. Deities would never be able to move about handily in any country. If one whom we recognized and adored as a god should go abroad in our streets, and the day it was to happen were known, all traffic would be blocked and business would come to a standstill.

This god is comfortably housed, and yet modestly, all things considered, for if he wanted to live in a palace he would only need to speak and his worshipers would gladly build it. Sometimes he sees devotees for a moment, and comforts them and blesses them, and they kiss his feet and go away happy. Rank is nothing to him, he being a god. To him all men are alike. He sees whom he pleases and denies himself to whom he pleases. Sometimes he sees a prince and denies himself to a pauper; at other times he receives the pauper and turns the prince away. However, he does not receive many of either class. He has to husband his time for his meditations. I think he would receive Rev. Mr. Parker at any time. I think he is sorry for Mr. Parker, and I think Mr. Parker is sorry for him; and no doubt this compassion is good for both of them.

When we arrived we had to stand around in the garden a little while and wait, and the outlook was not good, for he had been turning away Maharajas that day and receiving only the riff-raff, and we belonged in between, somewhere. But presently, a servant came out saying it was all right, he was coming.

And sure enough, he came, and I saw him—that object of the worship of millions. It was a strange sensation, and thrilling. I wish I could feel it stream through my veins again. And yet, to me he was not a god, he was only a Taj. The thrill was not my thrill, but had come to me secondhand from those invisible millions of believers. By a hand-shake with their god I had ground-circuited their wire and got their monster battery's whole charge.

He was tall and slender, indeed emaciated. He had a clean cut and conspicuously intellectual face, and a deep and kindly eye. He looked many years older than he really was, but much study and meditation and fasting and prayer, with the arid life he had led as hermit and beggar, could account for that. He is wholly nude when he receives natives, of whatever rank they may be, but he had white cloth around his loins now, a concession to Mr. Parker's Europe prejudices, no doubt.

As soon as I had sobered down a little we got along very well together, and I found him a most pleasant and friendly deity. He had heard a deal about Chicago, and showed a quite remarkable interest in it, for a god. It all came of the World's Fair and the Congress of Religions. If India knows about nothing else American, she knows about those, and will keep them in mind one while.

He proposed an exchange of autographs, a delicate attention which made me believe in him, but I had been having my doubts before. He wrote his in his book, and I have a reverent regard for that book, though the words run from right to left, and so I can't read it. It was a mistake to print in that way. It contains his voluminous comments on the Hindoo holy writings, and if I could make them out I would try for perfection myself. I gave him a copy of *Huckleberry Finn*. I thought it might rest him up a little to mix it in along with his meditations on Brahma, for he looked tired, and I knew that if it didn't do him any good it wouldn't do him any harm.

He has a scholar meditating under him—Mina Bahadur Rana—but we did not see him. He wears clothes and is very imperfect. He has written a little pamphlet about his master, and I have that. It contains a wood-cut of the master and himself seated on a rug in the garden. The portrait of the master is very good indeed. The posture is exactly that which Brahma himself affects, and it requires long arms and limber legs, and can be accumulated only by gods and the india-rubber man. There is a life-size marble relief of Shri 108, S.B.S. in the garden. It represents him in this same posture.

Dear me! It is a strange world. Particularly the Indian division of it. This pupil, Mina Bahadur Rana, is not a commonplace person, but a man of distinguished capacities and attainments, and, apparently, he had a fine worldly career in front of him. He was serving the Nepal Government in a high capacity at the Court of the Viceroy of India, twenty years ago. He was an able man, educated, a thinker, a man of property. But the longing to devote himself to a religious life came upon him, and he resigned his place, turned his back upon the vanities and comforts of the world, and went away into the solitudes to live in a hut and study the sacred writings and meditate upon virtue and holiness and seek to attain them. This sort of religion resembles ours. Christ recommended the rich to give away all their property and follow Him in poverty, not in worldly comfort. American and English millionaires do it every day, and thus verify and confirm to the world the tremendous forces that lie in religion. Yet many people scoff at them for this loyalty to duty, and many will scoff at Mina Bahadur Rana and call him a crank. Like many Christians of great character and intellect, he has made the study of his Scriptures and the writing of books of commentaries upon them the loving labor of his life. Like them, he has believed that his was not an idle and foolish waste of his life, but a most worthy and honorable employment of it. Yet, there are many people who will see in those others, men worthy of homage and deep reverence, but in him merely a crank. But I shall not. He has my reverence. And I don't offer it as a common thing and poor, but as an unusual thing and of value. The ordinary reverence, the reverence defined and explained by the dictionary costs nothing. Reverence for one's own sacred things—parents, religion, flag, laws, and respect for one's own beliefs—these are feelings which we cannot even help. They come natural to us; they are involuntary, like breathing. There is no personal merit in breathing. But the reverence which is difficult, and which has personal merit in it, is the respect which you pay, without compulsion, to the political or religious attitude of a man whose beliefs are not yours. You can't revere his gods or his politics, and no one expects you to do that, but you could respect his belief in them if you tried hard enough; and you could respect him, too, if you tried hard enough. But it is very, very difficult; it is next to impossible, and so we hardly ever try. If the man doesn't believe as we do, we say he is a crank, and that settles it. I mean it does nowadays, because now we can't burn him.

We are always canting about people's "irreverence," always charging this offense upon somebody or other, and thereby intimating that we are better than that person and do not commit that offense ourselves. Whenever we do this we are in a lying attitude, and our speech is cant; for none of us are reverent—in a meritorious way; deep down in our hearts we are all irreverent. There is probably not a single exception to this rule in the earth. There is probably not one person whose reverence rises higher than respect for his own sacred things; and therefore, it is not a thing to boast about and be proud of, since the most degraded savage has that—and, like the best of us, has nothing higher. To speak plainly, we despise all reverences and all objects of reverence which are outside the pale of our own list of sacred things. And yet, with strange inconsistency, we are shocked when other people despise and defile the things which are holy to us. Suppose we should meet with a paragraph like the following, in the newspapers:

"Yesterday a visiting party of the British nobility had a picnic at Mount Vernon, and in the tomb of Washington they ate their luncheon, sang popular songs, played games, and danced waltzes and polkas."

Should we be shocked? Should we feel outraged? Should we be

amazed? Should we call the performance a desecration? Yes, that would all happen. We should denounce those people in round terms, and call them hard names.

And suppose we found this paragraph in the newspapers:

"Yesterday a visiting party of American pork-millionaires had a picnic in Westminster Abbey, and in that sacred place they ate their luncheon, sang popular songs, played games, and danced waltzes and polkas."

Would the English be shocked? Would they feel outraged? Would they be amazed? Would they call the performance a desecration? That would all happen. The pork-millionaires would be denounced in round terms; they would be called hard names.

In the tomb at Mount Vernon lie the ashes of America's most honored son; in the Abbey, the ashes of England's greatest dead; the tomb of tombs, the costliest in the earth, the wonder of the world, the Taj, was built by a great Emperor to honor the memory of a perfect wife and perfect mother, one in whom there was no spot or blemish, whose love was his stay and support, whose life was the light of the world to him; in it her ashes lie, and to the Mohammedan millions of India it is a holy place; to them it is what Mount Vernon is to Americans, it is what the Abbey is to the English.

Major Sleeman wrote forty or fifty years ago (the italics are mine):

"I would here enter my humble protest against the *quadrille and lunch parties* which are sometimes given to European ladies and gentlemen of the station at this imperial tomb; drinking and dancing are no doubt very good things in their season, but they are sadly out of place *in a sepulchre.*"

Were there any Americans among those lunch parties? If they were invited, there were.

If my imagined lunch-parties in Westminster and the tomb of Washington should take place, the incident would cause a vast outbreak of bitter eloquence about Barbarism and Irreverence; and it would come from two sets of people who would go next day and dance in the Taj if they had a chance.

As we took our leave of the Benares god and started away we noticed a group of natives waiting respectfully just within the gate—a Rajah from somewhere in India, and some people of lesser consequence. The god beckoned them to come, and as we passed out the Rajah was kneeling and reverently kissing his sacred feet.

If Barnum—but Barnum's ambitions are at rest. This god will remain in the holy peace and seclusion of his garden, undisturbed. Barnum could not have gotten him, anyway. Still, he would have found a substitute that would answer.

Smyrna

FROM *The Innocents Abroad*, CHAPTER XXXIX

We inquired, and learned that the lions of Smyrna consisted of the ruins of the ancient citadel, whose broken and prodigious battlements frown upon the city from a lofty hill just in the edge of the town—the Mount Pagus of Scripture, they call it; the site of that one of the Seven Apocalyptic Churches of Asia which was located here in the first century of the Christian era; and the grave and the place of martyrdom of the venerable Polycarp, who suffered in Smyrna for his religion some eighteen hundred years ago.

We took little donkeys and started. We saw Polycarp's tomb, and then hurried on.

The "Seven Churches"—thus they abbreviate it—came next on the list. We rode there—about a mile and a half in the sweltering sun—and visited a little Greek church which they said was built upon the ancient site; and we paid a small fee, and the holy attendant gave each of us a little wax candle as a remembrancer of the place, and I put mine in my hat and the sun melted it and the grease all ran down the back of my neck; and so now I have not any thing left but the wick, and it is a sorry and a wilted-looking wick at that.

Several of us argued as well as we could that the "church" mentioned in the Bible meant a party of Christians, and not a building; that the Bible spoke of them as being very poor—so poor, I thought, and so subject to persecution (as per Polycarp's martyrdom) that in the first place they probably could not have afforded a church edifice, and in the second would not have dared to build it in the open light of day if they could; and finally, that if they had had the privilege of building it, common judgment would have suggested that they build it somewhere near the town. But the elders of the ship's family ruled us down and scouted our evidences. However, retribution came to them afterward. They found that they had been led astray and had gone to the wrong place; they discovered that the accepted site is in the city.

Riding through the town, we could see marks of the six Smyrnas that have existed here and been burned up by fire or knocked down by earthquakes. The hills and the rocks are rent asunder in places, excavations expose great blocks of building-stone that have lain buried for ages, and all the mean houses and walls of modern Smyrna along the way are spotted white with broken pillars, capitals and fragments of sculptured marble that once adorned the lordly palaces that were the glory of the city in the olden time.

The ascent of the hill of the citadel is very steep, and we proceeded rather slowly. But there were matters of interest about us. In one place, five hundred feet above the sea, the perpendicular bank on the upper side of the road was ten or fifteen feet high, and the cut exposed three veins of oyster shells, just as we have seen quartz veins exposed in the cutting of a road in Nevada or Montana. The veins were about eighteen inches thick and two or three feet apart, and they slanted along downward for a distance of thirty feet or more, and then disappeared where the cut joined the road. Heaven only knows how far a man might trace them by "stripping." They were clean, nice oyster shells, large, and just like any other oyster shells. They were thickly massed together, and none were scattered above or below the veins. Each one was a well-defined lead by itself, and without a spur. My first instinct was to set up the usual—

NOTICE:

> We, the undersigned, claim five claims of two hundred feet each (and one for discovery), on this ledge or lode of oyster-shells, with all its dips, spurs, angles, variations and sinuosities, and fifty feet on each side of the same, to work it, etc., etc., according to the mining laws of Smyrna.

They were such perfectly natural-looking leads that I could hardly keep from "taking them up." Among the oyster-shells were mixed many fragments of ancient, broken crockery ware. Now how did those masses of oyster-shells get there? I cannot determine. Broken crockery and oyster-shells are suggestive of restaurants—but then they could have had no such places away up there on that mountain side in our time, because nobody has lived up there. A restaurant would not pay in such a stony, forbidding, desolate place. And besides, there were no champagne corks among the shells. If there ever was a restaurant there, it must have been in Smyrna's palmy days, when the hills were covered with palaces. I could believe in one restaurant, on those terms; but then how about the three? Did they have restaurants there at three different periods of the world?—because there are two or three feet of solid earth between the oyster leads. Evidently, the restaurant solution will not answer.

The hill might have been the bottom of the sea, once, and been lifted up, with its oyster-beds, by an earthquake—but, then, how about the crockery? And moreover, how about three oyster beds, one above another, and thick strata of good honest earth between?

That theory will not do. It is just possible that this hill is Mount Ararat, and that Noah's Ark rested here, and he ate oysters and threw the shells overboard. But that will not do, either. There are the three layers again and the solid earth between—and, besides, there were only eight in Noah's family, and they could not have eaten all these oysters in the two or three months they staid on top of that mountain. The beasts—however, it is simply absurd to suppose he did not know any more than to feed the beasts on oyster suppers.

It is painful—it is even humiliating—but I am reduced at last to one slender theory: that the oysters climbed up there of their own accord. But what object could they have had in view?—what did they want up there? What could any oyster want to climb a hill for? To climb a hill must necessarily be fatiguing and annoying exercise for an oyster. The most natural conclusion would be that the oysters climbed up there to look at the scenery. Yet when one comes to reflect upon the nature of an oyster, it seems plain that he does not care for scenery. An oyster has no taste for such things; he cares nothing for the beautiful. An oyster is of a retiring disposition, and not lively—not even cheerful above the average, and never enterprising. But above all, an oyster does not take any interest in scenery—he scorns it. What have I arrived at now? Simply at the point I started from, namely, those oyster shells are there, in regular layers, five hundred feet above the sea, and no man knows how they got there. I have hunted up the guide-books, and the gist of what they say is this: "They are there, but how they got there is a mystery."

Damascus

From *The Innocents Abroad,* CHAPTER XLIV

As the glare of day mellowed into twilight, we looked down upon a picture which is celebrated all over the world. I think I have read about four hundred times that when Mahomet was a simple camel-driver he reached this point and looked down upon Damascus for the first time, and then made a certain renowned remark. He said man could enter only one paradise; he preferred to go to the one above. So he sat down there and feasted his eyes upon the earthly paradise of Damascus, and then went away without entering its gates. They have erected a tower on the hill to mark the spot where he stood.

Damascus is beautiful from the mountain. It is beautiful even to foreigners accustomed to luxuriant vegetation, and I can easily understand how unspeakably beautiful it must be to eyes that are only used to the God-forsaken barrenness and desolation of Syria. I should think a Syrian would go wild with ecstacy when such a picture bursts upon him for the first time.

From his high perch, one sees before him and below him, a wall of dreary mountains, shorn of vegetation, glaring fiercely in the sun; it fences in a level desert of yellow sand, smooth as velvet and threaded far away with fine lines that stand for roads, and dotted with creeping mites we know are camel-trains and journeying men; right in the midst of the desert is spread a billowy expanse of green foliage; and nestling in its heart sits the great white city, like an island of pearls and opals gleaming out of a sea of emeralds. This is the picture you see spread far below you, with distance to soften it, the sun to glorify it, strong contrasts to heighten the effects, and over it and about it a drowsing air of repose to spiritualize it and make it seem rather a beautiful estray from the mysterious worlds we visit in dreams than a substantial tenant of our coarse, dull globe. And when you think of the leagues of blighted, blasted, sandy, rocky, sun-burnt, ugly, dreary, infamous country you have ridden over to get here, you think it is the most beautiful, beautiful picture that ever human eyes rested upon in all the broad universe! If I were to go to Damascus again, I would camp on Mahomet's hill about a week, and then go away. There is no need to go inside the walls. The Prophet was wise without knowing it when he decided not to go down into the paradise of Damascus.

There is an honored old tradition that the immense garden which Damascus stands in was the Garden of Eden, and modern writers have gathered up many chapters of evidence tending to show that it really was the Garden of Eden, and that the rivers Pharpar and Abana are the "two rivers" that watered Adam's Paradise. It may be so, but it is not paradise now, and one would be as happy outside of it as he would be likely to be within. It is so crooked and cramped and dirty that one cannot realize that he is in the splendid city he saw from the hill-top. The gardens are hidden by high mud-walls, and the paradise is become a very sink of pollution and uncomeliness. Damascus has plenty of clear, pure water in it, though, and this is enough, of itself, to make an Arab think it beautiful and blessed. Water is scarce in blistered Syria. We run railways by our large cities in America; in Syria they curve the roads so as to make them run by the meagre little puddles they call *fountains*, and which are not found oftener on a journey than every four hours. But the "rivers" of Pharpar and Abana of Scripture (mere creeks) run through Damascus, and so every house and every garden have their sparkling fountains and rivulets of water. With her forest of foliage and her abundance of water, Damascus must be a wonder of wonders to the Bedouin from the deserts. Damascus is simply an oasis— that is what it is. For four thousand years, its waters have not gone dry or its fertility failed. Now we can understand why the city has existed so long. It could not die. So long as its waters remain to it away out there in the midst of that howling desert, so long will Damascus live to bless the sight of the tired and thirsty wayfarer.

"Though old as history itself, thou art fresh as the breath of spring, blooming as thine own rose-bud, and fragrant as thine own orange flower, O Damascus, pearl of the East!"

Damascus dates back anterior to the days of Abraham, and is the oldest city in the world. It was founded by Uz, the grandson of Noah. "The early history of Damascus is shrouded in the mists of a hoary antiquity." Leave the matters written of in the first eleven chapters of the Old Testament out, and no recorded event has occurred in the world but Damascus was in existence to receive the news of it. Go back as far as you will into the vague past, there was always a Damascus. In the writings of every century for more than four thousand years, its name has been mentioned and its praises sung. To Damascus, years are only moments, decades are only flitting trifles of time. She measures time, not by days and months and years, but by the empires she has seen rise, and prosper and crumble to ruin. She is a type of immortality. She saw the foundations of Baalbec, and Thebes, and Ephesus laid; she saw these villages grow into mighty cities, and amaze the world with their grandeur—and she has lived to see them desolate, deserted, and given over to the owls and the bats. She saw the Israelitish empire exalted, and she saw it annihilated. She saw Greece rise, and flourish two thousand years, and die. In her old age she saw Rome built; she saw it overshadow the world with its power; she saw it perish. The few hundreds of years of Genoese and Venetian might and splendor were, to grave old Damascus, only a trifling scintillation hardly worth remembering. Damascus has seen all that has ever occurred on earth, and still she lives. She has looked upon the dry bones of a thousand empires, and will see the tombs of a thousand more before she dies. Though another claims the name, old Damascus is by right the Eternal City.

We reached the city gates just at sundown. They do say that one can get into any walled city of Syria, after night, for bucksheesh, except Damascus. But Damascus, with its four thousand years of respectability in the world, has many old fogy notions. There are no street lamps there, and the law compels all who go abroad at night to carry lanterns, just as was the case in old days, when heroes and heroines of the Arabian Nights walked the streets of Damascus, or flew away toward Bagdad on enchanted carpets.

It was fairly dark a few minutes after we got within the wall, and we rode long distances through wonderfully crooked streets, eight to ten feet wide, and shut in on either side by the high mud-walls of the gardens. At last we got to where lanterns could be seen flitting about here and there, and knew we were in the midst of the curious old city. In a little narrow street, crowded with our pack-mules and with a swarm of uncouth Arabs, we alighted, and through a kind of a hole in the wall entered the hotel. We stood in a great flagged court, with flowers and citron trees about us, and a huge tank in the centre that was receiving the waters of many pipes. We crossed the court and entered the rooms prepared to receive four of us. In a large marble-paved recess between the two rooms was a tank of clear, cool water, which was kept running over all the time by the streams that were pouring into it from half a dozen pipes. Nothing, in this scorching, desolate land could look so refreshing as this pure water flashing in the lamp-light; nothing could look so beautiful, nothing could sound so delicious as this mimic rain to ears long unaccustomed to sounds of such a nature. Our rooms were large, comfortably furnished, and even had their floors clothed with soft, cheerful-tinted carpets. It was a pleasant thing to see a carpet again, for if there is any thing drearier than the tomb-like, stone-paved parlors and bed-rooms of Europe and Asia, I do not know what it is. They make one think of the grave all the time. A very broad, gaily caparisoned divan, some twelve or fourteen feet long, extended across one side of each room, and opposite were single beds with spring mattresses. There were great looking-glasses and marble-top tables. All this luxury was as grateful to systems and senses worn out with an exhausting day's travel, as it was unexpected—for one can not tell what to expect in a Turkish city of even a quarter of a million inhabitants.

I do not know, but I think they used that tank between the rooms to draw drinking water from; that did not occur to me, however, until I had dipped my baking head far down into its cool depths. I thought of it then, and superb as the bath was, I was sorry I had taken it, and was about to go and explain to the landlord. But a finely curled and scented poodle dog frisked up and nipped the calf of my leg just then, and before I had time to think, I had soused him to the bottom of the tank, and when I saw a servant coming with a pitcher I went off and left the pup trying to climb out and not succeeding very well. Satisfied revenge was all I needed to make me perfectly happy, and when I walked in to supper that first night in Damascus I was in that condition. We lay on those divans a long time, after supper, smoking narghilies and long-stemmed chibouks, and talking about the dreadful ride of the day, and I knew then what I had sometimes known before—that it is worth while to get tired out, because one so enjoys resting afterward.

In the morning we sent for donkeys. It is worthy of note that we had to send for these things. I said Damascus was an old fossil, and she is. Any where else we would have been assailed by a clamorous army of donkey-drivers, guides, peddlers and beggars—but in Damascus they so hate the very sight of a foreign Christian that they want no intercourse whatever with him; only a year or two ago, his person was not always safe in Damascus streets. It is the most fanatical Mohammedan purgatory out of Arabia. Where you see one green turban of a Hadji elsewhere (the honored sign that my lord has made the pilgrimage to Mecca), I think you will see a dozen in Damascus. The Damascenes are the ugliest, wickedest looking villains we have seen. All the veiled women we had seen yet, nearly, left their eyes exposed, but numbers of these in Damascus completely hid the face under a close-drawn black veil that made the woman look like a mummy. If ever we caught an eye exposed it was quickly hidden from our contaminating Christian vision; the beggars actually passed us by without demanding bucksheesh; the merchants in the bazaars did not hold up their goods and cry out eagerly, "Hey, John!" or "Look this, Howajji!" On the contrary, they only scowled at us and said never a word.

The narrow streets swarmed like a hive with men and women in strange Oriental costumes, and our small donkeys knocked them right and left as we plowed through them, urged on by the merciless donkey-boys. These persecutors run after the animals, shouting and goading them for hours together; they keep the donkey in a gallop always, yet never get tired themselves or fall behind. The donkeys fell down and spilt us over their heads occasionally, but there was nothing for it but to mount and hurry on again. We were banged against sharp corners, loaded porters, camels, and citizens generally; and we were so taken up with looking out for collisions and casualties that we had no chance to look about us at all. We rode half through the city and through the famous "street which is called Straight" without seeing any thing, hardly. Our bones were nearly knocked out of joint, we were wild with excitement, and our sides ached with the jolting we had suffered. I do not like riding in the Damascus street-cars.

We were on our way to the reputed houses of Judas and Ananias. About eighteen or nineteen hundred years ago, Saul, a native of Tarsus, was particularly bitter against the new sect called Christians, and he left Jerusalem and started across the country on a furious crusade against them. He went forth "breathing threatenings and slaughter against the disciples of the Lord."

"And as he journeyed, he came near Damascus, and suddenly there shined round about him a light from heaven:

"And he fell to the earth and heard a voice saying unto him, 'Saul, Saul, why persecutest thou me?'

"And when he knew that it was Jesus that spoke to him he trembled, and was astonished, and said, 'Lord, what wilt thou have me to do?'"

He was told to arise and go into the ancient city and one would tell him what to do. In the meantime his soldiers stood speechless and awe-stricken, for they heard the mysterious voice but saw no man. Saul rose up and found that that fierce supernatural light had destroyed his sight, and he was blind, so "they led him by the hand and brought him to Damascus." He was converted.

Paul lay three days, blind, in the house of Judas, and during that time he neither ate nor drank.

There came a voice to a citizen of Damascus, named Ananias, saying, "Arise, and go into the street which is called Straight, and inquire at the house of Judas, for one called Saul, of Tarsus; for behold, he prayeth."

Ananias did not wish to go at first, for he had heard of Saul before, and he had his doubts about that style of a "chosen vessel" to preach the gospel of peace. However, in obedience to orders, he went into the "street called Straight" (how he found his way into it, and after he did, how he ever found his way out of it again, are mysteries only to be accounted for by the fact that he was acting under Divine inspiration). He found Paul and restored him, and ordained him a preacher; and from this old house we had hunted up in the street which is miscalled Straight, he had started out on that bold missionary career which he prosecuted till his death. It was not the house of the disciple who sold the Master for thirty pieces of silver. I make this explanation in justice to Judas, who was a far different sort of man from the person just referred to. A very different style of man, and lived in a very good house. It is a pity we do not know more about him.

I have given, in the above paragraphs, some more information for people who will not read Bible history until they are defrauded into it by some such method as this. I hope that no friend of progress and education will obstruct or interfere with my peculiar mission.

The street called Straight is straighter than a corkscrew, but not as straight as a rainbow. St. Luke is careful not to commit himself; he does not say it is the street which is straight, but the "street which is called Straight." It is a fine piece of irony; it is the only facetious remark in the Bible, I believe. We traversed the street called Straight a good way, and then turned off and called at the reputed house of Ananias. There is small question that a part of the original house is there still; it is an old room twelve or fifteen feet under ground, and its masonry is evidently ancient. If Ananias did not live there in St. Paul's time, somebody else did, which is just as well. I took a drink out of Ananias' well, and singularly enough, the water was just as fresh as if the well had been dug yesterday.

We went out toward the north end of the city to see the place where the disciples let Paul down over the Damascus wall at dead of night—for he preached Christ so fearlessly in Damascus that the people sought to kill him, just as they would to-day for the same offense, and he had to escape and flee to Jerusalem.

Then we called at the tomb of Mahomet's children and at a tomb which purported to be that of St. George who killed the dragon, and so on out to the hollow place under a rock where Paul hid during his flight till his pursuers gave him up; and to the mausoleum of the five thousand Christians who were massacred in Damascus in 1861 by the Turks. They say those narrow streets ran blood for several days, and that men, women and children were butchered indiscriminately and left to rot by hundreds all through the Christian quarter; they say, further, that the stench was dreadful. All the Christians who could get away fled from the city, and the Mohammedans would not defile their hands by burying the "infidel dogs." The thirst for blood extended to the high lands of Hermon and Anti-Lebanon, and in a short time twenty-five thousand more Christians were massacred and their possessions laid waste. How they hate a Christian in Damascus!—and pretty much all over Turkeydom as well. And how they will pay for it when Russia turns her guns upon them again!

The Sacred Sea of Galilee

FROM *The Innocents Abroad,* CHAPTER XLVIII

The celebrated Sea of Galilee is not so large a sea as Lake Tahoe—
(I measure all lakes by Tahoe, partly because I am far more familiar
with it than with any other, and partly because I have such a high admiration for it and such a world of pleasant recollections of it, that it is very
nearly impossible for me to speak of lakes and not mention it)—by a good
deal—it is just about two-thirds as large. And when we come to speak of
beauty, this sea is no more to be compared to Tahoe than a meridian of
longitude is to a rainbow. The dim waters of this pool can not suggest the
limpid brilliancy of Tahoe; these low, shaven, yellow hillocks of rocks and
sand, so devoid of perspective, can not suggest the grand peaks that compass Tahoe like a wall, and whose ribbed and chasmed fronts are clad with
stately pines that seem to grow small and smaller as they climb, till one
might fancy them reduced to weeds and shrubs far upward, where they join
the everlasting snows. Silence and solitude brood over Tahoe; and silence
and solitude brood also over this lake of Genessaret. But the solitude of the
one is as cheerful and fascinating as the solitude of the other is dismal and
repellant.

In the early morning one watches the silent battle of dawn and darkness upon the waters of Tahoe with a placid interest; but when the shadows
sulk away and one by one the hidden beauties of the shore unfold themselves in the full splendor of noon; when the still surface is belted like a
rainbow with broad bars of blue and green and white, half the distance
from circumference to centre; when, in the lazy summer afternoon, he lies
in a boat, far out to where the dead blue of the deep water begins, and
smokes the pipe of peace and idly winks at the distant crags and patches of
snow from under his cap-brim; when the boat drifts shoreward to the white
water, and he lolls over the gunwale and gazes by the hour down through
the crystal depths and notes the colors of the pebbles and reviews the finny
armies gliding in procession a hundred feet below; when at night he sees

moon and stars, mountain ridges feathered with pines, jutting white capes, bold promontories, grand sweeps of rugged scenery topped with bald, glimmering peaks, all magnificently pictured in the polished mirror of the lake, in richest, softest detail, the tranquil interest that was born with the morning deepens and deepens, by sure degrees, till it culminates at last in resistless fascination!

It is solitude, for birds and squirrels on the shore and fishes in the water are all the creatures that are near to make it otherwise, but it is not the sort of solitude to make one dreary. Come to Galilee for that. If these unpeopled deserts, these rusty mounds of barrenness, that never, never, never do shake the glare from their harsh outlines, and fade and faint into vague perspective; that melancholy ruin of Capernaum; this stupid village of Tiberias, slumbering under its six funereal plumes of palms; yonder desolate declivity where the swine of the miracle ran down into the sea, and doubtless thought it was better to swallow a devil or two and get drowned into the bargain than have to live longer in such a place; this cloudless, blistering sky; this solemn, sailless, tintless lake, reposing within its rim of yellow hills and low, steep banks, and looking just as expressionless and unpoetical (when we leave its sublime history out of the question) as any metropolitan reservoir in Christendom—if these things are not food for rock me to sleep, mother, none exist, I think.

But I should not offer the evidence for the prosecution and leave the defense unheard. Wm. C. Grimes deposes as follows:

> We had taken ship to go over to the other side. The sea was not more than six miles wide. Of the beauty of the scene, however, I cannot say enough, nor can I imagine where those travelers carried their eyes who have described the scenery of the lake as tame or uninteresting. The first great characteristic of it is the deep basin in which it lies. This is from three to four hundred feet deep on all sides except at the lower end, and the sharp slope of the banks, which are all of the richest green, is broken and diversified by the wadys and water-courses which work their way down through the sides of the basin, forming

dark chasms or light sunny valleys. Near Tiberias these banks are rocky, and ancient sepulchres open in them, with their doors toward the water. They selected grand spots, as did the Egyptians of old, for burial places, as if they designed that when the voice of God should reach the sleepers, they should walk forth and open their eyes on scenes of glorious beauty. On the east, the wild and desolate mountains contrast finely with the deep blue lake; and toward the north, sublime and majestic, Hermon looks down on the sea, lifting his white crown to heaven with the pride of a hill that has seen the departing footsteps of a hundred generations. On the north-east shore of the sea was a single tree, and this is the only tree of any size visible from the water of the lake, except a few lonely palms in the city of Tiberias, and by its solitary position attracts more attention than would a forest. The whole appearance of the scene is precisely what we would expect and desire the scenery of Genessaret to be, grand beauty, but quiet calm. The very mountains are calm.

It is an ingeniously written description, and well calculated to deceive. But if the paint and the ribbons and the flowers be stripped from it, a skeleton will be found beneath.

So stripped, there remains a lake six miles wide and neutral in color; with steep green banks, unrelieved by shrubbery; at one end bare, unsightly rocks, with (almost invisible) holes in them of no consequence to the picture; eastward, "wild and desolate mountains"; (low, desolate hills, he should have said); in the north, a mountain called Hermon, with snow on it; peculiarity of the picture, "calmness"; its prominent feature, one tree.

No ingenuity could make such a picture beautiful—to one's actual vision.

I claim the right to correct misstatements, and have so corrected the color of the water in the above recapitulation. The waters of Genessaret are of an exceedingly mild blue, even from a high elevation and a distance of five miles. Close at hand (the witness was sailing on the lake), it is hardly proper to call them blue at all, much less "deep" blue. I wish to state, also, not as a correction, but as matter of opinion, that Mount Hermon is not a striking or picturesque mountain by any means, being too near the height of its immediate neighbors to be so. That is all. I do not object to the witness dragging a mountain forty-five miles to help the scenery under consideration, because it is entirely proper to do it, and besides, the picture needs it.

"C. W. E." (of "Life in the Holy Land") deposes as follows:

A beautiful sea lies unbosomed among the Galilean hills, in the midst of that land once possessed by Zebulon and Naphtali, Asher and Dan. The azure of the sky penetrates the depths of the lake, and the waters are sweet and cool. On the west, stretch broad fertile plains; on the north the rocky shores rise step by step until in the far distance tower the snowy heights of Hermon; on the east through a misty veil are seen the high plains of Perea, which stretch away in rugged mountains leading the mind by varied paths toward Jerusalem the Holy. Flowers bloom in this terrestrial paradise, once beautiful and verdant with waving trees; singing birds enchant the ear; the turtle-dove soothes with its soft note; the crested lark sends up its song toward heaven, and the grave and stately stork inspires the mind with thought, and leads it on to meditation and repose. Life here was once idyllic, charming; here were once no rich, no poor, no high, no low. It was a world of ease, simplicity, and beauty; now it is a scene of desolation and misery.

This is not an ingenious picture. It is the worst I ever saw. It describes in elaborate detail what it terms a "terrestrial paradise," and closes with the startling information that this paradise is "a scene of desolation and misery."

I have given two fair, average specimens of the character of the testimony offered by the majority of the writers who visit this region. One says, "Of the beauty of the scene I can not say enough," and then proceeds to cover up with a woof of glittering sentences a thing which, when stripped for inspection, proves to be only an unobtrusive basin of water, some mountainous desolation, and one tree. The other, after a conscientious effort to build a terrestrial paradise out of the same materials, with the addition of a "grave and stately stork," spoils it all by blundering upon the ghastly truth at the last.

Nearly every book concerning Galilee and its lake describes the scenery as beautiful. No—not always so straightforward as that. Sometimes the impression intentionally conveyed is that it is beautiful, at the same time that the author is careful not to say that it is, in plain Saxon. But a careful analysis of these descriptions will show that the materials of which they are formed are not individually beautiful and cannot be wrought into combinations that are beautiful. The veneration and the affection which some of these men felt for the scenes they were speaking of, heated their fancies and biased their judgment; but the pleasant falsities they wrote were full of honest sincerity, at any rate. Others wrote as they did, because they feared it would be unpopular to write otherwise. Others were hypocrites and deliberately meant to deceive. Any of them would say in a moment, if asked, that it was always right and always best to tell the truth. They would say that, at any rate, if they did not perceive the drift of the question.

But why should not the truth be spoken of this region? Is the truth harmful? Has it ever needed to hide its face? God made the Sea of Galilee and its surroundings as they are. Is it the province of Mr. Grimes to improve upon the work?

Pilgrims, sinners and Arabs are all abed, now, and the camp is still. Labor in loneliness is irksome. Since I made my last few notes, I have been sitting outside the tent for half an hour. Night is the time to see Galilee. Genessaret under these lustrous stars has nothing repulsive about it. Genessaret, with the glittering reflections of the constellations flecking its surface, almost makes me regret that I ever saw the rude glare of the day upon it. Its history and its associations are its chiefest charm, in any eyes, and the spells they weave are feeble in the searching light of the sun. Then, we scarcely feel the fetters. Our thoughts wander constantly to the practical concerns of life, and refuse to dwell upon things that seem vague and unreal. But when the day is done, even the most unimpressible must yield to the dreamy influences of this tranquil starlight. The old traditions of the place steal upon his memory and haunt his reveries, and then his fancy clothes all sights and sounds with the supernatural. In the lapping of the waves upon the beach, he hears the dip of ghostly oars; in the secret noises of the night he hears spirit voices; in the soft sweep of the breeze, the rush of invisible wings. Phantom ships are on the sea, the dead of twenty centuries come forth from the tombs, and in the dirges of the night wind the songs of old forgotten ages find utterance again.

In the starlight, Galilee has no boundaries but the broad compass of the heavens, and is a theatre meet for great events; meet for the birth of a religion able to save a world; and meet for the stately Figure appointed to stand upon its stage and proclaim its high decrees. But in the sunlight, one says: Is it for the deeds which were done and the words which were spoken in this little acre of rocks and sand eighteen centuries gone, that the bells are ringing to-day in the remote islands of the sea and far and wide over continents that clasp the circumference of the huge globe?

One can comprehend it only when night has hidden all incongruities and created a theatre proper for so grand a drama.

Church of the Holy Sepulchre

FROM *The Innocents Abroad,* CHAPTER LIII

When one enters the Church of the Holy Sepulchre, the Sepulchre itself is the first thing he desires to see, and really is almost the first thing he does see. The next thing he has a strong yearning to see is the spot where the Saviour was crucified. But this they exhibit last. It is the crowning glory of the place. One is grave and thoughtful when he stands in the little Tomb of the Saviour—he could not well be otherwise in such a place—but he has not the slightest possible belief that ever the Lord lay there, and so the interest he feels in the spot is very, very greatly marred by that reflection. He looks at the place where Mary stood, in another part of the church, and where John stood, and Mary Magdalene; where the mob derided the Lord; where the angel sat; where the crown of thorns was found, and the true Cross; where the risen Saviour appeared—he looks at all these places with interest, but with the same conviction he felt in the case of the Sepulchre, that there is nothing genuine about them, and that they are imaginary holy places created by the monks. But the place of the Crucifixion affects him differently. He fully believes that he is looking upon the very spot where the Saviour gave up his life. He remembers that Christ was very celebrated, long before he came to Jerusalem; he knows that his fame was so great that crowds followed him all the time; he is aware that his entry into the city produced a stirring sensation, and that his reception was a kind of ovation; he can not overlook the fact that when he was cruci-fied there were very many in Jerusalem who believed that he was the true Son of God. To publicly execute such a personage was sufficient in itself to make the locality of the execution a memorable place for ages; added to this, the storm, the darkness, the earthquake, the rending of the vail of the Temple, and the untimely waking of the dead, were events calculated to fix the execution and the scene of it in the memory of even the most thought-less witness. Fathers would tell their sons about the strange affair, and point out the spot; the sons would transmit the story to their children, and thus a period of three hundred years would easily be spanned at which time Helena came and built a church upon Calvary to commemorate the death and burial of the Lord and preserve the sacred place in the memories of men; since that time there has always been a church there. It is not pos-sible that there can be any mistake about the locality of the Crucifixion. Not half a dozen persons knew where they buried the Saviour, perhaps, and a burial is not a startling event, any how; therefore, we can be pardoned for unbelief in the Sepulchre, but not in the place of the Crucifixion. Five hundred years hence there will be no vestige of Bunker Hill Monument left, but America will still know where the battle was fought and where Warren fell. The crucifixion of Christ was too notable an event in Jerusalem, and the Hill of Calvary made too celebrated by it, to be forgotten in the short space of three hundred years. I climbed the stairway in the church which brings one to the top of the small inclosed pinnacle of rock, and looked upon the place where the true cross once stood, with a far more absorbing interest than I had ever felt in any thing earthly before. I could not believe that the three holes in the top of the rock were the actual ones the crosses stood in, but I felt satisfied that those crosses had stood so near the place now occupied by them, that the few feet of possible difference were a matter of no consequence.

When one stands where the Saviour was crucified, he finds it all he can do to keep it strictly before his mind that Christ was not crucified in a Catholic Church. He must remind himself every now and then that the great event transpired in the open air, and not in a gloomy, candle-lighted cell in a little corner of a vast church, up-stairs—a small cell all bejeweled and bespangled with flashy ornamentation, in execrable taste.

Under a marble altar like a table, is a circular hole in the marble floor, corresponding with the one just under it in which the true Cross stood. The first thing every one does is to kneel down and take a candle and examine this hole. He does this strange prospecting with an amount of gravity that can never be estimated or appreciated by a man who has not seen the operation. Then he holds his candle before a richly engraved picture of the Saviour, done on a messy slab of gold, and wonderfully rayed and starred with diamonds, which hangs above the hole within the altar, and his solemnity changes to lively admiration. He rises and faces the finely wrought figures of the Saviour and the malefactors uplifted upon their crosses behind the altar, and bright with a metallic lustre of many colors. He turns next to the figures close to them of the Virgin and Mary Magdalen; next to the rift in the living rock made by the earthquake at the time of the Crucifixion, and an extension of which he had seen before in the wall of one of the grottoes below; he looks next at the show-case with a figure of the Virgin in it, and is amazed at the princely fortune in precious gems and jewelry that hangs so thickly about the form as to hide it like a garment almost. All about the apartment the gaudy trappings of the Greek Church offend the eye and keep the mind on the rack to remember that this is the Place of the Crucifixion—Golgotha—the Mount of Calvary. And the last thing he looks at is that which was also the first—the place where the true Cross stood. That will chain him to the spot and compel him to look once more, and once again, after he has satisfied all curiosity and lost all interest concerning the other matters pertaining to the locality.

And so I close my chapter on the Church of the Holy Sepulchre—the most sacred locality on earth to millions and millions of men, and women, and children, the noble and the humble, bond and free. In its history from the first, and in its tremendous associations, it is the most illustrious edifice in Christendom. With all its clap-trap side-shows and unseemly impostures of every kind, it is still grand, reverend, venerable—for a god died there; for fifteen hundred years its shrines have been wet with the tears of pilgrims from the earth's remotest confines; for more than two hundred, the most gallant knights that ever wielded sword wasted their lives away in a struggle to seize it and hold it sacred from infidel pollution. Even in our own day a war, that cost millions of treasure and rivers of blood, was fought because two rival nations claimed the sole right to put a new dome upon it. History is full of this old Church of the Holy Sepulchre—full of blood that was shed because of the respect and the veneration in which men held the last resting-place of the meek and lowly, the mild and gentle, Prince of Peace!

PART VII

Fantasies

Satan's Letter

FROM *Letters from the Earth*

This is a strange place, and extraordinary place, and interesting. There is nothing resembling it at home. The people are all insane, the other animals are all insane, the earth is insane, Nature itself is insane. Man is a marvelous curiosity. When he is at his very very best he is a sort of low grade nickel-plated angel; at his worst he is unspeakable, unimaginable; and first and last and all the time he is a sarcasm. Yet he blandly and in all sincerity calls himself the "noblest work of God." This is the truth I am telling you. And this is not a new idea with him, he has talked it through all the ages, and believed it. Believed it, and found nobody among all his race to laugh at it.

Moreover—if I may put another strain upon you—he thinks he is the Creator's pet. He believes the Creator is proud of him; he even believes the Creator loves him; has a passion for him; sits up nights to admire him; yes, and watch over him and keep him out of trouble. He prays to Him, and thinks He listens. Isn't it a quaint idea? Fills his prayers with crude and bald and florid flatteries of Him, and thinks He sits and purrs over these extravagancies and enjoys them. He prays for help, and favor, and protection, every day; and does it with hopefulness and confidence, too, although no prayer of his has ever been answered. The daily affront, the daily defeat, do not discourage him, he goes on praying just the same. There is something almost fine about this perseverance. I must put one more strain upon you: he thinks he is going to heaven!

He has salaried teachers who tell him that. They also tell him there is a hell, of everlasting fire, and that he will go to it if he doesn't keep the Commandments. What are Commandments? They are a curiosity. I will tell you about them by and by. . . .

"I have told you nothing about man that is not true." You must pardon me if I repeat that remark now and then in these letters; I want you to take seriously the things I am telling you, and I feel that if I were in your place and you in mine, I should need that reminder from time to time, to keep my credulity from flagging.

For there is nothing about man that is not strange to an immortal. He looks at nothing as we look at it, his sense of proportion is quite different from ours, and his sense of values is so widely divergent from ours, that with all our large intellectual powers it is not likely that even the most gifted among us would ever be quite able to understand it.

For instance, take this sample: he has imagined a heaven, and has left entirely out of it the supremest of all his delights, the one ecstasy that stands first and foremost in the heart of every individual of his race—and of ours—sexual intercourse!

It is as if a lost and perishing person in a roasting desert should be told by a rescuer he might choose and have all longed-for things but one, and he should elect to leave out water!

His heaven is like himself: strange, interesting, astonishing, grotesque. I give you my word, it has not a single feature in it that he actually values. It consists—utterly and entirely—of diversions which he cares next to nothing about, here in the earth, yet is quite sure he will like them in heaven. Isn't it curious? Isn't it interesting? You must not think I am exaggerating, for it is not so. I will give you details.

Most men do not sing, most men cannot sing, most men will not stay when others are singing if it be continued more than two hours. Note that.

Only about two men in a hundred can play upon a musical instrument, and not four in a hundred have any wish to learn how. Set that down.

Many men pray, not many of them like to do it. A few pray long, the others make a short cut.

More men go to church than want to.

To forty-nine men in fifty the Sabbath Day is a dreary, dreary bore.

Of all the men in a church on a Sunday, two-thirds are tired when the service is half over, and the rest before it is finished.

The gladdest moment for all of them is when the preacher uplifts his hands for the benediction. You can hear the soft rustle of relief that sweeps the house, and you recognize that it is eloquent with gratitude.

All nations look down upon all other nations.

All nations dislike all other nations.

All white nations despise all colored nations, of whatever hue, and oppress them when they can.

White men will not associate with "niggers," nor marry them.

They will not allow them in their schools and churches.

All the world hates the Jew, and will not endure him except when he is rich.

I ask you to note all those particulars.

Further. All sane people detest noise.

All people, sane or insane, like to have variety in their life. Monotony quickly wearies them.

Every man, according to the mental equipment that has fallen to his share, exercises his intellect constantly, ceaselessly, and this exercise makes up a vast and valued and essential part of his life. The lowest intellect, like the highest, possesses a skill of some kind and takes a keen pleasure in testing it, proving it, perfecting it. The urchin who is his comrade's superior in games is as diligent and as enthusiastic in his practice as are the sculptor, the painter, the pianist, the mathematician and the rest. Not one of them could be happy if his talent were put under an interdict.

Now then, you have the facts. You know what the human race enjoys, and what it doesn't enjoy. It has invented a heaven out of its own head, all by itself: guess what it is like! In fifteen hundred eternities you couldn't do it. The ablest mind known to you or me in fifty million aeons couldn't do it.

Cannibalism in the Cars

FROM *Sketches, New and Old*

I visited St. Louis lately, and on my way West, after changing cars at Terre Haute, Indiana, a mild, benevolent-looking gentleman of about forty-five, or maybe fifty, came in at one of the way-stations and sat down beside me. We talked together pleasantly on various subjects for an hour, perhaps, and I found him exceedingly intelligent and entertaining. When he learned that I was from Washington, he immediately began to ask questions about various public men, and about Congressional affairs; and I saw very shortly that I was conversing with a man who was perfectly familiar with the ins and outs of political life at the Capital, even to the ways and manners, and customs of procedure of Senators and Representatives in the Chambers of the national Legislature. Presently two men halted near us for a single moment, and one said to the other:

"Harris, if you'll do that for me, I'll never forget you, my boy."

My new comrade's eye lighted pleasantly. The words had touched upon a happy memory, I thought. Then his face settled into thoughtfulness—almost into gloom. He turned to me and said,

"Let me tell you a story; let me give you a secret chapter of my life—a chapter that has never been referred to by me since its events transpired. Listen patiently, and promise that you will not interrupt me."

I said I would not, and he related the following strange adventure, speaking sometimes with animation, sometimes with melancholy, but always with feeling and earnestness.

THE STRANGER'S NARRATIVE

On the 19th of December, 1853, I started from St. Louis on the evening train bound for Chicago. There were only twenty-four passengers, all told. There were no ladies and no children. We were in excellent spirits, and pleasant acquaintanceships were soon formed. The journey bade fair to be a happy one; and no individual in the party, I think, had even the vaguest presentiment of the horrors we were soon to undergo.

"At 11 P.M. it began to snow hard. Shortly after leaving the small village of Welden, we entered upon that tremendous prairie solitude that stretches its leagues on leagues of houseless dreariness far away toward the jubilee Settlements. The winds, unobstructed by trees or hills, or even vagrant rocks, whistled fiercely across the level desert, driving the falling snow before it like spray from the crested waves of a stormy sea. The snow was deepening fast; and we knew, by the diminished speed of the train, that the engine was plowing through it with steadily increasing difficulty. Indeed, it almost came to a dead halt sometimes, in the midst of great drifts that piled themselves like colossal graves across the track. Conversation began to flag. Cheerfulness gave place to grave concern. The possibility of being imprisoned in the snow, on the bleak prairie, fifty miles from any house, presented itself to every mind, and extended its depressing influence over every spirit.

"At two o'clock in the morning I was aroused out of an uneasy slumber by the ceasing of all motion about me. The appalling truth flashed upon me instantly—we were captives in a snow-drift! 'All hands to the rescue!' Every man sprang to obey. Out into the wild night, the pitchy darkness, the billowy snow, the driving storm, every soul leaped, with the consciousness that a moment lost now might bring destruction to us all. Shovels, hands, boards—anything, everything that could displace snow, was brought into instant requisition. It was a weird picture, that small company of frantic men fighting the banking snows, half in the blackest shadow and half in the angry light of the locomotive's reflector.

"One short hour sufficed to prove the utter uselessness of our efforts. The storm barricaded the track with a dozen drifts while we dug one away. And worse than this, it was discovered that the last grand charge the engine had made upon the enemy had broken the fore-and-aft shaft of the driving-wheel! With a free track before us we should still have been helpless. We entered the car wearied with labor, and very sorrowful. We gathered about the stoves, and gravely canvassed our situation. We had no provisions whatever—in this lay our chief distress. We could not freeze, for there was a good supply of wood in the tender. This was our only comfort. The discussion ended at last in accepting the disheartening decision of the conductor, viz., that it would be death for any man to attempt to travel fifty miles on foot through snow like that. We could not send for help, and even if we could it would not come. We must submit, and await, as patiently as we might, succor or starvation! I think the stoutest heart there felt a momentary chill when those words were uttered.

"Within the hour conversation subsided to a low murmur here and there about the car, caught fitfully between the rising and falling of the blast; the lamps grew dim; and the majority of the castaways settled themselves among the flickering shadows to think—to forget the present, if they could—to sleep, if they might.

"The eternal night—it surely seemed eternal to us—wore its lagging hours away at last, and the cold gray dawn broke in the east. As the light grew stronger the passengers began to stir and give signs of life, one after another, and each in turn pushed his slouched hat up from his forehead, stretched his stiffened limbs, and glanced out of the windows upon the cheerless prospect. It was cheerless, indeed!—not a living thing visible anywhere, not a human habitation; nothing but a vast white desert; uplifted sheets of snow drifting hither and thither before the wind—a world of eddying flakes shutting out the firmament above.

"All day we moped about the cars, saying little, thinking much. Another lingering dreary night—and hunger.

"Another dawning—another day of silence, sadness, wasting hunger, hopeless watching for succor that could not come. A night of restless slumber, filled with dreams of feasting—wakings distressed with the gnawings of hunger.

"The fourth day came and went—and the fifth! Five days of dreadful imprisonment! A savage hunger looked out at every eye. There was in it a sign of awful import—the foreshadowing of a something that was vaguely shaping itself in every heart—a something which no tongue dared yet to frame into words.

"The sixth day passed—the seventh dawned upon as gaunt and haggard and hopeless a company of men as ever stood in the shadow of death. It must out now! That thing which had been growing up in every heart was ready to leap from every lip at last! Nature had been taxed to the utmost—she must yield. RICHARD H. GASTON of Minnesota, tall, cadaverous, and pale, rose up. All knew what was coming. All prepared—every emotion, every semblance of excitement—was smothered—only a calm, thoughtful seriousness appeared in the eyes that were lately so wild.

"'Gentlemen: It cannot be delayed longer! The time is at hand! We must determine which of us shall die to furnish food for the rest!'

"MR. JOHN J. WILLIAMS of Illinois rose and said: 'Gentlemen—I nominate the Rev. James Sawyer of Tennessee.'

"MR. Wm. R. ADAMS of Indiana said: 'I nominate Mr. Daniel Slote of New York.'

"MR. CHARLES J. LANGDON: 'I nominate Mr. Samuel A. Bowen of St. Louis.'

"MR. SLOTE: 'Gentlemen—I desire to decline in favor of Mr. John A. Van Nostrand, Jun., of New Jersey.'

"MR. GASTON: 'If there be no objection, the gentleman's desire will be acceded to.'

"MR. VAN NOSTRAND objecting, the resignation of Mr. Slote was rejected. The resignations of Messrs. Sawyer and Bowen were also offered, and refused upon the same grounds.

"MR. A. L. BASCOM of Ohio: 'I move that the nominations now close, and that the House proceed to an election by ballot.'

"MR. SAWYER: 'Gentlemen—I protest earnestly against these proceedings. They are, in every way, irregular and unbecoming. I must beg to move that they be dropped at once, and that we elect a chairman of the meeting and proper officers to assist him, and then we can go on with the business before us understandingly.'

"MR. BELL of Iowa: 'Gentlemen—I object. This is no time to stand upon forms and ceremonious observances. For more than seven days we have been without food. Every moment we lose in idle discussion increases our distress. I am satisfied with the nominations that have been made— every gentleman present is, I believe—and I, for one, do not see why we should not proceed at once to elect one or more of them. I wish to offer a resolution—'

"MR. GASTON: 'It would be objected to, and have to lie over one day under the rules, thus bringing about the very delay you wish to avoid. The gentleman from New Jersey—'

"MR. VAN NOSTRAND: 'Gentlemen—I am a stranger among you; I have not sought the distinction that has been conferred upon me, and I feel a delicacy—'

"MR. MORGAN of Alabama (interrupting): 'I move the previous question.'

"The motion was carried, and further debate shut off, of course. The motion to elect officers was passed, and under it Mr. Gaston was chosen chairman, Mr. Blake, secretary, Messrs. Holcomb, Dyer, and Baldwin a committee on nominations, and Mr. R. M. Howland, purveyor, to assist the committee in making selections.

"A recess of half an hour was then taken, and some little caucusing followed. At the sound of the gavel the meeting reassembled, and the committee reported in favor of Messrs. George Ferguson of Kentucky, Lucien Herrman of Louisiana, and W. Messick of Colorado as candidates. The report was accepted.

"MR. ROGERS of Missouri: 'Mr. President The report being properly before the House now, I move to amend it by substituting for the name of Mr. Herrman that of Mr. Lucius Harris of St. Louis, who is well and honorably known to us all. I do not wish to be understood as casting the least reflection upon the high character and standing of the gentleman from Louisiana, far from it. I respect and esteem him as much as any gentleman here present possibly can; but none of us can be blind to the fact that he has lost more flesh during the week that we have lain here than any among us—none of us can be blind to the fact that the committee has been derelict in its duty, either through negligence or a graver fault, in thus offering for our suffrages a gentleman who, however pure his own motives may be, has really less nutriment in him—'

"THE CHAIR: 'The gentleman from Missouri will take his seat. The Chair cannot allow the integrity of the committee to be questioned save by the regular course, under the rules. What action will the House take upon the gentleman's motion?'

"MR. HALLIDAY of Virginia: 'I move to further amend the report by substituting Mr. Harvey Davis of Oregon for Mr. Messick. It may be urged by gentlemen that the hardships and privations of a frontier life have rendered Mr. Davis tough; but, gentlemen, is this a time to cavil at toughness? Is this a time to be fastidious concerning trifles? Is this a time to dispute about matters of paltry significance? No, gentlemen, bulk is what we desire—substance, weight, bulk—these are the supreme requisites now—not talent, not genius, not education. I insist upon my motion.'

"MR. MORGAN (excitedly): 'Mr. Chairman—I do most strenuously object to this amendment. The gentleman from Oregon is old, and furthermore is bulky only in bone—not in flesh. I ask the gentleman from Virginia if it is soup we want instead of solid sustenance? if he would delude us with shadows? if he would mock our suffering with an Oregonian specter? I ask him if he can look upon the anxious faces around him, if he can gaze into our sad eyes, if he can listen to the beating of our expectant hearts, and still thrust this famine-stricken fraud upon us? I ask him if he can think of our desolate state, of our past sorrows, of our dark future, and still unpityingly foist upon us this wreck, this ruin, this tottering swindle, this gnarled and blighted and sapless vagabond from Oregon's hospitable shores? Never!'

"The amendment was put to vote, after a fiery debate, and lost. Mr. Harris was substituted on the first amendment. The balloting then began. Five ballots were held without a choice. On the sixth, Mr. Harris was elected, all voting for him but himself. It was then moved that his election should be ratified by acclamation, which was lost, in consequence of his again voting against himself.

"MR. RADWAY moved that the House now take up the remaining candidates, and go into an election for breakfast. This was carried.

"On the first ballot—there was a tie, half the members favoring one candidate on account of his youth, and half favoring the other on account of his superior size. The President gave the casting vote for the latter, Mr. Messick. This decision created considerable dissatisfaction among the friends of Mr. Ferguson, the defeated candidate, and there was some talk of demanding a new ballot; but in the midst of it a motion to adjourn was carried, and the meeting broke up at once.

"The preparations for supper diverted the attention of the Ferguson faction from the discussion of their grievance for a long time, and then, when they would have taken it up again, the happy announcement that Mr. Harris was ready drove all thought of it to the winds.

"We improvised tables by propping up the backs of car-seats, and sat down with hearts full of gratitude to the finest supper that had blessed our vision for seven torturing days. How changed we were from what we had been a few short hours before! Hopeless, sad-eyed misery, hunger, feverish anxiety, desperation, then; thankfulness, serenity, joy too deep for utterance now. That I know was the cheeriest hour of my eventful life. The winds howled, and blew the snow wildly about our prison house, but they were powerless to distress us any more. I liked Harris. He might have been better done, perhaps, but I am free to say that no man ever agreed with me better than Harris, or afforded me so large a degree of satisfaction. Messick was very well, though rather high-flavored, but for genuine nutritiousness and delicacy of fiber, give me Harris. Messick had his good points—I will not attempt to deny it, nor do I wish to do it but he was no more fitted for breakfast than a mummy would be, sir—not a bit. Lean?—why, bless me!— and tough? Ah, he was very tough! You could not imagine it—you could never imagine anything like it."

"Do you mean to tell me that—"

"Do not interrupt me, please. After breakfast we elected a man by the name of Walker, from Detroit, for supper. He was very good. I wrote his wife so afterward. He was worthy of all praise. I shall always remember

Walker. He was a little rare, but very good. And then the next morning we had Morgan of Alabama for breakfast. He was one of the finest men I ever sat down to;+ handsome, educated, refined, spoke several languages fluently; a perfect gentleman, he was a perfect gentleman, and singularly juicy. For supper we had that Oregon patriarch, and he was a fraud, there is no question about it—old, scraggy, tough, nobody can picture the reality. I finally said, gentlemen, you can do as you like, but I will wait for another election. And Grimes of Illinois said, 'Gentlemen, I will wait also. When you elect a man that has something to recommend him, I shall be glad to join you again.' It soon became evident that there was general dissatisfaction with Davis of Oregon, and so, to preserve the good will that had prevailed so pleasantly since we had had Harris, an election was called, and the result of it was that Baker of Georgia was chosen. He was splendid! Well, well—after that we had Doolittle, and Hawkins, and McElroy (there was some complaint about McElroy, because he was uncommonly short and thin), and Penrod, and two Smiths, and Bailey (Bailey had a wooden leg, which was a clear loss, but he was otherwise good), and an Indian boy, and an organ-grinder, and a gentleman by the name of Buckminster—a poor stick of a vagabond that wasn't any good for company and no account for breakfast. We were glad we got him elected before relief came."

"And so the blessed relief did come at last?"

"Yes, it came one bright, sunny morning, just after election. John Murphy was the choice, and there never was a better, I am willing to testify; but John Murphy came home with us, in the train that came to succor us, and lived to marry the widow Harris—"

"Relict of—"

"Relict of our first choice. He married her, and is happy and respected and prosperous yet. Ah, it was like a novel, sir—it was like a romance. This is my stopping-place, sir; I must bid you goodby. Any time that you can make it convenient to tarry a day or two with me, I shall be glad to have you. I like you, sir; I have conceived an affection for you. I could like you as well as I liked Harris himself, sir. Good day, sir, and a pleasant journey."

He was gone. I never felt so stunned, so distressed, so bewildered in my life. But in my soul I was glad he was gone. With all his gentleness of manner and his soft voice, I shuddered whenever he turned his hungry eye upon me; and when I heard that I had achieved his perilous affection, and that I stood almost with the late Harris in his esteem, my heart fairly stood still!

I was bewildered beyond description. I did not doubt his word; I could not question a single item in a statement so stamped with the earnestness of truth as his; but its dreadful details overpowered me, and threw my thoughts into hopeless confusion. I saw the conductor looking at me. I said, "Who is that man?"

"He was a member of Congress once, and a good one. But he got caught in a snow-drift in the cars, and like to have been starved to death. He got so frost-bitten and frozen up generally, and used up for want of something to eat, that he was sick and out of his head two or three months afterward. He is all right now, only he is a monomaniac, and when he gets on that old subject he never stops till he has eat up that whole car-load of people he talks about. He would have finished the crowd by this time, only he had to get out here. He has got their names as pat as A B C. When he gets them all eat up but himself, he always says: 'Then the hour for the usual election for breakfast having arrived; and there being no opposition, I was duly elected, after which, there being no objections offered, I resigned. Thus I am here.'"

I felt inexpressibly relieved to know that I had only been listening to the harmless vagaries of a madman instead of the genuine experiences of a bloodthirsty cannibal.

A Curious Pleasure Excursion

FROM *Sketches, New and Old*

ADVERTISEMENT

This is to inform the public that in connection with Mr. Barnum I have leased the comet for a term of years; and I desire also to solicit the public patronage in favor of a beneficial enterprise which we have in view.

We propose to fit up comfortable, and even luxurious, accommodations in the comet for as many persons as will honor us with their patronage, and make an extended excursion among the heavenly bodies. We shall prepare 1,000,000 state-rooms in the tail of the comet (with hot and cold water, gas, looking-glass, parachute, umbrella, etc., in each), and shall construct more if we meet with a sufficiently generous encouragement. We shall have billiard-rooms, card-rooms, music-rooms, bowling-alleys and many spacious theaters and free libraries; and on the main deck we propose to have a driving park, with upward of 100,000 miles of roadway in it. We shall publish daily newspapers also.

DEPARTURE OF THE COMET

The comet will leave New York at 10 P.M. on the 20th inst., and therefore it will be desirable that the passengers be on board by eight at the latest, to avoid confusion in getting under way. It is not known whether passports will be necessary or not, but it is deemed best that passengers provide them, and so guard against all contingencies. No dogs will be allowed on board. This rule has been made in deference to the existing state of feeling regarding these animals, and will be strictly adhered to. The safety of the passengers will in all ways be jealously looked to. A substantial iron railing will be put up all around the comet, and no one will be allowed to go to the edge and look over unless accompanied by either my partner or myself.

THE POSTAL SERVICE

will be of the completest character. Of course the telegraph, and the telegraph only, will be employed; consequently friends occupying state-rooms 20,000,000 and even 30,000,000 miles apart will be able to send a message and receive a reply inside of eleven days. Night messages will be half-rate. The whole of this vast postal system will be under the personal superintendence of Mr. Hale of Maine. Meals served at all hours. Meals served in staterooms charged extra.

Hostility is not apprehended from any great planet, but we have thought it best to err on the safe side, and therefore have provided a proper number of mortars, siege-guns, and boarding-pikes. History shows that small, isolated communities, such as the people of remote islands, are prone to be hostile to strangers, and so the same may be the case with

THE INHABITANTS OF STARS

of the tenth or twentieth magnitude. We shall in no case wantonly offend the people of any star, but shall treat all alike with urbanity and kindliness, never conducting ourselves toward an asteroid after a fashion which we could not venture to assume toward Jupiter or Saturn. I repeat that we shall not wantonly offend any star; but at the same time we shall promptly resent any injury that may be done us, or any insolence offered us, by parties or governments residing in any star in the firmament. Although averse to the shedding of blood, we shall still hold this course rigidly and fearlessly, not only toward single stars, but toward constellations. We shall hope to leave a good impression of America behind us in every nation we visit, from Venus to Uranus. And, at all events, if we cannot inspire love we shall at least compel respect for our country wherever we go. We shall take with us, free of charge,

A GREAT FORCE OF MISSIONARIES,

and shed the true light upon all the celestial orbs which, physically aglow, are yet morally in darkness. Sunday-schools will be established wherever practicable. Compulsory education will also be introduced.

The comet will visit Mars first, and proceed to Mercury, Jupiter, Venus, and Saturn. Parties connected with the government of the District of Columbia and with the former city government of New York, who may desire to inspect the rings, will be allowed time and every facility. Every star of prominent magnitude will be visited, and time allowed for excursions to points of interest inland.

THE DOG STAR

has been stricken from the program. Much time will be spent in the Great Bear, and, indeed, in every constellation of importance. So, also, with the Sun and Moon and the Milky Way, otherwise the Gulf Stream of the Skies. Clothing suitable for wear in the sun should be provided. Our program has been so arranged that we shall seldom go more than 100,000,000 of miles at a time without stopping at some star. This will necessarily make the stoppages frequent and preserve the interest of the tourist. Baggage checked through to any point on the route. Parties desiring to make only a part of the proposed tour, and thus save expense, may stop over at any star they choose and wait for the return voyage.

After visiting all the most celebrated stars and constellations in our system and personally, inspecting the remotest sparks that even the most powerful telescope can now detect in the firmament, we shall proceed with good heart upon

A STUPENDOUS VOYAGE

of discovery among the countless whirling worlds that make turmoil in the mighty wastes of space that stretch their solemn solitudes, their unimaginable vastness billions upon billions of miles away beyond the farthest verge of telescopic vision, till by comparison the little sparkling vault we used to gaze at on Earth shall seem like a remembered phosphorescent flash of spangles which some tropical voyager's prow stirred into life for a single instant, and which ten thousand miles of phosphorescent seas and tedious lapse of time had since diminished to an incident utterly trivial in his recollection. Children occupying seats at the first table will be charged full fare.

FIRST-CLASS FARE

from the Earth to Uranus, including visits to the Sun and Moon and all the principal planets on the route, will be charged at the low rate of $2 for every 50,000,000 miles of actual travel. A great reduction will be made where parties wish to make the round trip. This comet is new and in thorough repair and is now on her first voyage. She is confessedly the fastest on the line. She makes 20,000,000 miles a day, with her present facilities; but, with a picked American crew and good weather, we are confident we can get 40,000,000 out of her. Still, we shall never push her to a dangerous speed, and we shall rigidly prohibit racing with other comets. Passengers desiring to diverge at any point or return will be transferred to other comets. We make close connections at all principal points with all reliable lines. Safety can be depended upon. It is not to be denied that the heavens are infested with

OLD RAMSHACKLE COMETS

that have not been inspected or overhauled in 10,000 years, and which ought long ago to have been destroyed or turned into hail-barges, but with these we have no connection whatever. Steerage passengers not allowed abaft the main hatch.

Complimentary round-trip tickets have been tendered to General

Butler, Mr. Shepherd, Mr. Richardson, and other eminent gentlemen, whose public services have entitled them to the rest and relaxation of a voyage of this kind. Parties desiring to make the round trip will have extra accommodation. The entire voyage will be completed, and the passengers landed in New York again, on the 14th of December, 1991. This is, at least, forty years quicker than any other comet can do it in. Nearly all the back-pay members contemplate making the round trip with us in case their constituents will allow them a holiday. Every harmless amusement will be allowed on board, but no pools permitted on the run of the comet—no gambling of any kind. All fixed stars will be respected by us, but such stars as seem to need fixing we shall fix. If it makes trouble, we shall be sorry, but firm.

Mr. Coggia having leased his comet to us, she will no longer be called by his name, but by my partner's. N. B.—Passengers by paying double fare will be entitled to a share in all the new stars, suns, moons, comets, meteors, and magazines of thunder and lightning we may discover. Patent-medicine people will take notice that

WE CARRY BULLETIN-BOARDS

and a paint-brush along for use in the constellations, and are open to terms. Cremationists are reminded that we are going straight to—some hot places—and are open to terms. To other parties our enterprise is a pleasure excursion, but individually we mean business. We shall fly our comet for all it is worth.

FOR FURTHER PARTICULARS,

or for freight or passage, apply on board, or to my partner, but not to me, since I do not take charge of the comet until she is under way. It is necessary, at a time like this, that my mind should not be burdened with small business details.

Captain Stormfield's Visit to Heaven

FROM *Captain Stormfield's Visit to Heaven,* CHAPTER I

Well, when I had been dead about thirty years I begun to get a little anxious. Mind you, had been whizzing through space all that time, like a comet. LIKE a comet! Why, Peters, I laid over the lot of them! Of course there warn't any of them going my way, as a steady thing, you know, because they travel in a long circle like the loop of a lasso, whereas I was pointed as straight as a dart for the Hereafter; but I happened on one every now and then that was going my way for an hour or so, and then we had a bit of a brush together. But it was generally pretty one-sided, because I sailed by them the same as if they were standing still. An ordinary comet don't make more than about 200,000 miles a minute. Of course when I came across one of that sort—like Encke's and Halley's comets, for instance—it warn't anything but just a flash and a vanish, you see. You couldn't rightly call it a race. It was as if the comet was a gravel-train and I was a telegraph despatch. But after I got outside of our astronomical system, I used to flush a comet occasionally that was something LIKE. WE haven't got any such comets—ours don't begin. One night I was swinging along at a good round gait, everything taut and trim, and the wind in my favor—I judged I was going about a million miles a minute—it might have been more, it couldn't have been less—when I flushed a most uncommonly big one about three points off my starboard bow. By his stern lights I judged he was bearing about northeast-and-by-north-half-east. Well, it was so near my course that I wouldn't throw away the chance; so I fell off a point, steadied my helm, and went for him. You should have heard me whiz, and seen the electric fur fly! In about a minute and a half I was fringed out with an electrical nimbus that flamed around for miles and miles and lit up all space like broad day. The comet was burning blue in the distance, like a sickly torch, when I first sighted him, but he begun to grow bigger and bigger as I crept up on him. I slipped up on him so fast that when I had gone about 150,000,000 miles I was close enough to be swallowed up in the phosphorescent glory of his wake, and I couldn't see anything for the glare. Thinks I, it won't do to run into him, so I shunted to one side and tore along. By and by I closed up abreast of his tail. Do you know what it was like? It was like a gnat closing up on the continent of America. I forged along. By and by I had sailed along his coast for a little upwards of a hundred and fifty million miles, and then I could see by the shape of him that I hadn't even got up to his waistband yet. Why, Peters, WE don't know anything about comets, down here. If you want to see comets that ARE comets, you've got to go outside of our solar system—where there's room for them, you understand. My friend, I've seen comets out there that couldn't even lay down inside the ORBITS of our noblest comets without their tails hanging over.

Well, I boomed along another hundred and fifty million miles, and got up abreast his shoulder, as you may say. I was feeling pretty fine, I tell you; but just then I noticed the officer of the deck come to the side and hoist his glass in my direction. Straight off I heard him sing out—"Below there, ahoy! Shake her up, shake her up! Heave on a hundred million billion tons of brimstone!"

"Ay-ay, sir!"

"Pipe the stabboard watch! All hands on deck!"

"Ay-ay, sir!"

"Send two hundred thousand million men aloft to shake out royals and sky-scrapers!"

"Ay-ay, sir!"

"Hand the stuns'ls! Hang out every rag you've got! Clothe her from stem to rudder-post!"

"Ay-ay, sir!"

In about a second I begun to see I'd woke up a pretty ugly customer, Peters. In less than ten seconds that comet was just a blazing cloud of red-hot canvas. It was piled up into the heavens clean out of sight—the old thing seemed to swell out and occupy all space; the sulphur smoke from the furnaces—oh, well, nobody can describe the way it rolled and tumbled up into the skies, and nobody can half describe the way it smelt. Neither can anybody begin to describe the way that monstrous craft begun to crash along. And such another powwow—thousands of bo's'n's whistles screaming at once, and a crew like the populations of a hundred thousand worlds like ours all swearing at once. Well, I never heard the like of it before.

We roared and thundered along side by side, both doing our level best, because I'd never struck a comet before that could lay over me, and so I was bound to beat this one or break something. I judged I had some reputation in space, and I calculated to keep it. I noticed I wasn't gaining as fast, now, as I was before, but still I was gaining. There was a power of excitement on board the comet. Upwards of a hundred billion passengers swarmed up from below and rushed to the side and begun to bet on the race. Of course this careened her and damaged her speed. My, but wasn't the mate mad! He jumped at that crowd, with his trumpet in his hand, and sung out—

"Amidships! amidships, you! or I'll brain the last idiot of you!"

Well, sir, I gained and gained, little by little, till at last I went skimming sweetly by the magnificent old conflagration's nose. By this time the captain of the comet had been rousted out, and he stood there in the red glare for'ard, by the mate, in his shirt-sleeves and slippers, his hair all rats' nests and one suspender hanging, and how sick those two men did look! I just simply couldn't help putting my thumb to my nose as I glided away and singing out:

"Ta-ta! ta-ta! Any word to send to your family?"

Peters, it was a mistake. Yes, sir, I've often regretted that—it was a mistake. You see, the captain had given up the race, but that remark was too tedious for him—he couldn't stand it. He turned to the mate, and says he—

"Have we got brimstone enough of our own to make the trip?"

"Yes, sir."

"Sure?"

"Yes, sir—more than enough."

"How much have we got in cargo for Satan?"

"Eighteen hundred thousand billion quintillions of kazarks."

"Very well, then, let his boarders freeze till the next comet comes.

Lighten ship! Lively, now, lively, men! Heave the whole cargo overboard!"

Peters, look me in the eye, and be calm. I found out, over there, that a kazark is exactly the bulk of a HUNDRED AND SIXTY-NINE WORLDS LIKE OURS! They hove all that load overboard. When it fell it wiped out a considerable raft of stars just as clean as if they'd been candles and somebody blowed them out. As for the race, that was at an end. The minute she was lightened the comet swung along by me the same as if I was anchored. The captain stood on the stern, by the after-davits, and put his thumb to his nose and sung out—

"Ta-ta! ta-ta! Maybe YOU'VE got some message to send your friends in the Everlasting Tropics!"

Then he hove up his other suspender and started for'ard, and inside of three-quarters of an hour his craft was only a pale torch again in the distance. Yes, it was a mistake, Peters—that remark of mine. I don't reckon I'll ever get over being sorry about it. I'd 'a' beat the bully of the firmament if I'd kept my mouth shut.

But I've wandered a little off the track of my tale; I'll get back on my course again. Now you see what kind of speed I was making. So, as I said, when I had been tearing along this way about thirty years I begun to get uneasy. Oh, it was pleasant enough, with a good deal to find out, but then it was kind of lonesome, you know. Besides, I wanted to get somewhere. I hadn't shipped with the idea of cruising forever. First off, I liked the delay, because I judged I was going to fetch up in pretty warm quarters when I got through; but towards the last I begun to feel that I'd rather go to—well, most any place, so as to finish up the uncertainty.

Well, one night—it was always night, except when I was rushing by some star that was occupying the whole universe with its fire and its glare—light enough then, of course, but I necessarily left it behind in a minute or two and plunged into a solid week of darkness again. The stars ain't so close together as they look to be. Where was I? Oh yes; one night I was sailing along, when I discovered a tremendous long row of blinking lights away on the horizon ahead. As I approached, they begun to tower and swell and look like mighty furnaces. Says I to myself—

"By George, I've arrived at last—and at the wrong place, just as I expected!"

Then I fainted. I don't know how long I was insensible, but it must have been a good while, for, when I came to, the darkness was all gone and there was the loveliest sunshine and the balmiest, fragrantest air in its place. And there was such a marvelous world spread out before me—such a glowing, beautiful, bewitching country. The things I took for furnaces were gates, miles high, made all of flashing jewels, and they pierced a wall of solid gold that you couldn't see the top of, nor yet the end of, in either direction. I was pointed straight for one of these gates, and a-coming like a house afire. Now I noticed that the skies were black with millions of people, pointed for those gates. What a roar they made, rushing through the air! The ground was as thick as ants with people, too—billions of them, I judge.

I lit. I drifted up to a gate with a swarm of people, and when it was my turn the head clerk says, in a business-like way—

"Well, quick! Where are you from?"

"San Francisco," says I.

"San Fran—WHAT?" says he.

"San Francisco."

He scratched his head and looked puzzled, then he says—

"Is it a planet?"

By George, Peters, think of it! "PLANET?" says I; "it's a city. And moreover, it's one of the biggest and finest and—"

"There, there!" says he, "no time here for conversation. We don't deal in cities here. Where are you from in a GENERAL way?"

"Oh," I says, "I beg your pardon. Put me down for California."

I had him AGAIN, Peters! He puzzled a second, then he says, sharp and irritable—

"I don't know any such planet—is it a constellation?"

"Oh, my goodness!" says I. "Constellation, says you? No—it's a State."

"Man, we don't deal in States here. WILL you tell me where you are from IN GENERAL—AT LARGE, don't you understand?"

"Oh, now I get your idea," I says. "I'm from America,—the United States of America."

Peters, do you know I had him AGAIN? If I hadn't I'm a clam! His face was as blank as a target after a militia shooting-match. He turned to an under clerk and says—

"Where is America? WHAT is America?"

The under clerk answered up prompt and says—

"There ain't any such orb."

"ORB?" says I. "Why, what are you talking about, young man? It ain't an orb; it's a country; it's a continent. Columbus discovered it; I reckon likely you've heard of HIM, anyway. America—why, sir, America—"

"Silence!" says the head clerk. "Once for all, where—are—you—FROM?"

"Well," says I, "I don't know anything more to say—unless I lump things, and just say I'm from the world."

"Ah," says he, brightening up, "now that's something like! WHAT world?"

Peters, he had ME, that time. I looked at him, puzzled, he looked at me, worried. Then he burst out—

"Come, come, what world?"

Says I, "Why, THE world, of course."

"THE world!" he says. "H'm! there's billions of them! Next!"

That meant for me to stand aside. I done so, and a sky-blue man with seven heads and only one leg hopped into my place. I took a walk. It just occurred to me, then, that all the myriads I had seen swarming to that gate, up to this time, were just like that creature. I tried to run across somebody I was acquainted with, but they were out of acquaintances of mine just then. So I thought the thing all over and finally sidled back there pretty meek and feeling rather stumped, as you may say.

"Well?" said the head clerk.

"Well, sir," I says, pretty humble, "I don't seem to make out which world it is I'm from. But you may know it from this—it's the one the Saviour saved."

He bent his head at the Name. Then he says, gently—

"The worlds He has saved are like to the gates of heaven in number—none can count them. What astronomical system is your world in?—perhaps that may assist."

"It's the one that has the sun in it—and the moon—and Mars"—he shook his head at each name—hadn't ever heard of them, you see—"and Neptune—and Uranus—and Jupiter—"

"Hold on!" says he—"hold on a minute! Jupiter...Jupiter...Seems to me we had a man from there eight or nine hundred years ago—but people from that system very seldom enter by this gate." All of a sudden he begun to look me so straight in the eye that I thought he was going to bore through me. Then he says, very deliberate, "Did you come STRAIGHT HERE from your system?"

"Yes, sir," I says—but I blushed the least little bit in the world when I said it.

He looked at me very stern, and says—

"That is not true; and this is not the place for prevarication. You wandered from your course. How did that happen?"

Says I, blushing again—

"I'm sorry, and I take back what I said, and confess. I raced a little with a comet one day—only just the least little bit—only the tiniest lit—"

"So—so," says he—and without any sugar in his voice to speak of.

I went on, and says—

"But I only fell off just a bare point, and I went right back on my course again the minute the race was over."

"No matter—that divergence has made all this trouble. It has brought you to a gate that is billions of leagues from the right one. If you had gone to your own gate they would have known all about your world at once and there would have been no delay. But we will try to accommodate you." He turned to an under clerk and says—

"What system is Jupiter in?"

"I don't remember, sir, but I think there is such a planet in one of the little new systems away out in one of the thinly worlded corners of the universe. I will see."

He got a balloon and sailed up and up and up, in front of a map that was as big as Rhode Island. He went on up till he was out of sight, and by and by he came down and got something to eat and went up again. To cut a long story short, he kept on doing this for a day or two, and finally he came down and said he thought he had found that solar system, but it might be fly-specks. So he got a microscope and went back. It turned out better than he feared. He had rousted out our system, sure enough. He got me to describe our planet and its distance from the sun, and then he says to his chief—

"Oh, I know the one he means, now, sir. It is on the map. It is called the Wart."

Says I to myself, "Young man, it wouldn't be wholesome for you to go down THERE and call it the Wart."

Well, they let me in, then, and told me I was safe forever and wouldn't have any more trouble.

Then they turned from me and went on with their work, the same as if they considered my case all complete and shipshape. I was a good deal surprised at this, but I was diffident about speaking up and reminding them. I did so hate to do it, you know; it seemed a pity to bother them, they had so much on their hands. Twice I thought I would give up and let the thing go; so twice I started to leave, but immediately I thought what a figure I should cut stepping out amongst the redeemed in such a rig, and that made me hang back and come to anchor again. People got to eying me— clerks, you know—wondering why I didn't get under way. I couldn't stand this long—it was too uncomfortable. So at last I plucked up courage and tipped the head clerk a signal. He says—

"What! you here yet? What's wanting?"

Says I, in a low voice and very confidential, making a trumpet with my hands at his ear—

"I beg pardon, and you mustn't mind my reminding you, and seeming to meddle, but hain't you forgot something?"

He studied a second, and says—

"Forgot something? . . . No, not that I know of."

"Think," says I.

He thought. Then he says—

"No, I can't seem to have forgot anything. What is it?"

"Look at me," says I, "look me all over."

He done it.

"Well?" says he.

"Well," says I, "you don't notice anything? If I branched out amongst the elect looking like this, wouldn't I attract considerable attention?—wouldn't I be a little conspicuous?"

"Well," he says, "I don't see anything the matter. What do you lack?"

"Lack! Why, I lack my harp, and my wreath, and my halo, and my hymn-book, and my palm branch—I lack everything that a body naturally requires up here, my friend."

Puzzled? Peters, he was the worst puzzled man you ever saw. Finally he says—

"Well, you seem to be a curiosity every way a body takes you. I never heard of these things before."

I looked at the man awhile in solid astonishment; then I says—

"Now, I hope you don't take it as an offence, for I don't mean any, but really, for a man that has been in the Kingdom as long as I reckon you have, you do seem to know powerful little about its customs."

"Its customs!" says he. "Heaven is a large place, good friend. Large empires have many and diverse customs. Even small dominions have, as you doubtless know by what you have seen of the matter on a small scale in the Wart. How can you imagine I could ever learn the varied customs of the countless kingdoms of heaven? It makes my head ache to think of it. I know the customs that prevail in those portions inhabited by peoples that are appointed to enter by my own gate—and hark ye, that is quite enough knowledge for one individual to try to pack into his head in the thirty-seven millions of years I have devoted night and day to that study. But the idea of learning the customs of the whole appalling expanse of heaven—O man, how insanely you talk! Now I don't doubt that this odd costume you talk about is the fashion in that district of heaven you belong to, but you won't be conspicuous in this section without it."

I felt all right, if that was the case, so I bade him good-day and left. All day I walked towards the far end of a prodigious hall of the office, hoping to come out into heaven any moment, but it was a mistake. That hall was built on the general heavenly plan—it naturally couldn't be small. At last I got so tired I couldn't go any farther; so I sat down to rest, and begun to tackle the queerest sort of strangers and ask for information, but I didn't get any; they couldn't understand my language, and I could not understand theirs. I got dreadfully lonesome. I was so down-hearted and homesick I wished a hundred times I never had died. I turned back, of course. About noon next day, I got back at last and was on hand at the booking-office once more. Says I to the head clerk—

"I begin to see that a man's got to be in his own Heaven to be happy."

"Perfectly correct," says he. "Did you imagine the same heaven would suit all sorts of men?"

"Well, I had that idea—but I see the foolishness of it. Which way am I to go to get to my district?"

He called the under clerk that had examined the map, and he gave me general directions. I thanked him and started; but he says—

"Wait a minute; it is millions of leagues from here. Go outside and stand on that red wishing-carpet; shut your eyes, hold your breath, and wish yourself there."

"I'm much obliged," says I; "why didn't you dart me through when I first arrived?"

"We have a good deal to think of here; it was your place to think of it and ask for it. Good-by; we probably sha'n't see you in this region for a thousand centuries or so."

"In that case, o revoor," says I.

PART VIII

A Final Note

A Literary Nightmare

FROM *The Writings of Mark Twain*

[ALSO CALLED *"Punch, Brothers, Punch!"*]

Will the reader please to cast his eye over the following lines, and see if he can discover anything harmful in them?

Conductor, when you receive a fare, Punch in the presence of the passenjare! A blue trip slip for an eight-cent fare, A buff trip slip for a six-cent fare, A pink trip slip for a three-cent fare, Punch in the presence of the passenjare!

CHORUS

Punch, brothers! punch with care! Punch in the presence of the passenjare!

I came across these jingling rhymes in a newspaper, a little while ago, and read them a couple of times. They took instant and entire possession of me. All through breakfast they went waltzing through my brain; and when, at last, I rolled up my napkin, I could not tell whether I had eaten anything or not. I had carefully laid out my day's work the day before—thrilling tragedy in the novel which I am writing. I went to my den to begin my deed of blood. I took up my pen, but all I could get it to say was, "Punch in the presence of the passenjare." I fought hard for an hour, but it was useless. My head kept humming, "A blue trip slip for an eight-cent fare, a buff trip slip for a six-cent fare," and so on and so on, without peace or respite. The day's work was ruined—I could see that plainly enough. I gave up and drifted down-town, and presently discovered that my feet were keeping time to that relentless jingle. When I could stand it no longer I altered my step. But it did no good; those rhymes accommodated themselves to the new step and went on harassing me just as before. I returned home, and suffered all the afternoon; suffered all through an unconscious and unrefreshing dinner; suffered, and cried, and jingled all through the evening; went to bed and rolled, tossed, and jingled right along, the same as ever; got up at midnight frantic, and tried to read; but there was nothing visible upon the whirling page except "Punch! punch in the presence of the passenjare." By sunrise I was out of my mind, and every-body marveled and was distressed at the idiotic burden of my ravings—"Punch! oh, punch! punch in the presence of the passenjare!"

Two days later, on Saturday morning, I arose, a tottering wreck, and went forth to fulfil an engagement with a valued friend, the Rev. Mr. ———, to walk to the Talcott Tower, ten miles distant. He stared at me, but asked no questions. We started. Mr. ——— talked, talked, talked as is his wont. I said nothing; I heard nothing. At the end of a mile, Mr. ——— said "Mark, are you sick? I never saw a man look so haggard and worn and absent-minded. Say something, do!"

Drearily, without enthusiasm, I said: "Punch brothers, punch with care! Punch in the presence of the passenjare!"

My friend eyed me blankly, looked perplexed, they said:

"I do not think I get your drift, Mark. There does not seem to be any relevancy in what you have said, certainly nothing sad; and yet—maybe it was the way you said the words—I never heard anything that sounded so pathetic. What is—"

But I heard no more. I was already far away with my pitiless, heart-breaking "blue trip slip for an eight-cent fare, buff trip slip for a six-cent fare, pink trip slip for a three-cent fare; punch in the presence of the pas-senjare." I do not know what occurred during the other nine miles. However, all of a sudden Mr. ——— laid his hand on my shoulder and shouted:

"Oh, wake up! wake up! wake up! Don't sleep all day! Here we are at the Tower, man! I have talked myself deaf and dumb and blind, and never got a response. Just look at this magnificent autumn landscape! Look at it! look at it! Feast your eye on it! You have traveled; you have seen boaster landscapes elsewhere. Come, now, deliver an honest opinion. What do you say to this?"

I sighed wearily; and murmured:

"A buff trip slip for a six-cent fare, a pink trip slip for a three-cent fare, punch in the presence of the passenjare."

Rev. Mr. ——— stood there, very grave, full of concern, apparently, and looked long at me; then he said:

"Mark, there is something about this that I cannot understand. Those are about the same words you said before; there does not seem to be anything in them, and yet they nearly break my heart when you say them. Punch in the—how is it they go?"

I began at the beginning and repeated all the lines.

My friend's face lighted with interest. He said:

"Why, what a captivating jingle it is! It is almost music. It flows along so nicely. I have nearly caught the rhymes myself. Say them over just once more, and then I'll have them, sure."

I said them over. Then Mr. ——— said them. He made one little mistake, which I corrected. The next time and the next he got them right. Now a great burden seemed to tumble from my shoulders. That torturing jingle departed out of my brain, and a grateful sense of rest and peace descended upon me. I was light-hearted enough to sing; and I did sing for half an hour, straight along, as we went jogging homeward. Then my freed tongue found blessed speech again, and the pent talk of many a weary hour began to gush and flow. It flowed on and on, joyously, jubilantly, until the fountain was empty and dry. As I wrung my friend's hand at parting, I said:

"Haven't we had a royal good time! But now I remember, you haven't said a word for two hours. Come, come, out with something!"

The Rev. Mr. ——— turned a lack-luster eye upon me, drew a deep sigh, and said, without animation, without apparent consciousness:

"Punch, brothers, punch with care! Punch in the presence of the passenjare!"

A pang shot through me as I said to myself, "Poor fellow, poor fellow! he has got it, now."

I did not see Mr. —— for two or three days after that. Then, on Tuesday evening, he staggered into my presence and sank dejectedly into a seat. He was pale, worn; he was a wreck. He lifted his faded eyes to my face and said:

"Ah, Mark, it was a ruinous investment that I made in those heartless rhymes. They have ridden me like a nightmare, day and night, hour after hour, to this very moment. Since I saw you I have suffered the torments of the lost. Saturday evening I had a sudden call, by telegraph, and took the night train for Boston. The occasion was the death of a valued old friend who had requested that I should preach his funeral sermon. I took my seat in the cars and set myself to framing the discourse. But I never got beyond the opening paragraph; for then the train started and the car-wheels began their 'clack, clack-clack-clack-clack! clack-clack!—clack-clack-clack!' and right away those odious rhymes fitted themselves to that accompaniment. For an hour I sat there and set a syllable of those rhymes to every separate and distinct clack the car-wheels made. Why, I was as fagged out, then, as if I had been chopping wood all day. My skull was splitting with headache. It seemed to me that I must go mad if I sat there any longer; so I undressed and went to bed. I stretched myself out in my berth, and—well, you know what the result was. The thing went right along, just the same. 'Clack-clack- clack, a blue trip slip, clack-clack-clack, for an eight cent fare; clack-clack-clack, a buff trip slip, clack-clack-clack, for a six-cent fare, and so on, and so on, and so on punch in the presence of the passenjare!' Sleep? Not a single wink! I was almost a lunatic when I got to Boston. Don't ask me about the funeral. I did the best I could, but every solemn individual sentence was meshed and tangled and woven in and out with 'Punch, brothers, punch with care, punch in the presence of the passenjare.' And the most distressing thing was that my delivery dropped into the undulating rhythm of those pulsing rhymes, and I could actually catch absent-minded people nodding time to the swing of it with their stupid heads. And, Mark, you may believe it or not, but before I got through the entire assemblage were placidly bobbing their heads in solemn unison, mourners, undertaker, and all. The moment I had finished, I fled to the anteroom in a state bordering on frenzy. Of course it would be my luck to find a sorrowing and aged maiden aunt of the deceased there, who had arrived from Springfield too late to get into the church. She began to sob, and said:

"'Oh, oh, he is gone, he is gone, and I didn't see him before he died!'

"'Yes!' I said, 'he is gone, he is gone, he is gone—oh, will this suffering never cease!'

"'You loved him, then! Oh, you too loved him!'

"'Loved him! Loved who?'

"'Why, my poor George! my poor nephew!'

"'Oh—him! Yes—oh, yes, yes. Certainly—certainly. Punch—punch—oh, this misery will kill me!'

"'Bless you! bless you, sir, for these sweet words! I, too, suffer in this dear loss. Were you present during his last moments?'

"'Yes. I—whose last moments?'

"'His. The dear departed's.'

"'Yes! Oh, yes—yes—yes! I suppose so, I think so, I don't know! Oh, certainly—I was there, I was there!'

"'Oh, what a privilege! what a precious privilege! And his last words—oh, tell me, tell me his last words! What did he say?'

"'He said—he said—oh, my head, my head, my head! He said—he said—he never said anything but Punch, punch, punch in the presence of the passenjare! Oh, leave me, madam! In the name of all that is generous, leave me to my madness, my misery, my despair!—a buff trip slip for a six-cent fare, a pink trip slip for a three-cent fare—endu—rance can no fur—ther go!—PUNCH in the presence of the passenjare!'"

My friend's hopeless eyes rested upon mine a pregnant minute, and then he said impressively:

"Mark, you do not say anything. You do not offer me any hope. But, ah me, it is just as well—it is just as well. You could not do me any good. The time has long gone by when words could comfort me. Something tells me that my tongue is doomed to wag forever to the jigger of that remorseless jingle. There—there it is coming on me again: a blue trip slip for an eight-cent fare, a buff trip slip for a—"

Thus murmuring faint and fainter, my friend sank into a peaceful trance and forgot his sufferings in a blessed respite.

How did I finally save him from an asylum? I took him to a neighboring university and made him discharge the burden of his persecuting rhymes into the eager ears of the poor, unthinking students. How is it with them, now? The result is too sad to tell. Why did I write this article? It was for a worthy, even a noble, purpose. It was to warn you, reader, if you should came across those merciless rhymes, to avoid them—avoid them as you would a pestilence.

ACKNOWLEDGMENTS

First, to Mark Twain's father, who, by his purchase of a large tract of land in Monroe County, Missouri, misled his son into thinking one day he would join the landed gentry in a life of idleness. When life surprised him, and his patrimony turned out to be worthless, young Sam Clemens had nothing to live on but his wits, with which he was amply supplied. So thanks, John Clemens, for the lousy land deal.

Also, for her counsel and good cheer, Shelley Fisher Fishkin of Stanford University, who, in addition to being a justly renowned Twain scholar, is no doubt the most amiable professor in the history of American literature. My fellow executive producers of the Kennedy Center Mark Twain Prize for American Humor: my dear brother Bob Kaminsky, and my almost-brothers Mark Krantz, and Cappy McGarr. At the Kennedy Center, the unwavering support of Michael Kaiser and his team: Marie Mattson, Robert Pullen, Leslie Miller, and the person who brought us there, Ann Stock. Of course PBS and CPB and especially our colleagues at WETA: Sharon Rockefeller, Dalton Delan, David Thompson, Jim Corbley, Cecily van Praagh, Krystal Fogg, and Anne Kaufman.

Carlo Devito for his confidence, comraderie, wine and cheese. Philip Turner for his deeply literate sense of nuance and playfulness (qv the title of this book) and Iris Blasi, who carried this project over the finish line while Wall Street tanked and the publishing industry absorbed some punishing body blows.

That a fun book should have emerged while chaos, cupidity, and crassness were loosed upon the land seems, to me, to be rightly Twainish, which is something my wonderful agent, Lisa Queen, always gets right.

BIBLIOGRAPHY

PART I: THE MISSISSIPPI

The Lure of the River

Clemens, Samuel Langhorne. *Life on the Mississippi*. Boston: James R. Osgood and Co., 1883.

More River Thoughts

Twain, Mark. *The Adventures of Huckleberry Finn*. New York: Charles L. Webster and Co., 1884.

Steamboat Magic and a Small Town Boy

Clemens, Samuel Langhorne. *Life on the Mississippi*. Boston: James R. Osgood and Co., 1883.

The Face of the Water

Clemens, Samuel Langhorne. *Life on the Mississippi*. Boston: James R. Osgood and Co., 1883.

Goin' to the Theater in the Big City (A Letter from "Thomas Jefferson Snodgrass," 1856)

Keokuk Saturday Post, November 1, 1856.
(http://www.twainquotes.com/Keokuk/18561101.html)

Mardi Gras in New Orleans (A Letter to Pamela A. Moffet, 1859)

Written March 9–11, 1859, in New Orleans, Louisiana
Twain, Mark. *Mark Twain's Letters, Volume 1: 1853–1866*. Edited by Edgar Marquess

Bibliography

Branch, Michael B. Frank, Kenneth M. Sanderson, Harriet Elinor Smith, Lin
Salamo, and Richard Bucci. *The Mark Twain Papers*. Berkeley, Los Angeles, London:
University of California Press, 1988.
(http://www.marktwainproject.org/xtf/view?docId=letters/UCCL00019.xml;style=letter)

A Tour of New Orleans

Clemens, Samuel Langhorne. *Life on the Mississippi*. Boston: James R. Osgood and Co.,
1883.

The Scene of the Battle: Vicksburg

Clemens, Samuel Langhorne. *Life on the Mississippi*. Boston: James R. Osgood and
Co., 1883.

PART II: THE WEST

"Roughing It" Lecture

State Republican, (Lansing, Michigan), December 21, 1871. Transcribed text of Mark
Twain's lecture, given December 14, 1871.
(http://etext.virginia.edu/railton/roughingit/lecture/rilectsr.html)

Among the Miners

Twain, Mark. *Roughing It*. Hartford: American Publishing Co., 1872.

The Killing of Julius Caesar, "Localized"

Twain, Mark. *The Celebrated Jumping Frog of Calaveras County, and Other Sketches*. New
York: C. H. Webb, 1867.

A Trip to Tahoe

Twain, Mark. *Roughing It*. Hartford: American Publishing Co., 1872.

Off for San Francisco

Twain, Mark. *Roughing It*. Hartford: American Publishing Co., 1872.

Bibliography

A San Francisco Day Trip

"Early Rising, As Regards Excursions to the Cliff House," *The Golden Era.* July 3, 1864.
(http://www.twainquotes.com/Era/18640703.html)

San Francisco Weather and Other Natural Events

Twain, Mark. *The Celebrated Jumping Frog of Calaveras County, and Other Sketches.* New
York: C. H. Webb, 1867.

PART III: BACK EAST

Philadelphia: The First Visit

Written December 4, 1853

Muscatine Journal, December 16, 1953, 1, in the P.M. Musser Public Library, Muscatine,
Iowa (IaMu), and the Historical Library, State Historical Society of Iowa, Des
Moines.
(http://www.marktwainproject.org/xtf/view?docId=letters/UCCL00004.xml;style=letter)

New York: The Overgrown Metropolis

Written February 2, 1867, in New York
San Francisco *Alta California,* March 28, 1867.
(http://www.twainquotes.com/18670328.html)

New York: The Dreadful Russian Bath

Written February 23rd, 1867 in New York
San Francisco *Alta California,* April 5, 1867.
(http://www.twainquotes.com/18670405.html)

New York: Changes in the City

Written February 23rd, 1867 in New York
San Francisco *Alta California,* April 5, 1867.
(http://www.twainquotes.com/18670405.html)

New York: Street People

Written June 2, 1867, in New York

San Francisco *Alta California*, August 4, 1867.

(http://www.twainquotes.com/18670804.html)

New York: Personal Ads

Written May 19TH, 1867, in New York

San Francisco *Alta California*, June 30, 1867.

(http://www.twainquotes.com/18670630.html)

Plymouth Rock and the Pilgrims

Speech given in Philadelphia on December 22, 1881.

Twain, Mark. *Mark Twain's Speeches*. New York: Harper & Brothers, 1910.

(http://etext.virginia.edu/railton/onstage/pilgrims.html)

First Visit to Boston

Written July 1869

San Francisco *Alta California*, July 25, 1869.

(http://www.twainquotes.com/18690725.html)

Boston: A Modern Cretan Labyrinth

Written July 1869

San Francisco *Alta California*, July 25, 1869.

(http://www.twainquotes.com/18690725.html)

Boston Antiquities

Written July 1869

San Francisco *Alta California*, July 25, 1869.

(http://www.twainquotes.com/18690725.html)

Boston Politeness

Written July 1869

San Francisco *Alta California*, July 25, 1869.

(http://www.twainquotes.com/18690725.html)

Bibliography

The Weather of New England
New York Times, December 23, 1876.
(http://www.twainquotes.com/18761223.html)

Niagara
Twain, Mark. *Sketches, New and Old.* New York: Harper & Brothers, 1917. Written 1871.

Traveling with a Reformer
Twain, Mark. *The Man Who Corrupted Hadleyburg, and Other Stories.* New York: Harper
  Collins, 1900.

PART IV: TRAVELS IN THE PACIFIC

Our Fellow Citizens of the Sandwich Islands
Fatout, Paul. *Mark Twain Speaking.* Iowa City: University of Iowa Press, 1976.
First given in San Francisco, October 2, 1866.

Letters from Hawaii
Written in Honolulu, March 1866.
Sacramento *Daily Union,* April 21, 1866.
(http://www.twainquotes.com/18660421u.html)

Australians and Americans
Twain, Mark. *Following the Equator.* American Publishing Co., 1897.

Entering Sydney
Twain, Mark. *Following the Equator.* American Publishing Co., 1897.

Town of Wauganui
Twain, Mark. *Following the Equator.* American Publishing Co., 1897.

The Weet-Weet
Twain, Mark. *Following the Equator.* American Publishing Co., 1897.

Bibliography

PART V: EUROPE

The American Vandal Abroad

Mark Twain's Speeches, ed. Albert Bigelow Paine. New York: Harper & Brothers, 1923, pages 21–30.

Old Master Worshippers

Written in Constantinople, August 23, 1867

San Francisco *Alta California,* October 23, 1867.

(http://etext.virginia.edu/railton/innocent/alta18.html)

Old Saint Paul's

Clemens, Samuel L. *Mark Twain's Sketches. Number One.* Authorized edition. New York: American News Co., 1874.

Concerning Chambermaids

Twain, Mark. *The Celebrated Jumping Frog of Calaveras County and Other Sketches.* New York: C. H. Webb, 1867.

Mark Twain's Map of Paris

The Galaxy, November 1870.

(http://www.twainquotes.com/Galaxy/187011a.html)

The Chicago of Europe

Mark Twain's Travel Letters from 1891–92. *Chicago Daily Tribune,* April 3, 1892. [Often retitled "The German Chicago"]

The Awful German Language

Twain, Mark. *A Tramp Abroad.* Hartford, CT: The American Publishing Co., 1880.

An Austrian Health Factory

Mark Twain's Travel Letters from 1891–92. *Chicago Daily Tribune,* February 7, 1892. [Often retitled "Marienbad—A Health Factory"]

Bibliography

Bayreuth
Mark Twain's Travel Letters from 1891–92. *Chicago Daily Tribune,* December 6, 1891.
   [Often retitled "At the Shrine of St. Wagner"]

The Knighted Knave of Bergen
Twain, Mark. *A Tramp Abroad.* Hartford, CT: American Publishing Co., 1880.

The Matterhorn and the Glacier
Twain, Mark. *A Tramp Abroad.* Hartford, CT: American Publishing Co., 1880.

Rafting Down the Neckar
Twain, Mark. *A Tramp Abroad.* Hartford, CT: American Publishing Co., 1880.

The Cave of the Specter
Twain, Mark. *A Tramp Abroad.* Hartford, CT: American Publishing Co., 1880.

The Belated Russian Passport
Twain, Mark. *The Man Who Corrupted Hadleyburg, and Other Stories.* New York: Harper
   Collins, 1900.

Nude Bathers
Written in Odessa, Russia, August 22, 1867.
San Francisco *Alta California,* November 3, 1867.
(http://etext.virginia.edu/railton/innocent/alta22.html)

Mark Twain in the Cradle of Liberty
Mark Twain's Travel Letters from 1891–92. *Chicago Daily Tribune,* March 6, 1892.

A Holiday Flight through France
Twain, Mark. *The Innocents Abroad.* Hartford, CT: American Publishing Co., 1869.

Versailles
Twain, Mark. *The Innocents Abroad.* Hartford, CT: American Publishing Co., 1869.

The Story of Abelard and Heloise
Twain, Mark. *The Innocents Abroad.* Hartford, CT: American Publishing Co., 1869.

Bibliography

The Famous Gondola
Twain, Mark. *The Innocents Abroad.* Hartford, CT: American Publishing Co., 1869.

Italian without a Master
Twain, Mark. *The $30,000 Bequest and Other Stories.* New York: Harper & Brothers, 1906.

The Chief Charm of European Life
Twain, Mark. *The Innocents Abroad.* Hartford, CT: American Publishing Co., 1869.

PART VI: AFRICA, INDIA, AND THE HOLY LAND

The Taj Mahal
Twain, Mark. *Following the Equator.* Hartford, CT: American Publishing Co., 1897.

Another Living God
Twain, Mark. *Following the Equator.* Hartford, CT: American Publishing Co., 1897.

Smyrna
Twain, Mark. *The Innocents Abroad.* Hartford, CT: American Publishing Co., 1869.

Damascus
Twain, Mark. *The Innocents Abroad.* Hartford, CT: American Publishing Co., 1869.

The Sacred Sea of Galilee
Twain, Mark. *The Innocents Abroad.* Hartford, CT: American Publishing Co., 1869.

The Church of the Holy Sepulchre
Twain, Mark. *The Innocents Abroad.* Hartford, CT: American Publishing Co., 1869.

Bibliography

PART VII: FANTASIES

Satan's Letter
Twain, Mark. *Letters from the Earth.* Harper & Row, 1962.

Cannibalism in the Cars
Twain, Mark. *Sketches, New and Old.* New York: Harper & Brothers, 1917. Written 1871.

A Curious Pleasure Excursion
Twain, Mark. *Sketches, New and Old.* New York: Harper & Brothers, 1917. Written 1871.

Captain Stormfield's Visit to Heaven
Extracts from *Captain Stormfield's Visit to Heaven. Harper's Magazine,* 1907.

PART VIII: A FINAL NOTE

A Literary Nightmare
Twain, Mark. *Punch, Brothers, Punch! and Other Stories.* New York: Slote, Woodman & Co., 1878.

INDEX

Index

Index

Index

Index

ABOUT THE EDITOR

PETER KAMINSKY is the former managing editor of *National Lampoon* and one of the creators of the Kennedy Center Mark Twain Prize for American Humor as well as the Library of Congress Gershwin Prize for Popular Song. With his brother, Bob, he wrote and produced numerous network comedy specials with John Candy, Jerry Seinfeld, Mary Tyler Moore, Bob Newhart, and many others. His "Outdoors" column has run in the *New York Times* for more than two decades, and he is a well-known cookbook author and food journalist. He is the author of numerous books, including *The Moon Pulled Up an Acre of Bass*, *Pig Perfect: Encounters with Remarkable Swine,* and most recently, *Seven Fires: Grilling the Argentine Way*. His father, Lucian, wrote for Jackie Gleason.